Lecture Notes in Computer Science 16434

The series Lecture Notes in Computer Science (LNCS), including its subseries Lecture Notes in Artificial Intelligence (LNAI) and Lecture Notes in Bioinformatics (LNBI), has established itself as a medium for the publication of new developments in Computer Science research, teaching, and education.

The series enjoys close cooperation with the international research community, publishing the proceedings of many prestigious conferences and collaborating with important societies.

Proposals

A conference or workshop applying for publication in LNCS should have an international program committee, a coherent subject scope limited to related computer science topics, and an appropriate plan for reviewing the submitted papers. To submit a proposal to LNCS please contact lncs@springer.com.

Publishing Service

LNCS offers a full publishing service, including typesetting of papers, making most content available in PDF, HTML, print, and ePub formats. Authors can embed videos in their content, or add electronic supplementary material to be made available in our digital library (SpringerLink).

Open Access

Conference organisers may opt for gold open access of all content in proceedings volumes. Alternatively individual author teams may select gold open access for their proceedings papers. Please contact lncs@springer.com to enquire about terms.

Societies, Communities

LNCS cooperates with prestigious computer science societies and communities, publishing the proceedings of flagship conferences across all major fields. Among the events and associations are ECCV (European Conference on Computer Vision), IACR (International Association for Cryptologic Research), MICCAI (Medical Image Computing and Computer Assisted Intervention Society), the China Computer Federation (CCF), DASFAA (International Conference on Database Systems for Advanced Applications), PRICAI (Pacific Rim International Conference on Artificial Intelligence), IFIP (International Federation for Information Processing), ETAPS (International Joint Conferences on Theory and Practice of Software), ECML PKDD (European Conf. on Machine Learning and Principles and Practice of Knowledge Discovery in Databases), and IAPR (International Association for Pattern Recognition).

Indexing and Distribution

LNCS submits the content and bibliographic metadata of proceedings volumes to the major abstracting and indexing services, including the Conference Proceedings Citation Index (CPCI, part of Clarivate Analytics' Web of Science), DBLP, Scopus, the EI Engineering (Compendex, Inspec), the ACM Digital Library, and Google Scholar. In addition to the indexing services listed above, Springer Nature content is available worldwide through key university and industry library subscription access, and through major distributors such as Amazon and Google Books.

Sublines

The **Formal Methods** subline (https://link.springer.com/series/15554) was established in cooperation with the Formal Methods Europe association, publishing proceedings and tutorials associated with high-quality events. The Advanced Research in Computing and Software Science (**ARCoSS**) subline was established in cooperation with the European Association for Theoretical Computer Science (EATCS) and the International Joint Conferences on Theory and Practice of Software (ETAPS), and it publishes proceedings of high-quality events in theoretical computer science and foundations of programming.

Special Collections

LNCS includes contributed edited works such as **Festschrifts**, dedicated to individuals who have made excellent contributions to the field of computer science, **State-of-the-Art Surveys**, and **Tutorials**. Please contact lncs@springer.com for further details about any of these volume types.

Transactions

We publish the LNCS Transactions in Large-Scale Data- and Knowledge-Centered Systems and the LNCS Transactions in Petri Nets and Other Models of Concurrency (ToPNoC). Please contact lncs@springer.com for further details.

SharedIt

Springer Nature can make shareable links to online PDFs of published proceedings papers available to authors. This encourages reading by users who otherwise don't have subscription access (for example, via a university library). These shareable links can be communicated via social channels, on institutional repositories, on author websites, or on scholarly collaborative networks.

Overleaf

The LaTeX2e Proceedings Templates are available in the scientific authoring platform Overleaf.

Other Benefits of Publishing

By default, conference **organisers and authors are not charged** for publishing in LNCS. Organisers and participants get **free online access** to the SpringerLink-published papers for 4 weeks during and following the conference. LNCS offers readers transparent reviewing data about all published volumes. Authors retain copyright to their papers and **authors can self-archive** their submitted papers. For more information on publishing service and conditions, please contact lncs@springer.com.

Publishing Policies

We require volume editors (conference organisers), authors of proceedings papers, and reviewers engaged to evaluate papers submitted to conferences to follow our publishing policies and respective codes of conduct (https://www.springernature.com/gp/policies/book-publishing-policies).

LNCS Editors

Elisa Bertino (Purdue University), Wen Gao (Peking University), Bernhard Steffen (TU Dortmund), and Moti Yung (Google and Columbia University).

LNAI (Lecture Notes in Artificial Intelligence)

This subseries (https://link.springer.com/series/1244) was established in 1988 as a topical subseries of LNCS devoted to artificial intelligence. The editors are Wolfgang Wahlster (DFKI, Berlin), Randy Goebel (University of Alberta, Edmonton), and Zhi-Hua Zhou (Nanjing University).

LNBI (Lecture Notes in Bioinformatics)

This subseries (https://link.springer.com/series/5381) was established in 2003 as a topical subseries of LNCS devoted to bioinformatics and computational systems biology. The editors are Sorin Istrail (Brown University), Pavel Pevzner (University of California, San Diego) and Michael Waterman (University of Southern California).

Ki-Woong Park · Jungsoo Park
Editors

Information Security Applications

26th International Conference, WISA 2025
Jeju Island, South Korea, August 20–22, 2025
Revised Selected Papers

Editors
Ki-Woong Park
Sejong University
Seoul, Korea (Republic of)

Jungsoo Park
Kangnam University
Yongin-si, Korea (Republic of)

ISSN 0302-9743 ISSN 1611-3349 (electronic)
Lecture Notes in Computer Science
ISBN 978-981-95-6856-7 ISBN 978-981-95-6857-4 (eBook)
https://doi.org/10.1007/978-981-95-6857-4

This Springer imprint is published by the registered company Springer Nature Singapore Pte Ltd.
The registered company address is: 152 Beach Road, #21-01/04 Gateway East, Singapore 189721, Singapore

Preface

The 26th World Conference on Information Security Applications (WISA 2025) was held from August 20–August 22, 2025. This year's conference was hosted by the KIISC (Korea Institute of Information Security and Cryptology) and ETRI (Electronics and Telecommunications Research Institute).

The aim of this conference is to provide an international forum for the latest results of research, development, and applications within the field of information security and cryptology. This year, we received 66 submissions and were able to accept 24 papers at the conference. The challenging review and selection processes were successfully conducted by program committee (PC) members and external reviewers via the EasyChair review system. For transparency, it is worth noting that each paper underwent a double-blind review by at least three PC members. For the LNCS post-proceeding, the authors of selected papers had a few weeks to prepare their final versions, based on the comments received from the reviewers.

The conference featured invited talks and keynotes, including stimulating presentations from Willy Susilo (University of Wollongong) and Jihoon Cho (Samsung SDS). We thank the invited speakers for their kind acceptance and illuminating discussions. We would like to thank all authors who submitted their papers to WISA 2025, as well as all PC members. It is a truly wonderful experience to work with such talented and hardworking researchers. We also appreciate the external reviewers for assisting the PC members. Finally, we would like to thank all attendees for their active participation and the organizing members who successfully managed this conference. We look forward to seeing you again at next year's WISA.

December 2025

Ki-Woong Park
Jungsoo Park

Organization

General Co-chairs

Young-Ho Park	Sejong Cyber University, South Korea
Seung Chan Bang	ETRI, South Korea

Program Committee Co-chairs

Ki-Woong Park	Sejong University, South Korea
Jungsoo Park	Kangnam University, South Korea

Program Committee

Bimal Roy	Indian Statistical Institute, Kolkata, India
Byoungjin Seok	Hansung University, South Korea
Byoungyoung Lee	Seoul National University, South Korea
Changhee Choi	Sejong University, South Korea
Changhoon Kim	Daegu University, South Korea
Changhoon Lee	Seoul National University of Science and Technology, South Korea
Chun-I Fan	National Sun Yat-sen University, Taiwan
Daehee Jang	Kyunghee University, South Korea
Daehee Seo	Sangmyung University, South Korea
Daeseon Choi	Soongsil University, South Korea
Daesung Moon	ETRI, South Korea
Deokgyu Lee	Seowon University, South Korea
Deukhun Kim	Ajou University, South Korea
Dong-Guk Han	Kookmin University, South Korea
Donghoon Chang	NIST, USA
Dongjae Lee	Kangwon National University, South Korea
Dooho Choi	Korea University, South Korea
Gunhee Lee	NSR, South Korea
Gwonsang Ryu	Kongju National University, South Korea
Hwajeong Seo	Hansung University, South Korea
Hwankuk Kim	Kookmin University, South Korea
Hyobeom Ahn	Kongju National University, South Korea

Hyojin Jo	Yonsei University, South Korea
Hyoungshick Kim	Sungkyunkwan University, South Korea
Hyungrok Jo	Yokohama National University, Japan
Hyunil Kim	Chosun University, South Korea
Il-Gu Lee	Sungshin Women's University, South Korea
Iraklis Leontiadis	Heliax, Switzerland
Jaeseung Song	Sejong University, South Korea
Ji Sun Shin	Sejong University, South Korea
Jin Kwak	Ajou University, South Korea
Jiwon Seo	Dankook University, South Korea
Jiyoon Kim	Gyeongsang National University, South Korea
Jong Hwan Park	Sangmyung University, South Korea
Jongchul Moon	NSR, South Korea
Jonghyouk Lee	Sejong University, South Korea
Jonghyun Kim	Sejong University, South Korea
Jongsung Kim	Kookmin University, South Korea
Joobeom Yun	Sejong University, South Korea
Jun Lee	KISTI, South Korea
Junbeom Hur	Korea University, South Korea
Jungtaek Seo	Gachon University, South Korea
Junji Shikata	Yokohama National University, Japan
Kihun Hong	Seowon University, South Korea
Kwangsu Lee	Sejong University, South Korea
Kyungho Joo	Soongsil University, South Korea
Miran Han	Korea University, South Korea
Mohsen Ali Alawami	Hankuk University of Foreign Studies, South Korea
Mun-Kyu Lee	Inha University, South Korea
Myungseo Park	Hansung University, South Korea
Namgyun Baek	Duksung Women's University, South Korea
Reza Azarderakhsh	Florida Atlantic University, USA
Seog Chung Seo	Kookmin University, South Korea
Seonghan Shin	AIST, Japan
Seongmin Kim	Sungshin Women's University, South Korea
Seunghyun Park	Hansung University, South Korea
Seung-Hyun Seo	Hanyang University, South Korea
Seungjin Ryu	NSR, South Korea
Seyoung Lee	Kangwon National University, South Korea
Sokjoon Lee	Gachon University, South Korea
Su-Hyun Kim	Soonchunhyang University, South Korea
Swee-Huay Heng	Multimedia University, Malaysia
Taejin Lee	Gachon University, South Korea

Taek-Young Youn	Dankook University, South Korea
Toshihiro Yamauchi	Okayama University, Japan
Wai-Kong Lee	Universiti Tunku Abdul Rahman, Malaysia
Wonsuk Choi	Korea University, South Korea
Young-Gab Kim	Sejong University, South Korea
Yuseok Jeon	Korea University, South Korea

Organizing Committee Co-chairs

Manhee Lee	Hannam University, South Korea
Haehyun Cho	Soongsil University, South Korea
Jae Deok Lim	ETRI, South Korea

Organizing Committee

Jeong-Nyeo Kim	ETRI, South Korea
Hwankuk Kim	Kookmin University, South Korea
Hayoung Seong	KISTI, South Korea
Jungseok Song	KISTI, South Korea
Jinyoung Oh	KISA, South Korea
Hyunggeun Oh	NSR, South Korea
Deok Gyu Lee	Seowon University, South Korea
Daewan Han	NSR, South Korea

Contents

Malware and Forensics

Quantum and Cryptography

AI/LLM for Security

Privacy and Anonymity

IoT and Traffic Analysis

System and Application Security

Crashing or Freezing the Bot: LiDAR Spoofing Attacks on ROS 2 UGV

Hwaseong Lee[1(✉)], Hyunwoo Lee[2], Yongki Jung[1], Seongdong Heo[1], Moosung Park[1], and Changon Yoo[1]

[1] Agency for Defense Development, Seoul, Korea
mail.hslee@gmail.com
[2] Cyber Operations Command of Republic of Korea, Seoul, Korea

Abstract. LiDAR sensors play a critical role in obstacle recognition and path planning within autonomous driving systems. On ROS 2-based platforms, LiDAR data is delivered through a multi-stage topic structure. While existing sensor attack research has primarily focused on physical spoofing using laser reflections, such methods require high-precision control and are subject to environmental constraints. This paper proposes two LiDAR spoofing attack scenarios that exploit the open communication architecture of ROS 2 by software-level falsification of sensor node topics, disrupting the sensor data flow. The first attack injects random data into the raw input topic, distorting the entire LiDAR processing pipeline and causing collision by preventing obstacle recognition. The second attack manipulates intermediate processed data to generate fake obstacles, leading the vehicle to stop unnecessarily. These attacks demonstrate that substantial physical impacts can be induced without directly tampering with sensor signals. This study experimentally verifies the vulnerability in the sensor data structure of a real ROS 2-based UGV environment and provides foundational insights for designing countermeasures to ensure sensor data integrity and system security.

Keywords: ROS · LiDAR Sensors · Spoofing

1 Introduction

Autonomous driving technology is rapidly being adopted in sectors such as logistics, defense, and industry, with the Robot Operating System (ROS) serving as a key technological foundation. ROS 2, in particular, has been actively adopted in real-world autonomous systems due to its improvements in real-time capability, scalability, and security. ROS 2-based autonomous UGVs (Unmanned Ground Vehicles) perceive their environments and plan paths using data from sensors such as LiDAR, GPS, and IMU, transmitted between nodes via ROS 2's pub/sub communication model. While this structure enhances flexibility and development efficiency, it also introduces security vulnerabilities [1–3]. An attacker with access to the ROS 2 network can impersonate existing nodes or create new ones to

K.-W. Park and J. Park (Eds.): WISA 2025 2025, LNCS 16434, pp. 3–14, 2026.
https://doi.org/10.1007/978-981-95-6857-4_1

spoof specific sensor topics, severely impacting the vehicle's perception, decision-making, and control. Even without physical sensor tampering, the attacker can falsify topic data published by sensor nodes to mimic real sensor outputs, presenting a novel threat model.

Although ROS 2 provides a distributed communication structure based on the Data Distribution Service (DDS), message integrity verification and node authentication are optional [4–7]. Since ROS 2 does not enforce access control by default, unauthorized nodes can freely publish to existing topics without being verified. Especially in the case of LiDAR sensors, the messages containing distance data are processed and refined through multiple stages before being used for autonomous decision-making. If a malicious node intervenes at a specific point in this data flow, it can affect the entire decision-making structure of the system. For example, injecting malformed data at the sensor input stage can distort all subsequent processing, potentially preventing the system from recognizing actual obstacles. Alternatively, inserting meaning fake data an intermediate processing stage may cause the system to stop or change its path even when no obstacle is present. These attacks demonstrate that perception logic can be manipulated without physical access to the sensors.

Previous studies focused on physical LiDAR spoofing techniques using laser reflections or angle disruptions, which are difficult to reproduce on actual platforms due to control complexity and environmental constraints [13,14]. Some research exists on ROS security, but it is mostly conceptual or simulation-based. Few studies experimentally analyze the physical effects of sensor data falsification using a real ROS 2 UGV platform.

This paper presents two spoofing scenarios that tamper with different stages of the LiDAR data flow in a real ROS 2-based UGV to induce navigation disruption. The first attack spoofs raw input data to trigger obstacle recognition failure, and the second manipulates processed scan data to insert fake obstacles. Both were executed during actual outdoor navigation and analyzed using visual observations. Although the experiments were conducted in plaintext communication environments, prior research has shown that even with ROS 2's security enabled (DDS-Security), topic-level spoofing remains possible due to issues in certificate management and policy configuration. We point out the proposed threat model remains valid regardless of whether encryption is used (e.g., with DDS-security enabled). The study experimentally demonstrates how ROS 2 can be exploited to induce physical effects without hardware manipulation and contributes practical insights for enhancing sensor security [15].

2 System Overview

2.1 ROS 2-Based UGV Platform

The experimental platform used in this study is a custom-developed autonomous ground robot named R-UGV (Research UGV). The chassis weighs approximately 250 kg, with a maximum payload capacity of 500 kg (see Figs. 1 and 2). The main controller is an Intel Phantom Canyon NUC with an i7-1165G7 processor,

Fig. 1. The physical R-UGV(right) and external controller(left)

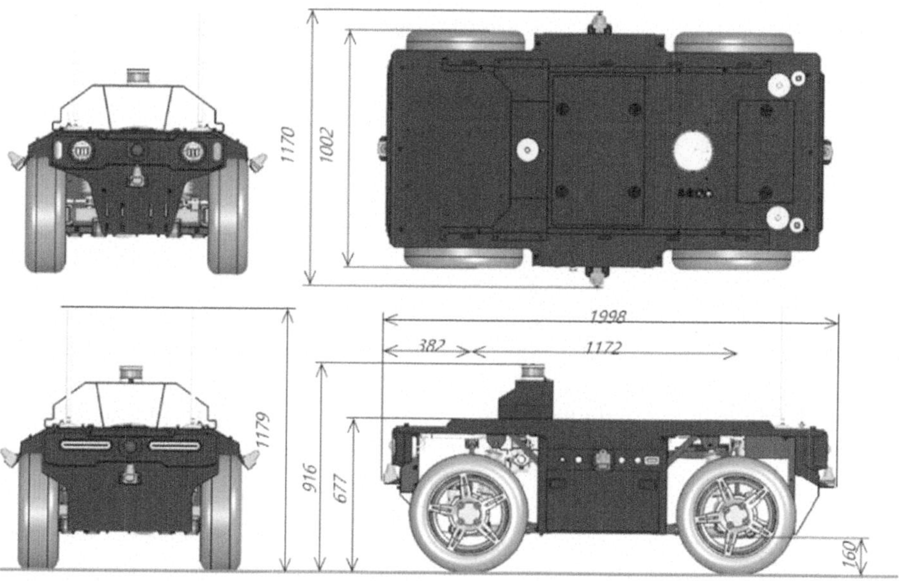

Fig. 2. Body outline of R-UGV

running Ubuntu 20.04 and ROS 2 Foxy. The R-UGV is equipped with essential sensors for autonomous driving, including 3D LiDAR, GPS, and IMU as shown in Table 1.

While ROS 2 supports encryption and authentication via DDS-Security, the R-UGV is configured to use plaintext communication with ROS 2 DDS security features disabled, considering the real-time performance and the limited computational resources of the NUC-based platform. Prior studies have reported real-time performance degradation with ROS 2 security features enabled [8]. Deng et a. demonstrated that topic spoofing remains feasible even in secured environments due to certificate and configuration issues [9]. Therefore, the spoofing attack conducted in this study can be regarded as a valid threat model even in environments where encrypted communication is applied. The R-UGV is designed for outdoor navigation. The process begins with SLAM-based mapping, followed by global path planning using designated waypoints. Real-time localization and obstacle avoidance are managed through a local planner that adapts paths based on current sensor data. The R-UGV communicates wirelessly with an external control station, and attack scenarios are executed via a custom injector node. This node connects to the ROS 2 network to spoof or publish sensor data. All attacks were carried out during live autonomous navigation in physical environments.

Table 1. Sensor Spec. in R-UGV

Sensor	Mfr.	Spec.	Iface.
LiDAR	Velodyne	– Detection range/Accuracy: 100 m/3cm – Vertical FoV: 30° – Vertical resolution: 2° (16 channels) – Horizon FoV: 360° – Horizontal resolution: 0.1°–0.4°	Ethernet
GPS	NovAtel	– Positioning accuracy: 1.0cm (based on RTK) – Support systems: GPS, GLONASS etc.	Serial
IMU	Phiget-Spatial	– Gyroscope speed max (X-Axis, Y-Axis): ±400°/s – Gyroscope speed max (Z-Axis): ±300°/s	USB

The R-UGV is connected to an external controller via wireless communication (see Fig. 3). The external controller consists of a laptop-based controller interface and a tablet style Remote Control Unit (RCU). All attack scenarios were executed during actual autonomous driving, and changes in physical behavior were observed in a real-world environment.

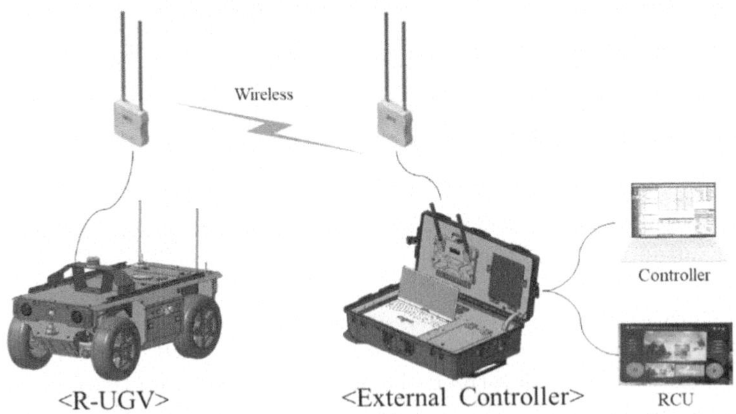

Fig. 3. System architecture of R-UGV

2.2 Sensor and Node Architecture

The sensor data in the R-UGV system is processed by corresponding ROS 2 nodes for each specific function [16]. The main nodes are as follows. Sensor data in the R-UGV system is handled by dedicated ROS 2 nodes:

- LiDAR Driver Node: Publishes raw distance data as packets.
- Transform & Point Cloud Nodes: Generate 3D point clouds via coordinate transformations.
- Laser Scan Node: Converts 3D data to 2D scans for obstacle avoidance.
- GPS & IMU Nodes: Provide location and orientation data.
- Control Nodes: Handle speed, direction, and waypoint following.

Each sensor's data is transmitted to multiple nodes via ROS 2's publish/subscribe architecture. In particular, LaserScan messages are directly tied to autonomous driving decisions and are treated as critical information, being subscribed to by various nodes.

2.3 LiDAR Data Flow Structure

The raw distance data from the LiDAR sensor is published by the drive node to the `/velodyne_packets` topic, transformed into a 2D scan (/scan) for use in navigation modules such as obstacle avoidance, stopping, and path adjustment. The LiDAR data processing pipeline is shown in Fig. 4. In this processing pipeline, injecting malformed data at the input stage or manipulating meaningful information at the processing stage can cause the entire autonomous driving system to malfunction. This study experimentally compares the disruption effects on autonomous driving by individually tampering with data topics at both stages-input and processing.

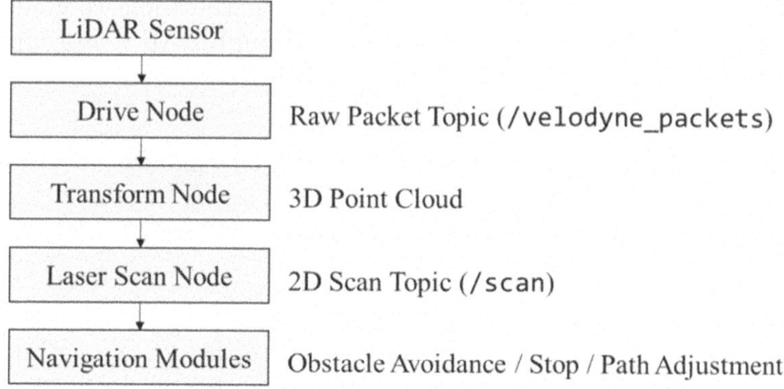

Fig. 4. LiDAR data processing flow in R-UGV

3 LiDAR Topic Spoofing Attack Model

This section describes the design and implementation of two LiDAR topic spoofing attack scenarios carried out on a ROS 2-based autonomous UGV. Without physically interfering with the sensor layer, the attacker exploits ROS 2's internal publish/subscribe architecture to spoof data published by sensor nodes. Though this, the attacker aims to induce errors in the system's perception and decision-making processes, ultimately causing physical effects during actual operation.

3.1 Attacker Assumptions and Threat Model

In this study, the attacker is assumed to already have access to ROS 2 network. This access could be obtained through prior compromise, insider threats, or external connections in the absence of communication security [10,11]. The attacker's goal is to manipulate the flow of LiDAR sensor data so that the autonomous system either fails to recognize actual obstacles or incorrectly identifies non-existent ones. As a result, the vehicle may experience physical malfunctions such as collisions, abrupt strops, or deviation from its intended path.

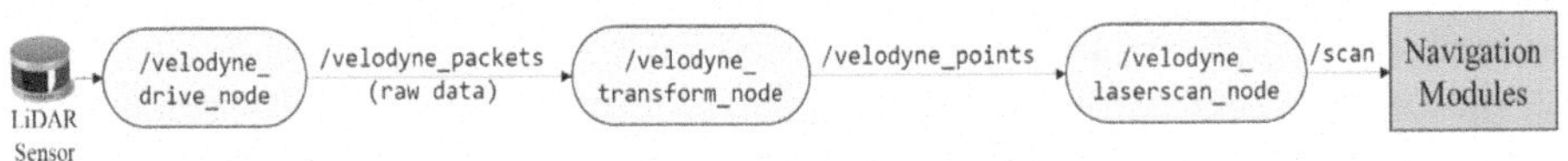

Fig. 5. Topic communication between nodes from LiDAR sensor input

3.2 Attack Scenarios

Figure 5 presents a portion of `rqt_graph`, showing the topic communication structure (pub/sub relationships) between nodes from LiDAR sensor input. The attacker targets two specific points within this flow:

- Input stage: `/velodyne_packets` (raw distance data published by the sensor drive)
- Processing stage: `/scan` (final decision-making data converted into 2D range information).

Attack Scenario 1 (Inducing collisions via raw data spoofing): This attack injects abnormal data at the sensor input stage to distort the entire LiDAR data processing pipeline. The goal is to prevent proper obstacle recognition, which results in a physical outcome such as a collision caused by the failure to detect actual obstacles. The attack node uses the same message type as `/velodyne_packets` (i.e., `/velodyne_msgs/VelodyneScan`) and publishes packet messages containing random by patterns to the ROS 2 network. Since the attack distorts data at the input topic stage, it affects the subsequent point cloud generation and scan transformation. As a result, the autonomous system may fail to recognize the presence of obstacles and continue driving, leading to a collision.

Attack Scenario 2 (Inducing stops via fake obstacle injection): This attack falsifies the `/scan` topic to make it appear as though there are obstacle at close range, even when node exist. The system misinterprets this as a real threat and reacts with inappropriate behaviors such as emergency stops or route changes. The attack node uses the same message type as `/scan` (`sensor_msgs/LaserScan`) and construct messages as fol lows:

- `ranges[]`: Insert short distance values (less than 0.2 m) within a 180-degree forward field of view.
- `intensities[]`: Insert high values in the corresponding range indices.

The message period and structure are kept identical to legitimate `/scan` message so that decision-making nodes subscribing to `/scan` interpret them as valid distance readings. The system responds by avoiding or stopping for nonexistent obstacles. In the experiment, `RViz2` [12] visualizations showed arc-shaped fake obstacles and vehicle was observed to suddenly stop in the middle of navigation. This attack methodology can be extended to other sensors with similar pub/sub structures. For example, falsifying GPS messages on the topic `/ublox/fix` could mislead localization or perception modules, resulting in navigation failure or unsafe behavior

4 Experiments

This section presents the results of real-world spoofing attacks conducted on a ROS 2 based UGV system. The goal of experiments was to verify the physical effects of LiDAR topic spoofing on actual autonomous navigation. The attacks were executed using Python-based ROS 2 publisher nodes, and the results were analyzed through RViz2 visualizations and on-site images.

Table 2. Attack scenario summary

'Type	Attack Scenario 1	Attack Scenario 2
Attack ID	A1	A2
Target topic	`/velodyne_packets`	`/scan`
Attack method	Random packet injection	False obstacle injection
Expected impact	Collision	Navigation halt/UGV stop

4.1 Experiment Setup

The experiments were conducted in an outdoor environment where the R-UGV followed predefined waypoints autonomously. Two types of attacks were carried out: (i) injecting random data into the `/velodyne_packets` topic to corrupt raw sensor input, and (ii) publishing false obstacles to the /scan topic to interfere with obstacle avoidance behavior. Each scenarios followed the same procedure: baseline navigation and attack injection then behavioral observation. The two attacks scenarios are summarized in Table 2. These attacks were implemented using Python with `rclpy` library. The publisher node generated forged messages and published them periodically to the target topic. Figure 6 shows an actual image of the R-UGV during experiment.

Fig. 6. Outdoor experiment scenes with R-UGV

4.2 RViz2 Visualization and Experimental Results

`RViz2` is a 3D visualization tool used in ROS 2 that enables real-time monitoring of sensor data, including LiDAR, IMU, and odometry. In this experiment, `RViz2` was used to visualize the `/scan` topic, which reflects processed LiDAR data, allowing clear observation of false obstacle patterns during the spoofing attack. In the outdoor experiments, clear behavior changes were observed following each attack. In the /scan spoofing scenario(A2), false obstacle points appeared in `RViz2`, even though there were no real obstacles. Based on the perceived distance of false obstacle, the R-UGV either stopped or deviated from its planned path in an attempt to avoid them. Although the `/velodyne_packets` topic is not directly visualized in `RViz2`, its impact was evident in the A1 attack scenario through disrupted downstream sensor outputs. Its corruption affected downstream topics such as `/scan`, ultimately causing the R-UGV to stop moving due to failure in LiDAR data processing.

Figure 7 compares the sensor outputs before and after the attack while the R-UGV remained stationary, using `RViz2`. The left column presents Scenario A1, and the right column presents Scenario A2. In each case, the top row displays the normal sensor state, while the bottom row reflects the system's

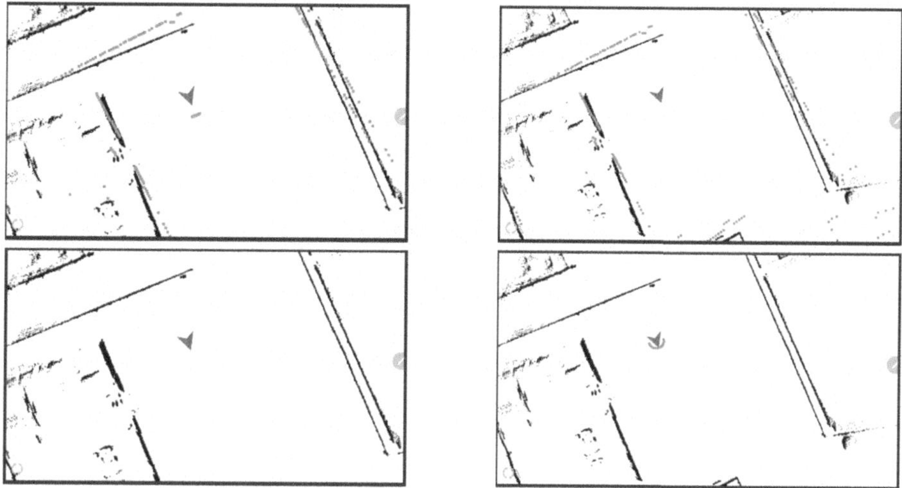

Fig. 7. Sensor output before/after the attack under stationary conditions (`RViz2`). A1(left) and A2(right). Pre-attack state(top) and post-attack state(bottom). Red arrow indicates R-UGV's position/heading, blue dots present perceived objects

response after the spoofing attack. In scenario A1, random data was injected into `/velodyne_packets` topic, disrupting the LiDAR data processing pipeline. As a result, the R-UGV failed to recognize nearby obstacles. In scenario A2, forged obstacle data was injected directly into the /scan topic. In the bottom right image, `RViz2` displays false obstacle points (blue dots) that do not exist in the physical environment.

Figure 8 shows how the UGV responded during active navigation when spoofing at tacks were executed. Each column presents an attack scenario: A1 on the left A2 on the right. The rows present three stages: before the attack (top), at the moment of attack (middle), and after attack (bottom). In Scenario A1, random packets were published to the `/velodyne_packets` topic. As a result, the local planner re-generated a new path under the false assumption that no obstacles were present. The UGV then followed this shortest path, which led to a collision. In Scenario A2, arc-shaped fake obstacles were repeatedly injected into the /scan topic. As seen in the bottom right image, the R-UGV identified a curved wall of objects and continuously adjusted its local path to avoid them. However, due to persistent spoofed objects, the R-UGV could not completed its planned navigation task and ultimately failed to proceed.

This experiment demonstrated that even simple top-based spoofing attacks can significantly disrupt autonomous navigation in ROS 2-based UGV system. The spoofing attack halted the robot by corrupting raw sensor input and caused semantic misinterpretation, resulting in inappropriate obstacle avoidance behavior.

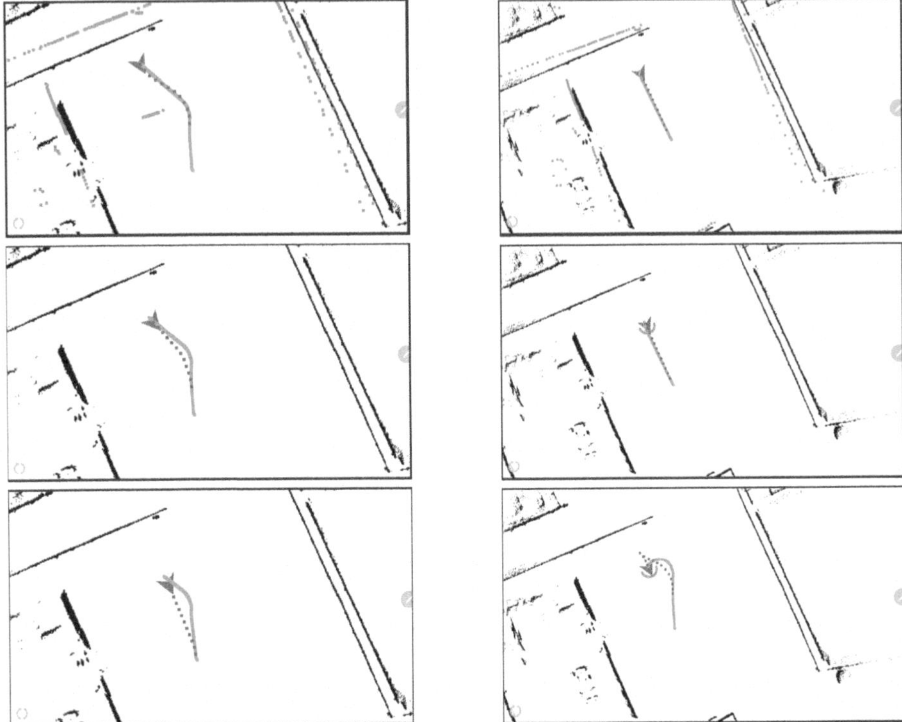

Fig. 8. Sensor output before/after the attack under autonomous driving (`Rviz2`). A1(left) and A2(right). Pre-attack state(top), attack onset(middle), and post-attack state(bottom), respectively. Red arrow indicates R-UGV's position/heading, blue dots present perceived objects, green solid line shows the global path, and red dashed line represents the local path

This type of attack can be monitored in real time by integrating with a rule-based or a machine-learning-based detection system. This was demonstrated in [17], where the proposed attack scenario was applied to a rule-based method and effectively distinguished between normal and abnormal behaviors.

5 Conclusion

This study conducted real-world spoofing experiments on a custom-built ROS 2-based UGV(R-UGV) to evaluate the impact of LiDAR topic manipulation. Two attack scenarios targeting different stages of the sensor data flow were implemented without any physical access to the sensors. The result shows that even without direct sensor tampering, false data injection alone can disrupt autonomous driving by altering perceive obstacles and path planning. These results highlight the structural vulnerabilities of ROS 2's pub/sub model. By validating these attacks on an actual robotic platform, this work bridges the gap between theoretical vulnerabilities and practical exploitation, and provides a concrete basis for developing lightweight, real-time defenses in future ROS based systems. Future work includes extending the attack model to other sensor modalities and integrating detection mechanisms based on rule-based and machine learning approaches.

References

1. Abed, M.S., Al-Doori, Q.F., Abdullah, A.T., Abdallah, A.A.: Security vulnerabilities and threats in robotic systems: a comprehensive review. Int. J. Saf. Secur. Eng. **13**(3), 555–563 (2023)
2. Dieber, B., Breiling, B., Taurer, S., Kacianka, S., Rass, S., Schartner, P.: Security for the robot operating system. Robot. Auton. Syst. **98**, 192–203 (2017)
3. Botta, A., Rotbei, S., Zinno, S., Ventre, G.: Cyber security of robots: a comprehensive survey. Intell. Syst. Appl. **18**, (2023)
4. Portugal, D., Rocha, R.P., Castilho, J.P.: Inquiring the robot operating system community on the state of adoption of the ROS 2 robotics middleware. Int. J. Intell. Robot. Appl. **8**(1), 100–115 (2024)
5. Open Robotics, ROS 2 Design Overview. https://design.ros2.org/. Accessed 30 Sept 2025
6. SROS. https://github.com/ros2/sros2. Accessed 30 Sept 2025
7. Specification, O.M.G.: The real-time publish-subscribe protocol (RTPS) DDS interoperability wire protocol specification. Object Management Group Ptc-18-09-03 (2018)
8. Kim, J., Smereka, J.M., Cheung, C., Nepal, S., Grobler, M.: Security and performance considerations in ROS 2: a balancing act (2018). arXiv:1809.09566
9. Deng, G., Xu, G., Zhou, Y., Zhang, T., Liu, Y.: On the (In)security of secure ROS2. In: Proceeding of the 2022 ACM SIGSAC Conference on Computer and Communications Security, pp. 739–753 (2022)
10. Patel, Y., Rughani, P.H., Desai, D.: Analyzing security vulnerability and forensic investigation of ROS2: a case study. In: Proceeding of the 8th International Conference on Robotics and Artificial Intelligence, pp. 6–12 (2022)
11. Kaasen, A.D., Grov, G., Mancini, F., Baksaas, M.: Toward data-driven autonomous cyber defence for military unmanned vehicles-threats and attack. In: Proceeding of the IEEE Military Communications Conference, pp. 861–866 (2022)
12. RViz2. https://turtlebot.github.io/turtlebot4-user-manual/software/rviz.html. Accessed 30 Sept 2025
13. Cao, Y., Xiao, C., Cyr, B., Zhou, Y., Park, W., Rampazzi, S., Mao, Z.M.: Adversarial sensor attack on lidar-based perception in autonomous driving. In: Proceeding of the 2019 ACM SIGSAC Conference on computer and Communications Security, pp. 2267–2281 (2019)
14. Cao, Y., Bhupathiraju, S.H., Naghavi, P., Sugawara, T., Mao, Z.M., Rampazzi, S.: You can't see me: physical removal attacks on lidar-based autonomous vehicles driving frame works. In: Proceeding of the 32nd USENIX Security Symposium, pp. 2993–3010 (2023)

15. Değirmenci, E., Kırca, Y.S., Özçelik, İ, Yazıcı, A.: ROSIDS23: network intrusion detection dataset for robot operating system. Data Brief **51**, 109739 (2023)
16. ROS 2 Documentation: Sensor Integration. https://docs.ros.org/en/foxy/index.html. Accessed 30 Sept 2025
17. Lee, H., Jung, Y., Heo, S., Park, M., Yoo, C.: Light weight rule-based detection for operation in UGV environments. J. Korean Inst. Inf. Technol. **23**(8), 87–95 (2025)

PodBeater: Exploiting Multi-value Affinity for Efficient Co-location Attacks in Kubernetes

Yiju Jung, Hyerean Jang, and Youngjoo Shin(✉)

School of Cybersecurity, Korea University, Seoul 02841, Republic of Korea
{wjddlwn2637,hr_jang,syoungjoo}@korea.ac.kr

Abstract. Kubernetes supports multi-tenancy by allowing multiple users to share physical infrastructure. However, this design leads to co-location attacks, where an attacker deploys attack pods onto the same node as victim pods to exploit shared hardware resources. While previous work demonstrates the feasibility of such attacks, it assumes that the attacker has sufficient knowledge of the victim pod's configuration. This paper presents PodBeater, a novel co-location attack that exploits Kubernetes's multi-value affinity feature to steer the scheduler's pod placement decisions. Unlike previous work, PodBeater is designed to operate even under a realistic threat model where the attacker lacks knowledge of the victim pod's configuration. We evaluate PodBeater on both a small-scale cluster with 20 nodes and 350 pods and a large-scale cluster with 40 nodes and 800 pods, demonstrating its effectiveness under both previous and more realistic threat models. Our results show that PodBeater achieves co-location with fewer attack pods compared to previous works.

Keywords: Kubernetes · Co-location attack · Affinity mechanism

1 Introduction

Kubernetes [7] has become the de facto standard for container orchestration in modern cloud infrastructures. A core component of the Kubernetes architecture is the scheduler, which assigns pods to suitable nodes based on resource availability and user-specified scheduling requirements. While this scheduling mechanism offers flexibility and efficiency, it also introduces new security challenges [5]. Moreover, Kubernetes supports multi-tenancy by allowing multiple users to share the same physical infrastructure. This design leads to co-location attacks [1,10,15], where an attacker deliberately deploys attack pods on the same node as target pods. Once co-located, the attacker can exploit shared hardware resources to mount microarchitectural side-channel [9] or denial-of-service attacks [14].

K.-W. Park and J. Park (Eds.): WISA 2025 2025, LNCS 16434, pp. 15–27, 2026.
https://doi.org/10.1007/978-981-95-6857-4_2

Previous work, REPTTACK [5], demonstrates the feasibility of co-location attacks in Kubernetes cluster. Specifically, it exploits the Kubernetes scheduler by allowing an attacker to influence pod placement decisions through carefully crafted user-specified scheduling requirements. By replicating the victim pod's scheduling requirements, the attacker can deliberately steer the scheduler to co-locate attack pods on the same node as the victim pod.

However, REPTTACK has two main limitations. First, it assumes a threat model in which the attacker possesses sufficient knowledge of the victim pod's scheduling requirements, which is strong in practical settings. This assumption does not reflect the real-world Kubernetes cluster, as such information is typically not exposed to unprivileged users. Second, previous work does not account for additional scheduling requirements, such as multi-value affinity conditions, which can significantly influence the scheduler's placement decisions.

To overcome these limitations, we improve the previous work by presenting *PodBeater*, a co-location attack exploiting multi-value affinity. In Kubernetes, nodes and pods are labeled with user-specified attributes (e.g., location or hardware type), which the scheduler uses to identify nodes that meet a pod's scheduling requirements. Multi-value affinity enables a pod to specify multiple values for a given label, expanding the set of candidate nodes. As a result, the scheduler considers more nodes for placement, increasing the probability that a pod is scheduled on the same node as the victim. PodBeater exploits this scheduling behavior to achieve co-location with the victim pod using fewer attack pods.

We evaluate PodBeater under two threat models: (1) $\mathcal{T}_u$, which is the same as the previous work [5] where the attacker has sufficient knowledge of the victim pod's scheduling requirements and (2) $\mathcal{T}_r$, where the attacker lacks knowledge of the victim pod's scheduling requirements, more realistic than $\mathcal{T}_u$. We design multiple attack strategies and assess them on both small- and large-scale clusters. We evaluate our work under $\mathcal{T}_u$ to compare it with REPTTACK. Under $\mathcal{T}_r$, we analyze PodBeater's effectiveness using both single-value and multi-value affinity condition. In our experiment, PodBeater consistently achieves co-location with fewer attack pods than the previous work and single-value affinity strategies, demonstrating superior efficiency in reducing attack cost. Finally, we discuss several mitigations against the proposed attack.

Contributions. Our main contributions are as follows:

- We present PodBeater, a co-location attack that leverages multi-value affinity in the scheduling process of Kubernetes.
- We evaluate PodBeater under various threat models, demonstrating that it achieves co-location with fewer attack pods compared to the previous attack.
- We perform large-scale experiments on a 40-node Kubernetes cluster with 800 pods to quantitatively evaluate how different attack strategies affect the number of attack pods required to achieve co-location.

2 Related Work

Co-location attack in Kubernetes. Previous work [5] introduces a co-location attack that exploits the scheduling behavior of Kubernetes. It assumes the attacker has sufficient knowledge of the victim pod's scheduling requirements. By replicating these requirements, the attacker achieves co-location with the victim pod by deploying a small number of attack pods. In contrast, our work explores multi-value affinity to enable more efficient co-location attacks in Kubernetes, and demonstrates that PodBeater outperforms REPTTACK. We further evaluate PodBeater under realistic threat models, and propose diverse attack strategies to quantitatively assess its effectiveness.

Co-location attacks beyond Kubernetes. Co-location attacks have been studied in various cloud environments. Zhao et al. [15] exploit the load balancer of Google Cloud Run to spread attack instances across multiple physical machines. Makrani et al. [10] used fake traces that mimic the victim's behavior to induce co-location. Atya et al. [1] demonstrated brute-force methods in Amazon EC2 by repeatedly launching VMs until co-location is achieved. Other studies analyzed how placement policies affect attack performance. Han et al. [6] showed that attackers can improve the success rate of co-location by adjusting the number of VM launches based on allocation policies. Varadarajan et al. [13] showed that manipulating deployment parameters such as launch timing and instance count can improve the success rate of co-location in public cloud.

Affinity policy in cloud. Affinity policy has also been employed in the cloud to improve placement decisions and optimize system performance. Pachorkar et al. [12] and Chen et al. [2] both proposed an affinity-aware placement mechanisms to optimize resource usage and reduce network overhead. Moreno-Vozmediano et al. [11] proposed a new affinity-based placement policy to improve orchestration mechanisms for deploying high-availability services.

Unlike previous work, our work shows that attackers can influence scheduling decisions by exploiting affinity-based configurations. While affinity policies are designed to optimize resource usage and service availability, our findings reveal that they can be exploited to perform co-location attacks.

3 Background

3.1 Kubernetes Orchestration Mechanism

Kubernetes is an orchestration platform that automates the deployment and management of containerized applications in the cloud. A Kubernetes cluster consists of *nodes* (i.e., physical or virtual machines) that provide resources to run *pods*, the smallest scheduling units that encapsulate one or more containers.

Kubernetes provides an efficient scheduling mechanism to deploy pods onto appropriate nodes within the cluster. Users can specify scheduling requirements by attaching labels (i.e., user-specified key-value pairs), which are expressed as

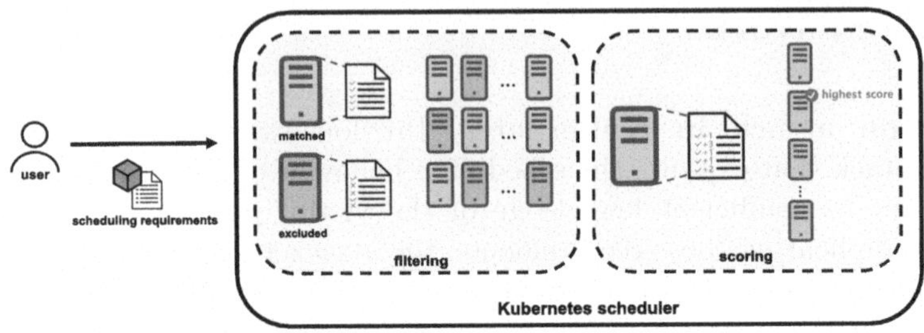

Fig. 1. Workflow of Kubernetes scheduler to determine a suitable node.

affinity conditions. These requirements, defined in the pod specification, influence the scheduler's decision to select a suitable node.

Overview of Kubernetes scheduler. The Kubernetes scheduler determines pod placement based on the current state of cluster resources and user-specified scheduling requirements. As shown in Fig. 1, users specify these scheduling requirements using labels within the pod specification. The scheduling process comprises two phases. In the filtering phase, the scheduler excludes nodes that fail to meet the pod's resource requirements. In the scoring phase, it evaluates the remaining candidates and assigns scores. The scheduler then selects the node with the highest score for pod placement.

Affinity scheduling mechanism in Kubernetes. Kubernetes provides an affinity mechanism to reflect user-specified scheduling requirements. Affinity allows users to define placement conditions that constrain a pod to run on a specific node or be co-located with, or explicitly separated from, other pods. There are three types of affinity: nodeAffinity, podAffinity, and podAntiAffinity. *nodeAffinity* restricts a pod to nodes with specific labels. *podAffinity* places a pod on nodes already hosting pods with matching labels. *podAntiAffinity* ensures separation from pods with specified labels, often used to improve availability or reduce resource contention. Users define these conditions in the pod specification using key-value labels.

Affinity conditions are evaluated during both the filtering and scoring phases of the scheduling process, directly influencing pod placement decisions. User can specify affinity conditions with either a single value or multiple values for a given key. The condition is satisfied if any of the specified values match the corresponding label on the node, making it eligible for scheduling. For example, if a pod is expected to be placed on nodes labeled `disktype=ssd`, this requirement can be specified using nodeAffinity. Similarly, if the podAffinity specifies the key `color` with a single value `red`, the pod will be scheduled on a node that already hosts another pod labeled `color=red`. When multiple values are specified for the key `color`, such as `values: [red, orange, yellow]`, then any node hosting a pod labeled one of these values (e.g., `color=orange`) satisfies the condition.

3.2 Co-location Attack

Orchestration systems such as Kubernetes operate in multi-tenant environments, allowing pods from different users to share the same nodes. Co-location attack exploits this environmental characteristic by intentionally placing the attack pod on the same node as the victim pod, forcing them to share physical resources.

Once co-located, the attacker can exploit shared hardware to perform various threats, such as cache-based side-channel or denial-of-service (DoS) attacks, potentially leaking information or degrading service availability. Since co-location enables these threats, it is a significant security concern.

4 PodBeater Attack

In this section, we propose PodBeater, a co-location attack that exploits Kubernetes's multi-value affinity to reduce the attack cost by minimizing the number of pods required to achieve co-location with a victim pod. In Sect. 4.1, we present the motivation behind PodBeater. In Sect. 4.2, we describe the attack procedure for conducting PodBeater in Kubernetes.

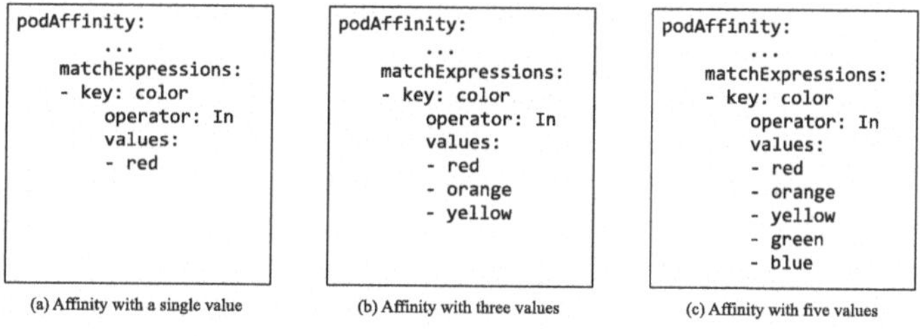

Fig. 2. Comparison of single-value and multi-value affinity.

4.1 Motivation

Previous work demonstrates that Kubernetes's affinity-based scheduling mechanism can be exploited to co-locate with a victim pod on the same node. However, it assumes that the attacker has sufficient knowledge of the victim pod's scheduling requirements and considers only a single strategy with fixed affinity conditions. In real-world cloud environments, attackers typically lack such knowledge, and affinity conditions are often configured with multiple values.

Therefore, it is necessary to evaluate attack strategies under more realistic threat models and to explore attack strategies that leverage multi-value affinity configurations. Unlike previous work, we consider a more realistic threat model in which the attacker lacks such knowledge. Moreover, since Kubernetes supports multi-value affinity, we leverage this feature to design various attack strategies that achieve co-location with fewer attack pods than both previous work and single-value affinity strategies. To this end, we introduce PodBeater, a co-location attack that employs multi-value affinity strategies and evaluates their effectiveness under both $\mathcal{T}_r$ and $\mathcal{T}_u$.

4.2 Attack Procedure

PodBeater exploits Kubernetes's multi-value affinity, which influences the scheduler's placement decision to select a suitable node. The attacker performs the attack through the following steps.

Step 1 The attacker defines a pod specification with an affinity condition that includes N affinity values to steer the scheduler's placement decision.
Step 2 The attacker submits the pod specification, and the scheduler deploys the attack pod to a suitable node based on the provided affinity values.
Step 3 The attacker verifies whether the attack pod is co-located with the victim pod on the same node.
Step 4 Steps 1–3 are repeated until the attack pod is successfully co-located with the victim pod.

Since affinity feature influences the scheduler's placement decision to assign a pod to a suitable node, the performance of PodBeater can vary depending on the number of affinity values N specified in the pod specification. Figure 2(a) illustrates an example of the single-value affinity, where the affinity condition specifies only one value. Figure 2(b) and (c) illustrate multi-value affinity, where the affinity condition specifies three and five values, respectively. Whenever we deploy attack pods across different nodes, we specify a unique label used exclusively by the attack pods and configure an additional *podAntiAffinity* condition based on this label. This prevents unnecessary concentration on the same node and increases the chances of reaching the victim pod.

5 Evaluation

In this section, we evaluate the PodBeater attack. In Sect. 5.1, we describe our experimental setup. In Sect. 5.2, we evaluate PodBeater under $\mathcal{T}_u$. In Sect. 5.3, we evaluate PodBeater under $\mathcal{T}_r$.

Table 1. Kubernetes cluster configurations.

	# of master nodes	# of worker nodes	# of pods
Small-scale cluster	1	20	350
Large-scale cluster	1	40	400

5.1 Experimental Setup

To evaluate the impact of cluster size on the efficiency of co-location attacks, we conduct experiments across two deployment scales as shown in Table 1: (1) a small-scale cluster with one master node and 20 worker nodes, and (2) a large-scale cluster with one master node and 40 worker nodes. To enable a direct comparison with previous work [5], we adopted the same large-scale configuration and constructed a small-scale cluster with half its size to analyze the impact of scale. The clusters are configured using containerd [3] as the container runtime, and all interactions are performed through the Kubernetes command-line tool `kubectl`. Each node was randomly assigned key-value labels representing hardware characteristics, including CPU type, GPU type, disk type, and memory capacity. Labels are assigned using the command "`kubectl label nodes <nodeName> <key>=<value>`".

To simulate realistic clusters, we selected 25 of the most widely used services on Docker Hub [4] and deployed them as benign pods. For each pod, labels were randomly assigned based on the Recommended Labels and Example Labels provided by the Kubernetes documentation [8]. The pods are defined using YAML-formatted manifest files and deployed using the command "`kubectl apply -f <pod manifest file>`". To evaluate the impact of label diversity, we configured two settings with label counts of 9 and 5, representing high and low diversity, respectively. These labels were selected based on documentation applicable to our environment.

5.2 PodBeater on Threat Model $\mathcal{T}_u$

In this section, we evaluate the performance of PodBeater in $\mathcal{T}_u$, where the attacker has sufficient knowledge of the victim pod's scheduling requirement. We evaluate PodBeater with different attack strategies and compare its results against previous work.

Threat model. We assume a strong attacker with sufficient knowledge of the victim pod's scheduling requirements (i.e., affinity conditions) in the target cluster. Leveraging this knowledge, the attacker can deploy an attack pod to the target cluster by replicating the victim's affinity conditions. The attacker can also specify multi-value affinity in the pod specification to influence the scheduler's placement decisions. The scheduler selects a suitable node for each pod solely based on its scheduling requirements. We further assume that the attacker can determine whether co-location with the victim pod has been achieved. This can be verified through side-channel attacks, however, detailed analysis of this technique is beyond the scope of this work.

Experimental design. To conduct a thorough evaluation, we propose two attack strategies and compare their results against REPTTACK. We describe REPTTACK and each strategy as follows:

- **REPTTACK.** The attacker replicates the victim pod's scheduling requirements and repeatedly deploys attack pods with the same affinity condition.

Algorithm 1 PodBeater on threat model $\mathcal{T}_u$.

Require: Label count $L = 9$, maximum attempts N
1: Generate label pool $\mathcal{P}$
2: Deploy *initial* pods with randomly assigned labels from $\mathcal{P}$
3: Deploy *benign* pods with randomly generated affinity conditions
4: Select target victim pod $V \in$ *benign*
5: **for** $i \leftarrow 1$ **to** N **do**
6:     Generate attack pod A_i based on V's affinity condition
7:     Deploy A_i
8:     **if** A_i is placed on the same node as V **then**
9:         Record number of attempts i
10:         **Break**
11:     **end if**
12: **end for**

- **Strategy 1. Deploying an attack pod with an identical multi-value affinity condition.** The attacker extends the victim pod's affinity condition by appending additional values from the labels of pods likely to be co-located with the victim. This extended condition remains fixed across all attack attempts. We denote this strategy as $PodBeater_{same}$.
- **Strategy 2. Deploying an attack pod with a distinct multi-value affinity condition.** Similar to Strategy 1, the attacker extends the victim pod's affinity condition with additional values. However, in each attempt, the attacker randomly selects new values to explore different placement opportunities. We denote this strategy as $PodBeater_{random}$.

We perform our experiment based on Algorithm 1. The experiment begins by initializing the label pool $\mathcal{P}$, where the size of the label pool L is configured to 9 (Line 1 in Algorithm 1). We then deploy initial pods that reference labels from $\mathcal{P}$ but do not specify affinity conditions (Line 2). These initial pods serve as anchors, ensuring that the affinity conditions of subsequently deployed benign pods can be satisfied. This prevents benign pods from remaining in a Pending state due to unsatisfiable affinity conditions. After the initial pods are successfully deployed, the benign pods are deployed with randomly generated affinity conditions (Line 3). Then the attacker selects a victim pod V from benign pods (Line 4). In each trial, the attacker generates an attack pod by replicating the victim pod's affinity condition and appending additional affinity values inferred from other pods that are likely scheduled on the same node as the victim (Line 6). The attacker then deploys it iteratively (Line 7) until co-location is achieved (Line 8). The number of attack pods required to achieve co-location is recorded (Line 9). The experiment was repeated 10 times under identical settings.

Experimental result. Table 2 presents our experimental results on different cluster scales. In the large-scale cluster, PodBeater demonstrated better performance than the REPTTACK. Specifically, REPTTACK required an average of 2.9 attack pods, while $PodBeater_{same}$ and $PodBeater_{random}$ required 2.2 and 2.1 pods to achieve co-location with the victim pod, respectively. On the other

Table 2. Average number of attack pods required to achieve co-location on $\mathcal{T}_u$

Cluster setting	REPTTACK	PodBeater$_{same}$	PodBeater$_{random}$
Small-scale cluster	1.0	1.0	1.0
Large-scale cluster	2.9	2.2	2.1

Algorithm 2 PodBeater on threat model $\mathcal{T}_r$.

Require: Label count $L \in \{5, 9\}$, maximum attempts N
Generate label pool $\mathcal{P}$ of size L
Deploy *benign* pods with randomly assigned labels from $\mathcal{P}$
Select target victim pod $V \in$ *benign*
for $i \leftarrow 1$ **to** N **do**
    Generate attack pod A_i with randomly specified affinity conditions
    Deploy A_i
    if A_i is placed on same node as V **then**
        Record number of attempts i
        Break
    end if
end for

hand, in the small-scale cluster, all attack strategies achieved co-location with the victim pod by deploying a single attack pod, This performance improvement originates from using node affinity, which effectively narrows down the candidate nodes for placement. Moreover, having fewer nodes and higher pod density in the small-scale cluster makes it more likely that the scheduler places both the victim pod and the attacker's pod on the same node, even with minimal attempts.

5.3 PodBeater on Threat Model $\mathcal{T}_r$

In this section, we evaluate the performance of PodBeater in $\mathcal{T}_r$, where the attacker lacks knowledge of the victim pod's scheduling requirement. We evaluate PodBeater with different attack strategies and discuss their results.

Threat model. We assume an unprivileged attacker who lacks knowledge of the scheduling requirements of any pod in the target cluster. Consequently, the attacker should inevitably deploy attack pods by randomly specifying label values in the affinity condition. All other assumptions are identical to those of $\mathcal{T}_u$.

Experimental design. To conduct a thorough evaluation, we propose three attack strategies and compare their results. We describe each strategy as follows:

- **Strategy 1. Deploying an attack pod with a single value affinity.** The attacker defines an affinity condition with a single affinity value to steer the scheduler's placement decision. We denote this strategy as $\mathcal{V}_1$.
- **Strategy 2. Deploying an attack pod with three-value affinity.** The attacker defines an affinity condition with three affinity values. We denote this strategy as PodBeater$_{\mathcal{V}_3}$.

– **Strategy 3. Deploying an attack pod with five-value affinity.** The attacker defines an affinity condition with five affinity values. We denote this strategy as PodBeater$_{\mathcal{V}_5}$.

We design an experiment based on Algorithm 2. In this experiment, a label pool $\mathcal{P}$ is first generated with a size of label pool $L \in 5, 9$ (Line 1 in Algorithm 2) to reflect cluster diversity by simulating different levels of label diversity. We then deploy benign pods with randomly assigned labels from this pool (Line 2) and select the victim pod V from the benign pods (Line 3). In each trial, the attacker generates attack pod by randomly selecting three or five values from the label pool to construct the affinity conditions (Line 5). This setup allows us to evaluate two types of PodBeater: PodBeater$_{\mathcal{V}_3}$ and PodBeater$_{\mathcal{V}_5}$. The attacker deploys the generated attack pod (Line 6) and checks whether it is placed on the same node as the victim (Line 7). The attacker continues to deploy additional attack pods until the co-location is achieved (Line 4–8). The number of attack pods required to achieve co-location is recorded for each trial (Line 9). We repeat the experiment 120 and 240 times for $L = 5$ and $L = 9$, respectively, to ensure reliable results and mitigate scheduling variability.

Table 3. Average number of attack pods required to achieve co-location in the small-scale cluster.

Label count	$\mathcal{V}_1$	PodBeater$_{\mathcal{V}_3}$	PodBeater$_{\mathcal{V}_5}$
5 labels	14.44	10.52	10.99
9 labels	17.57	15.62	8.64

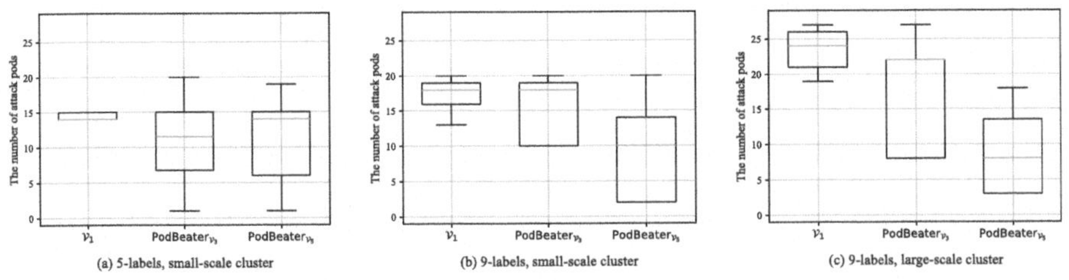

Fig. 3. Distribution of attack pods across attack strategies.

Experimental result. We evaluate PodBeater with respect to two key factors. First, we vary the total number of labels assigned to benign pods to assess how the size of the label pool influences the attack cost. Second, we configure clusters at two different scales to examine the effect of cluster size on the cost of

Table 4. Average number of attack pods required to achieve co-location on $\mathcal{T}_r$

Cluster setting	$\mathcal{V}_1$	PodBeater$_{\mathcal{V}_3}$	PodBeater$_{\mathcal{V}_5}$
Small-scale cluster	17.57	15.62	8.64
Large-scale cluster	23.31	18.02	10.14

co-location attacks. Based on these two factors, we determine which of the three proposed attack strategies is the most effective.

Table 3 presents the average number of attack pods required to achieve co-location with the victim pod in the small-scale cluster under two different label counts. The results show that PodBeater consistently reduces the number of required attack pods compared to $\mathcal{V}_1$. Specifically, with a label count of 5, $\mathcal{V}_1$ required an average of 14.44 pods, whereas PodBeater$_{\mathcal{V}_3}$ and PodBeater$_{\mathcal{V}_5}$ reduced this to 10.52 and 10.99, respectively. A similar result is observed with a label count of 9, where both PodBeater$_{\mathcal{V}_3}$ and PodBeater$_{\mathcal{V}_5}$ outperformed $\mathcal{V}_1$. Figure 3(a) and (b) show the distribution of required attack pods under the 5-label and 9-label settings, respectively. In the 5-label setting (cf., Fig. 3a), PodBeater$_{\mathcal{V}_3}$ is the most efficient, while PodBeater$_{\mathcal{V}_5}$ required slightly more pods. However, in the 9-label setting (cf., Fig. 3b), PodBeater$_{\mathcal{V}_5}$ proved to be the most efficient. These results indicate that increasing the number of affinity values does not always improve attack efficiency. To minimize the attack cost, an attacker must carefully tune the number of affinity values based on the cluster characteristics.

Table 4, Fig. 3(b) and (c) compare the impact of cluster scale. Using 9 labels, we conducted experiments in both small- and large-scale clusters. As the cluster size increased, all strategies required more attack pods to achieve co-location. Specifically, the attack cost increased by approximately 33% for $\mathcal{V}1$, 15% for PodBeater$_{\mathcal{V}_3}$, and 17% for PodBeater$_{\mathcal{V}_5}$.

In summary, PodBeater consistently reduces attack cost more effectively than $\mathcal{V}_1$ across different label counts and cluster scales. However, using an excessive number of affinity values may diminish attack efficiency. These findings suggest that attackers must adapt affinity configurations based on the characteristics of the target cluster to optimize attack performance.

6 Mitigation

This section presents mitigation approaches to prevent the PodBeater attack.

Enforcing access control over affinity configuration. Kubernetes allows an unprivileged user to specify affinity conditions that influence pod placement. PodBeater exploits this property to efficiently achieve co-location with victim pods. To mitigate this, affinity configurations can be restricted to authorized users, such as specific service accounts, through access control mechanisms. For instance, *PodSecurityAdmission* or *ValidatingAdmissionWebhook* can enforce policies that permit only users in designated RBAC groups to define or modify affinity fields, preventing unauthorized abuse. In addition, integrity checks on affinity conditions can prevent attack pods from being deployed into the cluster.

Detecting and thwarting anomalous behavior. PodBeater achieves co-location by repeatedly launching pods with identical affinity conditions. To mitigate this, the scheduler can monitor affinity usage patterns and restrict repetitive scheduling behavior. For example, the scheduler may delay or reject pods that reuse the same affinity conditions within a short time window. Furthermore, specific affinity conditions can be blocked or restricted through policy to prevent attackers from steering placement toward victim pods.

7 Conclusion

In this paper, we presented *PodBeater*, a co-location attack that exploits Kubernetes's multi-value affinity feature to achieve efficient co-location. While previous work considers only a threat model in which the attacker has sufficient knowledge of the victim pod referred to as $\mathcal{T}_u$, our work explores both $\mathcal{T}_u$ and a more realistic threat model, $\mathcal{T}_r$, where the attacker lacks such knowledge. In addition, we evaluate PodBeater in both small- and large-scale cluster settings. We first show that, under the $\mathcal{T}_u$, PodBeater requires fewer attack pods than previous work to achieve co-location, demonstrating higher attack efficiency. We then demonstrate that, under the $\mathcal{T}_r$, PodBeater reduces the number of attack pods required to achieve co-location compared to the $\mathcal{V}_1$. However, using too many affinity values can degrade efficiency, suggesting that attackers must tune the number of affinity values based on cluster characteristics. This study provides a systematic analysis of Kubernetes scheduling vulnerabilities under varying attacker models and cluster scales, offering insights to guide the design of more secure orchestration systems.

Acknowledgements. This research was supported by a National Research Foundation of Korea (NRF) grant, funded by the Korean government (MSIT) (RS-2023-NR077166, RS-2023-00227165). This research was supported by the Korea University Grant.

References

1. Atya, A.O.F., Qian, Z., Krishnamurthy, S.V., La Porta, T., McDaniel, P., Marvel, L.M.: Catch me if you can: a closer look at malicious co-residency on the cloud. IEEE/ACM Trans. Netw. **27**(2), 560–576 (2019). https://doi.org/10.1109/TNET.2019.2891528
2. Chen, Z., Jiang, F., Chen, B., Li, Y., Zhang, Y., Huang, C., Yang, R., Jiang, F., Chen, J., Xiang, W., et al.: Resource allocation with service affinity in large-scale cloud environments. In: 2024 IEEE 40th International Conference on Data Engineering (ICDE), pp. 5280–5293. IEEE (2024)

3. Containerd Authors: Containerd: an industry-standard container runtime (2025). https://containerd.io/. Accessed 14 May 2025
4. Docker Inc.: Docker hub (2025). https://hub.docker.com/. Accessed 14 May 2025
5. Fang, C., Wang, H., Nazari, N., Omidi, B., Sasan, A., Khasawneh, K.N., Rafatirad, S., Homayoun, H.: REPTTACK: exploiting cloud schedulers to guide co-location attacks. In: Proceedings of the Network and Distributed System Security Symposium (NDSS) (2022). https://doi.org/10.14722/ndss.2022.23149
6. Han, Y., Chan, J., Alpcan, T., Leckie, C.: Using virtual machine allocation policies to defend against co-resident attacks in cloud computing. IEEE Trans. Dependable Secure Comput. **14**(1), 95–108 (2015)
7. Kubernetes Authors: Kubernetes: production-grade container orchestration (2025). https://kubernetes.io. Accessed 10 May 2025
8. Kubernetes Authors: objects in kubernetes—labels (2025). https://kubernetes.io/docs/concepts/overview/working-with-objects/. Accessed 10 May 2025
9. Liu, F., Yarom, Y., Ge, Q., Heiser, G., Lee, R.B.: Last-level cache side-channel attacks are practical. In: 2015 IEEE Symposium on Security and Privacy, pp. 605–622. IEEE (2015). https://doi.org/10.1109/SP.2015.43
10. Makrani, H.M., Sayadi, H., Nazari, N., Khasawneh, K.N., Sasan, A., Rafatirad, S., Homayoun, H.: Cloak & co-locate: adversarial railroading of resource sharing-based attacks on the cloud. In: 2021 International Symposium on Secure and Private Execution Environment Design (SEED), pp. 1–13. IEEE (2021)
11. Moreno-Vozmediano, R., Montero, R.S., Huedo, E., Llorente, I.M.: Orchestrating the deployment of high availability services on multi-zone and multi-cloud scenarios. J. Grid Comput. **16**, 39–53 (2018)
12. Pachorkar, N., Ingle, R.: Affinity aware VM colocation mechanism for cloud. Int. J. Adv. Comput. Res. **4**(4), 956 (2014)
13. Varadarajan, V., Zhang, Y., Ristenpart, T., Swift, M.: A placement vulnerability study in multi-tenant public clouds. In: 24th USENIX Security Symposium (USENIX Security 15), pp. 913–928 (2015)
14. Zhang, T., Zhang, Y., Lee, R.B.: Dos attacks on your memory in cloud. In: Proceedings of the 2017 ACM on Asia Conference on Computer and Communications Security, pp. 253–265 (2017). https://doi.org/10.1145/3052973.3052978
15. Zhao, Z.N., Morrison, A., Fletcher, C.W., Torrellas, J.: Everywhere all at once: co-location attacks on public cloud FaaS. In: Proceedings of the 29th ACM International Conference on Architectural Support for Programming Languages and Operating Systems, vol. 1, pp. 133–149 (2024). https://doi.org/10.1145/3617232.3624867

GUARD-CAN: Graph-Understanding and Recurrent Architecture for CAN Anomaly Detection

Hyeong Seon Kim and Huy Kang Kim(✉)

School of Cybersecurity, Korea University, Seoul, Republic of Korea
{ccloseon,cenda}@korea.ac.kr

Abstract. Modern in-vehicle networks face various cyber threats due to the lack of encryption and authentication in the Controller Area Network (CAN). To address this security issue, this paper presents **GUARD-CAN**, an anomaly detection framework that combines graph-based representation learning with time-series modeling. **GUARD-CAN** splits CAN messages into fixed-length windows and converts each window into a graph that preserves message order. To detect anomalies in the time-aware and structure-aware context at the same window, **GUARD-CAN** takes advantage of overcomplete Autoencoder (AE) and Graph Convolutional Network (GCN) to generate graph embedding vectors. The model groups these vectors into sequences and feeds them into the Gated Recurrent Unit (GRU) to detect temporal anomaly patterns across the graphs. **GUARD-CAN** performs anomaly detection at both the sequence level and the window level, and this allows multi-perspective performance evaluation. The model also verifies the importance of window size selection through an analysis based on Shannon entropy. As a result, **GUARD-CAN** shows that the proposed model detects four types of CAN attacks (flooding, fuzzing, replay and spoofing attacks) effectively without relying on complex feature engineering.

Keywords: Controller Area Network · Graph Convolutional Network · Intrusion Detection System

1 Introduction

Recent vehicle systems focus on automation, electrification, and connectivity. This trend increases the complexity and importance of in-vehicle networks. A representative example is the Controller Area Network (CAN) [1], which is widely used based on its real-time performance and lightweight protocol.

However, from a security perspective, CAN lacks encryption and authentication functions, making it vulnerable to various cyberattacks [2]. In July 2015, Miller *et al.* disclosed a remote hacking case involving a Jeep Cherokee [3]. They showed that a real vehicle could be controlled through network intrusion, which raised strong awareness of vehicle security in both academia and industry. In

K.-W. Park and J. Park (Eds.): WISA 2025 2025, LNCS 16434, pp. 28–39, 2026.
https://doi.org/10.1007/978-981-95-6857-4_3

addition, Tencent Keen Security Lab proved remote hacking by injecting malicious messages into the CAN bus of Tesla Model S and Model X vehicles through wireless (Wi-Fi/cellular) networks [4]. As vehicles are transforming from simple means of transportation into complex cyber-physical systems, the importance of CAN-based anomaly detection and real-time security systems continues to grow. Given these trends, various intrusion detection systems (IDSs) have been proposed to detect security threats in CAN. Statistical, machine learning-based, and deep learning-based methods have been used, but existing studies often require domain knowledge of the CAN bus and have the limitation of requiring additional feature engineering.

This paper proposes **GUARD-CAN**, which detects temporal anomalous patterns in CAN bus attacks. **GUARD-CAN** divides CAN messages into fixed-size windows and converts each window into a graph. It combines overcomplete Autoencoder (AE) and Graph Convolutional Network (GCN) to encode patterns embedded in the data. The encoded graph embedding vectors are formed into a sequence and input into Gated Recurrent Unit (GRU) to learn and detect anomalous patterns in the temporal context. The main contributions of this study are as follows:

- **Arbitration ID independent algorithm**: **GUARD-CAN** only uses DLC and Data field as graph node features. That means **GUARD-CAN** does not need a full description of DBC, which is regarded as a private intellectual property.
- **Structure-aware graph embedding with GCN**: We combine overcomplete AE with GCN to encode each graph into a graph embedding vector. This process extracts structural and temporal patterns from the data.
- **Temporal context learning with GRU over graph sequences**: We group graph embedding vectors by sequence length and use them as input to GRU. This enables anomaly detection that reflects temporal characteristics across graphs.

2 Background

2.1 Controller Area Network (CAN)

CAN is an in-vehicle communication protocol widely used in modern vehicles. Based on its durability and efficiency, it supports real-time data transmission and reception between various Electronic Control Units (ECUs) [1]. However, CAN lacks message authentication and does not apply message encryption. Furthermore, as all ECUs are connected to a common network and communicate via broadcast, they are exposed to many security threats [2]. The dataset used in this study [5] includes a total of four types of CAN bus attacks, which are as follows:

- **Flooding**: Transmits an excessive number of messages to overwhelm the CAN bus and exhaust its communication bandwidth.

- **Fuzzing**: Randomly injects arbitrary messages to cause system malfunctions.
- **Replay**: Reuses previously recorded normal CAN messages to disguise malicious activity as legitimate traffic.
- **Spoofing**: Alters specific CAN IDs and data based on traffic analysis to manipulate vehicle functions.

2.2 Graph Convolutional Network (GCN)

GCN [6] is a neural network model designed to effectively process graph data with irregular structures. It extends the concept of Convolutional Neural Networks, which are primarily used in image processing, to the graph domain. GCN integrates not only the features of each node but also the features of neighboring nodes and their connection structure. GCN performs convolution operations on the graph at each layer and updates the node feature representations accordingly. In particular, GCN learns meaningful patterns from data without complex feature engineering by aggregating information from directly connected neighboring nodes.

In this study, we combine overcomplete AE and GCN. This model extracts graph embedding vectors that effectively capture the structural and temporal features in CAN bus graph data. Thereby, GCN contributes to the stability and performance improvement of anomaly detection.

3 Related Work

Existing IDS for CAN studies can be classified into statistical anomaly detection, machine learning-based detection, and deep learning-based detection. Song et al. [7] proposed a lightweight IDS for CAN by analyzing the time interval between CAN messages. Lee et al. [8] proposed an IDS that detects attacks on CAN networks through response pattern analysis based on remote frames. The authors used the offset and time interval between request and response messages as key features. Song et al. [9] proposed an IDS for CAN based on a deep convolutional neural network with a lightweight Inception-ResNet structure. This method achieved high performance by extracting meaningful patterns from CAN traffic data without complex feature engineering.

Ye et al. [10] proposed three graph-based features (time difference, betweenness centrality, and graph density) that can be applied to intrusion detection. They used these features to perform anomaly detection using Classification and Regression Trees. Song et al. [11] introduced DGIDS, which builds a dynamic graph based on the arrival order of messages. Instead of using a fixed-length window, they used the message cycle of a base ID as the window. The system runs both offline and online phases simultaneously and detects anomalies by using multiple features. Devnath proposed GCNIDS [12], a GCN-based IDS designed to detect mixed attacks in CAN bus data. The method constructs graphs using Arbitration IDs within each window and uses only the maximum in-degree and out-degree as node features. GCN extracts node embeddings and performs graph-level binary classification.

However, existing studies [7,8,10,11] require domain knowledge of CAN bus data and may have limitations in learning complex patterns embedded in the data. This study considers these points and allows GCN to learn meaningful patterns without complex feature engineering. In addition, the existing method [12] only analyzes graphs from individual time steps without considering temporal continuity. This study addresses this by using sequences to reflect temporal characteristics between graphs.

4 Methodology

This section presents the overall methodology of **GUARD-CAN**. The proposed framework consists of four main steps, and the overall pipeline is illustrated in Fig. 1.

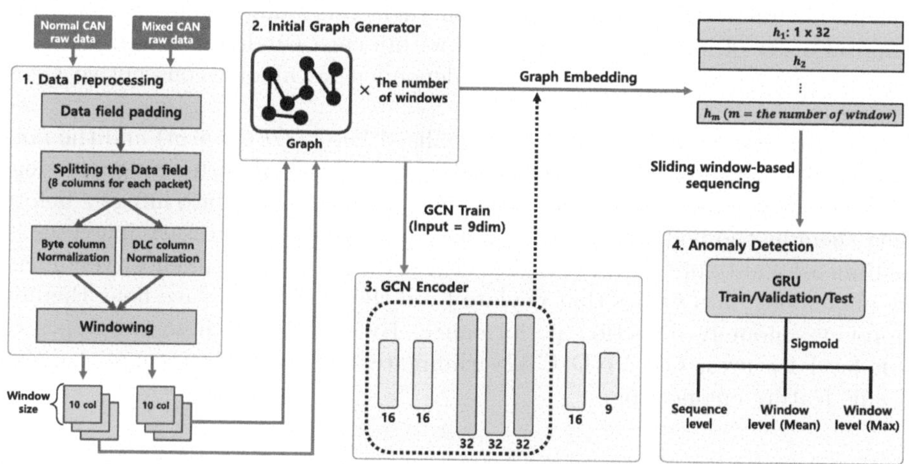

Fig. 1. Overview of **GUARD-CAN**.

4.1 Data Preprocessing

In this study, we applied a series of preprocessing steps to convert raw CAN data into a form suitable for model training. A raw CAN packet typically consists of the Timestamp, the Arbitration ID, the Data Length Code (DLC), and the Data field.

In the first step of preprocessing, we add 0x00 bytes to the end of the data field when its length is shorter than 8 bytes. After padding, we split each data field into eight columns from byte1 to byte8. Then, we convert each byte value from hexadecimal to decimal and normalize it to a real value in the range [0, 1]. The DLC value is normalized in the same manner. This normalization process mitigates the scale differences between the integer-based DLC field and the byte-based Data field. This aims to prevent potential instability in model training.

Following feature transformation, we segment the CAN messages into fixed-size windows using a non-overlapping windowing strategy based on a predefined window size. If the last window contains fewer packets than the specified window size, it is discarded. For example, with a window size of 100, a final window containing only 79 packets would not be used in training or evaluation. Simultaneously, we assign labels to each window. If any packet within a window is labeled as an attack, the entire window is marked as abnormal.

4.2 Initial Graph Generator

The Initial Graph Generator takes the preprocessed windows and converts each window into a graph. The model uses these graphs as input to GCN and learns the structural characteristics of the CAN data flow. It constructs edges by sequentially connecting packets based on their timestamps and preserves the temporal order of message transmissions within each window. This edge design helps the model capture the temporal dependencies among consecutive CAN messages.

The node features consist of the normalized DLC (DLC_norm) and the normalized values of the CAN payload (byte1–byte8) obtained during preprocessing. At this point, we convert the processed CAN payload values into integers before using them as the node features. This design prevents unnecessary increases in the dimensionality of GCN. With these features, the model can effectively identify anomalous data values that deviate from the normal message flow, thereby improving anomaly detection performance. By leveraging these two types of node-level features, **GUARD-CAN** eliminates the need for manual domain-specific feature engineering.

4.3 GCN Encoder

GCN takes each window-level graph as input and performs encoding to generate a graph embedding vector. **GUARD-CAN** uses only normal data to train GCN and applies the trained GCN to encode graphs that contain both normal and attack data. In this study, we combine overcomplete AE with GCN to improve its training effectiveness. **GUARD-CAN** does not rely on complex feature engineering. Instead, it extracts features that reflect both temporal and structural characteristics within the graph using reconstruction loss from the AE. By using this structure, the model produces more generalized representations and improves training stability compared to using GCN alone.

First, we use the node features (DLC_norm, binarized byte1 to byte8) as input to the AE encoder. The encoder consists of two linear layers and applies ReLU activation function after each layer. It takes a 9-dimensional input and embeds it into a 16-dimensional latent space. AE encoder transforms the input features into expressive vectors. During this process, it extracts a latent vector that reflects the characteristics of each node and helps GCN learn more effectively.

The embedding vectors extracted from the AE encoder are used as inputs to GCN. GCN consists of three GCNConv layers, each followed by ReLU. All three layers output 32-dimensional embedding vectors. Through the graph structure, each node updates its latent vector by aggregating features from itself and its neighboring nodes. Additionally, the edge connections based on temporal order allow GCN to indirectly capture sequential patterns. This process enables the generation of graph-level representations that incorporate the overall context of the graph.

Finally, AE decoder takes the graph embedding vector from GCN as input and reconstructs it into the original input feature space. It consists of two linear layers. The first layer converts a 32-dimensional to 16-dimensional. After applying ReLU, the final layer transforms the 16-dimensional vector into the original input dimension of 9. This process trains the model to reconstruct the original node features. The model evaluates reconstruction accuracy using Mean Squared Error (MSE) loss.

When embedding mixed data, the model loads the saved parameters and uses only AE encoder and GCN. AE encoder maps node features into 16-dimensional vectors, and GCN updates these vectors based on graph context. Then it applies global mean pooling to generate a 1×32 graph embedding vector for each window. The anomaly detection model takes these graph embedding vectors as input.

4.4 Anomaly Detection

Creating Sequences This study aims to reflect the temporal characteristics and patterns among graph embedding vectors in anomaly detection. For this purpose, we organize graph embedding vectors into fixed-length sequences and feed them into the GRU-based anomaly detection model. **GUARD-CAN** constructs the sequences using a method similar to a sliding window. For example, when the sequence length is 3, the sequences are generated as follows: $S_0 = [h_0, h_1, h_2]$, $S_1 = [h_1, h_2, h_3]$, $\cdots$, $S_n = [h_{(m-2)}, h_{(m-1)}, h_m]$, where S_n represents the n-th sequence and h_m denotes the graph embedding vector encoded by GCN. The variable m indicates the total number of windows. The model assigns a label to each sequence based on the labels of all the graphs that form the sequence. If the sequence includes even one graph labeled as an attack, the model treats that sequence as anomalous.

GRU Model Configuration The GRU model receives input in the form of [*batch_size*, *sequence_length*, *feature_dim*]. *batch_size* denotes the number of sequences; *sequence_length* indicates the number of windows in each sequence; and *feature_dim* represents the dimension of the graph embedding vector generated for each window. We set the *feature_dim* to 32 because the graph embedding vector extracted by GCN has a shape of 1×32.

The model uses two GRU layers to learn temporal dependencies within each sequence. We set the hidden dimension of GRU to 64 and apply a dropout rate of 0.3 to prevent overfitting. The GRU output passes through two fully connected (FC) layers to produce the final prediction. The first FC layer compresses the GRU output into a 32-dimensional representation, and the second FC layer generates binary classification probabilities for each sequence. We apply sigmoid activation function to obtain the final probability values.

This study evaluates anomaly detection performance at both the sequence-level and the window-level. Sequence-level detection captures anomalies by considering the temporal flow between graphs, while window-level detection focuses on identifying anomalies within each graph. In this study, optimization is performed using Binary Cross Entropy (BCE) loss based on the sequence-level predictions.

Sequence-Level Anomaly Detection A sequence consists of a set of graph embedding vectors, and we regard each sequence as an independent unit. The sequence-level anomaly probability output by GRU ranges between 0 and 1. We apply a threshold of 0.5 to determine whether an anomaly is detected. As a result, the final output of the sequence-level anomaly detection is returned as a binary value of 0 or 1.

Window-Level Anomaly Detection A window refers to a group of CAN packets, and each window forms a single graph. This study also evaluates anomaly detection performance at the window-level, which is a finer unit than the sequence. Through this approach, we analyze how the temporal characteristics between graphs affect detection performance. Window-level anomaly detection is performed based on the window-level anomaly probability output from the GRU model. Each sequence uses overlapping graph embedding vectors, so a single window can appear in multiple sequences. Therefore, we perform window-level anomaly detection using two approaches.

The first approach determines anomalies based on the average of all predicted values for each graph embedding vector h. The second approach determines anomalies based on the maximum predicted value for each h. For both approaches, the anomaly detection threshold is set to 0.5, and the final output for each window is a binary value of 0 or 1.

5 Experiment

This section evaluates the performance of **GUARD-CAN**. We first describe the dataset used in the experiments and then evaluate the performance based on changes in window size and sequence length. Experiments are performed on MS Windows 10, Intel(R) Core(TM) i7-10700K CPU @ 3.80 GHz, 64.0 GB RAM, NVIDIA GeForce RTX 3080 Ti (12GB). And we implement **GUARD-CAN** using Python 3.12.2, torch 2.4.1, and torch-geometric 2.6.1.

5.1 Dataset

In this study, we conducted experiments using the Car Hacking: Attack & Defense Challenge 2020 dataset [5,13], provided by HCRL, Korea University. GCN learns the temporal characteristics and graph structure of normal data during training. For anomaly detection, we use a dataset that contains both normal data and four types of attack data. This dataset was split into training, validation, and test sets in a 6:2:2 ratio. The composition of the raw dataset, including the normal and four attack types, is shown in Table 1.

Table 1. Distribution of normal and attack records by dataset.

Dataset	Type	Number of records (Ratio)
GCN training	Normal	179,346 (100%)
Anomaly detection	Normal	1,799,046 (89.92%)
Anomaly detection	Flooding	96,559 (4.83%)
Anomaly detection	Fuzzing	44,770 (2.24%)
Anomaly detection	Replay	37,869 (1.89%)
Anomaly detection	Spoofing	22,489 (1.12%)

5.2 Window Size Analysis

In this study, we divide each packet according to the designated window size during the data preprocessing step. Then, using the initial graph generator, we convert each window into a graph based on the order of messages. Therefore, the window size serves as a key parameter that defines the unit of the graph. If the window size is too small, the graph lacks sufficient information, which limits what GCN can learn. In contrast, if the window size is too large, the graph may include excessive and diluted information, which can negatively affect model training.

Therefore, we analyze the entropy of each window to determine an appropriate window size. In general, when the IDs appear more evenly within a window, the entropy value increases. This implies that the information is evenly distributed across the window. Selecting a proper window size helps GCN extract meaningful features and ultimately improves anomaly detection performance. To support this process, we perform an analysis using Shannon entropy about window sizes ranging from 10 to 400.

We calculated the following statistical values for each window divided by the designated size: mean, median, minimum, maximum, and standard deviation of entropy. Based on these statistics, we also analyzed the entropy growth rate by window size. Figure 2 shows the average entropy values and growth rate trends for each window size.

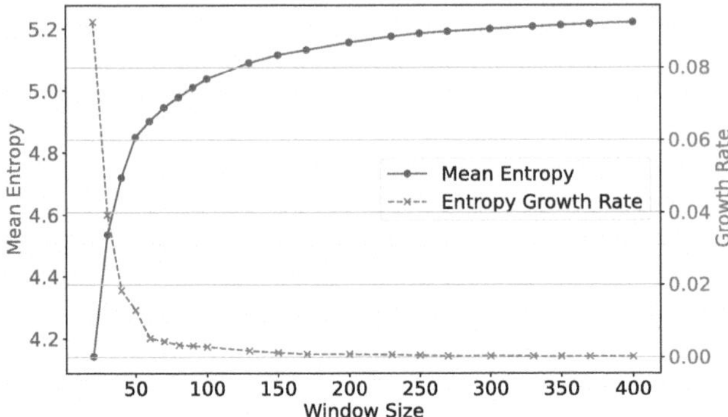

Fig. 2. Entropy average and growth rate by window size. This graph shows the values between window sizes 20 and 400, excluding window size 10 for which the growth rate cannot be calculated.

As shown in Fig. 2, when the window size is less than 50, the entropy increases rapidly. In cases where the amount of information increases sharply, the graph may still lack enough information for GCN to learn effectively. In addition, it can be observed that for window sizes over 150, the growth rate nearly converges to zero. Therefore, this study conducted performance evaluations of the proposed model using five window sizes: 50, 75, 100, 125, and 150. In addition, the sequence length determines the temporal context that GRU can use to detect anomalies. Short sequences help capture local anomalies, and long sequences provide broader context but may dilute the influence of recent abnormal patterns. To evaluate performance under different levels of temporal dependency, we selected sequence lengths of 30, 50, 100, 120, and 150 for the experiments.

This evaluation uses the following performance metrics: accuracy, precision, recall, F1-score, and Area Under the Curve (AUC). Figure 3 presents the overall performance of **GUARD-CAN** proposed in this paper.

In addition, the best performance result for each window size is shown in Table 2. Win and Seq columns represent window size and sequence length, respectively. In addition, the Type column indicates three methods for anomaly detection: sequence, mean and max.

5.3 Result Analysis

Table 2 shows that the performance of **GUARD-CAN** tends to decrease as the window size increases. In the experiments, the model achieved 0.9702 accuracy and 0.9930 AUC when the window size was 50 and the sequence length was 50. This result supports our earlier analysis. A larger window size causes the information within each graph to become diluted, which prevents GCN from extracting meaningful features. Meanwhile, window sizes of 100 and 150 showed their best performance when the sequence length was relatively long. However, the performance remained lower than that of experiments using smaller window

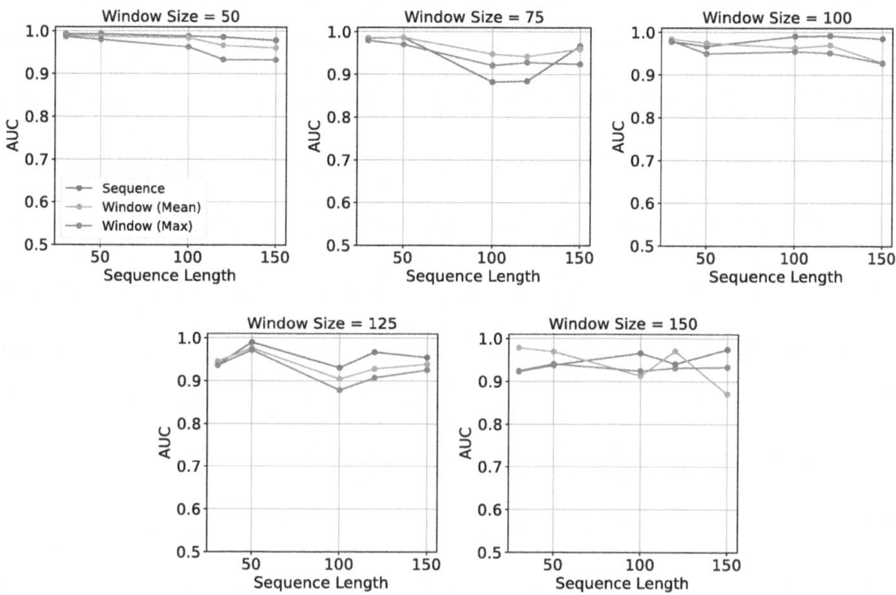

Fig. 3. AUC variation by sequence length for each window size. The figure shows the anomaly detection results (AUC) for each sequence length with five window size values, including sequence-level, window-level (mean), and window-level (max).

Table 2. Performance comparison of the best results by window size.

Win	Seq	Type	Accuracy	Precision	Recall	F1-score	AUC
50	50	Sequence	0.9702	0.9902	0.9559	0.9727	0.9930
		Mean	0.8682	0.9867	0.7571	0.8544	0.9877
		Max	0.9279	0.9557	0.9064	0.9258	0.9803
75	50	Sequence	0.9588	0.9904	0.9372	0.9630	0.9864
		Mean	0.9342	0.9759	0.8958	0.9340	0.9867
		Max	0.9513	0.9389	0.9696	0.9540	0.9697
100	120	Sequence	0.9578	0.9964	0.9400	0.9673	0.9917
		Mean	0.8870	0.9256	0.8552	0.8854	0.9693
		Max	0.8937	0.8874	0.9239	0.9019	0.9509
125	50	Sequence	0.9645	0.9881	0.9532	0.9700	0.9895
		Mean	0.9035	0.9628	0.8482	0.8987	0.9758
		Max	0.9160	0.9483	0.8886	0.9145	0.9713
150	120	Sequence	0.8762	0.9604	0.8631	0.9079	0.9402
		Mean	0.7542	0.9523	0.5759	0.6066	0.9703
		Max	0.8756	0.8713	0.9054	0.8821	0.9309

and sequence settings. In addition, Fig. 3 further shows that shorter sequence lengths tend to reduce the variation across the three anomaly detection metrics for each window size. These findings indicate that **GUARD-CAN** can extract more meaningful features and achieve more stable training when using smaller window sizes and sequence lengths.

We also compare model performance when using normalized byte values (float values in the range [0, 1]) and when using binarized byte values (integer values of 0 or 1) as node features. Table 3 presents the top 3 sequence-level anomaly detection results of **GUARD-CAN** using normalized byte values. The results show that using binarized byte values leads to higher anomaly detection performance.

Using normalized byte values causes confusion for overcomplete AE and GCN because the value distribution becomes highly dense. In particular, the small differences among normal messages increase the reconstruction error and lead to false positives (FP). In addition, when attack messages such as replay and spoofing resemble the distribution of normal messages, the model can produce false negatives (FN). In addition, normal messages account for the majority of the dataset used in the experiments. This data imbalance remains a major cause of FP and FN even when using binarized byte values. To address this issue, future work will expand the research by applying oversampling techniques focused on anomalous data.

Table 3. Sequence-level anomaly detection performance with normalized byte values. This result shows that the overall performance when normalizing byte values is relatively lower than the case of binarized byte encoding.

Win	Seq	Type	Accuracy	Precision	Recall	F1-score	AUC
50	30	Sequence	0.8256	0.9254	0.7407	0.8194	0.9225
50	50	Sequence	0.8095	0.9331	0.7055	0.8031	0.9145
50	150	Sequence	0.8040	0.8820	0.7992	0.8339	0.8650

6 Conclusion

In this paper, we proposed **GUARD-CAN**, a CAN anomaly detection framework that combines graph-based learning and time-series modeling. The proposed model divides CAN messages into windows and converts each window into a graph. After embedding the graphs through GCN, a GRU-based time-series model detects anomalies while reflecting temporal patterns.

The model is designed to effectively learn the structural and temporal characteristics inherent in CAN traffic without complex feature engineering. We also analyzed its performance from multiple perspectives using both sequence-level and window-level evaluation criteria. Furthermore, we demonstrate the importance of selecting an appropriate learning unit through a window size analysis based on Shannon entropy. As a result, **GUARD-CAN** achieves high detection performance for four representative CAN attacks and especially shows the best performance under small window sizes and short sequence lengths.

In future work, we plan to improve the model by applying a combined loss function that can optimize both sequence-level and window-level detection. In addition, we will also improve **GUARD-CAN** by modifying the structure to directly use arbitration IDs as node identifiers in GCN learning.

Acknowledgments. This work was supported by a grant (UI247022TD) from the Agency for Defense Development, South Korea.

References

1. Refat, R.U.D., Elkhail, A.A., Hafeez, A., Malik, H.: Detecting can bus intrusion by applying machine learning method to graph based features. In: Intelligent Systems and Applications: Proceedings of the 2021 Intelligent Systems Conference (IntelliSys), vo. 3, pp. 730–748. Springer (2022)
2. Young, C., Zambreno, J., Olufowobi, H., Bloom, G.: Survey of automotive controller area network intrusion detection systems. IEEE Des. Test **36**(6), 48–55 (2019)
3. WIRED: Hackers remotely kill a jeep on the highway—with me in it. https://www.wired.com/2015/07/hackers-remotely-kill-jeep-highway/. Accessed 24 Jul 2025
4. Nie, S., Liu, L., Yuefeng, D.: Free-fall: hacking tesla from wireless to can bus. Brief. Black Hat USA **25**(1), 16 (2017)
5. Kang, H., Kwak, B.I., Lee, Y.H., Lee, H., Lee, H., Kim, H.K.: Car hacking and defense competition on in-vehicle network. In: Workshop on Automotive and Autonomous Vehicle Security (AutoSec), vol. 2021, p. 25. NDSS, San Diego, CA (2021)
6. Kipf, T.N., Welling, M.: Semi-supervised classification with graph convolutional networks (2016). arXiv:1609.02907
7. Song, H.M., Kim, H.R., Kim, H.K.: Intrusion detection system based on the analysis of time intervals of can messages for in-vehicle network. In: 2016 International Conference on Information Networking (ICOIN), pp. 63–68 (2016)
8. Lee, H., Jeong, S.H., Kim, H.K.: OTIDS: a novel intrusion detection system for in-vehicle network by using remote frame. In: 2017 15th Annual Conference on Privacy, Security and Trust (PST), pp. 57–5709 (2017)
9. Song, H.M., Woo, J., Kim, H.K.: In-vehicle network intrusion detection using deep convolutional neural network. Veh. Commun. **21**, 100198 (2020)
10. Ye, P., Liang, Y., Bie, Y., Qin, G., Song, J., Wang, Y., Liu, W.: GDT-IDS: graph-based decision tree intrusion detection system for controller area network. J. Supercomput. **81**(4), 591 (2025)
11. Song, J., Qin, G., Liang, Y., Yan, J., Sun, M.: DGIDS: dynamic graph-based intrusion detection system for can. Comput. Secur. **147**, 104076 (2024)
12. Devnath, M.K.: GCNIDS: graph convolutional network-based intrusion detection system for can bus (2023). arXiv:2309.10173
13. IEEE Dataport: Car hacking: attack & defense challenge 2020 dataset. https://dx.doi.org/10.21227/qvr7-n418. Accessed 24 Jul 2025

5G and Network Security

A Real-World Dataset to Enhance Intrusion Detection in SDN-IoT Systems

Chau Nguyen(✉), Hoang Anh Nguyen, Yang-Wai Chow, and Willy Susilo

Institute of Cybersecurity and Cryptology (IC2), University of Wollongong, Wollongong 2522, Australia
{chaun,hoanganhng,caseyc,wsusilo}@uow.edu.au

Abstract. The convergence of the Internet of Things (IoT) and Software-Defined Networking (SDN) has enabled scalability, dynamic resource allocation, and centralized management of SDN-IoT infrastructures. However, the integration introduces critical security challenges such as cross-layer threats and IoT-specific exploits. While Machine Learning (ML)based Intrusion Detection Systems (IDS) offer promising defense, their effectiveness is hindered by inadequate and outdated datasets that lack realistic SDN control-plane dynamics and IoT heterogeneity within integrated SDN-IoT environments. Critically, no existing dataset simultaneously captures three dimensions, including SDN control-plane behaviour, IoT device traffic, and cross-layer attack vectors essential for securing modern converged networks. To address the gap, we propose a novel dataset generated from a real-world SDN-IoT testbed. The dataset is validated using five ML models with two classification schemes. The experimental results show high detection performance, with 100% accuracy across attack categories and 88.5% accuracy across individual attack types.

Keywords: SDN-IoT Dataset · ML-based Intrusion Detection System · Real-world testbed

1 Introduction

The rapid evolution of the Internet of Things (IoT) has revolutionized the digital landscape, enabling billions of devices to communicate, sense, and act autonomously in diverse domains such as smart cities, healthcare, and industrial automation [12]. As IoT deployments scale, the underlying network infrastructure faces unprecedented demands for flexibility, scalability, and efficient management. Software-Defined Networking (SDN) has emerged as a transformative technology, decoupling control and data planes to provide centralized, programmable, and dynamic control over large and heterogeneous networks. The integration of SDN with IoT, which forms SDN-IoT architectures, has thus become a compelling solution to address the complexity and resource constraints

K.-W. Park and J. Park (Eds.): WISA 2025 2025, LNCS 16434, pp. 43–56, 2026.
https://doi.org/10.1007/978-981-95-6857-4_4

inherent in massive IoT environments [7]. This convergence empowers network operators with fine-grained traffic management, dynamic resource allocation, and the ability to adapt policies in real time, paving the way for next-generation large-scale IoT systems.

However, the benefits of SDN-IoT integration are accompanied by significant security challenges [8]. The programmable nature of SDN, while enhancing network agility, also introduces new attack surfaces, particularly at the control plane. Simultaneously, IoT devices, often resource-constrained and lacking robust security features, remain attractive targets for adversaries. This duality gives rise to complex, cross-layer threats such as SDN-assisted distributed denial-of-service (DDoS) attacks and IoT-specific exploits like device spoofing and firmware manipulation.

To encounter these evolving threats, Machine learning (ML)-based intrusion detection systems (IDS) have emerged as an adaptive and intelligent security solution. ML-based IDS can analyze vast amounts of network and device data to detect both known and novel attack patterns. However, the effectiveness of these systems is fundamentally dependent on the availability of high-quality, up-to-date datasets that accurately reflect the operational realities of SDN-IoT environments. Existing public datasets are often inadequate, suffering from a lack of realistic SDN control-plane features, insufficient representation of IoT device behaviors, limited coverage of contemporary attack vectors, imbalanced class distributions, and insufficient labeling. These shortcomings hinder the development and benchmarking of robust ML-based IDS solutions, leaving critical gaps in the SDN-IoT security research.

Addressing these dataset limitations is essential to advance ML-driven IoT security and ensure robust, scalable intrusion detection in increasingly complex and heterogeneous IoT ecosystems. This research presents a novel dataset generated from a real SDN-IoT testbed that integrates physical IoT devices with SDN emulation. The dataset is designed to capture both benign and malicious traffic relevant to modern SDN-IoT environments. The key contributions of this research are as follows.

- Development of a representative SDN-IoT testbed designed to capture realistic cross-layer attacks and IoT-specific exploits within integrated SDN-IoT environments.
- Creation of a novel SDN-IoT dataset that integrates SDN control-plane features, newly introduced VLAN-related features, and diverse IoT traffic enriched with two protocol-specific details.
- Design of two attack scenarios specifically crafted to capture cross-layer attack vectors, highlighting the interaction between SDN and IoT layers.
- Comprehensive evaluation of the dataset using five different machine learning models under two classification schemes.

The remainder of the paper is as follows. Section 2 reviews related work. Section 3 presents details of the proposed SDN-IoT testbed. Section 4 introduces the proposed SDN-IoT dataset. Section 5 presents the experimental results and discussion. Section 6 concludes the study with direction for future work.

2 Related Work

Over the last decade, a range of datasets have been developed to support Intrusion and Prevention Systems (IDS/IPS) across both Software-defined Networking (SDN) and Internet of Things (IoT) domains. The datasets were created with specific objectives and were gathered from diverse environments, including real-world testbed, simulated settings, or combination of both.

CIC-IDS-2017 [10] and CSE-CIC-IDS-2018 [1] are widely used in general IDS research, offering detailed flow-level statistics such as packet, byte counts, protocol types, and port number. They cover various attacks including DDoS, brute-force, and web-based attacks. However, they lack SDN controller logs and IoT-specific traffic, limiting their relevance for hydrid SDN-IoT environments. Moreover, as highlighted in [5], both datasets contain undocumented errors that may degrade the performance of machine learning-based IDS models. Notably, the 2018 version is mainly tailored for cloud environments like AWS.

In the SDN space, the CIC-DDoS-2019 [11] focuses on 13 DDoS variants (e.g., SYN Flood, UDP Fragmentation) and incorporates SDN-specific features such as flow entropy and packet length distribution. Despite its SDN alignment, it excludes IoT traffic, making it unsuitable for IoT-targeted attack analysis. Similarly, the InSDN dataset [3] captures flow tables, controller logs, and topology changes. While it enables SDN-specific attack detection as flow rule manipulation, it neglects IoT device interactions and protocol-level vulnerabilities.

Conversely, several datasets focus on IoT scenarios. CIC-IoT-2023 [6] captures the heterogeneity of IoT environments by including 33 attack types such as Mirai, spoofing, and man-in-the-middle (MITM) and traffic from 105 real IoT devices using protocols like Zigbee, Z-Wave, MQTT, and CoAP. However, lacking SDN-layer metadata limits its applicability in security frameworks with SDN integration.

Other datasets incorporate both SDN and IoT features. The TON_IoT dataset [2] excels in IIoT realism but treats SDN as an abstract concept and the dataset does not include explicit SDN features such as flow table states, controller logs, or SDN protocol events. The centralized control is simulated without actual SDN protocol as OpenFlow. Similarly, Edge-IoT dataset [4] offers comprehensive IoT/IIoT coverage and has limited SDN features and cross-domain threat analysis. While, the novel SDN dataset [9] pioneers SDN-IoT features integration but sacrifies IoT realism through simulation.

3 The Proposed SDN-IoT Testbed

3.1 Testbed Overview

The testbed captures realistic SDN- and IoT-specific traffic, including benign and malicious scenarios, within an integrated SDN-IoT setup. It emulates a large-scale architecture with a central SDN controller managing two IoT subsystems, each controlled individually, enabling realistic modeling of distributed control,

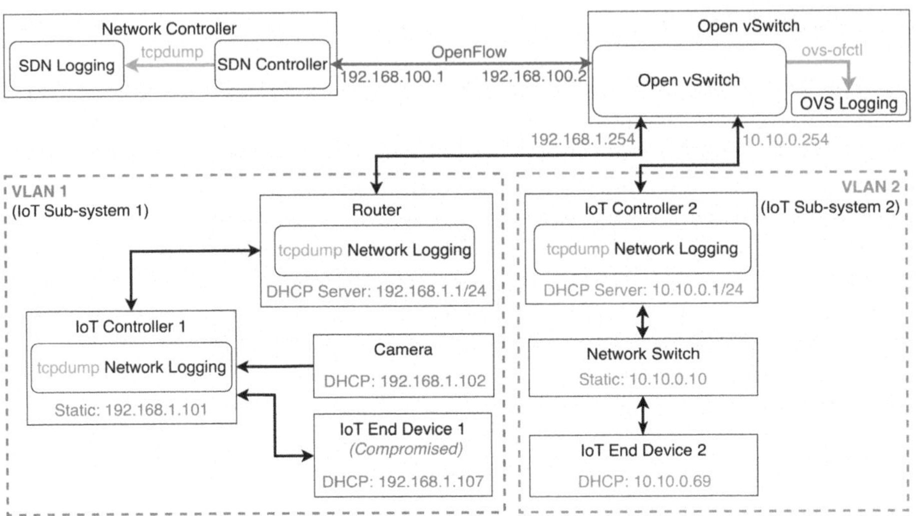

Fig. 1. The SDN-IoT testbed

cross-domain interactions, and multi-layer attacks. The testbed's architecture, IP addressing scheme, and logging points are illustrated in Fig. 1.

SDN provides logical IoT subsystem isolation over shared physical networks, eliminating dedicated hardware and enabling flexible, software-defined management. To enhance isolation and efficiency, the testbed uses VLANs to restrict broadcast traffic to designated segments. Specifically, the experimental network is partitioned into two VLANs including VLAN 1 and VLAN 2, each representing a distinct IoT subsystem under a unified SDN control plane.

To reflect real-world diversity, the testbed employs distinct IP assignment strategies across VLANs as illustrated in Fig. 1: VLAN 1 (192.168.1.0/24) uses a hardware-based DHCP router representing legacy networks, while VLAN 2 (10.10.0.0/24) adopts a software-based DHCP server typical of modern deployments. This hybrid setup improves realism, making the testbed applicable to heterogeneous SDN-IoT environments.

For data acquisition, a multi-point logging approach is used to capture ingress, egress, and SDN control-plane traffic for detailed analysis. Traffic logging is set at five strategic points as follows.

- **The SDN Controller**, which manages the whole network infrastructure and interacts with the Open vSwitch.
- **The Open vSwitch (OVS)**, which facilitates communication with the SDN controller, handling interactions across networks.
- **The Router**, which handles and monitors network traffic from inside VLAN 1 and outbound traffic to VLAN 2.
- **IoT Controller 1**, which manages IoT devices in VLAN 1.
- **IoT Controller 2**, which manages IoT devices and services in VLAN 2.

Internal traffic logging differs between VLANs. In VLAN 1, the Router captures all traffic, as it handles all device communication, while IoT Controller 1 is used only for device management. In VLAN 2, which lacks a dedicated gateway, IoT Controller 2 handles both device management and traffic capture.

3.2 Experimental Setup

The setup of the experiment is shown in Fig. 2.

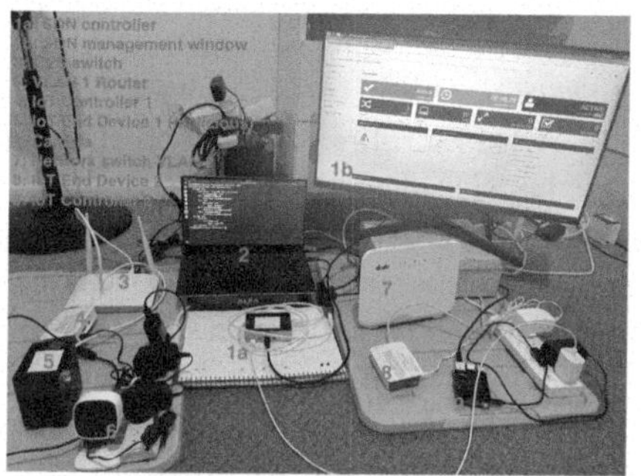

Fig. 2. The experiment setup

Table 1. Hardware specification

Component	Description
SDN Controller	Raspberry Pi 4, 8GB RAM
Open vSwitch	Dell i5, 8GB RAM
VLAN 1 router	D-Link DSL-2750U
IoT Controller 1	Raspberry Pi 3, 1GB RAM
IoT End Device 1	Raspberry Pi 4, 8GB RAM
Camera	Tapo C100
IoT Controller 2	Raspberry Pi 3, 2GB RAM
Network Switch	Huawei Gateway HG659
IoT End Device 2	Raspberry Pi 3, 1GB RAM

The experiment uses real devices to run testbed components, as detailed in Table 1. Each component runs a Linux-based OS with specific software for SDN and IoT functions. The SDN controller uses the Floodlight controller for centralised management and the virtual switch component runs Open-vSwitch. For IoT functionality, we developed custom programs to simulate HTTP and

MQTT traffic between IoT devices. Only IoT Controller 2 provides DHCP services. Notably, IoT End Device 1 is compromised and masquerades itself as a legitimate device. The security camera and the network switch use default vendor software.

3.3 Attack Scenarios and Attack Types

One key contribution of the work is the design of two attack scenarios, including Insider Attacks and Cross-Network Attacks, by which we can generate malicious traffic for cross-network attack detection. For the Insider Attack context, the compromised device acts maliciously within its own VLAN (VLAN 1). For the Cross-Network Attack one, the attacker targets devices in another VLAN (VLAN 2). While Insider Attacks reflect threats from compromised IoT nodes or privileged users within the SDN-IoT domain, exploiting trust relationships or misconfigurations, Cross-Network Attacks mirror adversaries moving laterally from one network segment into another. In both cases, the compromised device continues running normal services to conceal its malicious behaviour.

In the experiment, two types of attack are thoroughly studied, Reconnaissance and Denial-of-Services (DoS).

Reconnaissance attacks are a key initial phase in cyber intrusions, used to identify targets and vulnerabilities. In SDN-IoT environments, they are especially critical, as they reveal network topology, active devices, open ports, and communication patterns. Our work implements four types of reconnaissance attacks: IP Scanning (network-wide) and three device-targeted attacks, including Port Scanning, Service Discovery, and Device Fingerprinting.

An DoS attack disrupts system operations by overwhelming a target's resources with excessive traffic or requests. In the experiment, three common DoS types, including UDP Flood, SYN Flood, and ICMP Flood, are implemented.

In all scenarios and attack schemes, the compromised IoT End Device 1 targets all reachable networks and victims. Specifically, in the Insider Attack scenario, targets include VLAN 1, IoT Controller 1, and the camera. In the Cross-Network scenario, they are VLAN 2, IoT Controller 2, and IoT End Device 2. Attacks are executed using Nmap and hping3.

4 The Proposed SDN-IoT Dataset

This section presents the dataset generation process as illustrated in Fig. 3. Tcpdump and ovs-ofctl logs were first collected from five sources during each experiment. In the aggregation and annotation step, logs from the same instance were merged into comprehensive records capturing both SDN and IoT characteristics. The resulting traffic database was then pre-processed into an SDN-IoT dataset suitable for developing and evaluating the ML-based IDS.

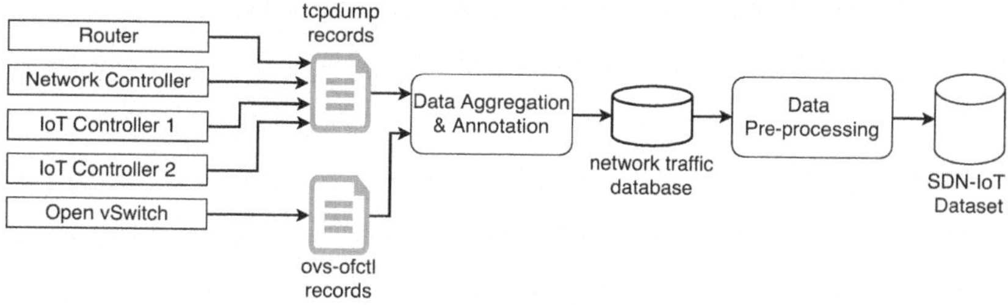

Fig. 3. The data generation framework

4.1 Data Collection

Our approach adopts two levels of attack classification: high-level categories and fine-grained types. This enables IDS models utilising our dataset to detect specific known attacks while retaining its ability to detect new or similar attack schemes from the general behaviours of such attack categories.

As mentioned in Sect. 3.3, we conducted our experiments under two distinct network scenarios: Insider and Cross-Network Attacks to capture network behaviour during these attacks. The traffic is collected at five key vantage points: the IoT Controller 1, the IoT Controller 2, the VLAN 1 Router, the SDN Controller, and the OVS as presented in Fig. 1.

Each data instance in the dataset was collected for at least 3 min, during which the associated attack was initiated and executed at a random point within the window. This approach was adopted to ensure a natural representation of network activity and to simulate realistic variations in attack timing. For port scanning attacks, the duration of each instance was extended to approximately 20 min, as preliminary tests indicated that such attacks require significantly more time to complete. In contrast, for benign traffic, a single uninterrupted session lasting 90 min was recorded, capturing a broad and stable range of legitimate network behaviours and providing a reliable baseline for comparison.

4.2 Data Aggregation and Annotation

The recorded logs from OVS includes more than 230 million packets, while the other four data loggers captured approximately 2.5 million packets. Instead of gauging draw traffic and total networking packets, we aggregated them, as the data alone do not fully reflect network traffic characteristics and behaviours. While a single record can capture up to millions of network packets, individual packets or small batches of them often struggle to portray the overall network's pattern, especially in the presence of network inconsistencies. In contrast, since a high-traffic network can accumulate as much data over a short period as a low-traffic system can over a long period, the total count of packets cannot accurately reflect the traffic intensity. Therefore, we calculated and included the average traffic volume per second to normalise and compare activity across

Table 2. Features of SDN-IoT dataset

Feature category	Data logger					Feature types
	Ctl1	Ctl2	Router	SDN	OVS	
Record ID	✓	✓	✓	✓	✓	None
Scenario	✓	✓	✓	✓	✓	SDN
Attack type	✓	✓	✓	✓	✓	Label
Attack category	✓	✓	✓	✓	✓	Label
Total packets (captured/received/dropped)	✓	✓	✓	✓		SDN & IoT
Total unique IPs/ports	✓	✓	✓	✓		SDN & IoT
Packets traffic per second	✓	✓	✓	✓		SDN & IoT
Directional packets per second [1]	✓	✓	✓	✓		SDN & IoT
Packets per second per protocol [2]	✓	✓	✓	✓		SDN & IoT
Average packet length per packet type (IP/ARP/Other)	✓	✓	✓	✓		SDN & IoT
Average number of flags per second per TCP flag	✓	✓	✓	✓		SDN & IoT
Total records					✓	SDN
Total IP packets per type [3]					✓	SDN
Total actions performed per targets (controller, LAN, output, other)					✓	SDN
Total times of flags raise per flag					✓	SDN
Total unique in_ports					✓	SDN
Total unique source and destination IPs/ports					✓	SDN
Total sent packets and bytes[4]					✓	SDN

[1] Directional packet types: Received, Sent, Internal, Routing, Other
[2] Protocol types: IP, ARP, UDP, TCP, ICMP, BOOTP/DHCP, OpenFlow
[3] IP packet types: IP, ARP, UDP, TCP, Other
[4] excluding those sent to the controller

records. Additionally, a maximum number of packets per second is recorded to identify sudden spikes that may indicate suspicious behaviour.

Afterwards, we derived a comprehensive feature set combining both IoT-centric and SDN-centric attributes from all five data loggers (as listed in Table 2). The collected features include standard traffic metrics, such as total packets captured, received, and dropped, along with protocol-specific statistics for IP, ARP, and OpenFlow, including the average and maximum packet rates, the average packet length, and the frequency of TCP flags. The tick denotes whether the data is collected by any of the five data loggers, and controllers 1 and 2 are abbreviated as Ctl1 and Ctl2, respectively. Besides the aforementioned general IoT and SDN characteristics, the feature set also includes SDN-specific features extracted solely from the OVS, such as the number of flow records, controller-directed actions, and the distribution of port activities. We assign labels using the ground truth defined for each experimental scenario.

The resulting database comprises 259 labeled entries and a feature-rich structure of 165 features, combining both fundamental and aggregated traffic statistics. The dataset is saved as a CSV file and uploaded to the GitHub repository for further analysis and evaluation.

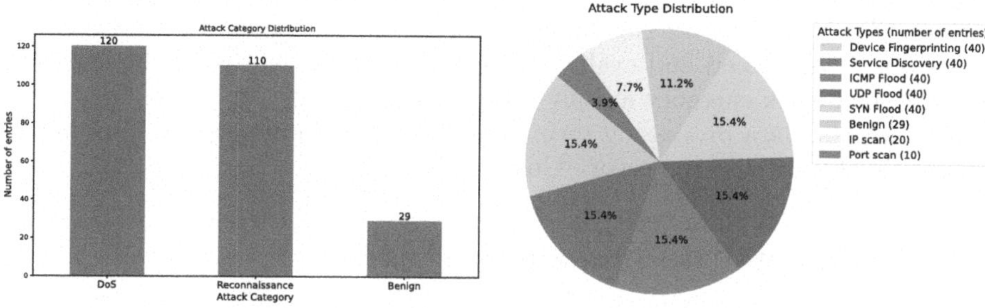

(a) Label according to attack category (b) Label according to attack types

Fig. 4. The data distribution of the dataset among label categories

4.3 Data Preprocessing

We performed several adjustments to prepare the dataset for machine learning analysis. The Record ID column was removed, as it served only as an internal reference during data collection and held no predictive value. Although the total number of packets captured was reliably extracted, the total number of packets received and dropped was missing in several records from the IoT and SDN controllers. These values were available only in the summary output of the tcpdump command and could not be reconstructed or inferred from the packet logs themselves. We suspect that this issue occurred due to the tcpdump process being overloaded during high-volume traffic situations such as DoS attacks, leading to incomplete summaries. Given the inconsistency and lack of a reliable imputation strategy, these fields were temporarily excluded from the final dataset to maintain data integrity.

After the cleaning step, we derived the final dataset with 156 feature columns, excluding the labels. Two distinct label sets were maintained to support the two experimental classification tasks: one for attack categories (Benign, DoS, Reconnaissance) and the other for attack types (IP Scan, Port Scan, Service Discovery, Device Fingerprinting, ICMP Flood, SYN Flood, UDP Flood, and Benign). Figure 4 shows the distribution of the dataset among categories.

4.4 Model Training

For training and evaluation, the dataset was split into training and testing sets using an 80:20 ratio, assuring no data leakage between training and testing sets and preserving the validity of model evaluation. Moreover, we applied stratified sampling to preserve the proportional representation of labels in both sets. This approach helps prevent overfitting or undertraining on specific classes, given the presence of multiple attack types and the relatively limited dataset size.

We evaluated the dataset with five widely used machine learning algorithms in this study: Logistic Regression (LR), Random Forest (RF), Support Vector Machine (SVM), K-Nearest Neighbours (KNN), and Gradient Boosting (XGB). Each model was trained and evaluated under two aforementioned classification scenarios: by attack category and by attack type.

All datasets, data processing scripts, and model training pipelines are made available in the GitHub repository Gong SDN-IoT.[1]

5 Experimental Results and Discussion

5.1 Experimental Results

The section presents the evaluation results of the five ML models on the attack category and attack type classifications. The four evaluation metrics are: Accuracy, Recall, Precision, and F1-score.

Table 3. Attack classification results

Model	Attack category				Attack type			
	Accuracy	Recall	Precision	F1-score	Accuracy	Recall	Precision	F1-score
LR	**1.000**	**1.000**	**1.000**	**1.000**	0.423	0.423	0.429	0.366
RF	**1.000**	**1.000**	**1.000**	**1.000**	0.788	0.788	0.790	0.785
SVM	0.885	0.885	0.792	0.833	0.327	0.327	0.196	0.243
KNN	**1.000**	**1.000**	**1.000**	**1.000**	0.750	0.750	0.761	0.742
XGB	**1.000**	**1.000**	**1.000**	**1.000**	**0.885**	**0.885**	**0.888**	**0.884**

Table 3 illustrates high performance across most models on the attack-category classification task. LR, RF, KNN, and XGB, each achieved perfect scores across all metrics, indicating that the three categories are well separated in the feature space. This high performance can be attributed to the simplicity of the task (three classes) and the inherent differences between benign, reconnaissance, and DoS traffic, particularly in terms of packet volume, traffic frequency, protocol usage, and flow behaviour. However, SVM underperformed with an F1-score of 0.833 and an accuracy of 0.885, which is likely due to its sensitivity to unscaled features, potential kernel mismatches, and its limited support vectors failing to represent all classes in the dataset.

[1] The project repository: https://github.com/hoanganhnguyen1198/gongSDNIoT25.

The results for the attack-type classification task present a greater challenge. As shown in Table 3, the XGB model outperformed all other models with an accuracy of 0.885 and an F1-score of 0.884. Its ability to manage complex, non-linear interactions and perform well on smaller datasets gave it a clear advantage. Additionally, its boosting process and regularisation mechanisms helped it generalise effectively, even with complex labels. RF and KNN also performed relatively well, with F1 scores of 0.785 and 0.742, respectively, benefitting from their non-linear decision-making abilities and being well-suited to capturing class clusters. LR and SVM performed poorly, with F1-scores of 0.366 and 0.243, respectively. These results highlight the limitations of linear models when dealing with overlapping, high-dimensional class boundaries and limited data per class.

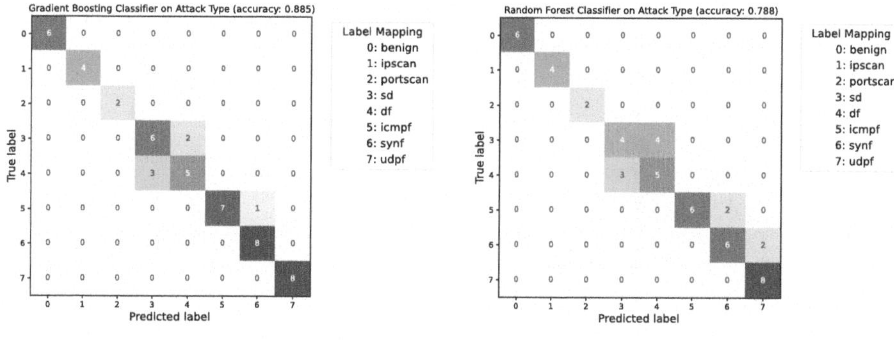

(a) The Gradient Boosting (XGB) model (b) The Random Forest (RF) model

Fig. 5. Attack type classification confusion matrices

An analysis of the XGB confusion matrix (Fig. 5a) further illustrates some of the challenges associated with fine-grained classification. For instance, the model misclassified two instances of service discovery as device fingerprinting and three instances of device fingerprinting as service discovery. This confusion is understandable, given that both attacks rely on probing techniques that involve similar protocols (e.g., TCP, UDP), scattered low-rate packets, and comparable traffic volumes, resulting in overlapping patterns in feature space. Additionally, one ICMP flood was misclassified as a SYN flood, likely due to their shared characteristics as DoS attacks: high packet volumes, short durations, and frequent, unidirectional bursts of traffic. Despite a poorer performance, the confusion matrix of the RF model faces similar issues, as shown in Fig. 5b, further reinforcing the aforementioned arguments.[2]

[2] Due to the paper's length restriction, the feature importance of the two models is included in the GitHub repository.

5.2 Discussion

Table 4 presents a comparative analysis of publicly available IoT and SDN-integrated datasets commonly used. The comparison covers attack diversity, SDN component usage, real device installation, protocol-level coverage, and the comprehensiveness of evaluation and attack scenarios. These factors are crucial for assessing a dataset's suitability for real-world use and MLbased IDSs. Here, "Y" means Yes, "N" means No, and "N/A" indicates missing information.

Our work stands out across nearly all criteria. In terms of attack diversity, our dataset includes three DoS attack types and four reconnaissance attack types.

Table 4. Comparison between datasets

Dataset	Attack types		SDN features		IoT features		Evaluation scenarios	Attack scenarios
	DoS	Recon	Usage	VLAN	Real devices	Protocols		
CIC-IDS-2017	N/A	1	N	N	N	N	1	1
CIC-IDS-2018	N/A	1	N	N	N	N	N	1
CIC-DDoS-2019	0	0	N	N	N	N	1	1
CIC-IoT-2023	**4**	**4**	N	N	Y	N/A	**3**	1
TON_IoT	N/A	1	Y	N	Y	1	1	1
Edge_IIoT	0	2	Y	N	N	N/A	N	1
Novel SDN	2	3	Y	N	N	1	**3**	1
Our work	3	**4**	**Y**	**Y**	**Y**	**2**	2	**2**

Crucially, our dataset includes explicit SDN-related features, especially VLAN configurations, which reflect the behaviour of SDN-based networks, in contrast to the few existing datasets that offer partial SDN support but do not include VLAN features, such as TON_IoT and Novel SDN. Furthermore, our dataset was constructed using real IoT devices deployed in a functional environment, including a rich set of protocol-level features covering multiple protocol types.

From an evaluation perspective, our work goes beyond simple binary classification by implementing two evaluation modes: by attack category and by attack type. Moreover, our dataset is the only one in the comparison to include two distinct attack scenarios: an insider attack targeting the local network, and a cross-network attack reaching a neighbouring VLAN via an SDN-enabled switch. This dual-scenario design reflects realistic threat models and enables more nuanced model evaluation in various environments.

6 Conclusion and Future Work

The work introduced a novel SDN-IoT dataset integrating explicit SDN features (such as VLAN configurations) and real IoT device traffic to support ML-based IDS in SDN-IoT environments. The dataset addresses key limitations of existing datasets by including diverse Reconnaissance and DoS attack types, along with realistic insider and cross-network attack scenarios, enabling detailed and practical ML-based IDS evaluations.

For future work, we plan to expand the dataset with additional attack types such as ARP Spoofing, MAC Flooding, and Packet Sniffing and support more IoT protocols including CoAP and WebSocket. We also aim to explore real-time data collection and labelling methods, and apply advanced ML techniques (e.g., CNNs, RNNs, Transformers) to improve intrusion detection performance in dynamic SDN-IoT contexts.

Acknowledgment. The work is funded by the University of Wollongong via the AEGiS grant.

References

1. A realistic cyber defense dataset (cse-cic-ids2018) (1999). https://www.registry.opendata.aws/cse-cic-ids2018/
2. Alsaedi, A., Moustafa, N., Tari, Z., Mahmood, A., Anwar, A.: Ton_IoT telemetry dataset: a new generation dataset of IoT and IIoT for data-driven intrusion detection systems. IEEE Access **8**, 165130–165150 (2020)
3. Elsayed, M.S., Le-Khac, N.A., Jurcut, A.D.: InSDN: a novel SDN intrusion dataset. IEEE Access **8**, 165263–165284 (2020)
4. Ferrag, M.A., Friha, O., Hamouda, D., Maglaras, L., Janicke, H.: Edge-IIoTset: a new comprehensive realistic cyber security dataset of IoT and IIoT applications for centralized and federated learning. IEEe Access **10**, 40281–40306 (2022)
5. Liu, L., Engelen, G., Lynar, T., Essam, D., Joosen, W.: Error prevalence in nids datasets: a case study on cic-ids-2017 and cse-cic-ids-2018. In: 2022 IEEE Conference on Communications and Network Security (CNS), pp. 254–262 (2022). https://doi.org/10.1109/CNS56114.2022.9947235
6. Neto, E.C.P., Dadkhah, S., Ferreira, R., Zohourian, A., Lu, R., Ghorbani, A.A.: CICIoT 2023: a real-time dataset and benchmark for large-scale attacks in IoT environment. Sensors **23**(13), 5941 (2023)
7. Piroddi, A., Fonti, R., et al.: SDN-driven innovations in MANETs and IoT: a path to smarter networks. J. Adv. Inf. Technol. **16**(3), 411–425 (2025)
8. Rahdari, A., Jalili, A., Esnaashari, M., Gheisari, M., Vorobeva, A.A., Fang, Z., Sun, P., Korzhuk, V.M., Popov, I., Wu, Z., Tahaei, H.: Security and privacy challenges in SDN-enabled IoT systems: Causes, proposed solutions, and future directions. Comput. Mater. & Contin. **80**(2), 2511–2533 (2024). https://doi.org/10.32604/cmc.2024.052994
9. Sarica, A.K., Angin, P.: A novel SDN dataset for intrusion detection in IoT networks. In: 2020 16th International conference on network and service management (CNSM), pp. 1–5. IEEE (2020)
10. Sharafaldin, I., Lashkari, A.H., Ghorbani, A.A., et al.: Toward generating a new intrusion detection dataset and intrusion traffic characterization. ICISSp **1**(2018), 108–116 (2018)
11. Sharafaldin, I., Lashkari, A.H., Hakak, S., Ghorbani, A.A.: Developing realistic distributed denial of service (DDoS) attack dataset and taxonomy. In: 2019 international Carnahan Conference on Security Technology (ICCST), pp. 1–8. IEEE (2019)

12. Sharmila Kumari, N., Vimala, H.S., Pruthvi, C.N., Shreyas, J.: Holistic survey on security in iot application layer: attacks, protocols, and applications. IEEE Access **12**, 186957–187014 (2024). https://doi.org/10.1109/ACCESS.2024.3462170

Toward a Stealth Mode of 5G-AKA

SeongHan Shin(✉)

National Institute of Advanced Industrial Science and Technology (AIST), 2-3-26 Aomi, Koto-ku, Tokyo 135-0064, Japan
seonghan.shin@aist.go.jp

Abstract. For the 5G primary authentication, 5G-AKA (5G Authentication and Key Agreement) has been designed and standardized in the 3GPP consortium. In this paper, we propose a stealth mode of 5G-AKA (for short, Stealth-5G-AKA) protocol that is compatible with the current 3GPP standard. In the Stealth-5G-AKA protocol, UE and SN share a stealth anchor key in addition to a (regular) anchor key. Also, we discuss several security properties of the Stealth-5G-AKA protocol. Moreover, we compare the 5G-AKA [3] with relevant 3GPP-compatible protocols (5G-AKA' [22], 5G-AKA-FS [23] and Stealth-5G-AKA) with respect to security properties and efficiency in terms of computation costs and communication costs.

Keywords: 5G-AKA · Stealth key exchange · Forward secrecy · UE unlinkability

1 Introduction

Currently, the fifth generation (5G) mobile network and telecommunication standard has been developed to meet the needs of enhanced mobile broadband, massive machine-type communications, and ultra-reliable and low-latency communications. Among several building blocks in this standard, 5G-AKA (5G Authentication and Key Agreement) [3] and EAP-AKA' (Improved Extensible Authentication Protocol Method for 3rd Generation Authentication and Key Agreement) [3], developed by the 3GPP consortium, are of utmost importance, which allow a User Equipment (UE) and a Home Network (HN) to authenticate each other and establish key materials (i.e., anchor keys) for protecting subsequent 5G communications. The 5G-AKA protocol is a new version of the AKA variants used for 3G and 4G networks. A distinctive feature of the 5G-AKA protocol is that a SUPI (SUbscriber Permanent Identifier) of UE is sent to HN in the form of encrypted by using the ECIES (Elliptic Curve Integrated Encryption Scheme) KEM (Key Encapsulation Mechanism) with HN's public key.

In [5], Basin et al. provided a comprehensive formal model of the 5G-AKA protocol and evaluated the model with respect to the 5G security goals using the security protocol verification tool Tamarin [18]. Then, they found that some crit-

K.-W. Park and J. Park (Eds.): WISA 2025 2025, LNCS 16434, pp. 57–69, 2026.
https://doi.org/10.1007/978-981-95-6857-4_5

ical security goals for the 5G-AKA protocol were not met. In [8], Borgaonkar et al. showed a new privacy attack on subscriber privacy against all the AKA variants (including 5G-AKA) by exploiting a logical vulnerability in the protection mechanism of SQN (Sequence Number). Also, Koutsos [17] showed that all the known privacy attacks (except the IMSI-catcher attack) are possible in the 5G-AKA protocol and then proposed a modified 5G-AKA protocol that satisfies the unlinkability property and is proven in the Bana-Comon logic model [4]. After describing that the 5G-AKA protocol is still vulnerable to a series of active linkability attacks, Wang et al. [22] proposed a privacy-preserving 5G-AKA (called 5G-AKA') that is secure against active linkability attacks by encrypting a random challenge of HN with an ECIES-KEM key, and is compatible with the SIM cards and Serving Networks (SNs). By using Tamarin [18], they also proved that the 5G-AKA' protocol achieves privacy, authentication, and secrecy. Recently, IETF EMU WG has been working on an EAP-AKA' (EAP-AKA' FS [13]) protocol that provides forward secrecy. The EAP-AKA' FS protocol is a simple combination of the EAP-AKA' [15] and Diffie-Hellman key exchange [10]. Very recently, You et al. [23] proposed an augmentation to 5G-AKA (5G-AKA-FS) to achieve forward security and thwart linkability attacks.

1.1 Motivation and Our Contributions

Recently, Fischlin [11] introduced a notion of stealth key exchange and showed how to embed a covert key exchange sub-protocol into the regular TLS 1.3 execution [14], generating a stealth session key in addition to a regular session key. One prospective application of stealth key exchange is a sanitizable channel where a designated entity can partly access and modify payload data with a regular session key, while entities who share a stealth session key can covertly communicate in a channel protocol.

In this paper, we propose a stealth mode of 5G-AKA (for short, Stealth-5G-AKA) protocol that is compatible with the current 3GPP standard [3] with small modifications. In the Stealth-5G-AKA protocol, UE and SN share a stealth anchor key in addition to a (regular) anchor key. A main idea of the Stealth-5G-AKA protocol is that we set an embedded (elliptic curve) Diffie-Hellman public key as a random challenge, and an (elliptic curve) Diffie–Hellman key is used as a key material of a stealth anchor key for forward secrecy and unlinkability. Also, we discuss several security properties of the Stealth-5G-AKA protocol. Moreover, we compare the 5G-AKA [3] with relevant 3GPP-compatible protocols (5G-AKA' [22], 5G-AKA-FS [23] and Stealth-5G-AKA) with respect to security properties (stealthiness, security of stealth key, forward secrecy, UE anonymity/unlinkability and security of anchor key) and efficiency in terms of computation costs and communication costs.

2 Preliminaries

Table 1 shows abbreviations and notations to be used throughout this paper.

Table 1. Abbreviations and notations

	Meanings
UE (ME, SIM)	User Equipment (Mobile Equipment, Subscriber Identity Modules)
HN	Home Network
SN	Serving Network
SUPI	SUbscriber Permanent Identifier
SUCI	SUbscriber Concealed Identifier
KEM	Key Encapsulation Mechanism
DEM	Data Encapsulation Mechanism
AMF	Access Management Function
AUSF	AUthentication Server Function
SEAF	SEcurity Anchor Function
k	A permanent key shared between UE and HN
K_{AUSF}	A master session key derived from Stealth-5G-AKA
K'_{AUSF}	A master stealth session key derived from Stealth-5G-AKA
K_{SEAF}	An anchor key derived from Stealth-5G-AKA
K'_{SEAF}	A stealth anchor key derived from Stealth-5G-AKA
k_{UE}	UE's shared key established by ECIES-KEM
k_{HN}	HN's shared key established by ECIES-KEM
(PK_{HN}, sk_{HN})	HN's ECIES public-private key pair where $PK_{HN} = sk_{HN} \cdot G$
ID_{SN}	A unique identifier of SN
ID_{HN}	A unique identifier of HN
SQN_{UE}	A sequence number of UE
SQN_{HN}	A sequence number of HN
$RAND$	A random challenge of HN

2.1 Elliptic Curve Integrated Encryption Scheme

The Elliptic Curve Integrated Encryption Scheme (ECIES) [9,16,19,21] is a well-known hybrid encryption scheme consisting of a Key Encapsulation Mechanism (KEM) and a Data Encapsulation Mechanism (DEM) where messages of arbitrary length can be encrypted. This scheme is a key component of 5G-AKA.

The ECIES-KEM has the following three algorithms:

- **ECIES.KeyGen**(pp): On input of a public parameter pp, the algorithm outputs a private-public key pair (sk, PK) such that $PK = sk \cdot G$, where pp is an elliptic curve parameter standardized in [20], and $G \in pp$ is a base point.
- **ECIES.Encap**(PK): On input of a public key PK, the algorithm generates an ephemeral private-public key pair (r, R) such that $R = r \cdot G$, and then outputs a ciphertext $C_0 = R$ and a shared key $k_s = \mathsf{KDF}(r \cdot PK)$, where KDF is a key derivation function.
- **ECIES.Decap**(sk, C_0): On input of a private key sk and a ciphertext C_0, the algorithm outputs the shared key $k_s = \mathsf{KDF}(sk \cdot C_0)$.

The ECIES-DEM has the following two algorithms:

- **ECIES.SEnc**(k_s, M): On input of a key k_s and a message M, the algorithm first parses k_s as $k_1||k_2$, computes $C_1 = \mathsf{ENC}(k_1, M)$ and $C_2 = \mathsf{MAC}(k_2, C_1)$, and then outputs (C_1, C_2), where ENC is an encryption part of a symmetric encryption scheme and MAC is a message authentication code.
- **ECIES.SDec**($k_s, (C_1, C_2)$): On input of a key k_s and a ciphertext (C_1, C_2), the algorithm first parses k_s as $k_1||k_2$. If $C_2 \neq \mathsf{MAC}(k_2, C_1)$, it outputs $\perp$. Otherwise, the algorithm outputs $M = \mathsf{DEC}(k_1, C_1)$, where DEC is a decryption part of a symmetric encryption scheme.

2.2 Stealth Key Exchange

Recently, Fischlin [11] introduced a notion of stealth key exchange and showed how to embed a covert key exchange sub-protocol into the regular TLS 1.3 execution [14], generating a stealth session key in addition to a regular session key. The basic idea is to use exchanged nonces, which ensure that a session is unique, to transport other Diffie-Hellman public keys. One prospective application of stealth key exchange is a sanitizable channel where a designated entity[1] can partly access and modify payload data with a regular session key, while entities who share a stealth session key can covertly communicate in a channel protocol (refer to [11] for the other applications).

A stealth key exchange protocol has the following security properties [11]:

Stealthiness: An outside attacker remains oblivious if a stealth mode has been used (i.e., a stealth session key has been generated) or not in the protocol execution.

Security of stealth key: A stealth session key should be secure even if an attacker can control a regular session key derived in the same protocol execution.

[1] For example, it can be a sanitizer, who monitors incoming packets for malicious contents (e.g., malware) and locates suspicious ones in quarantine, in an intrusion detection system.

3 A Stealth 5G-AKA Protocol

In this section, we propose a stealth mode of 5G-AKA (for short, Stealth-5G-AKA) protocol that is compatible with the current 3GPP standard [3] with small modifications. In the Stealth-5G-AKA protocol, UE and SN share a stealth anchor key K'_{SEAF} in addition to an anchor key K_{SEAF}. Also, the Stealth-5G-AKA protocol provides forward secrecy and unlinkability like [23]. Before executing the Stealth-5G-AKA protocol, UE holds $(k, PK_{HN}, SUPI, SQN_{UE})$ secretly and HN stores $(k, sk_{HN}, ID_{HN}, SQN_{HN})$ secretly. Also, SN stores ID_{SN}. Note that SN and HN are connected with a secure channel.

3.1 The Initiation Phase: Step 1

In this phase, UE sends its $SUPI$ as an encrypted form using ECIES [9,16,19,21] with HN's public key PK_{HN}. Correspondingly, HN decrypts $SUCI$ with its private key sk_{HN}. After successful completion of Step 1, we proceed to Step 2 by selecting Stealth-5G-AKA among various authentication methods.

Step 1.1 (UE) With HN's public key PK_{HN}, UE executes the followings:

1. Generate an ephemeral ECIES private-public key pair (r, R) such that $R = r \cdot G$
2. With PK_{HN}, compute a ciphertext $C_0 = R$ and a key $k_{UE} = \mathsf{KDF}(r \cdot PK_{HN})$
3. Parse the shared key k_{UE} as $k_1||k_2$
4. Compute $C_1 = \mathsf{ENC}(k_1, SUPI)$ and $C_2 = \mathsf{MAC}(k_2, C_1)$
5. Set $SUCI \leftarrow (C_0, C_1, C_2)$

UE sends $SUCI$ to SN.

Step 1.2 (SN) SN receives $SUCI$ from UE and then SN sends $(SUCI, ID_{SN})$ to HN.

Step 1.3 (HN) Upon receiving $(SUCI, ID_{SN})$ from SN, HN executes the followings:

1. Compute a shared key $k_{HN} = \mathsf{KDF}(sk_{HN} \cdot C_0)$
2. Parse the shared key k_{HN} as $k_1||k_2$

If $C_2 \neq \mathsf{MAC}(k_2, C_1)$, HN outputs $\perp$. Otherwise, it outputs $SUPI = \mathsf{DEC}(k_1, C_1)$, and retrieves the corresponding k and SQN_{HN} from its database.

3.2 The Challenge-Response Phase: Step 2

In this phase, UE and HN authenticate each other via a challenge-response method and establish anchor keys (i.e., K_{SEAF} and K'_{SEAF}) together with SN. A main idea of the Stealth-5G-AKA protocol is that we set an embedded (elliptic curve) Diffie-Hellman public key Y as a random challenge $RAND$, and an (elliptic curve) Diffie–Hellman key DHK is used as a key material of a stealth anchor key for forward secrecy and unlinkability. This phase uses a series of HMAC-SHA-256 cryptographic key derivation functions $\mathsf{f}_1, \mathsf{f}_2, \mathsf{f}_3, \mathsf{f}_4, \mathsf{f}_5, \mathsf{f}_1^*$, and f_5^*, as specified by TS 33.501 [3]. Also, we denote by $\mathsf{H}_{\text{SHA-256}}$ the SHA-256 cryptographic hash function.

Step 2.1 (HN) Using (k, SQN_{HN}), HN generates an authentication vector $SE\text{-}AV$ as follows:

1. Regular mode: Choose a random challenge $RAND \xleftarrow{\$} \{0,1\}^{256}$[2]
2. Stealth mode: Generate an ephemeral Diffie-Hellman private-public key pair (y, Y) such that $Y = y \cdot G$
3. Stealth mode: Set $RAND \leftarrow \mathsf{Embed}(Y)$ as a random challenge
4. Compute $MAC \leftarrow \mathsf{f}_1(k, SQN_{HN}, AMF, RAND)$ and an anonymous key $AK \leftarrow \mathsf{f}_5(k, RAND)$
5. Set $AUTN \leftarrow (AK \oplus SQN_{HN}, AMF, MAC)$
6. Compute $CK \leftarrow \mathsf{f}_3(k, RAND)$ and $IK \leftarrow \mathsf{f}_4(k, RAND)$
7. Compute expected responses $XRES \leftarrow \mathsf{f}_2(k, RAND)$, $XRES^* \leftarrow \mathsf{KDF}(CK||IK, ID_{SN}||RAND||XRES)$, and $HXRES^* \leftarrow \mathsf{LEFT}(128, \mathsf{H}_{\text{SHA-256}}(RAND||XRES^*))$
8. Derive $K_{AUSF} \leftarrow \mathsf{KDF}(CK||IK, ID_{SN}||AK \oplus SQN_{HN})$ and $K_{SEAF} \leftarrow \mathsf{KDF}(K_{AUSF}, ID_{SN})$
9. Increase SQN_{HN} by 1 (i.e., $SQN_{HN} \leftarrow SQN_{HN} + 1$)
10. Set $HE\text{-}AV \leftarrow (RAND, AUTN, XRES^*, K_{AUSF})$ and $SE\text{-}AV \leftarrow (RAND, AUTN, HXRES^*)$
11. Stealth mode: Compute a Diffie-Hellman key $DHK = y \cdot C_0$
12. Stealth mode: Compute $CK' \leftarrow \mathsf{f}_3(k, RAND \oplus DHK)$ and $IK' \leftarrow \mathsf{f}_4(k, RAND \oplus DHK)$
13. Stealth mode: Derive $K'_{AUSF} \leftarrow \mathsf{KDF}(CK'||IK', ID_{SN}||AK \oplus SQN_{HN})$ and $K'_{SEAF} \leftarrow \mathsf{KDF}(K'_{AUSF}, ID_{SN})$

HN sends $SE\text{-}AV$ to SN.

Step 2.2 (SN) SN receives $SE\text{-}AV$ from HN and stores $(RAND, HXRES^*)$. Then, SN sends $(RAND, AUTN)$ to UE.

[2] Here, we use a 256-bit $RAND$ instead of a 128-bit $RAND$ in the 3GPP standard [3].

Step 2.3 (UE) Upon receiving $(RAND, AUTN)$ from SN, UE executes the followings:

1. ME forwards $(RAND, AUTN)$ to SIM card.
2. Run SIM card command `AUTHENTICATE`$(RAND, AUTN)$
3. Compute $AK \leftarrow \mathsf{f}_5(k, RAND)$
4. Parse $AUTN$ as $(CONC, AMF, MAC)$
5. De-conceal $SQN_{HN} \leftarrow AK \oplus CONC$
6. Check $\mathsf{f}_1(k, SQN_{HN}, AMF, RAND) = MAC$
   - If this check does not pass, SIM card returns $\perp$ and then UE sends a failure message `Mac_Failure` to SN (see *Case i*).
   - Otherwise, proceed to the next step
7. Check $SQN_{UE} < SQN_{HN} < SQN_{UE} + \Delta$[3]
   - If this check does not pass, SIM card computes $MAC^* \leftarrow \mathsf{f}_1^*(k, SQN_{UE}, AMF, RAND)$ and returns $AUTS \leftarrow (AK^* \oplus SQN_{UE}, AMF, MAC^*)$ where $AK^* \leftarrow \mathsf{f}_5^*(k, RAND)$. Then, UE re-synchronizes with HN by sending a failure message `Sync_Failure` and $AUTS$ to SN (see *Case ii*).
   - Otherwise, proceed to the next step
8. Set $SQN_{UE} \leftarrow SQN_{HN}$
9. Compute $CK \leftarrow \mathsf{f}_3(k, RAND)$, $IK \leftarrow \mathsf{f}_4(k, RAND)$ and $RES \leftarrow \mathsf{f}_2(k, RAND)$
10. Stealth mode: Set $Y \leftarrow \mathsf{Embed}^{-1}(RAND)$
11. Stealth mode: Compute a Diffie-Hellman key $DHK = r \cdot Y$
12. Stealth mode: Compute $CK' \leftarrow \mathsf{f}_3(k, RAND \oplus DHK)$ and $IK' \leftarrow \mathsf{f}_4(k, RAND \oplus DHK)$
13. SIM card returns (CK, IK, RES, CK', IK') to ME.
14. ME computes $RES^* \leftarrow \mathsf{KDF}(CK||IK, ID_{SN}||RAND||RES)$, and derives $K_{AUSF} \leftarrow \mathsf{KDF}(CK||IK, ID_{SN}||CONC)$ and $K_{SEAF} \leftarrow \mathsf{KDF}(K_{AUSF}, ID_{SN})$.
15. Stealth mode: ME derives $K'_{AUSF} \leftarrow \mathsf{KDF}(CK'||IK', ID_{SN}||CONC)$ and $K'_{SEAF} \leftarrow \mathsf{KDF}(K'_{AUSF}, ID_{SN})$.
16. ME returns $(K_{SEAF}, K'_{SEAF}, RES^*)$.

UE stores (K_{SEAF}, K'_{SEAF}) and sends RES^* to SN (see *Case iii*).

[3] The first condition $SQN_{UE} < SQN_{HN}$ ensures the freshness of $(RAND, AUTN)$. Also, the second condition $SQN_{HN} < SQN_{UE} + \Delta$, which is optional in the non-normative Annex C of TS 33.102 [2], prevents a wrap-around of SQN_{UE}. For example, if Δ is too small (i.e., $\Delta = 2$), an attacker can make a synchronization failure by sending $SUCI$ computed by the attacker with a fake $SUPI$. After this attack, the honest UE and HN can no longer authenticate each other. In TS 33.102 [2], a recommended value of Δ is 2^{28} so as to decrease the synchronization failure rate.

Case i **(SIM card returns $\perp$)**: The UE sends a failure message `Mac_Failure` to the SN.

Case ii **(SIM card returns $AUTS$)**: The UE re-synchronizes with the HN by sending a failure message `Sync_Failure` and $AUTS$ to the SN. Upon receiving (`Sync_Failure`, $AUTS$), SN sends (`Sync_Failure`, $AUTS, RAND, SUCI$) to the HN. Then, HN parses $AUTS$ as $(AK^* \oplus SQN_{UE}, AMF, MAC^*)$, and de-conceals $SQN_{UE} \leftarrow AK^* \oplus SQN_{UE} \oplus \mathsf{f}_5^*(k, RAND)$. Next, HN checks its authenticity by comparing $MAC^* = \mathsf{f}_1^*(k, SQN_{UE}, AMF, RAND)$. If the check holds, HN re-sets SQN_{HN} by $SQN_{UE}{+}1$ (i.e., $SQN_{HN} \leftarrow SQN_{UE}{+}1$).

Case iii **(ME returns $(K_{SEAF}, K'_{SEAF}, RES^*)$)**: The UE stores (K_{SEAF}, K'_{SEAF}) and sends RES^* to the SN. Upon receiving RES^*, SN computes a hashed value $HRES^* \leftarrow \mathsf{LEFT}(128, \mathsf{H}_{\text{SHA-256}}(RAND||RES^*))$ and checks its validity by comparing $HRES^*$ with $HXRES^*$. If $HRES^* = HXRES^*$, SN forwards RES^* to the HN. Next, HN authenticates the UE by comparing RES^* with $XRES^*$. If $RES^* = XRES^*$, HN sends its result and $(SUPI, K_{SEAF}, K'_{SEAF})$ to the SN. The SN continues the protocol only if both checks hold, and aborts the protocol otherwise. When all checks pass, UE and SN communicate with session keys derived from anchor keys (i.e., (K_{SEAF}, K'_{SEAF})) in the subsequent 5G procedures. According to TS 33.501 [3], UE and SN should confirm the keys agreed and the identities of each other implicitly through the successful use of keys in subsequent procedures, which can be expressed by a key-confirmation round trip with K_{SEAF}.

Remark 1. In the Stealth-5G-AKA protocol, we use the elliptic curve `Curve25519` [6] for Diffie-Hellman key exchange parts instead of the recommended elliptic curves (e.g., `secp256k1` and `secp256r1`) in [20]. For Embed, we use the embedding technique Elligator 2 [7], which allows us to efficiently create elliptic curve points that are statistically indistinguishable from uniform random bit strings (see the Elligator webpage [1] for more details). Note that Elligator 2 is more general and works well with `Curve25519` while Elligator 1 based on [12] works for some elliptic curves. In [7], Bernstein et al. discussed an issue that the NIST elliptic curve `P-256` may not easily yield almost uniform random bit strings since the order of `P-256` is not sufficiently close to a power of 2. Also, the other option for Embed can be found in [11], where the random mapping Embed maps a large portion of elliptic curve points to strings that are statistically close to uniform bit strings.

4 Security of Stealth-5G-AKA

Due to the lack of space, we informally discuss several security properties of the Stealth-5G-AKA protocol.

4.1 Stealthiness

Here, we show that the Stealth-5G-AKA protocol provides stealthiness by giving a reduction to the security of Embed. Let $\text{transcript}_{\text{Regular}}$ (resp., $\text{transcript}_{\text{Stealth}}$)

be a communication transcript $(SUCI, (RAND, AUTN), RES^*)$ of the regular (resp., stealth) mode of Stealth-5G-AKA. Also, let $\mathscr{B}$ be an attacker who can distinguish an embedded elliptic curve point from a uniform random bit string. The only difference between $\text{transcript}_{\text{Regular}}$ and $\text{transcript}_{\text{Stealth}}$ is that $RAND \xleftarrow{\$} \{0,1\}^{256}$ is used in the regular mode and $RAND \leftarrow \mathsf{Embed}(Y)$ is used in the stealth mode. We assume that there exists an outside attacker $\mathscr{A}$ who can distinguish the regular mode from the stealth mode in the Stealth-5G-AKA protocol execution. By using $\mathscr{A}$, we can trivially construct an attacker $\mathscr{B}$ who breaks the security of Embed. In other words, the outside attacker remains oblivious if the stealth mode has been used or not in the Stealth-5G-AKA protocol execution.

4.2 Security of Stealth Key

Next, we show that a stealth anchor key is secure even if an attacker can control a (regular) anchor key derived in the same Stealth-5G-AKA protocol execution. We assume that there exists an attacker who can control the anchor key K_{SEAF} derived in the Stealth-5G-AKA protocol. Thanks to the security of KDF and the master stealth session key K'_{AUSF}, it is clear that the stealth anchor key K'_{SEAF} is secure against the attacker.

4.3 Forward Secrecy

In the Stealth-5G-AKA protocol, forward secrecy should be discussed in two flavors: an anchor key and a stealth anchor key. Regarding the stealth anchor key K'_{SEAF}, the Stealth-5G-AKA protocol guarantees forward secrecy since the ephemeral (elliptic curve) Diffie-Hellman key exchange [10] is inherent in its construction. Specifically, the ephemeral Diffie-Hellman public key on the UE (resp., HN) side is $R = r \cdot G$ in **Step 1.1** (resp., $Y = y \cdot G$ in **Step 2.1**) and the ephemeral Diffie–Hellman key $DHK = y \cdot C_0$ in **Step 2.1** (resp., $DHK = r \cdot Y$ in **Step 2.3**) is used as a key material of the stealth anchor key K'_{SEAF} on the HN (resp., UE) side. Note that KEM can be generally understood as the Diffie-Hellman key exchange.

Regarding the anchor key K_{SEAF}, the Stealth-5G-AKA protocol does not provide forward secrecy because the computation of K_{SEAF} is the same as the 5G-AKA protocol. This problem arises from the fact that the 5G-AKA protocol itself has no forward secrecy [23]. A fix to this problem is to use $RAND \oplus DHK$ instead of $RAND$ in the computations of $\mathsf{f}_1, \mathsf{f}_2, \mathsf{f}_3, \mathsf{f}_4, \mathsf{f}_5, \mathsf{f}_1^*$, and f_5^*. However, this fix requires modifications to the 3GPP standard [3].

4.4 UE Unlinkability

Similar to Sect. 4.3, UE unlinkability in the Stealth-5G-AKA protocol should be discussed in two flavors: an anchor key and a stealth anchor key. Regarding the stealth anchor key K'_{SEAF}, the Stealth-5G-AKA protocol guarantees UE unlinkability since the ephemeral (elliptic curve) ECIES public key $R = r \cdot G$ in **Step 1.1** on the UE side is used in the ephemeral Diffie–Hellman key $DHK = y \cdot R$ in **Step 2.1** which is subsequently used as a key material of the stealth anchor key K'_{SEAF} on the HN side.

Regarding the anchor key K_{SEAF}, the Stealth-5G-AKA protocol does not provide UE unlinkability because the computation of K_{SEAF} is the same as the 5G-AKA protocol. This problem arises from the fact that the 5G-AKA protocol itself is susceptible to UE linkability attacks (e.g., [22]). Basically, this problem can be solved by tightly relating $SUCI$ to the subsequent computations on the HN side. As in Sect. 4.3, a fix to this problem is to use $RAND \oplus DHK$ instead of $RAND$ in the computations of $\mathsf{f}_1, \mathsf{f}_2, \mathsf{f}_3, \mathsf{f}_4, \mathsf{f}_5, \mathsf{f}_1^*$, and f_5^*. However, this fix also requires modifications to the 3GPP standard [3].

5 Comparison

In this section, we compare the 5G-AKA [3] with relevant 3GPP-compatible protocols (5G-AKA' [22], 5G-AKA-FS [23] and Stealth-5G-AKA) with respect to several security properties (stealthiness, security of stealth key, forward secrecy, UE anonymity/unlinkability and security of anchor key) and efficiency in terms of computation costs and communication costs. We summarize comparative results in Tables 2 and 3.

Table 2. Security comparison of the 5G-AKA and relevant 3GPP-compatible protocols

Protocols	Stealthiness	Security of Stealth Key	Forward Secrecy	UE Anonymity / Unlinkability	Security of Anchor Key
5G-AKA [3]	No	No	No	Yes / No	Yes
5G-AKA' [22]	No	No	No	Yes / Yes	Yes
5G-AKA-FS [23]	No	No	Yes	Yes / Yes	Yes
Stealth-5G-AKA	Yes	Yes	Yes	Yes / Yes	Yes

From Table 2, it is clear that the only Stealth-5G-AKA protocol provides stealthiness and security of stealth anchor key. In Table 3, $RAND$ in the 5G-AKA [3] protocol is a 128-bit random challenge while $RAND$ in the 5G-AKA-FS [23] and Stealth-5G-AKA protocols is a 256-bit random challenge. For Embed, we use the embedding technique Elligator 2 [7], which needs two trials to find a suitable elliptic curve point on average and an inversion for the embedding. Note that two elliptic curve modular multiplications (i.e., R and k_{UE}) on the UE side, and one elliptic curve modular multiplication (i.e., Y) and Embed on the HN side can be pre-computed in the Stealth-5G-AKA protocol. From Tables 2 and 3, one

Table 3. Efficiency comparison of the 5G-AKA and relevant 3GPP-compatible protocols where Mul is an elliptic curve modular multiplication and $|l|$ indicates a bit-length of l

Protocols	Computation costs of		Communication costs between UE and SN
	UE	HN	
5G-AKA [3]	2Mul	1Mul	$\|SUCI\| + \|RAND\| + \|AUTN\| + \|RES^*\|$
5G-AKA' [22]	2Mul	1Mul	$\|SUCI\| + \|\mathsf{ENC}\| + \|AUTN\| + \|RES^*\|$
5G-AKA-FS [23]	3Mul	3Mul	$\|SUCI\| + \|RAND\| + \|AUTN\| + \|RES^*\|$
Stealth-5G-AKA	3Mul+ Embed^{-1}	3Mul+ Embed	$\|SUCI\| + \|RAND\| + \|AUTN\| + \|RES^*\|$

can see that there is a trade-off of security and efficiency between the 5G-AKA-FS [23] and Stealth-5G-AKA protocols. Also, we stress that the Stealth-5G-AKA protocol is fully compatible with the 3GPP standard [3] with small modifications to achieve stealthiness in the 5G-AKA protocol.

6 Conclusion

In this paper, we proposed a stealth mode of 5G-AKA (for short, Stealth-5G-AKA) protocol that is compatible with the current 3GPP standard [3] with small modifications. In the Stealth-5G-AKA protocol, UE and SN share a stealth anchor key in addition to a (regular) anchor key. Also, we discussed several security properties of the Stealth-5G-AKA protocol. Moreover, we compared the 5G-AKA [3] with relevant 3GPP-compatible protocols (5G-AKA' [22], 5G-AKA-FS [23] and Stealth-5G-AKA) with respect to security properties (stealthiness, security of stealth key, forward secrecy, UE anonymity/unlinkability and security of anchor key) and efficiency in terms of computation costs and communication costs. As in [11], we expect that the Stealth-5G-AKA protocol can be applied to a sanitizable channel (e.g., for private 5G) where a designated entity can partly access and modify payload data with a (regular) anchor key, while entities who share a stealth anchor key can covertly communicate in a channel protocol.

Future works of the Stealth-5G-AKA protocol include formal security analysis using security verification tools (e.g., Tamarin or ProVerif) and experimental performance evaluation on a realistic 5G testbed or a simulation framework for deployment feasibility in practical settings.

Acknowledgments. We sincerely appreciate the anonymous reviewers' constructive and valuable comments on this paper. This paper is based on results obtained from a project, JPNP23013, commissioned by the New Energy and Industrial Technology Development Organization (NEDO).

References

1. Elligator: Hiding cryptographic key exchange as random noise. https://elligator.org/
2. 3GPP TS 33.102: 3G security; Security architecture (Release 16). https://portal.3gpp.org/desktopmodules/Specifications/SpecificationDetails.aspx?specificationId=2262. Accessed July (2020)
3. 3GPP TS 33.501: Security architecture and procedures for 5G system (Release 18.2). https://portal.3gpp.org/desktopmodules/Specifications/SpecificationDetails.aspx?specificationId=3169. Accessed June (2023)
4. Bana, G., C.-Lundh, H.: A computationally complete symbolic attacker for equivalence properties. In: CCS 2014, pp. 609–620. ACM (2014)
5. Basin, D., Dreier, J., Hirschi, L., Radomirovic, S., Sasse, R., Stettler, V.: A formal analysis of 5G authentication. In: CCS 2018, pp. 1383–1396. ACM (2018)
6. Bernstein, D.J.: Curve25519: New Diffie-Hellman speed records. In: PKC 2006, pp. 207–228. Springer (2006)
7. Bernstein, D.J., Hamburg, M., Krasnova, A., Lange, T.: Elligator: elliptic-curve points indistinguishable from uniform random strings. In: CCS 2013, pp. 967–980. ACM (2013)
8. Borgaonkar, R., Hirschi, L., Park, S., Shaik, A.: New privacy threat on 3G, 4G, and upcoming 5G AKA protocols. Proc. Priv. Enhanc. Technol. (PoPETs) **2019**(3), 108–127 (2019)
9. BSI TR-02102-1: Cryptographic Mechanisms: Recommendations and Key Lengths. https://www.bsi.bund.de/SharedDocs/Downloads/EN/BSI/Publications/TechGuidelines/TG02102/BSI-TR-02102-1.html. Accessed Jan. (2024)
10. Diffie, W., Hellman, M.: New directions in cryptography. IEEE Trans. Inf. Theory **22**(6), 644–654 (1976)
11. Fischlin, M.: Stealth key exchange and confined access to the record protocol data in TLS 1.3. In: CCS 2023, pp. 2901–2914. ACM (2023)
12. Fouque, P.A., Joux, A., Tibouchi, M.: Injective encodings to elliptic curves. In: ACISP 2013, pp. 203–218. Springer (2013)
13. IETF Internet-Draft: Forward Secrecy for the Extensible Authentication Protocol Method for Authentication and Key Agreement (EAP-AKA' FS). https://www.ietf.org/archive/id/draft-ietf-emu-aka-pfs-12.html. Accessed Feb. (2024)
14. IETF RFC 8446: The Transport Layer Security (TLS) Protocol Version 1.3. https://www.rfc-editor.org/rfc/rfc8446.html. Accessed Aug. (2018)
15. IETF RFC 9048: Improved Extensible Authentication Protocol Method for 3GPP Mobile Network Authentication and Key Agreement (EAP-AKA'). https://www.rfc-editor.org/rfc/rfc9048.html. Accessed Oct. (2021)
16. ISO/IEC 18033-2:2006: Information technology—Security techniques—Encryption algorithms—Part 2: Asymmetric ciphers. https://www.iso.org/standard/37971.html. Accessed May (2006)
17. Koutsos, A.: The 5G-AKA authentication protocol privacy. In: EuroS&P 2019, pp. 464–479. IEEE (2019)
18. Meier, S., Schmidt, B., Cremers, C., Basin, D.: The TAMARIN prover for the symbolic analysis of security protocols. In: Computer Aided Verification (CAV) 2013, pp. 696–701. Springer (2013)
19. SECG SEC 1: Elliptic Curve Cryptography. https://www.secg.org/sec1-v2.pdf. Accessed May (2009)

20. SECG SEC 2: Recommended Elliptic Curve Domain Parameters. https://www.secg.org/sec2-v2.pdf. Accessed Jan. (2010)
21. Shoup, V.: A Proposal for an ISO Standard for Public Key Encryption (version 2.1). https://www.shoup.net/papers/iso-2_1.pdf. Accessed Dec. (2001)
22. Wang, Y., Zhang, Z., Xie, Y.: Privacy-Preserving and standard-compatible AKA protocol for 5G. In: USENIX Security Symposium 2021, pp. 3595–3612. USENIX Association (2021)
23. You, I., Kim, G., Shin, S., Kwon, H., Kim, J., Baek, J.: 5G-AKA-FS: a 5G authentication and key agreement protocol for forward secrecy. Sensors **24**(1)(159) (2024). https://doi.org/10.3390/s24010159

Cybersecurity Education and Model Security

Real Environment Tolerance Curve (RETC): Assessing Machine Learning Model Performance Degradation Under Extreme Class Imbalance

Yuki Tanaka and Mamoru Mimura(✉)

National Defense Academy of Japan, 1-10-20 Hashirimizu, Yokosuka, Kanagawa, Japan
mim@nda.ac.jp

Abstract. Evaluating machine learning models in cybersecurity often involves datasets with an equal ratio of benign and malicious samples. Previous studies employing conventional evaluation methods have assessed performance at a single, fixed class ratio. However, this evaluation approach has a critical flaw. It fails to show how its performance degrades when the class imbalance becomes severe. This issue causes a mismatch when deploying the model in a real environment. Therefore, we propose a new evaluation methodology: the Real Environment Tolerance Curve (RETC). RETC is a systematic method to assess model robustness under varying degrees of class imbalance. It involves generating test datasets with an increasing proportion of benign data and plotting key performance metrics against the imbalance ratio. The resulting visualization, the RETC plot, enables a quantitative evaluation of the ability of a model to maintain performance in benign-dominated environments. In this study, we first establish the theoretical foundation of the RETC method through mathematical analysis, clarifying how each metric behaves as class ratios change. Next, empirical experiments on network traffic and URL datasets demonstrate that RETC reveals critical performance differences missed by conventional single-ratio evaluations. Experiments with URL datasets revealed a model whose false positive rate surged by more than three times (2.5% to 8.7%) as the imbalance ratio increased from 1 to 10. This capability helps diagnose whether performance degradation is an apparent effect of metric properties or an essential weakness in model generalization. In conclusion, the RETC is a reliable diagnostic tool for predicting performance in real operations.

Keywords: Evaluation metrics · Imbalanced dataset · Binary classification

K.-W. Park and J. Park (Eds.): WISA 2025 2025, LNCS 16434, pp. 73–85, 2026.
https://doi.org/10.1007/978-981-95-6857-4_6

1 Introduction

Recent years have seen a surge in research on threat detection using machine learning and AI in cybersecurity [4]. The application of machine learning to cybersecurity threat detection has become increasingly prevalent. However, a significant gap exists between model evaluation in academic settings and the performance of the model in real-world operations. This gap largely arises from the well-known problem of class imbalance. Cybersecurity datasets, such as those containing network traffic, emails, or URLs, are inherently imbalanced, where benign data vastly outnumbers malicious ones [1,2,12]. Despite this fundamental characteristic, standard evaluation protocols in academic research often rely on balanced datasets, where the ratio of benign to malicious samples is artificially set to 1:1 [5,11]. While this approach simplifies model comparison and ensures reproducibility, it fails to assess the behavior of the model under the realistic conditions of extreme class imbalance. This approach can lead to a significant overestimation of their practical utility and mask critical weaknesses of models. For instance, a model that reports a low false positive rate (FPR) on a balanced test set may generate an unsustainable number of false alerts when deployed in a production environment, overwhelming security analysts [16].

Conventional, single-ratio evaluations do not adequately capture this performance degradation as class imbalance intensifies. Furthermore, while some previous studies have explored varying imbalance ratios, they often lack a theoretical foundation to support their findings. This omission makes it difficult to distinguish whether an observed performance drop is an inherent mathematical property of a metric or a genuine weakness in the generalization ability of a model. Therefore, to determine the true operational effectiveness of the models, it is critical to have a methodology that systematically evaluates their robustness against varying degrees of class imbalance.

To address this issue, our study proposes a new evaluation method: the Real Environment Tolerance Curve (RETC). However, simply observing performance changes under increasing imbalance is not sufficient. A key challenge is to distinguish between performance degradation that is an apparent effect stemming from the mathematical properties of the metrics and degradation that reflects a genuine weakness in the generalization ability of a model. To evaluate the RETC method as a tool for this purpose, this study aims to answer the following research questions (RQs):

- RQ1: What are the inherent characteristics of the behavior of standard evaluation metrics on the RETC as the class imbalance ratio changes?
- RQ2: What new insights into model robustness does the RETC method provide that are missed by conventional single-ratio evaluations?
- RQ3: Which features of the RETC plot (such as its shape and slope) indicate the robustness of the model?

The contributions of this paper are as follows:

- We propose a novel evaluation method: Real Environment Tolerance Curve (RETC), designed to assess model performance under varying class imbalance.
- We mathematically analyzed ideal classifiers to clarify the theoretical behavior of standard evaluation metrics under increasing class imbalance.
- We showed that the RETC method can detect performance differences between models that are often overlooked by conventional single-ratio evaluation through two empirical experiments.
- We established a clear criterion for diagnosing whether a performance degradation stems from the mathematical properties of metrics or an inherent weakness in the generalization ability of the models, by observing the transitions of the RETC plot, especially the plot of FPR.

This paper is structured as follows: Sect. 2 provides an overview of related research. Section 3 provides definitions that serve as the premise for the discussion in this study. Section 4 explains the specific steps of the proposed method, the RETC. Section 5 performs theoretical analysis and conducts demonstration experiments using actual datasets to evaluate the effectiveness of the proposed method. Section 6 considers the results obtained from various perspectives, and finally, Sect. 7 provides conclusions and future work.

2 Literature Review

Performance evaluation of machine learning models, especially in domains with significant class imbalance such as cybersecurity, has been an important research topic for many years. To clarify the position of this research, we will provide an overview of related research divided into three categories.

First, we study standard evaluation metrics for classification models. $Accuracy$, $Precision$, $Recall$, and F_1 are the most basic metrics calculated from a confusion matrix and are widely used [15]. In addition, the receiver operating characteristic (ROC) curve is a standard method for visualizing the performance of a classifier when the discrimination threshold is varied [7]. However, it has been pointed out that these metrics, especially $Accuracy$, cannot correctly evaluate the bias toward the majority class when the class ratio is imbalanced, and may lead to erroneous conclusions [6]. In response to this problem, the Matthews Correlation Coefficient (MCC) has been proposed as a more robust metric for imbalanced data because it takes into account all four confusion matrix elements [17]. The RETC proposed in this study uses these existing metrics as evaluation axes, while adding depth to their interpretation by introducing a new dimension, the class ratio.

Second, there is research on how to deal with class-imbalanced data. Attempts to address this issue have been made mainly at the learning stage, with data-level approaches such as oversampling, such as Synthetic Minority Oversampling Technique (SMOTE), which increases the data of minority classes, and undersampling, which reduces the data of majority classes, are the mainstream approaches [9,10]. There is also cost-aware learning, which weights the cost of misclassification by class, as an algorithm-level approach. These methods improve the *learning* of models. However, the problem of how to *evaluate* them remains. Even if a model is trained using these methods, it is necessary to verify whether it can withstand extreme imbalances in real environments, and the *evaluation* method proposed in this study plays a complementary role in measuring the effectiveness of these learning methods in a more practical manner.

Third, there are studies that attempt evaluation taking into account real environments. In the field of cybersecurity, it has been pointed out that the discrepancy between experimental and real environments undermines the reliability of model performance evaluation [3,14]. Based on this recognition, there are previous studies that take a similar approach to this study. For example, in executable file classification, there is a study [12] that evaluated the change in accuracy by sequentially adding benign samples to the test data, and a study [13] that used a similar method to evaluate a classification model for cross-site scripting attacks. However, since these previous studies rely on a single evaluation metric, they may not be able to capture the multifaceted changes in the performance of the model. In addition, there is a lack of in-depth discussion of the characteristics of each evaluation metric, and it is difficult to say that the interpretation of the observed performance degradation is sufficiently accurate.

Although these previous studies are an important step, they lack theoretical justification to support the behavior of the model. Therefore, in this study, we systematically track changes in performance after analyzing the characteristics of multiple metrics and provide theoretical justification to support the behavior. As described above, this research solves the issues of previous research. The proposed RETC method visualizes performance from multiple angles by plotting multiple key evaluation metrics simultaneously, and enables reliable diagnosis of the robustness of the model by interpreting the curves based on theoretical analysis of the behavior of the metrics. This provides a systematic evaluation method for more accurately predicting performance in real environments.

3 Preliminaries

This section establishes the formal definitions that underpin the proposed RETC method. A rigorous mathematical definition is essential for precisely describing the composition of test data under varying class imbalance ratios, which is a core component of our study. We begin by defining the universe of data, the datasets derived from it, and the classification process. We then formalize the elements of the confusion matrix.

Consider a universal set $U = \{\boldsymbol{x}_1, \boldsymbol{x}_2, \boldsymbol{x}_3 \dots \boldsymbol{x}_N\}$ of features of the data to be handled in real environments. Here, in cybersecurity, $\boldsymbol{x}_i$ is made from various data such as port number, text vector, URL, etc. Next, define binary label y for $\boldsymbol{x} \in U$.

$$y = \begin{cases} 0\ (benign) & U_0 = \{\boldsymbol{x} \in U | y = 0\} \\ 1\ (malicious) & U_1 = \{\boldsymbol{x} \in U | y = 1\} \end{cases} \tag{1}$$

The number of elements for each label is $N_0 = |U_0|$, $N_1 = |U_1|$, with the total number of elements being $N = N_0 + N_1$. Consequently, the proportion of each label is $P_0 = N_0/N$, $P_1 = N_1/N$. Given the nature of real environment data in the cybersecurity field, benign samples are typically more numerous than malicious ones, meaning that $P_0 \geq P_1$ holds in most cases. We define a dataset D as a subset of U: $D \subseteq U$. This dataset D consists of a selection of samples from U. Let D_0 be the set of benign samples in D, and D_1 be the set of malicious samples in D, such as $D_0 = D \cap U_0 = \{\boldsymbol{x} \in D | y = 0\}$, $D_1 = D \cap U_1 = \{\boldsymbol{x} \in D | y = 1\}$.

We also define the number of samples in D. Let n be the total number of samples in D. n_0 be the number of benign samples in D as : $n_0 = |D_0|$, and n_1 be the number of malicious samples in dataset: $n_1 = |D_1|$. Thus, it holds that $n = |D| = n_0 + n_1$. Since D is a subset of U, it naturally follows that $n_0 \leq N_0, n_1 \leq N_1$, and consequently $n \leq N$. Furthermore, the proportions of benign and malicious samples within the dataset D can be denoted as $p_0 = n_0/n$ and $p_1 = n_1/n$, respectively. Assuming $n > 0$, it follows that $p_0 + p_1 = 1$. We now define the classifier as a function $f : D \to [0, 1]$, which outputs a confidence score or probability that a given input $\boldsymbol{x} \in D$ belongs to the malicious class.

To obtain a binary prediction $\hat{y} \in \{0, 1\}$, we apply a threshold $\tau \in [0, 1]$ as follows:

$$\hat{y} = \begin{cases} 0 & \text{if } f(\boldsymbol{x}) < \tau \\ 1 & \text{if } f(\boldsymbol{x}) \geq \tau \end{cases} \tag{2}$$

Based on the true label $y \in \{0, 1\}$ and the predicted label $\hat{y} \in \{0, 1\}$, we define the confusion matrix elements such as True Positive (TP), False Negative (FN), True Negative (TN), False Positive (FP) as follows:

$$TP = \{\boldsymbol{x} \in D |\ y = 1, \hat{y} = 1\}, \quad FN = \{\boldsymbol{x} \in D |\ y = 1, \hat{y} = 0\}$$
$$TN = \{\boldsymbol{x} \in D |\ y = 0, \hat{y} = 0\}, \quad FP = \{\boldsymbol{x} \in D |\ y = 0, \hat{y} = 1\}$$

The confusion matrix is defined by the number of elements of these four sets. The total number of elements n is the sum of the total number of malicious classes n_1 and the total number of benign classes n_0

$$n_{TP} = |TP|, \quad n_{FN} = |FN|, \quad n_{TN} = |TN|, \quad n_{FP} = |FP| \tag{3}$$
$$n = (n_{TP} + n_{FN}) + (n_{TN} + n_{FP}) = n_1 + n_0 \tag{4}$$

These definitions serve as the fundamental building blocks for the methodology and analysis presented in the following sections. They establish the clear and theoretically grounded framework necessary for a reproducible and rigorous evaluation of model performance.

4 Methodology

This section explains the methodology of our proposed evaluation method: RETC. The RETC is a systematic method for quantitatively and visually assessing the robustness of a model against class imbalance in the test data. The primary output of the RETC method is a *RETC plot*, a visualization that plots multiple performance metrics as a function of the class imbalance ratio. This plot reveals how robust the performance of a model is under various practical conditions, which often exhibit a high prevalence of benign samples. The novelty of the RETC method does not simply lie in varying the class ratio. Instead, its primary strength is the formalization of this process into a comprehensive evaluation method that yields an easily interpretable visualization. Unlike conventional methods that evaluate performance at a single, fixed point (typically a malicious:benign=1:1 ratio), the RETC provides a continuous view of performance, allowing for a deeper understanding of the operational characteristics of a model. The scope of our proposal covers the definition of the data composition process, the generation of the RETC plot, and the methodology for interpreting this plot to assess model robustness. The RETC method consists of the following three steps, outlined in Fig. 1:

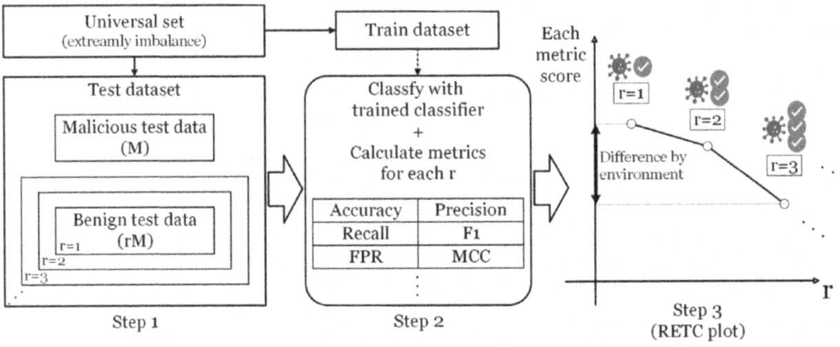

Fig. 1. Flow of methodology

Step1: Controlled Composition of Test Data

1. First, the number of malicious test samples is fixed at a constant value, $n_1^{test} = M$, where $M \in \mathbb{N}$. Fixing this value establishes a stable baseline for evaluation.
2. Second, the number of benign test samples is defined as $n_0^{test} = rM$. The parameter r represents the ratio of benign to malicious samples (n_0^{test}/n_1^{test}). In practice, the maximum value of r is constrained by the total number of available benign samples n_0, such as $r \leq n_0/M$.

Step2: Calculation of Performance Metrics For each value of the parameter r, a confusion matrix is generated by applying the model to the composed test data. From this matrix, a set of key performance metrics is calculated. In this study, we calculated $Accuracy, Precision, Recall, F_1, FPR,$ and MCC. This step creates a series of data points, with each point corresponding to a specific imbalance ratio r and the performance of the model at that ratio.

Step3: Generation and Interpretation of the RETC As a final step, we visualize the robustness of the model. The RETC plot is a two-dimensional plot with r on the horizontal axis and the evaluation metric value on the vertical axis. By plotting multiple models on the same graph, we can comprehensively and intuitively grasp the behavior of each model. A robust model is expected to show minimal performance degradation as r increases, which is reflected by a small absolute slope of the curves on the RETC plot.

When applying the RETC method, it is crucial to consider the source of the benign samples added to increase the ratio r. The selection of these samples can significantly affect the evaluation of the generalization capabilities of models. For instance, using benign samples that were part of the original training set (although held out from the actual training process) may produce different results compared to using benign samples from an entirely new dataset. Therefore, the source and characteristics of the additional benign samples must be clearly defined and reported to ensure the reproducibility and validity of the evaluation results.

5 Evaluation

This section evaluates the RETC method by addressing the research questions established in the Introduction. We begin by analyzing the theoretical properties of the evaluation metrics to provide a baseline for interpreting the RETC plot (addressing RQ1). We then apply the RETC method to actual datasets and models to demonstrate its practical advantages (addressing RQ2) and establish how to interpret its curves for robust model diagnosis (addressing RQ3).

5.1 Theoretical Properties and Visualization of the RETC

To properly interpret the RETC plot, we must first understand how the evaluation metrics themselves behave as a function of the class imbalance ratio r. This theoretical analysis provides a crucial baseline for separating the inherent mathematical behavior of metrics from the true performance of the models. Answering RQ1, this subsection details these inherent characteristics. First, we assume an ideal binary classifier whose performance at a given operational threshold τ is characterized by a fixed TPR and FPR. This idealization allows us to isolate and analyze the pure impact of changes in r on the evaluation metrics. Based on this assumption, we express standard evaluation metrics as functions of r. Table 1 shows the formula, monotonicity, and limit behavior of each metric.

To visualize these theoretical properties, we conducted a numerical experiment. We defined a Baseline model (TPR=0.95, FPR=0.02) and created two groups by varying either FPR or TPR, then generated the RETC plots for $r \in [1, 1000]$. The results are presented in Figs. 2 and 3. As predicted by our analysis, *Precision*, F_1, and MCC all decrease as r increases, even for an ideal classifier. This directly answers RQ1: the key characteristic of these metrics on the RETC is a mathematically inevitable decline with increasing class imbalance. Additionally, the plots in Fig. 2, where the FPR was varied, showed greater

Table 1. Formula, monotonicity, and limit behavior of each metric

Metric	Formula(function of r)	Monotonicity (trend as r increases)	Limit behavior $\lim_{r \to \infty} f(r)$
Accuracy	$\frac{TPR + (1 - FPR)r}{1 + r}$	$1 - FPR > TPR$: Increasing $1 - FPR < TPR$: Decreasing $1 - FPR = TPR$: Constant	$1 - FPR$
Precision	$\frac{TPR}{TPR + FPR \cdot r}$	Decreasing	0
Recall/ True Positive Rate (TPR)	TPR	Constant	$Recall(TPR)$ does not depend on r
False Positive Rate (FPR)	FPR	Constant	FPR does not depend on r
F_1	$\frac{2TPR}{1 + TPR + FPR \cdot r}$	Decreasing	0
Matthew Correlation Coefficient (MCC)	$\frac{\sqrt{r}(TPR - FPR)}{\sqrt{(TPR + FPR \cdot r)((1 - FPR)r + 1 - TPR)}}$	Decreasing	0

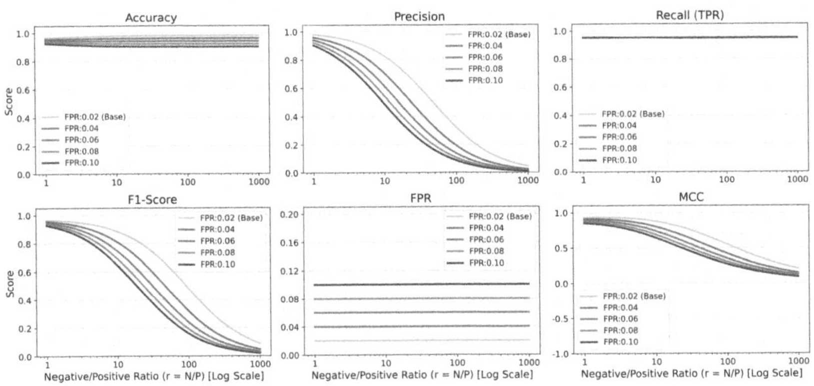

Fig. 2. The RETC plots on each metric fixed $TPR = 0.95$

changes in *Precision*, F_1, and MCC than the plots in Fig. 3, where the TPR was varied.

5.2 Empirical Evaluation Using Actual Datasets

We evaluated several machine learning models on two datasets: A (Network traffic logs) and B (URLs), as summarized in Table 2. The number of samples was fixed at $M = 1500$ anomalous samples for dataset A and $M = 15000$ malicious samples for dataset B, respectively. For each dataset, we varied the ratio r from 1 to 10.

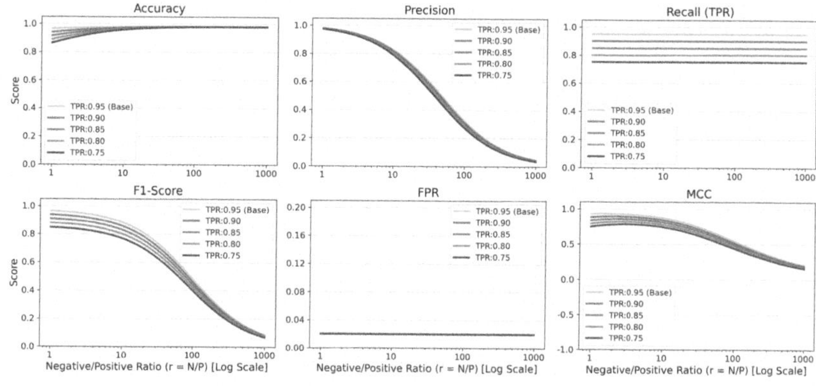

Fig. 3. The RETC plots on each metric fixed $FPR = 0.02$

Table 2. Datasets and models

Dataset	Feature	Anomaly/Malicious	Normal/Benign	Model
A [8]	Network traffic logs	3,007	576,710	SVM, RandomForest, XGBoost
B [13]	URL	33,426	482,780	CNN, RNN, LSTM

Performance Evaluation Results for Each Model The RETC plots for Dataset A and B are shown in Figs. 4 and 5. In Fig. 4, the RandomForest and XGBoost models exhibit nearly identical F_1 at $r = 1$. However, the RETC plot reveals that as r increases, the performance of the Random Forest model degrades more slowly than XGBoost. In Fig. 5, all three neural network models show excellent and very similar performance at $r = 1$. However, on the corresponding RETC plot, the *Precision* and F_1 of the RNN curves decline more noticeably than those of the CNN and LSTM.

RETC Shape and Observation of FPR In Dataset A, the FPR curves for all models were almost flat. In Dataset B, the FPR curves showed a clear increase as r increased, especially for the RNN model. The *Precision* and F_1 of this model decreased more than those of the other models.

6 Discussion

6.1 Model Performance with the RETC Method

The experimental results of this study show how the RETC method reveals model performance that static evaluation metrics cannot capture. Figure 4 shows that the initially similar F_1 of each model at $r = 1$ diverges as r increases, revealing a clear difference in performance. In particular, the F_1 of XGBoost decreases more quickly, suggesting that this model may be relatively vulnerable to unknown benign data. In this way, the RETC method provides a basis for

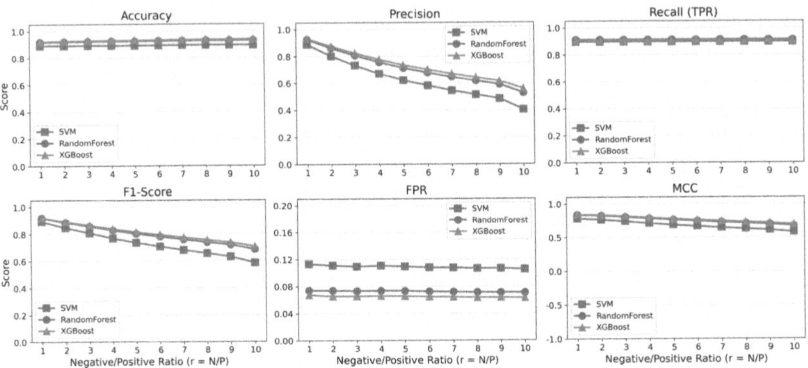

Fig. 4. The RETC plots on dataset A

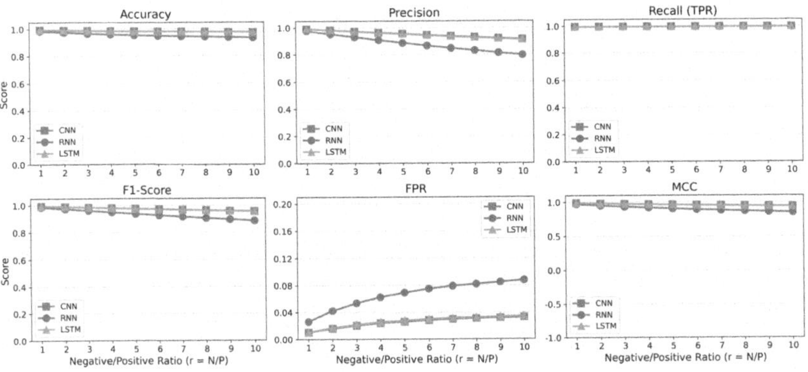

Fig. 5. The RETC plots on dataset B

determining which model is more stable and operationally viable. It achieves this by visualizing the performance impact of an increasing volume of benign data, which is expected in the real environment. More importantly, it is necessary to monitor the behavior of FPR. Theoretically, precision and F_1 naturally decrease with an increase in r. Therefore, it is premature to judge performance degradation based on a decrease in these metrics alone. However, if a decrease in these metrics is accompanied by an increase in FPR, as in the case of the RNN in Fig. 5, this is strong evidence that there is a fundamental problem with the generalization ability of the model. A major advantage of the RETC method is that by capturing dynamic changes in the FPR in this way, it is possible to analyze whether a performance decline is due to the mathematical properties of the metric or the true weaknesses of the model.

6.2 Correlation Between Data Characteristics and Performance Behavior

The behavior of the model observed by the RETC method is thought to be deeply related to the characteristics of the dataset. A comparison between the two datasets used in this study is useful for deepening this consideration. Dataset A (network traffic) is structured tabular data, and each model showed a relatively stable FPR. This can be interpreted as the separation boundary between normal and anomaly samples in the feature space is easy to learn, and the added normal samples do not deviate significantly from that boundary. In contrast, Dataset B (URL) has text data and linguistic features. The finding that the FPR of the RNN model significantly increased on this data is important in considering the interaction between model architecture and data characteristics. It is possible that the characteristics of the RNN, which learns sequential patterns in URLs, overfit unknown benign word combinations and syntax, making it more likely to cause false positives. The RETC method itself is universally applicable to any data format. However, the weaknesses of a model that it reveals strongly depend on the compatibility between the model architecture and the data characteristics.

6.3 Limitations

In order to correctly understand and apply the effectiveness of the proposed method, it is necessary to clearly recognize its prerequisites and limitations. First, there is a constraint on the size of the dataset. In order to ensure the reliability of the evaluation, this method requires a certain scale for both the malicious samples (M) fixed as a baseline and the benign samples to increase the ratio. If the number of samples in the original dataset is extremely small, it becomes difficult to set M to a statistically meaningful number, and the evaluation curve may become unstable. Second, there is the problem of the representativeness and diversity of the added benign data. In this study, available benign data were added randomly. In contrast, the distribution of benign data is not uniform in a real environment. If only benign data with a specific tendency is added, there is a risk that the evaluation results will be biased toward that characteristic. To evaluate the true generalization ability of the model, a multifaceted evaluation using benign data from various sources is desirable. Third, there is the scope of the evaluation. This study specializes in binary classification, where class imbalance is a problem. The applicability to multi-class classification problems and more complex scenarios where benign data, as well as unknown malicious data, change over time is beyond the scope of this work and is a topic for future study.

7 Conclusion

In this study, we proposed a new evaluation method: the RETC, to overcome the limitations of conventional evaluation methods, which often use balanced datasets that deviate from the real environment. The RETC method systematically changes the class imbalance ratio r of the test data and visualizes the trend of the performance metrics as the RETC plot. This makes it possible to reveal potential weaknesses of models that are likely to be overlooked at a single evaluation point. Through experiments, we confirmed that the RETC method can clearly show the difference in robustness between models. In particular, an important advantage of this method is its ability to distinguish whether a decrease in metrics such as F_1 is due to their mathematical properties or a deterioration in the performance of the model itself, accompanied by an increase in the FPR. In conclusion, the RETC method is a practical diagnostic tool for more realistic and multifaceted evaluation of the performance of models in the real environment, and provides a powerful guide for selecting and deploying truly reliable models in critical areas such as cybersecurity.

Future work will focus on dynamically generating anomalous data based on mathematical models to assess the robustness of models against temporal variations, leading to a more realistic verification of their reliability.

References

1. 2024 year in review. Technical report, cisco talos (2024). https://blog.talosintelligence.com/content/files/2025/03/2024YiR-report.pdf
2. Admass, W.S., et al.: Cyber security: state of the art, challenges and future directions. Cyber Secur. Appl. **2**, 100031 (2024). https://doi.org/10.1016/j.csa.2023.100031
3. Aghakhani, H., et al.: When malware is packin'heat; limits of machine learning classifiers based on static analysis features. In: Network and Distributed System Security Symposium (2020). https://doi.org/10.14722/ndss.2020.24310
4. Akuthota, U.C., et al.: The role of machine and deep learning in modern intrusion detection systems: a comprehensive review. Comput. Electr. Eng. **124**, 110318 (2025). https://doi.org/10.1016/j.compeleceng.2025.110318
5. Akuthota, V., et al.: Vulnerability detection and monitoring using llm. In: 2023 IEEE 9th International Women in Engineering (WIE) Conference on Electrical and Computer Engineering (WIECON-ECE), pp. 309–314 (2023). https://doi.org/10.1109/WIECON-ECE60392.2023.10456393
6. Bekkar, M., et al.: Evaluation measures for models assessment over imbalanced data sets. J. Inf. Eng. Appl. **3**(10) (2013)
7. Hoo, Z.H., et al.: What is an roc curve? Emerg. Med. J. **34**(6), 357–359 (2017). https://doi.org/10.1136/emermed-2017-206735
8. Kaggle: Cyber-security datasets. https://www.kaggle.com/discussions/general/335189
9. Lee, D., et al.: An efficient method to determine sample size in oversampling based on classification complexity for imbalanced data. Expert Syst. Appl. **184**, 115442 (2021). https://doi.org/10.1016/j.eswa.2021.115442

10. Lee, J.N., et al.: An efficient smote-based deep learning model for voice pathology detection. Appl. Sci. **13**(6), 3571 (2023). https://doi.org/10.3390/app13063571
11. Luu, G.H., et al.: Xsshield: a novel dataset and lightweight hybrid deep learning model for xss attack detection. Res. Eng. **24**, 103363 (2024). https://doi.org/10.1016/j.rineng.2024.103363
12. Mimura, M.: Impact of benign sample size on binary classification accuracy. Expert Syst. Appl. **211**, 118630 (2023). https://doi.org/10.1016/J.ESWA.2022.118630
13. Nakagawa, Y., et al.: Limitations of cross-site scripting attack detection methods based on linguistic features. IPSJ J. **65**, 1299–1308 (2024). https://doi.org/10.20729/00239245
14. Su, M., et al.: Bert-based approaches to identifying malicious urls. Sensors **23**(20), 8499 (2023). https://doi.org/10.3390/S23208499
15. Tharwat, A.: Classification assessment methods. Appl. Comput. Inf. **17**(1), 168–192 (2021). https://doi.org/10.1016/j.aci.2018.08.003
16. Zhang, J., et al.: Advancing face detection efficiency: utilizing classification networks for lowering false positive incidences. Array **22**, 100347 (2024). https://doi.org/10.1016/j.array.2024.100347
17. Zhu, Q.: On the performance of Matthews Correlation Coefficient (MCC) for imbalanced dataset. Pattern Recogn. Lett. **136**, 71–80 (2020). https://doi.org/10.1016/j.patrec.2020.03.030

TALOS: An Empirical Approach to Building Portable Hands-On Labs for Fundamental Cybersecurity Education Using Open-Source

Young Han Choi(✉) and Ki Tae Park

National Security Research Institute(NSR), Daejeon, South Korea
{yhch,parkkt}@nsr.re.kr

Abstract. The number and complexity of cyber attacks are increasing, making it very important to teach people of all ages and skill levels about cybersecurity. To address this issue, teaching methods are changing to include both basic ideas and practical, hands-on activities. Following well-known guidelines like CAE-C, REWIRE, and CSEC2017, we created a hands-on course that helps trainees learn practical skills, such as analyzing network data, finding website weaknesses, detecting attacks, making systems stronger, analyzing malware, and doing digital forensics. In this paper, we introduce a simple and organized way to teach beginner-level cybersecurity using open-source tools. We developed a portable and easy-to-use practice system called TALOS, which helps people learn important topics in operating systems and network security. TALOS was used in 19 training sessions with 367 participants, including university students and the general public. Survey results showed that most trainees were very satisfied, with 81.7% giving strong positive feedback about the training. These results suggest that portable, hands-on labs like TALOS are an effective and practical way to teach basic cybersecurity and could be used as a model for future training programs.

Keywords: Cybersecurity education · Hands-on labs · Cyber range

1 Introduction

As cyber threats keep increasing, it is more important than ever to have strong cybersecurity education. Cybersecurity education entails equipping individuals with the knowledge and skills necessary to protect systems, networks, and data from a wide range of cyber threats. The target audience for cybersecurity education is highly diverse, encompassing individuals ranging from young students to adults, with varying skill levels including beginner, intermediate, and advanced. To help people get ready for new cyber threats, it is important to combine classroom learning with real, hands-on exercise. Hands-on training enhances conceptual understanding and provides trainees with the technical skills required for

K.-W. Park and J. Park (Eds.): WISA 2025 2025, LNCS 16434, pp. 86–97, 2026.
https://doi.org/10.1007/978-981-95-6857-4_7

real-world application. To protect against different types of cyber threats, it is especially important for trainees to practice and build basic cybersecurity skills through hands-on exercises.

Cybersecurity frameworks have been developed to systematically define the various work roles within the cybersecurity domain and to classify the specific knowledge and skills required for each role [1,2]. In response to the growing demand for skilled cybersecurity professionals, numerous educational initiatives have incorporated these frameworks into their curricula. Frameworks such as the National Centers of Academic Excellence in Cybersecurity (CAE-C) [3], REWIRE [4], and Cybersecurity Curricular (CSEC) 2017 [5] have played a significant role in aligning educational content with industry standards and workforce needs. A key feature of these curricula is the emphasis on hands-on training, which is essential for enabling trainees to acquire and apply practical cybersecurity skills in realistic settings. To effectively deliver such experiential learning, the implementation of cyber ranges as hands-on labs for cybersecurity education has become increasingly important. A cyber range provides a controlled environment where trainees can both demonstrate existing competencies and develop new skills through immersive, scenario-based exercises [6].

In this paper, we propose a hands-on curriculum for acquiring fundamental cybersecurity skills and introduce a portable training environment suitable for small groups of trainees in various settings using open-source. We implemented the portable training environment in actual educational programs and received high satisfaction ratings from the participants. The contributions of this paper are as follows:

- We develop a hands-on educational program for fundamental cybersecurity education by conducting a comprehensive analysis of established cybersecurity frameworks such as CAE-C, REWIRE, and CSEC2017.
- We propose TALOS, a portable and practical cybersecurity training environment based on open-source tools, designed to work without an internet connection and at low cost. This approach makes advanced cybersecurity education accessible and affordable for a wide range of trainees.
- We conducted a series of practical cybersecurity training exercises in a small space using our training environment, and analysis of participant feedback indicated that the program achieved a high level of trainee satisfaction.

2 Related Work

This section reviews research on cybersecurity education and practical training environments.

Cybersecurity Education. The National Institute of Standards and Technology (NIST) [7] developed the National Initiative for Cybersecurity Education (NICE) Cybersecurity Workforce Framework [1] focused on cybersecurity work roles. NICE serves as a foundational reference for the CAE-C program by aligning academic curricula with national workforce needs.

ENISA [8] developed European Cybersecurity Skills Framework (ECSF) [2] as a structured reference model to define and standardize cybersecurity roles, skills, and competences across Europe. ECSF identifies 12 distinct cybersecurity roles. REWIRE has contributed to the development of a unified European approach to cybersecurity skills by supporting and expanding the ECSF through the alignment of training, education, and certification efforts with the framework.

A joint task force composed of ACM, IEEE-CS, AIS SIGSEC, and IFIP WG 11.8 established CSEC2017 as a global standard for undergraduate cybersecurity education by defining 8 core knowledge areas and emphasizing hands-on learning. CSEC2017 was adapted into the Cyber2yr2020 [9] curriculum by ACM CCECC to support practice-oriented cybersecurity education in two-year college programs, and its foundational concepts were also incorporated into security-related knowledge areas of Computing Curricula 2020 [10] to extend cybersecurity education across multiple computing disciplines.

Korea's National Competency Standards(NCS) [11] offer a nationally standardized framework for defining and developing occupational competencies across various industries. While NCS focuses on domestic workforce development and training alignment, NICE provides a globally recognized model specifically targeting the cybersecurity domain.

Cybersecurity Hands-on Labs. Recent studies have proposed innovative approaches to enhancing cybersecurity education by integrating realistic, hands-on training environments, such as cyber ranges, which provide trainees with diverse opportunities for practical experience [12].

Lazarov et al. [13] introduced an interactive, gamified cyber range approach to improve engagement and hands-on skills in cybersecurity education at various levels, using the BUTCA platform to deliver scenario-based exercises accessible via remote, automated environments. Dmytro [14] et al. developed a KVM-based simulation environment integrating open-source tools like pfSense and Security Onion to provide scalable, low-cost platforms for realistic, customizable cybersecurity training scenarios. Vykopal et al. [15] developed the KYPO Cyber Range Platform to provide scalable, data-driven, and customizable hands-on cybersecurity training through interactive scenarios and virtual labs.

Cybersecurity education requires the integration of adaptive, scalable, and interactive simulation-based environments, as practical training labs are essential for enhancing hands-on skill development, engagement, and personalized learning experiences that prepare diverse trainees for real-world cyber threats.

3 Our Approach

In this paper, we propose a portable hands-on lab environment for fundamental cybersecurity education utilizing open-source tools. We focus on practical training in fundamental cybersecurity skills and the development of a portable cyber training environment to enhance essential competencies for responding to cyber threats.

Hands-on Curricular. Fundamental cybersecurity skills refer to the basic abilities required to perform practical cybersecurity tasks, and these foundational skills can be expanded into more advanced competencies. To identify fundamental cybersecurity skills, we analyzed established cybersecurity frameworks, including CAE-C, REWIRE, and CSEC2017. This topic is discussed in detail in Sect. 4. These skills can be acquired through hands-on exercise using a variety of tools.

Portable Environment. To educate trainees in diverse environments, we proposed and implemented a portable training environment, which was used to conduct actual training sessions. This is discussed in Sects. 5. By developing a portable training platform for small groups, we were able to provide hands-on training environments to trainees in various locations, regardless of internet connectivity. Furthermore, by utilizing open-source software, we were able to reduce the overall cost burden.

4 Hands-On Curricular for Fundamental Cybersecurity

In this section, we examine existing cybersecurity education frameworks and design a curriculum focused on hands-on training for fundamental cybersecurity education.

4.1 Existing Cybersecurity Education Framework

We analyze three cybersecurity education frameworks (CAE-C, REWIRE, and CSEC2017) developed respectively by U.S. government agencies, European institutions, and international academic associations, as shown in Table 1.

CAE-C is grounded in the NICE Cybersecurity Workforce Framework developed by NIST, which categorizes cybersecurity work roles by tasks, knowledge, skills, and abilities. NICE defines 41 work roles across five categories and serves as the foundational reference for the CAE-C initiative. The CAE-C program, jointly managed by the NSA and DHS, designates academic institutions in three focus areas: Cyber Defense, Research, and Cyber Operations. Among these, the Centers of Academic Excellence in Cyber Defense (CAE-CD) outlines a structured curriculum consisting of 3 Foundational Knowledge Units(KUs), 5 Technical Core KUs, 5 Non-Technical Core KUs, and 56 Optional KUs. Technical Core KUs includes Basic Scripting and Programming, Basic Networking, Network Defense, Basic Cryptography, Operating Systems Concepts. In KUs, networking and operating systems represent the principal domains where hands-on exercise can be effectively conducted.

REWIRE is supported by ENISA and builds upon ECSF [8]. ECSF categorized the 12 role profiles to reflect the functional and skill-based demands of the European cybersecurity sector. Each role is defined in terms of specific tasks, knowledge, and skills REWIRE reduced the 51 NICE competencies to 29 cybersecurity competencies and classified them into three families: 7 cybersecurity skills, 7 IT skills, and 7 soft skills. Among these, network management,

Table 1. Comparison of Cybersecurity Education Frameworks: CAE-CD, REWIRE, and CSEC2017

Category	CAE-CD	REWIRE	CSEC2017
Overview	· NSA/DHS-certified academic program in cyber defense education	· EU project building cybersecurity skills and training framework	· Cybersecurity curriculum guidelines by global academic organizations
Background	· Reference: NICE · CAE-C: CAE-CD, CAE-CR, CAE-CO	· Reference: ESCF · Pre-project: CONCORDIA, SPARTA, ECHO, Cyber-Sec4Europe	· Follow-up: Cyber2yr2020, CC2020
Organizations	· NSA, DHS	· 12 European countries	· ACM, IEEE-CS, AIS SIGSEC, IFIP WG 11.8
Contents	· Knowledge Units (KUs) - Topics · (ex.) Network Defense – Network Operations – Network Analysis	· Role Profile – Skills (applying), Knowledge (understanding) · (ex.) Penetration Tester – Develop codes, scripts and programmes	· Knowledge Areas (KAs) – Knowledge Unit (KU) – Topic · (ex.) Connection Security – Network Defense – Network Traffic Analysis
Knowledges & Skills	· 3 Foundational KUs · 10 Core KUs (5 Tech, 5 Non-tech) · 60 Optional KUs	· 12 Role Profiles · 29 Skills (7 IT, 15 Cybersecurity, 7 Soft)	· 8 top-level KAs

software development, and operating systems are some of the most commonly needed skill areas in practice.

CSEC2017 was developed by a coalition of international academic associations and establishes global curriculum guidelines for undergraduate cybersecurity education. It centered on 8 core knowledge areas and emphasizing hands-on, practice-driven learning. Among the 8 core knowledge areas, five technically oriented domains (Data, Software, Component, Connection, and System) are closely related to networking, software, and operating system competencies.

Therefore, networking and operating systems should be included as key areas in cybersecurity fundamental training. This paper selects networking and operating systems as the primary areas for hands-on training in basic cybersecurity education. These areas are critical for developing foundational cybersecurity competencies, as they encompass practical tasks. Focusing on these areas enables training environments to offer realistic and application-oriented experiences that align with actual cybersecurity challenges.

4.2 Our Cybersecurity Education Program

We analyzed existing cybersecurity education curricula and selected operating systems and networks as the core areas for basic hands-on training. We classified practical topics that can be performed for each area, as shown in Table 2. We selected open-source tools that are widely used in practice, and ensured that sample files were readily available on the internet. The direction of hands-on exercise for each area is as follows:

- Network Area focuses on gaining a fundamental understanding of web vulnerabilities, network packets, and intrusion detection technologies.
- Operating System Area focuses on gaining a fundamental understanding of Windows, Linux, and malware.

Table 2. Our fundamental cybersecurity education program for hands-on labs

Areas	Topics	Related Tools
Network	Network Packet Analysis	Wireshark
	Web Hacking	DVWA, BurpSuite
	IDS	Snort
Operating System	System Hardening	Windows, Linux
	Windows OS	Sysinternals
	Reverse Engineering	Ghidra
	Ransomware	Python
	Disk Forensic	FTK Imager, Autopsy
	Memory Forensic	Volatility
	Artifacts	Powershell

Network Area. To achieve basic network security, trainees should be able to perform practical tasks such as web hacking, network packet analysis, and writing intrusion detection system rules.

Web hacking hands-on exercise utilizes `DVWA` [16], a vulnerable web application developed in PHP, and uses `Burp Suite` [17] to modify HTTP packets. Packet analysis is considered the core of network security hands-on exercise because it helps trainees understand network protocols. `Wireshark` [18] is a widely used tool for packet analysis, supporting the analysis of around 3,000 different protocols. trainees perform hands-on exercise using malicious packets provided by `malware traffic analysis` sites [19]. An intrusion detection system (IDS) is intended to identify and respond to network-based attacks, with `Snort` [20] being a representative and widely adopted solution. Using information gathered from packet analysis, trainees write detection rules and conduct hands-on detection exercises by examining dumped packet data.

Operating System Area. This area covers fundamental aspects of system security, providing hands-on exercise on the basics of Windows and malware.

For hands-on exercise, Windows is primarily chosen as the environment due to its ease of use, in contrast to Linux.

System hardening focuses on reviewing and optimizing system configuration settings, with practices applicable to both Linux and Windows platforms. To analyze behaviors of Windows and malware, monitoring tools from the Sysinternals suite [21] are utilized. For static analysis, `Ghidra` [22] is utilized to analyze executable files, including those using the PE (Portable Executable) file format. When studying ransomware, trainees are introduced to the basics of encryption and develop their own ransomware applications using Python as a practical exercise. In disk forensics, trainees perform practical exercises with `FTK Imager` [23] and `Autopsy` [24] to gain experience in examining disk layouts and file systems. Through the analysis of memory dump files with `Volatility` [25], practical exercises enable trainees to develop skills in memory forensics as well as the analysis of real-world malicious file behavior. Windows artifact analysis includes practical exercises in extracting various types of system information using PowerShell.

5 TALOS: Our Portable Hands-On Environment

TALOS is designed for installation and operation in a variety of locations to facilitate fundamental cybersecurity exercises. Specifically, it is implemented as a portable environment, enabling small groups to engage in effective hands-on exercise, as illustrated in Fig. 1. Moreover, by leveraging open-source software, TALOS significantly reduces operational costs, making it an accessible and cost-effective solution for cybersecurity training. We built TALOS on a Mac Studio (128GB RAM, 8TB disk) to facilitate easy portability.

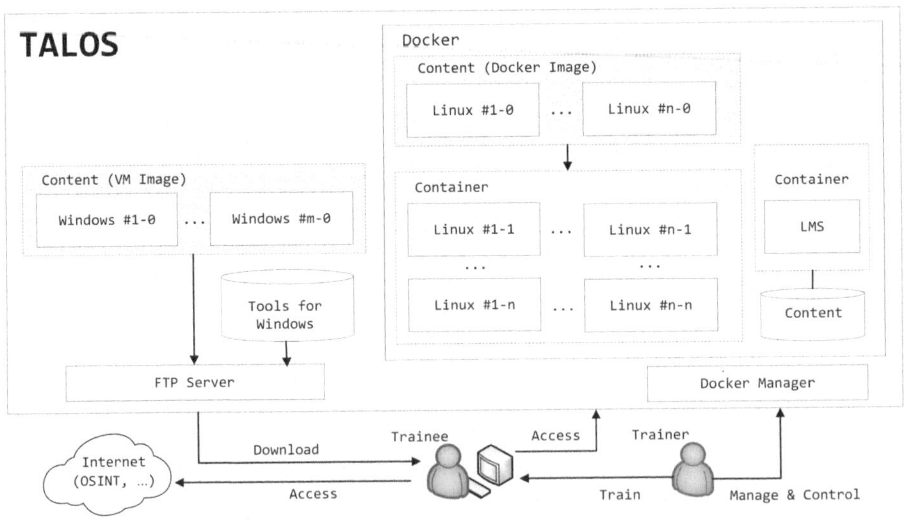

Fig. 1. The system architecture of TALOS.

Any service that can be installed on Linux can be deployed within Docker containers in TALOS. For Windows-based exercises, it is assumed that the trainee's access PC or laptop is running Windows, so the necessary tools are either installed directly on the trainee's device or provided through virtualization images. The installation of analysis-related programs can also be incorporated into the training curriculum.

The role of the initial access portal for trainees is performed by the LMS. We used `Moodle` [26] as the LMS. Through the LMS, participants receive dump files for hands-on exercises and the necessary information to access the servers.

Since operation is managed through docker, the basic environment is built on Linux, and the hands-on exercise environment is set up within docker images. We used Ubuntu 22.04 as the base Linux image. On the Ubuntu Linux, we installed `Snort`, `Volatility`, and `DVWA`. Containers are created according to the number of trainees, with each trainee assigned the same ID (`student`) and password (`password`), but distinguished by different port numbers. For example, the following code creates Linux containers for 25 students and opens both SSH and web ports.

```
#!/bin/bash
for i in {1..25}
   port1='expr 19300 + $i'
   port2='expr 19500 + $i'
   command="docker run -d --name trainee${i} -p ${port1}:22
      -p ${port2}:80 -it --platform linux/amd64 trainee_image:0.1"
   $command
done
```

Given that trainees mainly use Windows on their PCs, TALOS is focused on enabling Windows-related hands-on exercise on these computers. Depending on the practice content, trainees either use pre-built `VMWare` images or install necessary software directly on their PCs to perform hands-on exercises. The tools installed on Windows include FTK Imager, Ghidra, Wireshark, Burp Suite, Sysinternals suite, and so on. For disk forensics, a Virtual Hard Disk (VHD) is used to create a disk image, which is then subjected to analysis. Malicious packet analysis is conducted using dump files provided by the Malware Traffic Analysis website. For malware behavior analysis and memory forensics, publicly available memory dump files are utilized [27].

6 Implementation of Hands-on Training

We have conducted a total of 19 cybersecurity training sessions using TALOS, targeting 367 participants since 2024. The trainees included 80 high school students, 50 university students, and 237 security professionals from public institutions.

6.1 Portable Hands-on Environment Setup

Portable TALOS was installed in a practice room for small group (around 30 people), with laptops individually assigned. TALOS is configured to match the network of the physical classroom to which it is deployed (Fig. 2).

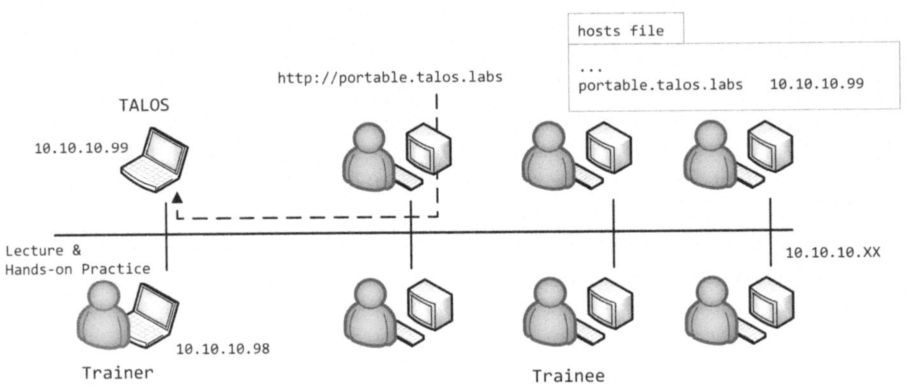

Fig. 2. An example of a practical training network.

For example, the network range uses the 10.10.10.xx, with TALOS assigned `10.10.10.99` and the instructor's laptop assigned `10.10.10.98`. The trainees' laptops are configured to access TALOS via the domain by setting `10.10.10.99` as `portable.talos.labs` in the hosts file. By doing so, trainees are able to access the TALOS domain and participate in hands-on exercises. Trainees benefit from the convenience of being able to freely participate in hands-on exercises through TALOS simply by adding a single domain entry to their host file.

6.2 Operation of Cybersecurity Education Program

We selected topics in the areas of networks and operating systems based on trainees' interests and proficiency levels.

Regardless of prior experience, the majority of trainees expressed strong interest in network-related subjects, particularly web hacking and packet analysis. Consequently, these two topics were consistently incorporated into the training curriculum.

For the operating systems component, Windows was utilized as the platform for practical exercises. Although Windows is widely used, many trainees encountered difficulties in comprehending its underlying mechanisms. Variations in trainees' skill levels significantly influenced their performance in operating system exercises. To address these challenges, system hardening activities were introduced to enhance trainees' understanding of Windows configuration. Subsequently, depending on trainees' preferences, additional exercises such as static and dynamic analysis or digital forensics were provided.

6.3 Participant Survey

Upon completion of the training, participants were surveyed on three aspects: satisfaction, perceived difficulty, and applicability of the training.

In terms of satisfaction, 81.7% of respondents indicated a high level of satisfaction, 17.9% reported an average level, and only 0.4% expressed low satisfaction. These results suggest that the majority of trainees were satisfied with the training program.

Regarding the perceived difficulty, 8.8% of participants found the training easy, 67.0% considered it moderate, and 24.2% rated it as difficult. The relatively high percentage of participants who found the training difficult may be attributed to their limited prior experience with the tools used in the practical exercises. This indicates a need for preliminary training or introductory materials, especially for those with less background in cybersecurity tools.

For the applicability of the training, a separate survey was conducted among professionals currently working in the field. The results showed that 46.9% of respondents rated the applicability as high, while 48.4% considered it average. These findings demonstrate that the training is generally perceived as relevant and useful for practical work in cybersecurity. However, the relatively moderate scores for applicability suggest that there is room for improvement in aligning the training content with the specific needs of professionals. Portable TALOS is primarily designed to provide fundamental hands-on experience in cybersecurity technologies. Therefore, to acquire more specialized skills required for particular job roles, it is necessary to develop more detailed and targeted training modules.

In conclusion, while Portable TALOS serves as an effective platform for basic cybersecurity training, further refinement and customization of the training curriculum are recommended to better meet the diverse needs of trainees (Fig. 3).

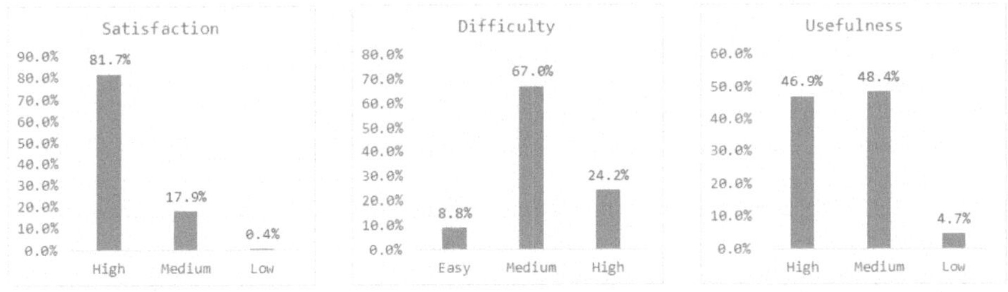

Fig. 3. Survey Analysis on Satisfaction, Difficulty, and Usefulness.

7 Conclusion and Future Work

This paper presented TALOS, a portable, open-source, Docker-based hands-on lab environment designed to enhance fundamental cybersecurity education. By systematically analyzing established frameworks such as CAE-CD, REWIRE, and CSEC2017, we developed a curriculum that emphasizes practical competencies in networking and operating systems, which are critical for entry-level cybersecurity roles. TALOS was deployed in 19 training sessions, engaging 367 participants from high schools, universities, and the professional sector. Survey results demonstrated a high level of satisfaction and perceived relevance among participants, confirming the effectiveness of TALOS in facilitating foundational cybersecurity skill acquisition. However, a significant proportion of trainees reported difficulty with the exercises, primarily due to limited prior experience with the required tools and concepts. This finding highlights the importance of providing preparatory materials and differentiated instruction to accommodate varying skill levels. While the training content was generally well-received, feedback from professional participants indicated the need for more specialized modules tailored to specific job roles and advanced topics. Overall, TALOS demonstrates strong potential as a scalable and accessible platform for practical cybersecurity education in diverse settings.

Future work will focus on refining the curriculum and expanding specialized training modules to better address the evolving needs of trainees and industry professionals.

References

1. NICE Workforce Framework for Cybersecurity (NICE Framework). https://niccs.cisa.gov/workforce-development/nice-framework. Accessed 12 May 2025
2. ENISA, European Cybersecurity Skills Framework (ECSF). https://www.enisa.europa.eu/topics/skills-and-competences/skills-development/ european-cybersecurity-skills-framework-ecsf. Accessed 16 May 2025
3. National Centers of Academic Excellence in Cybersecurity (NACE-C). https://www.nsa.gov/Academics/Centers-of-Academic-Excellence/. Accessed 23 June 2025
4. REWIRE - Cybersecurity Skills Alliance. https://rewireproject.eu. Accessed 23 June 2025
5. Cybersecurity Curricular Guidelines, CSEC 2017. https://cybered.hosting.acm.org/wp/ Accessed 23 June 2025
6. European Cyber Security Organisation (ECSO).: Understanding Cyber Ranges: From Hype to Reality. ECSO, Brussels (2020)
7. National Institute of Standard and Technology (NIST). https://www.nist.gov/. Accessed 19 May 2025
8. European Union Agency for Cybersecurity (ENISA). https://www.enisa.europa.eu/. Accessed 19 May 2025
9. Committee for Computing Education in Community Colleges (CCECC).: Cybersecurity Curricular Guidance for Associate-Degree Programs (Cyber2yr2020). ACM, New York (2020). ISBN 978-1-4503-7555-9. https://doi.org/10.1145/3381686

10. CC2020 Task Force.: Computing Curricula 2020: Paradigms for Global Computing Education. Association for Computing Machinery, New York (2020). ISBN 978-1-4503-9059-0. https://doi.org/10.1145/3467967
11. National Competency Standards (NCS). https://www.ncs.go.kr/index.do. Accessed 12 May 2025
12. 10 Hot Cyber Range Companies To Watch In 2025. https://cybersecurityventures.com/10-hot-cyber-range-companies-to-watch/. Accessed 11 June 2025
13. Lazarov, W., et al.: Lessons Learned from Using Cyber Range to Teach Cybersecurity at Different Levels of Education. Tech Know Learn (2025). https://doi.org/10.1007/s10758-025-09840-y
14. Dmytro, T., et al.: Interactive Cybersecurity Training System based on Simulation Environments. Meas. Comput. Devices Technol. Process. 4 (2024). https://arxiv.org/abs/2501.00186
15. Vykopal, J., et al.: Scalable Learning Environments for Teaching Cybersecurity Hands-on. In: Proceedings of the IEEE Frontiers in Education Conference (2021). https://doi.org/10.1109/FIE49875.2021.9637180
16. Damn Vulnerable Web Application (DVWA). https://github.com/digininja/DVWA Accessed 9 May 2025
17. PortSwigger. https://portswigger.net/burp Accessed 9 May 2025
18. Wireshark. https://www.wireshark.org/ Accessed 9 May 2025
19. Malware-Traffic-Analysis.NET. https://www.malware-traffic-analysis.net/ Accessed 9 May 2025
20. Snort. https://www.snort.org/ Accessed 9 May 2025
21. Sysinternals. https://learn.microsoft.com/en-us/sysinternals/ Accessed 9 May 2025
22. Ghidra. https://ghidra-sre.org/ Accessed 9 May 2025
23. FTK Imager. https://www.exterro.com/digital-forensics-software/ftk-imager Accessed 9 May 2025
24. Autopsy. https://www.autopsy.com/ Accessed 9 May 2025
25. Volatility. https://volatilityfoundation.org/ Accessed 9 May 2025
26. Moodle. https://moodle.org/ Accessed 9 May 2025
27. Memory Samples. https://github.com/volatilityfoundation/volatility/wiki/Memory-Samples Accessed 24 June 2025

Security Analysis and Verification

Impossible Differential Attack on SAND-64

Nobuyuki Sugio(✉)

Hokkaido University of Science, Sapporo, Japan
sugio-n@hus.ac.jp

Abstract. SAND is an AND-RX-based lightweight block cipher proposed by Chen et al. There are two variants of SAND, namely SAND-64 and SAND-128, due to structural differences. In this paper, we search for impossible differential distinguishers of SAND-64 using Constraint Programming (CP) and reveal 56 types of impossible differential distinguishers up to 11 rounds. Furthermore, we demonstrate a key recovery attack on 16-round SAND-64. The complexities for the attack require 2^{63} data, 2^{96} encryptions, and 2^{62} bytes of memory, respectively.

Keywords: Impossible differential attack · Lightweight cipher · SAND · Constraint programming

1 Introduction

SAND is proposed by Chen et al. in *Designs, Codes and Cryptography* 2022 [1]. SAND is a family of lightweight Feistel block ciphers (with 64- or 128-bit block size, both using a 128-bit key) designed using only AND, rotation, and XOR (AND-RX) operations, while enabling classical S-box-based cryptanalytic techniques.

For security evaluation, the designers analyzed differential attack [2], linear attack [3], and other cryptanalytic methods using Mixed Integer Linear Programming (MILP). In the previous research on SAND-64, the designers applied the method proposed in [4] to search for impossible differential distinguishers. They fixed the number of active S-boxes in the input and output differences as one, then performed an exhaustive search at nibble level. However, this method limits the search space, potentially overlooking other impossible differential distinguishers.

Hadipour et al. proposed a method to search for impossible differential distinguishers using deterministic differentials [5,6]. These approaches do not require predefined input and output differences,

1.1 Contributions of This Paper

We search for impossible differential distinguishers of SAND-64 using Hadipour et al.'s deterministic differentials and reveal 56 types of impossible differential distinguishers up to 11 rounds. Furthermore, we demonstrate a key recovery attack on 16-round SAND-64. The attack results are summarized in Table 1.

K.-W. Park and J. Park (Eds.): WISA 2025 2025, LNCS 16434, pp. 101–114, 2026.
https://doi.org/10.1007/978-981-95-6857-4_8

Table 1. Attack Results on SAND-64

Number of rounds	Type	Data	Time	Memory	Method
10	Distinguisher	–	–	–	Impossible Differential [1]
11	Distinguisher	–	–	–	Impossible Differential [12]
11	Distinguisher	–	–	–	Impossible Differential (**Ours**)
12	Distinguisher	2^{63}	-	-	Integral by CBDP [1]
12	Distinguisher	2^{63}	-	-	Integral by CBDP [14]
13	Distinguisher	–	–	–	Boomerang [15]
15	Key Recovery	2^{63}	2^{105}	2^{52}	Integral by CBDP [14]
15	Key Recovery	$2^{63.09}$	2^{56}	2^{59}	Boomerang [15]
16	Key Recovery	2^{63}	$2^{109.91}$	2^{85}	Integral by CBDP [14]
16	Key Recovery	2^{58}	2^{127}	2^{62}	Impossible Differential (**Ours**)
16	Key Recovery	2^{63}	2^{96}	2^{62}	Impossible Differential (**Ours**)

CBDP: Conventional Bit-based Division Property

1.2 Structure of This Paper

The structure of this paper is as follows. Section 2 provides related works on SAND-64. Section 3 explains an overview of impossible differential attack. Section 4 introduces constraint programming and the use of deterministic differentials in searching for impossible differential distinguishers. Sections 5 describes the structures of lightweight cipher SAND-64. In Sect. 6, we show a key recovery attack on SAND-64 using impossible differential distinguishers. Finally, Sect. 7 discusses a comparison with the previous attacks.

2 Related Works

The designers evaluated SAND's security against various attacks such as differential attack [2], linear attack [3], integral attack [7], impossible differential attack [8], and zero-correlation linear attack [10,11]. They searched for impossible differentials and zero-correlation linear approximations using a nibble-level search. As a result, they identified 10-round impossible differential distinguishers of SAND-64 [1].

Zhang et al. developed a systematic search framework for AND-RX ciphers to find impossible differential distinguishers [12]. Applying their method to SAND, they found 11-round impossible differential distinguishers of SAND-64.

Mirzaie et al. applied the conventional bit-based division property technique [13] to find integral distinguishers of SAND-64 [14]. As a result, they discovered a 12-round integral distinguisher with 23 balanced bits. The data complexity for the distinguisher is 2^{63}. Building on this distinguisher, Mirzaie et al. mounted key recovery attacks on 15- and 16-round SAND-64. The time complexities are 2^{105} encryptions for the 15-round attack and $2^{109.9}$ encryptions for the 16-round attack, respectively.

Li and Teh [15] introduced a boomerang-style attack on SAND using a novel AND-specific boomerang connectivity table. Their method led to 15-round key recovery attacks on SAND-64.

3 Impossible Differential Attack

Impossible differential attack was proposed by Biham et al. [8] and Knudsen [9]. Impossible differential was defined as the differential with probability zero. This attack eliminates the key candidates that generate differential with probability zero. In this technique, an attacker searches for an impossible output differential Δ_Y corresponding to a given input differential Δ_X over r-round of the cipher. If such a pair of input-output differentials (Δ_X, Δ_Y) exists, it is termed as an r-round impossible differential distinguisher. This distinguisher can be used to conduct a distinguishing attack or a key recovery attack against the target cipher.

Boura et al. have formalized the necessary number of data, time, and memory complexities for the impossible differential attack. The following outlines them. For more details, please refer to the reference [16].

The notations for an impossible differential attack are as follows. Let Δ_X and Δ_Y be input (resp. output) differences of the impossible differential. Let r_Δ be the number of rounds of the impossible differential. Let Δ_{in} and Δ_{out} be set of all possible input (resp. output) differences of the cipher. Let r_{in} and r_{out} be the number of rounds of the differential paths (Δ_X, Δ_{in}) or (Δ_Y, Δ_{out}).

The differential ($\Delta_X \to \Delta_{in}$) (resp. ($\Delta_Y \to \Delta_{out}$)) occurs with probability 1 while the differential ($\Delta_{in} \to \Delta_X$) (resp. ($\Delta_{out} \to \Delta_Y$)) is verified with probability $\frac{1}{2^{c_{in}}}$ (resp. $\frac{1}{2^{c_{out}}}$), where c_{in} (resp. c_{out}) is the number of bit-conditions that have to be verified to obtain Δ_X from Δ_{in} (resp. Δ_Y from Δ_{out}).

The probability that for a given key, a pair of inputs already satisfying the differences Δ_{in} and Δ_{out} verifies all the ($c_{in} + c_{out}$) bit-conditions is $2^{-(c_{in}+c_{out})}$. Therefore, the probability that a key trial is kept in the candidate keys set is $p_k = (1 - 2^{-(c_{in}+c_{out})})^N$ with N different input (or output) pairs.

Boura et al. have formalized the smallest value of N, denoted by N_{min}, verifying $p_k = (1 - 2^{-(c_{in}+c_{out})})^{N_{min}} < \frac{1}{2}$ is approximately $N_{min} = 2^{c_{in}+c_{out}}$. The cost of obtaining N pairs of ($\Delta_{in}, \Delta_{out}$) is evaluated as

$$C_N = \max\left\{ \min_{\Delta \in \{\Delta_{in}, \Delta_{out}\}} \left\{ \sqrt{N 2^{n+1-|\Delta|}} \right\}, N 2^{n+1-|\Delta_{in}|-|\Delta_{out}|} \right\}. \quad (1)$$

The cost C_N also represents the amount of needed data. The time complexity is

$$T = \left(C_N + \left(N + 2^{|k_{in} \cup k_{out}|} \frac{N}{2^{c_{in}+c_{out}}} \right) C'_E + 2^{|K|} p_k \right) C_E, \quad (2)$$

with N such that $p_k = (1 - 2^{-(c_{in}+c_{out})})^N < \frac{1}{2}$, and where C'_E is the ratio of the cost of partial encryption to the full encryption, and where the last term represents the brute-force search complexity.

The only elements that need to be stored are the N pairs. Therefore, the memory complexity for the attack is determined by N.

4 Constraint Programming and Its Application to Cryptanalysis

Hadipour et al. proposed cell-wise model [5] and bit-wise model [6] to search for impossible differential distinguishers using CP. In the bit-wise model, specific constraints were set to track the encryption and decryption processes for each round at the bit level, and an attacker could find bit-wise impossible differential distinguishers of a target cipher. Specifically, Hadipour et al. applied it to ASCON and this method discovered 5-round impossible differential distinguishers [6].

The following outlines the CP models for deterministic differential transitions. For more details, please refer to the references [5,6]. In the bit-wise models, let integer variables X and Y with the domain of $\{-1, 0, 1\}$ to indicate whether the differential is unknown, zero, or one, respectively.

CP model 1 (Branching) [6]

For $f : \mathbb{F}_2 \to \mathbb{F}_2^n$, $f(x) = (y_0, y_1, \cdots, y_{n-1})$, *where* $y_0 = y_1 = \cdots = y_{n-1} = x$, *the valid transitions for deterministic differential trails satisfy the following:*

$$\texttt{Branch}(X, Y_0, \cdots, Y_{n-1}) := \bigwedge_{i=0}^{n-1} (Y_i = X),$$

where X *and* Y_i *are integer variables with the domain of* $\{-1, 0, 1\}$ *for all* $0 \leq i \leq n-1$.

CP model 2 (XOR) [6]

For $f : \mathbb{F}_2^n \to \mathbb{F}_2$, $f(x_0, x_1, \cdots, x_{n-1}) = y$, *where* $y = x_0 \oplus x_1 \oplus \cdots \oplus x_{n-1}$, *the valid transitions for deterministic differential trails satisfy the following:*

$$\texttt{XOR}(X_0, \cdots, X_{n-1}, Y) := \begin{cases} \text{if} \bigvee_{i=0}^{n-1} (X_i = -1) \text{ then } Y = -1 \\ \text{else } Y = \sum_{i=0}^{n-1} X_i \bmod 2 \text{ endif} \end{cases}$$

where X_i *and* Y *are integer variables with the domain of* $\{-1, 0, 1\}$ *for all* $0 \leq i \leq n-1$.

CP model 3 (S-box) [6]

CP model for S-box can be derived from the differential distribution table (DDT).

The way how to encode deterministic behaviors of S-box using sbox analyzer is explained in Appendix N of [6].

CP models to search deterministic differential distinguishers are constructed as follows. We define integer variables $XU_{r,i}$ and $XL_{r,i}$, $(0 \leq r \leq R,\ 0 \leq i \leq n-1)$ to represent the differential pattern of the internal state after r rounds of a block cipher in the forward and backward directions. CP models for deterministic differential trails in forward and backward directions over R rounds are independently constructed. The constraints $\sum_{i=0}^{n-1} XU_{0,i} \neq 0$ and $\sum_{i=0}^{n-1} XL_{R,i} \neq 0$ are added to exclude all trivial solutions. The following constraints are added to ensure the inconsistency between the two deterministic differential propagations at least one point throughout the distinguisher:

$$\texttt{CSP} := \bigvee_{r=0}^{R-1} \left(\bigvee_{i=0}^{n-1} (XU_{r,i} + XL_{r,i} = 1) \right)$$

If CP models are feasible using a CP-solver, it means that there exist r-round impossible differentials. Otherwise, one can not find any impossible differential at r-round using deterministic differentials.

5 Lightweight Block Cipher SAND-64

SAND is a lightweight block cipher proposed by Chen et al. [1]. It employs an AND-RX structure and has two variants, SAND-64 and SAND-128, depending on the block size. In this paper, we focus on SAND-64, which has a block size of 64 bits and a secret key length of 128 bits. The recommended number of SAND-64 is 48. In the following description, we set $n = 32$.

5.1 Preliminaries

The notations used in the description of SAND-64 are defined as follows:

- $x = (x_{n-1}, x_{n-2}, \ldots, x_0)$: An n-bit variable, where x_{n-1} represents the most significant bit (MSB) and x_0 represents the least significant bit (LSB). The variable x is represented using a $4 \times \frac{n}{4}$ array. $x[i]$ is the i-th nibble (4-bit) of variable x.

$$x = \begin{bmatrix} x_{n-1} & \cdots & x_7 & x_3 \\ x_{n-2} & \cdots & x_6 & x_2 \\ x_{n-3} & \cdots & x_5 & x_1 \\ x_{n-4} & \cdots & x_4 & x_0 \end{bmatrix}, \quad \begin{cases} x[\frac{n}{4}-1] = (x_{n-1}, x_{n-2}, x_{n-3}, x_{n-4}), \\ \vdots \\ x[1] = (x_7, x_6, x_5, x_4), \\ x[0] = (x_3, x_2, x_1, x_0). \end{cases}$$

- $x||y$: Concatenation of variables x and y
- $x \ll s$: Left shift of variable x by s bits
- $x \lll t$: Left cyclic shift of variable x by t bits
- $x \odot y$: Bitwise AND operation
- $x \oplus y$: Bitwise XOR operation.

5.2 State Loading

Let $P = (Pl, Pr)$ be the plaintext, where $Pl = (Pl_{n-1}, \ldots, Pl_1, Pl_0)$ represents the left n-bit part and $Pr = (Pr_{n-1}, \ldots, Pr_1, Pr_0)$ represents the right n-bit part. The variables Pl and Pr are represented as $4 \times \frac{n}{4}$ arrays:

$$Pl = \begin{bmatrix} Pl_{n-1} & \ldots & Pl_7 & Pl_3 \\ Pl_{n-2} & \ldots & Pl_6 & Pl_2 \\ Pl_{n-3} & \ldots & Pl_5 & Pl_1 \\ Pl_{n-4} & \ldots & Pl_4 & Pl_0 \end{bmatrix} = \begin{bmatrix} x^0\{3\} \\ x^0\{2\} \\ x^0\{1\} \\ x^0\{0\} \end{bmatrix}, \quad Pr = \begin{bmatrix} Pr_{n-1} & \ldots & Pr_7 & Pr_3 \\ Pr_{n-2} & \ldots & Pr_6 & Pr_2 \\ Pr_{n-3} & \ldots & Pr_5 & Pr_1 \\ Pr_{n-4} & \ldots & Pr_4 & Pr_0 \end{bmatrix} = \begin{bmatrix} y^0\{3\} \\ y^0\{2\} \\ y^0\{1\} \\ y^0\{0\} \end{bmatrix}$$

The input (x^0, y^0) for the first round is assigned row by row from plaintext P:

$$x^0 = Pl_{n-1} \ldots Pl_7\ Pl_3 || \ldots || Pl_{n-4} \ldots Pl_4\ Pl_0 = x^0\{3\} || x^0\{2\} || x^0\{1\} || x^0\{0\},$$
$$y^0 = Pr_{n-1} \ldots Pr_7\ Pr_3 || \ldots || Pr_{n-4} \ldots Pr_4\ Pr_0 = y^0\{3\} || y^0\{2\} || y^0\{1\} || y^0\{0\}$$

Let $C = (Cl, Cr)$ be the ciphertext, where $Cl = (Cl_{n-1}, \ldots, Cl_1, Cl_0)$ represents the left n-bit part and $Cr = (Cr_{n-1}, \ldots, Cr_1, Cr_0)$ represents the right n-bit part. The ciphertext C is assigned row by row from the round R output (x^R, y^R):

$$Cl = \begin{bmatrix} Cl_{n-1} & \ldots & Cl_7 & Cl_3 \\ Cl_{n-2} & \ldots & Cl_6 & Cl_2 \\ Cl_{n-3} & \ldots & Cl_5 & Cl_1 \\ Cl_{n-4} & \ldots & Cl_4 & Cl_0 \end{bmatrix} = \begin{bmatrix} x^R\{3\} \\ x^R\{2\} \\ x^R\{1\} \\ x^R\{0\} \end{bmatrix}, \quad Cr = \begin{bmatrix} Cr_{n-1} & \ldots & Cr_7 & Cr_3 \\ Cr_{n-2} & \ldots & Cr_6 & Cr_2 \\ Cr_{n-3} & \ldots & Cr_5 & Cr_1 \\ Cr_{n-4} & \ldots & Cr_4 & Cr_0 \end{bmatrix} = \begin{bmatrix} y^R\{3\} \\ y^R\{2\} \\ y^R\{1\} \\ y^R\{0\} \end{bmatrix}$$

5.3 Round Function

The round function of SAND-64 is illustrated in Fig. 1. Let (x^r, y^r) denote the input of round r, sk^r denote the round key, and (x^{r+1}, y^{r+1}) denote the output. The round function consists of two types of nonlinear functions, G_0 and G_1, as well as a linear function P_n.

Table 2. Permutation p_8

j	0	1	2	3	4	5	6	7
$p_8(j)$	7	4	1	6	3	0	5	2

Let the input to G_0 and G_1 be an n-bit variable $x = x\{3\} || x\{2\} || x\{1\} || x\{0\}$ and the output be $y = y\{3\} || y\{2\} || y\{1\} || y\{0\}$. The function G_0 and G_1 are defined as follows:

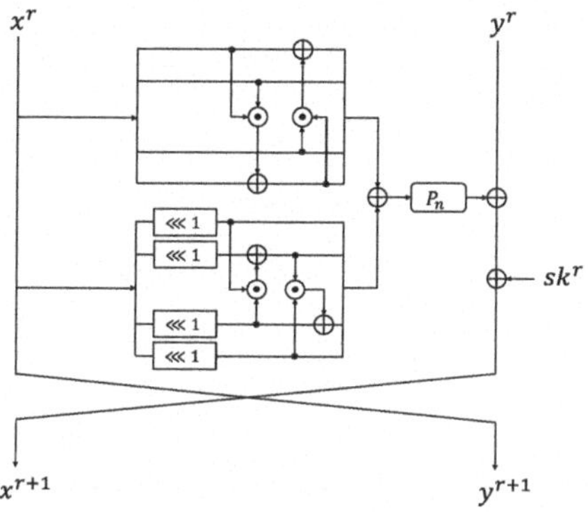

Fig. 1. Round function

$$G_0 := \begin{bmatrix} y\{3\} = y\{0\} \odot x\{1\} \oplus x\{3\} \\ y\{2\} = x\{2\} \\ y\{1\} = x\{1\} \\ y\{0\} = x\{3\} \odot x\{2\} \oplus x\{0\} \end{bmatrix}, \quad G_1 := \begin{bmatrix} y\{3\} = x\{3\} \\ y\{2\} = x\{3\} \odot x\{1\} \oplus x\{2\} \\ y\{1\} = y\{2\} \odot x\{0\} \oplus x\{1\} \\ y\{0\} = x\{0\} \end{bmatrix}.$$

The linear function P_n transforms the input word $x\{i\} = (x_{\frac{n}{4}\cdot i+\frac{n}{4}-1}, \dots, x_{\frac{n}{4}\cdot i+1}, x_{\frac{n}{4}\cdot i})$ into the output word $y\{i\}$ according to the following equation: $y_{\frac{n}{4}\cdot i+p_8(j)} = x_{\frac{n}{4}\cdot i+j}, \quad \text{for } 0 \leq j < \frac{n}{4},\ 0 \leq i < 4.$ The linear function P_n can be regarded as applying the permutation p_8 to each of the four $\frac{n}{4}$-bit words in parallel. The permutation p_8 is defined in Table 2.

5.4 Key Schedule

SAND-64 generates round keys from a 128-bit secret key K. The secret key is treated as a concatenation of four 32-bit words: $K = K^3||K^2||K^1||K^0$. Figure 2 and Fig. 3 illustrate the key schedule of SAND-64.

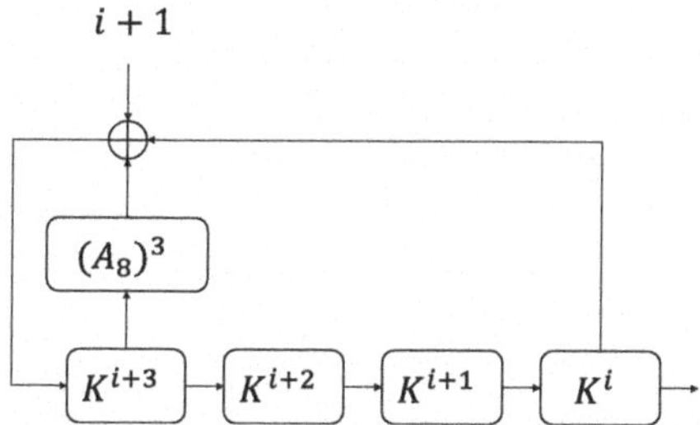

Fig. 2. Key schedule of SAND-64

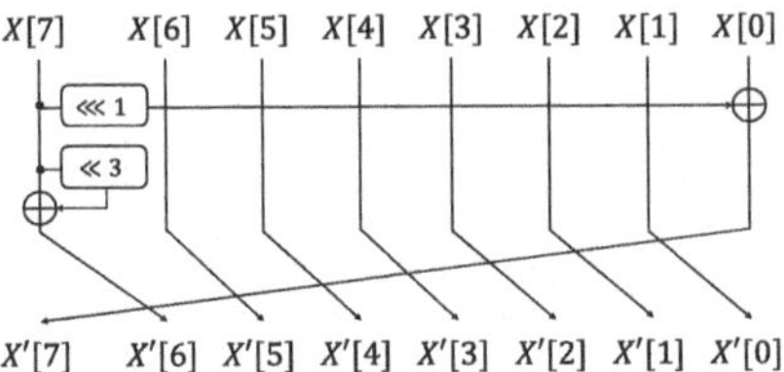

Fig. 3. Operation A_8

The constant $i+1$, $0 \leq i < R-4$ is a round-dependent constant. The update of the linear feedback shift register (LFSR) is defined as: $K^{i+4} \leftarrow (A_8)^3(K^{i+3}) \oplus K^i \oplus (i+1)$. The operation A_8 processes data in 4-bit units and is applied to K^{i+3} three times in succession. The round key sk^r $(0 \leq r < R)$ is derived from K^r as follows:

$$K^r = \begin{bmatrix} K^r_{31} \dots K^r_7 \; K^r_3 \\ K^r_{30} \dots K^r_6 \; K^r_2 \\ K^r_{29} \dots K^r_5 \; K^r_1 \\ K^r_{28} \dots K^r_4 \; K^r_0 \end{bmatrix}, \quad sk^r = K^r_{31} \dots K^r_3 || K^r_{30} \dots K^r_2 || K^r_{29} \dots K^r_1 || K^r_{28} \dots K^r_0.$$

6 Impossible Differential Attack on SAND-64

6.1 Construction of the CP Model

We construct a constraint programming (CP) model to search for impossible differential distinguishers of SAND-64 using deterministic differentials. For simplicity, the `StateLoading` process, which is linear permutation inserted in the 1st round input and last round output, is omitted. In the following, $n = 32$ for SAND-64.

The domain of the following integer variables is defined as $\{-1, 0, 1\}$, where each value represents an unknown, 0, and 1 difference, respectively. Based on the round function illustrated in Fig. 1, we define integer variables $XU_{r,i}$ and $YU_{r,i}$ $(0 \leq r \leq R, 0 \leq i \leq n-1)$, which represent i-th bit of the internal state differences in the forward (encryption) direction. Similarly, we define integer variables $XL_{r,i}$ and $YL_{r,i}$, which represent i-th bit of the internal state differences in the backward (decryption) direction. The variables $XU_{0,i}$ and $YU_{0,i}$ (as well as $XL_{0,i}$ and $YL_{0,i}$) represent the input differences, while $XU_{R,i}$ and $YU_{R,i}$ (as well as $XL_{R,i}$ and $YL_{R,i}$) represent the output differences after R rounds.

The construction of the CP model in the forward (encryption) direction using $XU_{r,i}$ and $YU_{r,i}$ is described below. We define integer variables $G_0U_{r,i}$ and $G_1U_{r,i}$ $(1 \leq r \leq R)$ to represent i-th bit of the output differences of the nonlinear functions G_0 and G_1, and impose the following constraints:

$$G_0U_{r,i} = G_0(XU_r)_i, \quad G_1U_{r,i} = G_1(XU_r)_i.$$

where $G_0(\cdot)_i$ (resp. $G_i(\cdot)_i$) denotes i-th bit of the output of G_0 (resp. G_1). The constraints for G_0 and G_1 can be derived from the differential distribution table (DDT). In this paper, we refer to Appendix N of [6] and use the S-box analyzer[1] to derive the constraints for G_0 and G_1.

We define integer variables $PU_{r,i}$ ($1 \leq r \leq R$) to represent i-th bit of the output differences of the linear function P_n, and impose the following constraint:

$$PU_{r,i} = P_n(\texttt{XOR}(G_0U_r, G_1U_r))_i.$$

where $P_n(\cdot)_i$ denotes i-th bit of the output P_n. For the round function output, the following constraints are imposed:

$$XU_{r+1,i} = \texttt{XOR}(YU_{r,i}, PU_{r,i}), \quad YU_{r+1,i} = XU_{r,i}.$$

By constructing these constraints for each round r ($0 \leq r \leq R$), the CP model for the forward (encryption) direction is completed. Similarly, the CP model for the backward (decryption) direction can be constructed using integer variables $XL_{r,i}$ and $YL_{r,i}$.

Additionally, we introduce the following constraints to eliminate trivial solutions:

$$\sum_{i=0}^{n-1} XU_{0,i} + \sum_{i=0}^{n-1} YU_{0,i} \neq 0, \quad \sum_{i=0}^{n-1} XL_{R,i} + \sum_{i=0}^{n-1} YL_{R,i} \neq 0.$$

Finally, to ensure that there is at least one contradiction between the deterministic difference propagation paths in the forward (encryption) and backward (decryption) directions, we introduce the following constraints:

$$\left\{ \bigvee_{r=0}^{R-1} \left(\bigvee_{i=0}^{n-1} (XU_{r,i} + XL_{r,i} = 1) \right) \right\} \vee \left\{ \bigvee_{r=0}^{R-1} \left(\bigvee_{i=0}^{n-1} (YU_{r,i} + YL_{r,i} = 1) \right) \right\}.$$

If the constructed CP model is satisfiable in a CP solver, it indicates the existence of an r-round impossible differential distinguisher.

6.2 Impossible Differential Distinguishers of SAND-64

We implemented the CP model constructed in the previous section using MiniZinc v2.9.2,[2] and employed OR-Tools CP-SAT 9.12.4544[3] as the CP solver. We obtained a solution in approximately 1 min and 30 s, revealing 56 types of 11-round impossible differential distinguishers. The results are presented in Table 3.

[1] https://github.com/hadipourh/sboxanalyzer.

[2] https://www.minizinc.org/.

[3] https://developers.google.com/optimization.

Table 3. 11-round impossible differential distinguishers of SAND-64

XU_0	0000 0000 0000 0000 0000 0000 0000 0000	YU_0	0000 0?00 0000 0?00 0000 0100 0000 0?00
XU_1	0000 0?00 0000 0?00 0000 0100 0000 0?00	YU_1	0000 0000 0000 0000 0000 0000 0000 0000
XU_2	0?00 00?0 0?00 00?0 0?00 0010 0?00 00?0	YU_2	0000 0?00 0000 0?00 0000 0100 0000 0?00
XU_3	00?? 0??0 00?? 0??0 00?1 0??0 00?? 0??0	YU_3	0?00 00?0 0?00 00?0 0?00 0010 0?00 00?0
XU_4	0??? ?0?? 0??? ?0?? 0??? 10?? 0??? ?0??	YU_4	00?? 0??0 00?? 0??0 00?1 0??0 00?? 0??0
XU_5	???? ???? ???? ???? ?1?? ???? ???? ????	YU_5	0??? ?0?? 0??? ?0?? 0??? 10?? 0??? ?0??
XL_5	???? ???? ???? ???? ?0?? ???? ???? ????	YL_5	???? ???? ???? ???? ???? ???? ???? ????
XL_6	0??? ?0?? 0??? ?0?? 0??? 00?? 0??? ?0??	YL_6	???? ???? ???? ???? ?0?? ???? ???? ????
XL_7	00?? 0??0 00?? 0??0 00?0 0??0 00?? 0??0	YL_7	0??? ?0?? 0??? ?0?? 0??? 00?? 0??? ?0??
XL_8	0?00 00?0 0?00 00?0 0?00 0000 0?00 00?0	YL_8	00?? 0??0 00?? 0??0 00?0 0??0 00?? 0??0
XL_9	0000 0?00 0000 0?00 0000 0000 0000 0?00	YL_9	0?00 00?0 0?00 00?0 0?00 0000 0?00 00?0
XL_{10}	0000 0000 0000 0000 0000 0000 0000 0000	YL_{10}	0000 0?00 0000 0?00 0000 0000 0000 0?00
XL_{11}	0000 0?00 0000 0?00 0000 0000 0000 0?00	YL_{11}	0000 0000 0000 0000 0000 0000 0000 0000

6.3 Key Recovery Attack on 16-Round SAND-64

Using the 11-round impossible differential distinguishers shown in Table 3, we perform a key recovery attack on 16-round SAND-64, as illustrated in Fig. 4. In Fig. 4, the locations where differences exist are highlighted in red or gray. The data, time, and memory complexities for the key recovery attack are estimated using the method of Boura et al. [16].

At $r_{in} = 3$, the bit conditions required to obtain the output difference at the 3rd round $(\Delta x^3, \Delta y^3)$ from the plaintext difference $(\Delta x^0, \Delta y^0)$ are $c_{in} = 36$. Additionally, the number of key bits involved is $k_{in} = 12$ bits ($sk^0 = 8$ bits$sk^1 =$ 4 bits).

Similarly, at $r_{out} = 2$, the bit conditions required to obtain the output difference at the 14th round $(\Delta x^{14}, \Delta y^{14})$ from the ciphertext difference $(\Delta x^{16}, \Delta y^{16})$ are $c_{out} = 21$. Additionally, the number of key bits involved is $k_{out} = 4$ bits ($sk^{15} = 4$ bits).

To reduce the number of key candidates by at least half, the necessary number of differential pairs $(\Delta_{in}, \Delta_{out})$ is $N_{min} = 2^{57}$. The computational complexity to obtain these pairs is estimated using Eq. (1) as follows:

$$C_N = \max\left\{\sqrt{2^{57}2^{64+1-40}}, 2^{57}2^{64+1-40-24}\right\} = 2^{58}$$

This computational complexity C_N also represents the necessary number of plaintexts. The total time complexity required for the key recovery attack is estimated using Eq. (2) as follows:

$$T = \left(2^{58} + \left(2^{57} + 2^{12+4}\right) \times \frac{5}{16} + 2^{128} \times \frac{1}{2}\right) = 2^{127}$$

which corresponds to the number of 16-round SAND-64 encryptions. Additionally, the memory required to store N_{min} differential pairs is estimated as: $M = 2^{57} \times 64 \times 4 \times \frac{1}{8} = 2^{62}$ bytes.

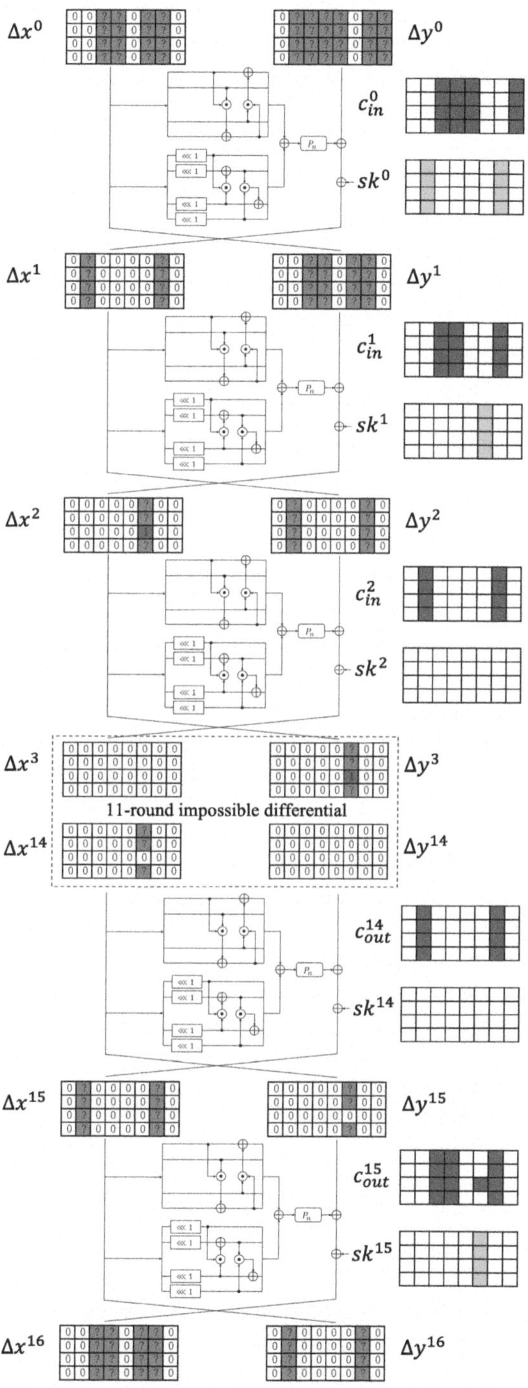

Fig. 4. Key Recovery Attack on 16-Round SAND-64

We can reduce the time complexity 2^{127} using plenty of plaintexts. For example, if we prepair 2^{63} plaintexts, we can generate $2^5 = 32$ sets of C_N. Because each data set of C_N can reduce the number of key candidates by at least half, the total time complexity is estimated as follows.

$$T = \left(2^{63} + 2^5 \times \left(2^{57} + 2^{12+4}\right) \times \frac{5}{16} + 2^{128} \times \left(\frac{1}{2}\right)^{32}\right) = 2^{96}$$

Because we can reuse a memory capacity for each data set of C_N, the memory complexity is 2^{62} bytes. The attack result is summarized in Table 1.

7 Discussion

7.1 Comparison with Zhang et al. [12]

The impossible differential distinguishers revealed in this paper differ from those reported by Zhang et al. [12] in both methodology and practical results. Specifically, the following points clarify why our differentials are either distinct or advantageous:

- **Search Methodology**: While Zhang et al. propose a framework based on differential propagation matrices and matrix threshold XOR-multiplication to evaluate provable and practical bounds, our method utilizes constraint programming (CP) models based on deterministic differentials [5,6].
- **Distinguisher Coverage**: Zhang et al. report 256 11-round impossible differentials for SAND64. Our method also reveals 56 distinct 11-round distinguishers, verified independently via a CP-solver (MiniZinc + OR-Tools), providing cross-validation and alternative derivations that demonstrate the same security bounds from a different model.
- **Solver Transparency and Extensibility**: Our approach is fully constraint-solver based and requires no custom symbolic computation or round-function-specific matrix derivation. This makes it readily adaptable to other AND-RX ciphers and promotes reproducibility.
- **Attack Relevance**: Based on the discovered 11-round distinguishers, we further constructed a full key recovery attack on 16-round SAND-64, with clearly defined data, time, and memory complexities. Zhang et al. only report boundary evaluations and do not demonstrate concrete key recovery results using the discovered distinguishers.

7.2 Comparison with the Previous Attacks [14,15]

Though our attack is higher time complexity than the boomerang attack [15], our attack can break 16-round SAND-64 which is longer round than the boomerang attack can reach. Our attack achieves lower time complexity than the integral attack [14]. Although the time complexity of 2^{96} is infeasible in practical attack, our result contributes to the theoretical understanding of SAND-64's structural weaknesses. Such analysis is crucial for cipher designers to evaluate the security margin and resistance to impossible differential attacks.

7.3 Application to SAND-128

Our attack method illustrated in Sect. 6 is similarly applicable to SAND-128. The details will be published in Proc. of 24th International Conference on Cryptology and Network Security, CANS 2025 [17].

References

1. Chen, S., Fan, Y., Sun, L., Fu, Y., Zhou, H., Li, Y., Wang, M., Wang, W., Guo, C.: SAND: an AND-RX Feistel lightweight block cipher supporting S-box-based security evaluations. Des. Codes Crypt. **90**, 155–198 (2022)
2. Biham, E., Shamir, A.: Differential Cryptanalysis of the Data Encryption Standard, pp. 79–88. Springer, New York (1993)
3. Matsui, M.: Linear Cryptanalysis Method for DES Cipher, Proceedings of the Workshop on the Theory and Application of Cryptographic Techniques, EUROCRYPT '93, vol. 765 of LNCS, pp. 386–397. Springer (1993)
4. Cui, T., Jia, K., Fu, K., Chen, S., Wang, M.: New automatic search tool for impossible differentials and zero-correlation linear approximations. IACR Cryptology ePrint Archive, Report 2016/689 (2016)
5. Hadipour, H., Sadeghi, S., Eichlseder, M.: Finding the impossible: automated search for full impossible differential, zero-correlation, and integral attacks. In: Proceedings of the EUROCRYPT 2023, vol. 14007 of LNCS, pp. 128–157. Springer (2023)
6. Hadipour, H., Gerhalter, S., Sadeghi, S., Eichlseder, M.: Improved search for integral, impossible differential and zero-correlation attacks, application to Ascon, for kSKINNY, SKINNY, MANTIS, PRESENT and QARMAv2. IACR Trans. Symmetric Cryptol. **2024**(1), 234–325 (2024)
7. Knudsen, L.R., Wagner, D.: Integral cryptanalysis, Proceedings of Fast Software Encryption, FSE2002, Vol.2365 of LNCS, pp. 112–127. Springer (2002)
8. Biham, E., Biryukov, A., Shamir, A.: Cryptanalysis of Skipjack reduced to 31 rounds using impossible differentials. Advances in Cryptology-EUROCRYPT'99, vol. 1592 of LNCS, pp. 12–23 (1999)
9. Knudsen, L.: DEAL-a 128-bit block cipher. Complexity **258**(2) (1998)
10. Bogdanov, A., Wang, M.: Zero Correlation Linear Cryptanalysis with Reduced Data Complexity, Proceedings of the 19th International Workshop on Fast Software Encryption, FSE 2012, vol. 7549 of LNCS, pp. 29–48 (2012)
11. Bogdanov, A., Rijmen, V.: Linear hulls with correlation zero and linear cryptanalysis of block ciphers. Des. Codes Crypt. **70**, 369–383 (2014)
12. Zhang, K., Wang, S., Lai, X., Wang, L., Guan, J., Hu, B.: Impossible differential cryptanalysis and a security evaluation framework for AND-RX ciphers. IEEE Trans. Inf. Theory **70**(8), 6025–6040 (2024)
13. Xiang, Z., Zhang, W., Bao, Z., Lin, D.: Applying MILP Method to Searching Integral Distinguishers Based on Division Property for 6 Lightweight Block Ciphers, Proceedings of the 22nd International Conference on the Theory and Application of Cryptology and Information Security, ASIACRYPT2016, vol. 10031 of LNCS, pp. 648–678, Springer (2016)
14. Mirzaie, A., Ahmadi, S., Aref, R.M.: Integral cryptanalysis of reduced-round SAND-64 based on bit-based division property. ISC Int. J. Inf. Secur. (ISeCure) **15**(3) (2023)

15. Li, Y., Teh, J.S.: Boomerang Cryptanalysis of SAND. J. Inf. Secur. Appl. **92**, 104086 (2025)
16. Boura, C., Lallemand, V., Naya-Plasencia, M., Suder, V.: Making the Impossible Possible, Cryptology, vol. 31, pp. 101–133. Springer (2018)
17. Sugio, N.: Impossible Differential Attack on SAND-128, Proceedings of the 24th International Conference on Cryptology and Network Security, CANS 2025 (2025)

Formal Verification of Labyrinth Encrypted Message Storage Protocol in Messenger

Kakeru Watanabe(✉) and Kazuki Yoneyama

Ibaraki University, Hitachi, Japan
{24nm771g,kazuki.yoneyama.sec}@vc.ibaraki.ac.jp

Abstract. Messenger, a messaging service, is widely used in the United States and around the world, with 947 million monthly active users as of February 2025. In December 2023, a default implementation of end-to-end encryption in Messenger and two accompanying technical white papers were released. Labyrinth Encrypted Message Storage Protocol is one of the protocols presented in these technical white papers and is intended to securely share message history between devices associated with each Messenger account. However, there has been no rigorous discussion of the security of Labyrinth to date, and the security model claimed in the technical white paper has some ambiguity. In this paper, we give the first formal verification of Labyrinth. First, we verify the confidentiality and integrity of the stored messages as the security claim in the specification (i.e., only considering outside adversaries). Next, considering the case of a device that has been revoked from an account and abused, we exhaustively verify under what conditions it is possible to break the confidentiality and integrity of a message. As a result of the verification, we clarify the conditions under which the confidentiality and integrity of stored messages can be broken by abusing a revoked device and the specific procedures for doing so while satisfying all the security claims made by the specification.

Keywords: Formal methods · Labyrinth · Messenger · Storage protocol

1 Introduction

1.1 Background

Social networking services (SNS) and other communication services are widely used, and ensuring their security is an important issue. Meta's Messenger [1] is estimated to have 947 million monthly active users as of February 2025, which is the fourth largest number in the world among messenger applications after WhatsApp, WeChat, and Telegram and widely used internationally [2]. In December 2023, Meta announced the introduction of end-to-end encryption (E2EE) in Messenger as a standard for all users [3], and in conjunction with this

K.-W. Park and J. Park (Eds.): WISA 2025 2025, LNCS 16434, pp. 115–127, 2026.
https://doi.org/10.1007/978-981-95-6857-4_9

announcement, published the specifications for the following two protocols: the core cryptographic protocol for transmitting messages between clients [4] and the protocol for end-to-end encrypting stored messaging history between devices on a user's account (Labyrinth Encrypted Message Storage Protocol) [5]. These two protocols have already begun to be used in Messenger at the time of this writing,[1], but no rigorous proof of security is known so far, including these technical white papers, and to clarify whether they truly meet the security claims made in the specifications and in the specific use cases envisioned is important.

In the past, handwritten security proofs were used to show the security of cryptographic protocols, but in recent years, verification using formal methods has been gaining popularity. The main advantages of formal verification are the automation of verification and the prevention of human error. By mathematically expressing the specifications to be verified and the security to be satisfied, the verification work itself can be delegated to a computer. Another advantage is that the verification itself does not have to be considered from scratch every time a minor setting is changed. The user only needs to consider how to change the input since the verification content passed to the computer as input can be reused, and security verification can be left to the computer.

With the above background, we examine the security of Labyrinth using formal methods in this paper.

1.2 Related Work and Motivating Problem

There are various known security verifications of cryptographic protocols using formal methods and security analysis of E2EE in SNS.

Formal Methods for Security Protocols. Formal methods are widely used for the security verification of real-world cryptographic protocols due to their good match with security fields. The major tools are ProVerif [7] and Tamarin Prover [8], and there are various known examples of verification of cryptographic protocols utilizing these tools: TLS 1.3 [9], QUIC [10], Bluetooth [11] and FIDO [12,13]. However, no formal verification of Labyrinth has been conducted to date.

Security Analysis of E2EE in SNS. LINE is a messaging application used mainly in the Asian region. The specification of E2EE in LINE messaging is published as a technical white paper [14,15], and several security analyses have been conducted to date.[2] Espinoza et al. [16] showed a replay attack (an attack in which a man-in-the-middle exploits an old session's encrypted messages) against E2EE of LINE. Isobe and Minematsu [17] showed a spoofing attack

[1] Note that E2EE has not yet been implemented in all use cases of Messenger, as noted in the Messenger Help Center [6].

[2] Note that all security analyses discussed here are for LINE Encryption Ver. 1.0 [14], which differs from the current specification [15].

(an attack that intercepts a session and impersonates a user) against E2EE of LINE. Moreover, Shi and Yoneyama [18] gave an exhaustive formal verification using ProVerif to LINE encryption scheme and rediscovered the above attacks, as well as an attack in the Transport Encryption Protocol (TEP) to break forward secrecy of the client's data.

iMessage is a messaging service developed by Apple, and E2EE was implemented from the beginning of its use. In February 2024, Apple released PQ3 [19], a post-quantum secure protocol for iMessage, and Linker et al. [20] formally verified PQ3 by Tamarin since its design phase.

There are several other studies about the security of cryptographic protocols related to SNS, such as the security analysis of Zoom's E2EE [21] and the security analysis of WhatsApp's backup protocol [22]. However, no study on the security of Labyrinth is currently known.

Limitation on Security Requirements of Labyrinth. The Labyrinth specification [5] proposes several design goals in terms of Messenger as 'a product and privacy'. In Labyrinth, the concept of epoch is also defined to take into account cases where a device is revoked from an account. The epoch is renewed when one device is revoked, and it is guaranteed that messages stored in a new epoch cannot be decrypted using keys and other data handled in previous epochs. The listed design goals do not consider the case of attacks using revoked devices. Hence, we consider that the security claimed in the specification alone is only for limited cases and it is significant to consider what threats can appear by the misuse of revoked devices and the information they hold.[3]

1.3 Our Contribution

In this paper, we present the first formal verification of Labyrinth. For security verification, we use ProVerif [7], a generic verification tool for cryptographic protocols, because of its expressiveness of protocol features and security requirements. First, we formalize the protocol specification with the ProVerif language. Next, we verify the confidentiality and integrity of the messages stored by Labyrinth and whether the claims made in the specification are satisfied. Moreover, according to the cases where the information of the revoked device becomes known to the attacker, we verify whether the confidentiality and integrity of the stored messages can be satisfied in such cases. The verification results show that while the security (confidentiality and integrity) as claimed in the specification is met, the security regarding the latter cases can be breached by misusing a revoked device. See Sect. 4 for details on the conditions necessary to break

[3] In the specification [5, pp. 36], the limitation on epoch integrity is discussed. Note that the attacks described there are based on the assumption that malicious servers do not provide the information necessary for protocol execution for a device, which is clearly different from legitimate protocol execution and the abusability of a revoked device, which we verify in this paper.

the above security requirements, etc., obtained through the verification in this study. We reported the attacks we discovered through Meta Bug Bounty [23]. The response from Meta was that these attacks were weaknesses that were known from the time of design and were accepted during the design process.

Labyrinth also claims that it uses AES-GCM-Extended, Labyrinth's own method of extending AES-GCM, as part of the components to make up the protocol, as an approach to avoid nonce reuse. Verification of Labyrinth as a protocol using a strict formalization of AES-GCM-Extended would require an enormous amount of time for verification, hence, we separate the abstraction level of verification according to such a part. First, we verify Labyrinth with an ideal AEAD.[4] Next, to show that AES-GCM-Extended does not differ in cryptographic security from an ideal AEAD, the confidentiality (observational equivalence with an ideal AEAD) and integrity are verified and shown as the security of AES-GCM-Extended as well.

1.4 Our Key Technique for Formalization

Labyrinth is a stateful protocol where devices can be added or revoked at any time without limit, as it is a protocol to ensure security in the storage of messages in a single account. On the other hand, while ProVerif has the advantage of being able to express cryptographic protocol specifications in a more natural way, it does not support stateful protocol descriptions. We focused on the fact that all epochs in Labyrinth are linked in a chain, taking over information from previous epochs, and formalized and verified with ProVerif based on a specific pattern of events that can occur when there is only one device connected to an account. In the formalization using ProVerif, the situation of epochs defined in Labyrinth is realized using the `phase` command, and the messages stored in each epoch are formalized as being stored in the database across epochs by using `table`. Based on these assumptions, the behavior of each entity is formalized as a sub-process, and in the case of a revoked device being used by an attacker, it is formalized to take this into account to achieve security verification by using ProVerif.

2 Labyrinth

In this section, we give a cryptographic description of the Labyrinth protocol's structure related to this work directly based on the white paper published by Meta [5]. Although the protocol in the white paper is described with the natural language, we organize the protocol algorithmically as a common manner for the cryptographic protocols.

[4] Note that ideally secure AEAD here refer to symbolically secure AEAD. This assumes an encryption scheme where the outputs are independent for different inputs even if nonce re-use occurs.

2.1 Cryptographic Primitives (and Its Concrete Specifications)

Authen ticated Symmetric Encryption (AES-GCM-Extended). Labyrinth uses an extension of AES-GCM named AES-GCM-Extended. The syntax used in the protocol description is $\texttt{ciphertext} \leftarrow \mathsf{encrypt}(\texttt{key}, \texttt{aad}, \texttt{plaintext})$ and $\texttt{plaintext} \leftarrow \mathsf{decrypt}(\texttt{key}, \texttt{aad}, \texttt{ciphertext})$, where aad is additional authenticated data.

Public Key Encryption (Labyrinth HPKE). Labyrinth uses an authenticated public key cryptosystem named Labyrinth HPKE (Hybrid Public Key Encryption). The syntax used in the protocol description is $(\texttt{priv\_key\_enc}, \texttt{pub\_key\_enc}) \leftarrow \mathsf{pk\_enc\_keygen}()$, $(\texttt{priv\_key\_auth}, \texttt{pub\_key\_auth}) \leftarrow \mathsf{pk\_auth\_keygen}()$, $\texttt{ciphertext} \leftarrow \mathsf{pk\_encrypt}(\texttt{pub\_key\_enc}, \texttt{pub\_key\_auth}, \texttt{priv\_key\_auth}, \texttt{pre\_shared\_key}, \texttt{aad}, \texttt{plaintext})$ and $\texttt{plaintext} \leftarrow \mathsf{pk\_decrypt}(\texttt{pub\_key\_enc}, \texttt{priv\_key\_enc}, \texttt{pub\_key\_auth}, \texttt{pre\_shared\_key}, \texttt{aad}, \texttt{ciphertext})$.

It is required that plaintext cannot be decrypted if ciphertext is generated with priv_key_auth not corresponding to pub_key_auth in decryption. We note that no concrete decryption algorithm is given in the specification, whereas a specific encryption algorithm is given. In this paper, we assume that Labyrinth HPKE is ideally secure.[5]

Digital Signature (XEdDSA). Labyrinth uses XEdDSA as a digital signature. The syntax used in the protocol description is $(\texttt{priv\_key}, \texttt{pub\_key}) \leftarrow \mathsf{pk\_sig\_keygen}()$, $\texttt{signature} \leftarrow \mathsf{pk\_sign}(\texttt{priv\_key}, \texttt{use\_case\_byte}, \texttt{data})$ and $\texttt{is\_valid} \leftarrow \mathsf{pk\_verify}(\texttt{pub\_key}, \texttt{signature}, \texttt{use\_case\_byte}, \texttt{data})$.

Message Authentication Code (MAC) and Key Derivation Function (KDF)(HMAC-SHA256). Labyrinth uses HMAC-SHA256 as MAC and KDF. The syntax used in the protocol description is $\texttt{mac\_value} \leftarrow \mathsf{mac}(\texttt{key}, \texttt{data})$[6] and $(\texttt{key1}, \texttt{key2}, ...) \leftarrow \mathsf{kdf}(\texttt{ikm}, \texttt{salt}, \texttt{info})$.

2.2 Protocol Overview

Labyrinth is a protocol for secure sharing of message history between multiple devices owned by the same user in Meta's Messenger. Labyrinth has its own goals in terms of product and privacy.

[5] Ideally secure HPKE here refers to the fact that no partial information of the plaintext is leaked if correct decryption fails (i.e. this refers to having ideal symbolic security).

[6] In the white paper, the input of mac is defined as (data, key). However, in the protocol specification, private keys are inputted to the first argument. Hence, we describe the syntax based on the protocol.

Entities. The entities that appear in Labyrinth are as follows.

Client: Each device (including virtual devices described in Sect. 2.3 and [5]) is defined as a client. A client is associated with an account, has its own key and access rights to the epoch, and is responsible for storing and loading messages.

Server: The server held by Meta manages the access rights of the devices associated with each account, as well as the DB for storing and loading messages.

Product Goals.

1. allowing messaging history to be accessed on new devices
2. providing an efficiently queryable and writeable storage mechanism, so devices need not store their entire message history.
3. preventing Meta from accessing data stored in Labyrinth

Privacy Goals.[7]

Baseline Message Secrecy: Labyrinth is intended to protect the content of messages from the server side and all that can monitor communications.

Post-Revocation Message Secrecy: Labyrinth guarantees that no device removed from the account can subsequently decrypt encrypted and stored messages.

Attachment Unlinkability
Labyrinth in Messenger

Epoch. Epoch is a concept provided for Labyrinth key management, which is updated only when a device is revoked; within an epoch, devices can be added an unlimited number of times, but revocation can occur only once. When the epoch is updated, the key for message encryption is updated, and it is no longer possible to decrypt messages in the new epoch from the revoked device.

2.3 Protocol Details

For readability, public parameters are abbreviated as "..." in the algorithmic expressions that follow. For details, see the specification [5].

[7] Attachment Linkability and Labyrinth in Messenger describe the policy of storing attachments and messages in isolation and the position of Labyrinth in Messenger, respectively. Note that these are not directly related to the security verification that is the main focus of this study.

Protocol Components.

Setup: Each Labyrinth device has the following keys. `deviceKeyPriv`,`deviceKeyPub`: asymmetric signature key pair. `epochStorageKeyPriv`,`epochStorageKeyPub`: asymmetric encryption key pair. `epochStorageAuthKeyPriv`, `epochStorageAuthKeyPub`: asymmetric authentication key pair. Within the mailbox metastore, the server stores the following per device: `deviceKeyPub`, `epochStorageKeyPub`,`pk_sign(deviceKeyPriv`, ..., `epochStorageKeyPub)`, `epochStorageAuthKeyPub` and `pk_sign(deviceKeyPriv`, ..., `epochStorageAuthKeyPub)`.

Epochs: Each epoch is associated with the following. `epochRootKey`: a secret shared among devices, but unknown to the server. `epochID`: a value assigned by the Labyrinth metadata server, uniquely identifying the epoch. `epochSequenceID`: a value assigned by clients, used within the mailbox. `epochMetadata`: encrypted secrets of at least one previous epoch. `epochDeviceMac[]`: list of proofs of membership for each device.

Protocol Phases. Labyrinth protocol execution is carried out in several phases and Labyrinth is also a stateful protocol. Henceforth, the client refers to mobile devices and the server refers to Meta's servers. In addition, each communication is basically assumed to take place between the client and the server. See the specification [5] for details.

Initialization. It corresponds to initialization in the Labyrinth protocol, where the client generates the secret and registers it with the server.

Opening an Epoch. This phase occurs when a new Labyrinth session is started or when a device revocation occurs, which updates the epoch.

Generate core epoch values. Each epoch has a root key from which the various values are derived.

If a new Labyrinth session is started: `epochRootKey` := `random(32)`
Else: `newEpochEntropy` := `random(32)`,
(`epochChainingKey`, `epochDistributionPresharedKey`) :=
`kdf(previousEpochRootKey`, ..., `concat(`..., `previousEpochSequenceID`, ..., `previousEpochID))`, `epochRootKey` := `kdf(newEpochEntropy`, `epochChainingKey`, ...)

`epochSequenceID` is an integer counter, beginning at 0 and calculated as `epochSequenceID` := `previousEpochSequenceID` + 1.

Store epoch metadata. Each epoch derives `epochDataStorageKey` and `epochDeviceMacKey` using `epochRootKey` and `epochSequenceID` to refer to its qualifications for previous epochs. The client encrypts and uploads `encryptedPreviousEpochSequenceID` and `encryptedPreviousEpochRootKey` encrypted using `epochDataStorageKey` for the previous epoch to the server.

Authentication of each device. When updating epochs, epoch entropy is shared from one device to another by the method described below. The sender device computes the `expectedMac` := mac(`previousEpochDeviceMacKey`, `deviceKeyPub`) for each destination device. Each device receiving epoch entropy computes the `previousEpochDeviceMac` := mac(`epochDeviceMacKey`, `deviceKeyPub`) to indicate its membership for previous epochs. The sender device compares these and only shares the `newEpochEntropy` with the device for which the equality is established.

Distribute new epoch entropy. In Labyrinth, the `epochRootKey` is not shared directly, but the `newEpochEntropy` is shared and the epoch is updated by deriving the `epochRootKey` from this and `previousEpochChainingKey` as described above. The sender device verifies each device's public key and then encrypts the `newEpochEntropy` to `epochEntropyEncrypted` := pk_encrypt(`epochStorageKeyPub_recipient`, `epochStorageAuthKeyPub_self`, `epochStorageKeyPriv_self`, `epochDistributionPreSharedKey`, concat(..., `epochSequenceID`), `newEpochEntropy`). The receiver device verifies the sender's `epochStorageAuthKeyPub`, decrypts the `epochEntropyEncrypted` and derives the `newEpochRootKey`.

Generating Recovery Codes. When adding a new device to the account, Labyrinth publishes a 40-character recovery code from already registered devices and restores the history of previous messages from the recovery codes.

Generating Virtual Devices. The Virtual Device concept is introduced to restore information about past epochs when new devices are added using recovery codes. Virtual Device is derived from one existing device.

Adding a device. When a new device is added to Labyrinth, it accesses the virtual device via recovery codes to obtain secret information of previous epochs.

Device Revocation. In Labyrinth, the revocation is to ensure that subsequent messages cannot be decrypted even without requiring the revoked device to remove the key. The epoch is updated starting from one device that is not revoked.

Storing and Loading Messages. The client derives `messageKey` := kdf(`epochRootKey`, ..., concat(..., `epochSequenceID`, ...)) used for encrypting the message from the current `epochRootKey`. It then encrypts the message and uploads `encryptedMessageData` := encrypt(`messageKey`, ..., `messageData`) to the server. Loading process mirrors the storing one. Note that when loading, the `messageKey` of the corresponding epoch is required.

3 Our Formalization of Labyrinth Using ProVerif

This section shows an overview of our formalization of Labyrinth. See (https://github.com/xk-watanabe/Verification_Labyrinth) for the full ProVerif code of our formalization.

3.1 Main Idea

As mentioned in Sect. 2.3, Labyrinth is a stateful protocol. On the other hand, ProVerif does not support stateful protocol descriptions. However, we find that given that all epochs are formed by inheriting information from previous epochs, events such as the addition or revocation of a device can be generalized and captured. From such an insight, we formalize Labyrinth by covering the following specific flows using ProVerif. In particular, we need to be mindful of the differences that arise in the way `newEpochEntropy` is shared when updating epochs and the way epoch information is accessed when adding devices, and we consider flows that encompass these differences. Note that the devices in Labyrinth are capable of storing messages at the latest epoch and reading messages at any epoch at any time. Our comprehensively formalized flows are shown below and an illustration of each flow and its relationship is shown in Fig. 1.

1. Initialization
2. Initialization → Add a Device
3. Initialization → Add a Device → Revoke a Device ($\star$)
4. Initialization → Add a Device → Revoke a Device → Add a Device ($\star$)
5. Initialization → Add a Device → Add a Device
6. Initialization → Add a Device → Add a Device → Revoke a Device ($\star, *$)
7. Initialization → Add a Device → Add a Device → Revoke a Device → Add a Device ($\star, *$)

In addition to considering situations in the technical white paper, we think that it should be taken into account whether the information about the revoked device is available to the attacker. We perform two-way verifications that capture such a situation as the flow marked with $\star$. Furthermore, the behaviour of updating epochs should also be considered. The specification did not explicitly specify whether the sharing of `newEpochEntropy` from the device originating the epoch updating to other devices is communicated via a server or directly between devices. For flows marked with $*$, we give a verification covering both of these. All these cases are covered by formalizing, in each flow, the sub-processes corresponding to each device added to the account and to the server, and by controlling what information is given to the attacker inside it.

3.2 Revocation of Devices

The verification in this paper aims to evaluate the security impact of whether or not an attacker can abuse the information of a revoked device. In the case of allowing abuse, in the sub-process of the device to be revoked, immediately after updating the phase, disclose the device's private keys and recovery codes to a public channel to which the attacker has access. Given that an attacker can intervene as a man-in-the-middle in the device registration and epoch update process, it is possible to attack using information on devices that have been revoked by having access to recovery codes and other information. In the case of not allowing, the null process (`0.`) shall be executed after updating the phase in the sub-process of the device to be revoked.

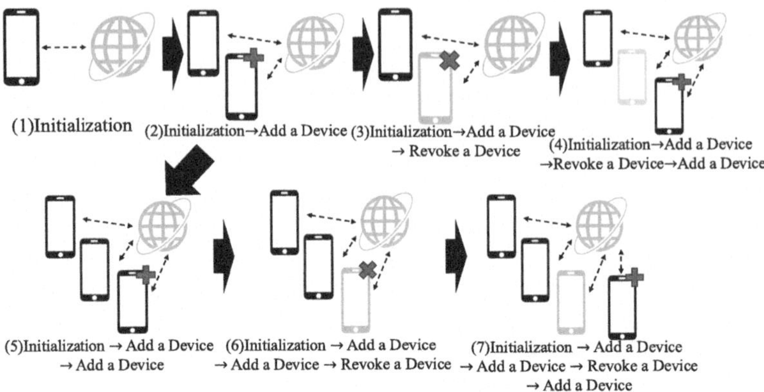

Fig. 1. Illustration of each verified flow (Arrows connecting each flow indicate the sequence of events. The practical protocol flows are all covered by these combinations.)

3.3 Sharing `newEpochEntropy`

If there are multiple devices remaining when updating an epoch, the `newEpochEntropy` created on one device must be shared with the other devices. However, the specification [5] does not explicitly specify the method of communication by which each device shares `newEpochEntropy`. In the verification of this paper, we verify both of the following for this bifurcation that occurs in the $*$ case of Sect. 3.1.

- communicated via a server
- directly between devices

The former is shared through the communication channel with the server's sub-process server as well as message storing and loading. For the latter, it formalizes the communication in a way that allows each targeted device sub-process access to the `private` channel and does not allow the attacker to intervene.

3.4 AEAD in Labyrinth

The original method AES-GCM-Extended is used as AEAD in Labyrinth. In the security verification of Labyrinth, AEAD is formalized as an ideally secure AEAD, rather than as the concrete scheme in the specification due to it requires an enormous amount of time for verification. We verify whether the concrete scheme AES-GCM-Extended is as secure as an ideally secure AEAD.

4 Verification Results

As a result of the security verification of Labyrinth, while the security claimed in the Labyrinth specification is satisfied, the use of a revoked device will definitively break the confidentiality and integrity of messages stored in previous epochs and conditionally[8] break the confidentiality and integrity of messages stored in the latest epoch. The specific conditions and the corresponding attacks are as follows.

1. At the time of device revocation, if there is only one non-revoked device remaining, the confidentiality of messages in previous epochs or the integrity of the remaining devices in reading back messages from previous epochs is broken.
2. When multiple non-revoked devices appear in the account at the time of device revocation and `newEpochEntropy` is shared from one device to the others,
   (a) if no adversary can intervene when `newEpochEntropy` is shared (e.g., the device owner transfers `newEpochEntropy` locally between devices), the same security as in 1. is broken.
   (b) if an adversary can intervene when sharing `newEpochEntropy` (e.g., the device owner sends `epochEntropyEncrypted` to the server and the server sends it to other devices), in addition to 1. and 2a., the confidentiality and the integrity of the messages in the new epoch are broken.

4.1 Intuitions of Attack Procedures

The security (confidentiality and integrity) of messages stored on previous epochs is broken by a natural attack considered by the availability of information on a revoked device. The security of messages stored in the latest epoch is only broken if `newEpochEntropy` is shared via a server (i.e., a situation where a intermediate party exists). In addition, the attack targets in this situation can be considered the sender and receiver of `newEpochEntropy`, respectively, both of which are attacks that aim to seize the messageKey of the latest epoch. Detailed procedures are omitted for reasons of space limitation.

5 Responsible Disclosure to Meta

We have reported to Meta via the Meta Bug Bounty [23] on the attack caused by the attacker's use of the revoked device, which is found in this study. The timeline and flow of the disclosure are as follows.

- On July 10, 2024, we sent Meta a report via the Meta Bug Bounty summarizing the series of attacks and stating that the security model should be extended to take into account the exploit of revoked devices.
- On October 8, 2024, after discussions of Meta Security with the corresponding product team, we were informed that the reported attack was a known vulnerability and was accepted during the design phase.

[8] The security is only broken if there is a man-in-the-middle adversary when sharing the epoch entropy. This corresponds to that obtained by the verification of the case of $*$ in Sect. 3.1.

- On November 11, 2024, we received permission from Meta to publish the results of this study.

Acknowledment. We would like to thank Meta Security for their consideration of our report. This work was supported by JST, CREST Grant Number JPMJCR22M1, Japan.

References

1. Messenger. https://www.messenger.com/
2. Most popular messaging apps 2025 — Statista. https://www.statista.com/statistics/258749/most-popular-global-mobile-messenger-apps/
3. Launching Default End-to-End Encryption on Messenger — Meta. https://about.fb.com/news/2023/12/default-end-to-end-encryption-on-messenger/
4. Messenger End-to-End Encryption Overview. https://engineering.fb.com/wp-content/uploads/2023/12/MessengerEnd-to-EndEncryptionOverview_12-6-2023.pdf
5. The Labyrinth Encrypted Message Storage Protocol. https://engineering.fb.com/wp-content/uploads/2023/12/TheLabyrinthEncryptedMessageStorageProtocol_12-6-2023.pdf
6. End-to-end encryption — Messenger Help Center. https://www.facebook.com/help/messenger-app/1084673321594605?helpref=hc_fnav
7. ProVerif. https://bblanche.gitlabpages.inria.fr/proverif/
8. Tamarin Prover. https://tamarin-prover.com/
9. Bhargavan, K., Blanchet, B., Kobeissi, N.: Verified models and reference implementations for the TLS 1.3 standard candidate. In: IEEE S&P (2017)
10. Sakurada, H., Yoneyama, K., Hanatani, Y., Yoshida, M.: Analyzing and fixing the QACCE security of QUIC. In: SSR (2016)
11. Jangid, M.K., Zhang, Y., Lin, Z.: Extrapolating formal analysis to uncover attacks in Bluetooth passkey entry pairing. In: NDSS (2023)
12. Feng, H., Guan, J., Li, H., Pan, X., Zhao, Z.: FIDO gets verified: a formal analysis of the universal authentication framework protocol. IEEE Trans. Dependable Secure Comput. **20**(5), 4291–4310 (2022)
13. Guan, J, Li, H., Ye, H., Zhao, Z.: A formal analysis of the FIDO2 protocols. In: ESORICS (2022)
14. LINE Encryption Overview (Ver. 1.0). https://scdn.line-apps.com/stf/linecorp/en/csr/line-encryption-whitepaper-ver1.0.pdf
15. LINE Encryption Overview (Ver. 2.1). https://scdn.line-apps.com/stf/linecorp/en/csr/line-encryption-whitepaper-ver2.1.pdf
16. Espinoza, A.M., Tolley, W.J., Crandall, J.R., Crete-Nishihata, M., Hilts, A.: Alice and Bob, who the FOCI are they?: Analysis of end-to-end encryption in the LINE messaging application. In: FOCI (2017)
17. Isobe, T., Minematsu, K.: Breaking message integrity of an end-to-end encryption scheme of LINE. In: ESORICS (2018)
18. Shi, C., Yoneyama, K.: Verification of LINE encryption version 1.0 using ProVerif. IEICE Transactions on Information and Systems (2019)
19. Blog - iMessage with PQ3: The new state of the art in quantum-secure messaging at scale - Apple Security Research. https://security.apple.com/blog/imessage-pq3/

20. Linker, F., Sasse, R., Basin., D.: A formal analysis of Apple's iMessage PQ3 protocol. In: USENIX Security (2025)
21. Isobe, T., Ito, R.: Security analysis of end-to-end encryption for zoom meetings. IEEE Access **9**, 90677–90689 (2021)
22. Davies, G.T., Faller, S., Gellert, K., Handirk, T., Hesse, J., Horváth, M., Jager, T.: Security analysis of the Whatsapp end-to-end encrypted backup protocol. In: CRYPTO (2023)
23. Program overview — Meta Bug Bounty. https://bugbounty.meta.com/

Automated VEX Generation and Vulnerability Prioritization Using Inter-Module Symbol Graphs

Jeongho Lee and Seyoung Lee(✉)

Kangwon National University, Kangwon, Republic of Korea
{jonglee32,seyoung}@kangwon.ac.kr

Abstract. In modern software supply chains, Software Bill of Materials(SBOM) based scanners can lead to *Alert Fatigue*. The Vulnerability Exploitability eXchange(VEX) standard involves a manual process for establishing justifications such as `vulnerable_code_not_in_execute_path`, which states that a component is not affected because the vulnerable code is not in the execution path. Automation of this process is limited due to Node.js's complex module system. This study proposes an automated VEX generation and vulnerability prioritization framework based on an *Inter-Module Symbol Graph* constructed using the static analysis tool CodeQL. This graph goes beyond package dependencies, considers Node.js's module resolution rules, and analyzes import and export information extracted from code to precisely track which component's API symbol calls another component's API symbol at the code level. The proposed system uses this graph to filter out vulnerabilities unreachable from the top-level application, reducing alerts by an average of 91.1% compared to existing Software Composition Analysis(SCA) tools. For the remaining actionable threats after filtering, structural metrics such as call depth and API utilization rate are analyzed to assess potential impact. Through this, the system automatically generates VEX documents and provides a prioritization model enabling developers and security teams to focus resources on specific threats amidst numerous alerts.

Keywords: Inter-module symbol graph · VEX · Software supply chain security · Static analysis · Node.js

1 Introduction

Modern software development is characterized by a deep reliance on the open-source ecosystem. Particularly in environments like Node.js, over 90% of application code can consist of Third-Party Libraries (TPLs) [4]. This complex supply chain structure has prompted the adoption of Software Bill of Materials (SBOM) to ensure transparency of software components. An SBOM is a data format that lists all components, libraries, and modules constituting a software product [7],

K.-W. Park and J. Park (Eds.): WISA 2025 2025, LNCS 16434, pp. 128–140, 2026.
https://doi.org/10.1007/978-981-95-6857-4_10

contributing to identifying and addressing affected software when vulnerabilities are found in specific components. However, SBOM-based automated scanners report vulnerabilities even in code not actually used by the project, leading to a side effect of severe *Alert Fatigue* for developers. Alert Fatigue is a phenomenon where repeated exposure to alerts reduces responsiveness to certain types of alerts [9]. In cybersecurity, it is recognized as a problem where excessive security alerts degrade the ability to respond to actual threats [11].

VEX (Vulnerability Exploitability eXchange), proposed to mitigate this alert fatigue problem, is a standard that provides an assertion about whether a specific product is affected by a known vulnerability. A VEX document specifies whether a component is affected or not_affected through the `status` field. When the status is not_affected, the reason is explicitly stated in the `justification` field. Representative justifications include vulnerable_code_not_present (vulnerable code is not present) and `vulnerable_code_not_in_execute_path` (vulnerable code is present but unreachable as it's not in the execution path) [1]. However, a major limitation of VEX is that the process of deriving these justifications, especially `vulnerable_code_not_in_execute_path`, is mostly manual [2].

The complexity of the Node.js environment further exacerbates this difficulty in automation. Node.js supports two distinct module systems, CommonJS (CJS) and ECMAScript Modules (ESM), each with differing behaviors and resolution rules, thus requiring precise consideration of both systems during static analysis [13]. In particular, the introduction of the `exports` field in `package.json` has increased the complexity of module resolution. This field allows fine-grained control over a package's public API, such as specifying entry points per subpath and providing conditional modules based on `import` and `require` statements. However, it makes it impossible to trace at the code level which file and `export` symbol a statement like `import "my-lib/feature"` actually connects to without Node.js's official module resolution algorithm [6]. These dynamic characteristics and diverse coding patterns make it a significant technical challenge to accurately determine call relationships solely through automated static analysis.

To address these issues, this study proposes a framework based on an *Inter-Module Symbol Graph* constructed using the static analysis tool CodeQL. CodeQL has been used to track inter-module dependencies or API usage flows in JavaScript/TypeScript code. The proposed symbol graph goes beyond a simple dependency map, precisely representing at the code level how specific API symbols from one component invoke API symbols of another.

The main contributions of this study are as follows:

First, unlike existing studies that focused on general call graph generation [5], this study presents a symbol graph construction methodology that precisely reflects the complex module resolution rules of the Node.js ecosystem, particularly the `exports` field, and accurately maps API call relationships between components at the symbol level based on extracted `import` and `export` information.

Second, going beyond SBOM-based component listing [8], it implements a framework that filters unreachable vulnerabilities based on this graph and automatically generates VEX documents including the `vulnerable_code_not_in_execute_path` justification.

Third, for the remaining actionable threats after filtering, it assesses potential impact using new structural metrics such as call depth and API utilization rate, and proposes a vulnerability prioritization model based on these metrics. This enables developers and security teams to focus resources on specific threats amidst numerous alerts.

2 Background

2.1 SBOM and VEX

An SBOM provides a formal, machine-readable inventory of software components and dependencies, enhancing supply chain transparency [7]. VEX complements SBOMs by providing an assertion about whether a specific product is affected by a known vulnerability. It aims to reduce alert fatigue by allowing producers to communicate exploitability status, using justifications like vulnerable_code_not_in_execute_path when a component is not affected [1]. This study focuses on automating the generation of such VEX statements.

2.2 CodeQL

Static analysis is a technique for finding errors or security vulnerabilities by analyzing source code without execution. This system adopts CodeQL, a powerful semantic code analysis engine. CodeQL builds a relational database from source code, representing complex code properties like data flow and control flow. Its ability to track inter-module dependencies in JavaScript/TypeScript through sophisticated queries provides the technical foundation for constructing the *Inter-Module Symbol Graph* proposed in this study [10].

3 Architecture

For VEX document generation, the proposed framework consists of four steps, as shown in Fig. 1: (1) Dependency Identification and Analysis Environment Setup, (2) Interface Extraction, (3) Inter-Module Symbol Graph Construction, and (4) Vulnerability Classification and Structural Risk Analysis. These steps enhance the precision of the analysis.

3.1 STEP 1: Dependency Identification and Analysis Environment Setup

The analysis environment setup identifies the analysis targets and lays the foundation for the framework. First, a CycloneDX SBOM is generated from the project [3] to identify direct and transitive dependency components and their relationships, and metadata such as name, version, and Package URL(PURL)

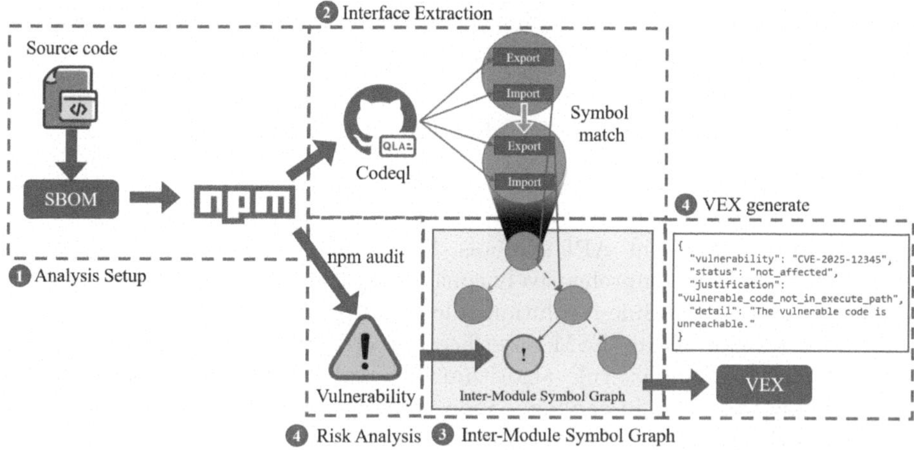

Fig. 1. Overall architecture of the proposed system.

are stored separately. By referencing the SBOM to download specified package versions from the npm registry and using the same source code that `npm install` fetches as the analysis target, both analysis reproducibility and accuracy are ensured. CodeQL databases are created from the acquired individual component source codes to complete the static analysis environment setup.

3.2 STEP 2: Interface Extraction

For symbol graph construction, each component's external interfaces—i.e., `export` / `import` statements—are identified at the code level. Using the CodeQL Databases generated in STEP 1, queries are executed to extract exported APIs and external module imports.

First, the component's Exported APIs are identified. CodeQL queries detect functions, classes, and variables exposed through CJS's `module.exports` assignments and `exports` object property additions, as well as ESM's `export` keyword. The extracted information includes API name, type, location, and relevant source code snippets. This algorithm analyzes source files to detect CommonJS `module.exports` and `exports` object assignment patterns and various ESM `export` syntaxes (default, named declaration, specifiers), and shows the procedure for extracting the module path, export name, type, location, and original code snippet for each export item.

Second, external module imports declared in the code are collected. CodeQL queries identify CJS `require()` and ESM `import` statements, and meticulously track used symbols, locations, and invocation methods (function calls, object instantiation, etc.). This is crucial for understanding actual call relationships between APIs. This algorithm describes how to find ESM `import` declarations and CommonJS `require()` calls in each source file, and collect the imported module path, used symbols (including aliases), import type (ES6/CJS), location information, and relevant code snippets.

3.3 STEP 3: Inter-Module Symbol Graph Construction

Based on the interface information from STEP 2, the *Inter-Module Symbol Graph* is constructed. This graph precisely represents code-level call/reference relationships between component API symbols. Semantic connections between symbols are extracted by comprehensively considering the extracted `import`/`export` statements, Node.js module resolution rules, and `package.json`.

Accurately identifying ESM interfaces is crucial. When resolving ESM, Node.js follows a complex rule algorithm [6] involving file extensions and the `type` and `exports` fields in `package.json`. This study utilizes this official specification and the `exports` field of each component's `package.json`. For example, the `exports` field determines which internal file a specific `import` path actually points to, or whether different files are provided based on conditions. This involves distinguishing and processing `bare specifiers` and relative paths separately, and ensuring that only explicitly allowed paths via the `exports` map are recognized as interfaces. A list of Node.js built-in modules clarifies the distinction from external packages, enhancing analysis accuracy.

Graph construction begins by analyzing the external module import information of each component. The system resolves identifiers specified in import statements according to Node.js module resolution rules to determine whether the reference is to an external package or an internal submodule of a package. Subsequently, by referring to the `exports` field defined in the target package's `package.json` to confirm intended API entry points and allowed paths, the candidate internal files that an import can point to are narrowed down, increasing connection accuracy. Node.js built-in modules are identified separately to distinguish them from external packages, and relative path imports are excluded from the analysis phase as they introduce unnecessary complexity in constructing the inter-module symbol graph.

After identifying the target callee module and candidate paths, it is necessary to match the symbols actually used by the **caller** with the symbols exported by the **callee**. This process is formalized as the SymbolMatch procedure in Algorithm 1. The algorithm takes as input (i) symbol name, alias, and usage type extracted from the `import` statement (`impD`), (ii) the list of exports exposed by the callee package (`expL`), (iii) the "`exports`" field of `package.json`, and (iv) the `import` subpath. It then scores path matches and type compatibility, returning the export with the highest score. Here, the `"exports"` field helps reduce the search space, thereby improving matching accuracy. The finally selected import/export pair is recorded as a graph edge, along with caller/callee information, call site, symbol context, and relationship type. As a result, an SBOM-level "A depends on B" relationship is refined to a code-level relationship like "A's `x.js` `foo()` calls B's `y.js` `Bar`", enhancing the precision of subsequent vulnerability propagation analysis.

3.4 STEP 4: Vulnerability Classification and Structural Risk Analysis

Finally, security analysis is performed using the symbol graph, consisting of vulnerability reachability-based classification and structural risk analysis.

First, classification based on vulnerability reachability assesses the actual impact of known vulnerabilities. Based on vulnerable components identified by npm audit, the existence of a call path from the top-level application to the vulnerable API on the symbol graph is determined. If no call path exists, it is classified as `vulnerable_code_not_in_execute_path`, becoming the basis for automatically generating a VEX document specifying `status: not_affected`. This filters out alerts for non-executable code, enhancing analysis accuracy.

Second, structural risk analysis supports the prioritization of *Actionable Threats* remaining after filtering. By analyzing topological metrics of the symbol graph, structural indicators such as reachability, average call depth, and API utilization rate are calculated for each threat-related component/API. These indicators quantitatively present the potential impact of vulnerabilities, helping to concentrate resources on critical threats. All analysis results and VEX information are provided in a comprehensive report.

Table 1. List of analyzed projects and summary of selection rationale

Project	Category	Trans. deps.	Weekly DLs	GH stars
Large-scale & Complex Projects				
`bower`	Package manager	207	280k	15.1k
`eslint`	Linter	153	58.2M	26k
`nodemon`	Dev utility	61	7.7M	26.2k
Widely-used & representative projects				
`jshint`	Linter	41	3.4M	8.6k
`prop-types`	Type checking	1	30M+	4.2k
`statsd`	Metrics daemon	5	N/A	17.4k
`grunt-cli`	Task runner CLI	32	240k	830
Minimal & focused projects				
`lodash`	Utility library	0	72.5M	60.6k
`is-odd`	Utility library	0	342k	N/A*
`chalk`	Terminal styling	2	325M	22.8k
`makeAppIcon`	Image utility	4	44	260
`generator`	Scaffolding tool	11	18k	342

The number of transitive dependencies, measured using 'npm ls –all'.

4 Evaluation

To validate the effectiveness and performance of the framework, we established three Research Questions (RQs): (1) How much does the system reduce alerts compared to existing Software Composition Analysis(SCA) tools (Actionable Threat Filtering)? (2) Do the extracted structural metrics help in assessing and prioritizing risk (Correlation Analysis)? and (3) Can the results aid the overall vulnerability management process (Practical Value)?

4.1 Experimental Design

The evaluation was conducted on 13 Node.js open-source projects selected considering various categories (linters, package managers, etc.), scales (0-207 transitive dependencies), and popularity (npm downloads, GitHub stars) (Table 1). These projects reflect the diversity and real-world complexity of the Node.js ecosystem and include benchmarks from prior studies [5,8] such as eslint and lodash to enhance objectivity. All experiments were conducted on Ubuntu 24.04.3 LTS using Node.js v22.16.0, npm v10.9.2, and CodeQL CLI v2.21.3. Vulnerability data was obtained through npm audit.

4.2 RQ1: Threat Filtering through Reachability Analysis

RQ1 evaluates how much `noise` (meaningless alerts) the proposed system removes from the warnings reported by existing tools. Tools widely used in the Node.js ecosystem, such as npm audit, report vulnerabilities considering only package dependencies, thus generating many false positives by alerting for vulnerabilities in libraries not actually used in the code. A prior study showed that utilizing call graphs can reduce false positives from npm audit by 81% [5]. Following this approach, vulnerabilities found in components unreachable by traversing the symbol graph from the top-level application were considered *Phantom Threats* and filtered out.

Table 2 shows that, as a result of the analysis, the proposed system automatically filtered an average of **91.1%** of vulnerability alerts across 12 projects. This figure surpasses the results of a prior study [5]. In 7 projects, including eslint and lodash, all reported vulnerabilities were unreachable, resulting in a 100% reduction rate. This means the system effectively removes alerts unrelated to the execution path, helping developers focus on actual threats, and can automatically generate VEX assertions with `status: not_affected` and `justification: vulnerable_code_not_in_execute_path`.

4.3 RQ2: Structural Metrics for Actionable Vulnerabilities

RQ2 verifies whether the proposed structural metrics contribute to the risk assessment of *actionable threats* remaining after filtering.

Table 2. Reduction rate of vulnerable component alerts through reachability analysis (RQ1)

Project	Total vuln. comp. (A) npm audit	Reachable vuln. comp. (B) Our System	Reduction rate (%) 100 * (1 - B/A)
`eslint`	12	0	**100%**
`lodash`	101	0	**100%**
`chalk`	7	0	**100%**
`prop-types`	47	0	**100%**
`statsd`	31	0	**100%**
`is-odd`	8	0	**100%**
`makeAppIcon`	1	0	**100%**
`jshint`	60	5	91.7%
`nodemon`	20	2	90.0%
`grunt-cli`	10	1	90.0%
`generator`	8	3	62.5%
`bower`	34	14	58.8%
Average			**91.1%**

Threat Proximity: Vulnerability Density at Call Depths. We hypothesized that actionable threats would be concentrated at shallow call depths. To verify this, we analyzed the **Vulnerability Density** at each call depth, i.e., the ratio of vulnerable components to the total reachable components at that depth (VulnDensity(D) $= N_{\text{vuln}}(D)/N_{\text{total}}(D)$). The comprehensive analysis showed that while the total number of components peaked at depth 2 (74 components), the vulnerability density was highest at depth 1 (**27.9%**), followed by 22.7% at depth 3, and decreased to below 5% at depths 4 and above. This suggests that components at depth 1, directly connected to the top-level application, structurally harbor high risk, and that call depth can be used as an indicator for assessing risk proximity.

Threat Impact: Invocation Frequency, Caller Diversity, and API Usage Rate. To assess component impact, we analyzed metrics such as **Invocation Frequency**, **Caller Diversity**, and **API Usage Rate (Export Usage Rate)**. For example, in the bower project, semver (call depth 1) was called 40 times from one component, while hoek (call depth 3) was called 50 times from 3 components, indicating a broader potential impact. Thus, these metrics provide clues for assessing the actual impact of vulnerabilities that cannot be determined by Common Vulnerability Scoring System(CVSS) scores alone. Furthermore, the average API usage rate per project reflected structural characteristics: the specific-purpose makeAppIcon (9.9%) showed high interdependency, while the complex eslint (1.8%) suggested loose coupling, aiding in the assessment of vulnerability propagation risk.

4.4 RQ3: A Practical Prioritization Model and Its Implications

RQ3 synthesizes the preceding analyses to present a framework that provides value to the vulnerability management process. In RQ1, *phantom threats* were eliminated, and in RQ2, risk assessment metrics for *actionable threats* were identified.

The Vulnerability Prioritization Matrix. RQ3 synthesizes the preceding analyses to present a framework that provides value to the vulnerability management process. For prioritizing actionable threats, we propose a 2x2 matrix model (Fig. 2) where the X-axis represents Risk Proximity (call depth) and the Y-axis represents Potential Impact (API usage rate). This model classifies threats into four actionable categories: (1) **Urgent Action** (top-left) for high-proximity, high-impact threats requiring immediate action; (2) **Core Dependency's Peripheral Threat** (top-right) for high-impact but low-proximity issues; (3) **Technical Debt** (bottom-right) for low-risk threats managed with lower priority; and (4) **Latent Supply Chain Risk** (bottom-left) for high-proximity threats with low current impact that require monitoring.

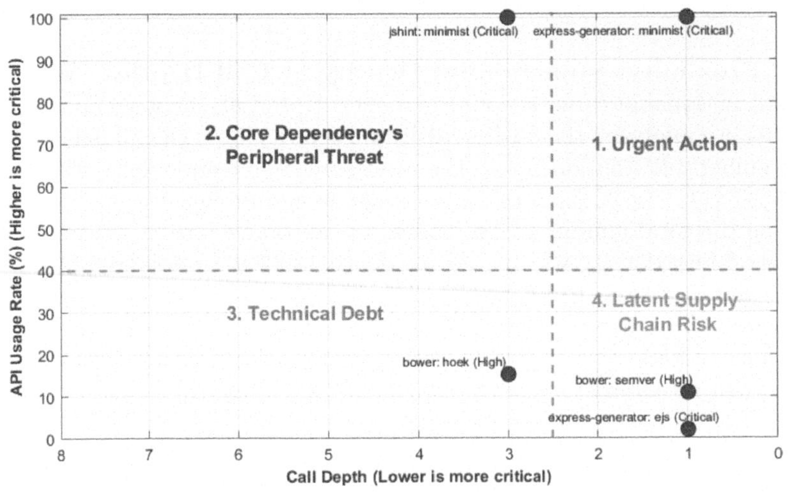

Fig. 2. Vulnerability prioritization matrix model

As a case study for applying the matrix, CVSS 9.8 Critical vulnerabilities (ejs, minimist) in express-generator are located at call depth 1 (highest risk density segment) and also have high API utilization, classifying them as **Quadrant 1 (Urgent Action)**, providing a basis for immediate action. In the case of bower, both semver (depth 1) and hoek (depth 3) have HIGH severity, but semver may be assessed as higher priority due to its higher risk proximity. jshint's minimist

(CRITICAL) is at call depth 3, but if its API utilization is low, it can be classified as **Quadrant 3 (Technical Debt)**, lowering its priority.

This framework (1) eliminates an average of 91.1% of alert noise, (2) assesses risk proximity through call depth, and (3) provides data-driven prioritization through the matrix, enabling effective allocation of limited security resources and improving the vulnerability management process. This is an approach that integrates the structural context of software beyond existing CVSS score-based management.

5 Related Work

Analyzing code reachability to reduce vulnerability alert noise is a core approach. A directly comparable prior work in this area proposed a modular call graph for Node.js applications, achieving an 81% reduction in false positive alerts reported by npm audit [5]. This was an important study demonstrating the effectiveness of call graphs for alert filtering. However, their research focused on call graph construction itself and did not directly link it to VEX document generation or vulnerability prioritization models. Building on this prior work, this study confirmed a 91.1% alert reduction rate through CodeQL's sophisticated semantic analysis, and further provides a comprehensive framework for automatically generating VEX documents based on filtered results and assessing structural risk.

One of the most recent studies proposed CovSBOM for the Java ecosystem, which integrates code coverage information into SBOMs to reduce false positives by approximately 72% [12]. This study shares the goal of assessing vulnerability effectiveness by analyzing actual code usage. However, CovSBOM measures code coverage, which relies on test execution, whereas our study performs purely static analysis to directly track symbol-level reachability, conducting an analysis specialized for Node.js's complex module systems (ESM/CJS). Furthermore, this study is differentiated by proposing a prioritization model using structural metrics that goes beyond simple filtering.

The fundamental need for such filtering approaches is clearly demonstrated in a large-scale study [4]. That research analyzed over 670,000 npm packages and statistically proved the *code bloat* problem, where, on average, only 9.5% of the code is actually used. This research provides strong evidence explaining why the majority of vulnerability alerts are unrelated to execution. Starting from the problem identified by that research, this study goes beyond merely measuring the existence of unused code to propose a concrete security solution that utilizes this insight to identify and manage actionable threats.

6 Conclusion and Future Work

This study addresses the problem of alert fatigue in software supply chains by proposing an automated framework for generating VEX documents and prioritizing vulnerabilities based on an *Inter-Module Symbol Graph*. The proposed system uses CodeQL to analyze module resolution rules in the Node.js ecosystem, identifying API call relationships between components at the symbol level.

Experimental evaluation demonstrated the effectiveness of this framework. First, through reachability analysis, it identified and filtered an average of 91.1% of vulnerability alerts reported by existing SCA tools as *phantom threats* unrelated to the execution path. This means that VEX assertions of vulnerable_code_not_in_execute_path can be automatically generated along with their justifications. Second, for the *actionable threats* remaining after filtering, risk was assessed by introducing new structural metrics such as call depth, API utilization rate, and invocation frequency. Vulnerability density analysis confirmed that risk proximity is a statistically significant indicator, which was used to determine the impact and urgency of vulnerabilities not ascertainable by CVSS scores alone. Finally, these metrics were integrated into a prioritization matrix model with two axes, risk proximity and `potential impact`, providing a data-driven decision-making framework for development teams to focus limited resources on specific threats.

This study has several limitations, which suggest directions for future research. The current framework relies on static analysis, making it difficult to trace code structures determined at runtime, such as `eval()` functions or dynamically generated **`require`** paths. Furthermore, the current framework focuses solely on the existence of call paths, i.e., reachability, to identify vulnerable_code_not_in_execute_path. Consequently, it has limitations in determining more granular VEX statuses, such as cases where vulnerable code is in the execution path but is not actually exploitable due to specific conditions or configurations (e.g., Vulnerable_code_cannot_be_controlled_by_adversary), or where defense mechanisms exist (e.g., `Inline_mitigations_already_exist`). Future research will explore introducing hybrid analysis combining static and dynamic analysis (such as taint analysis) to improve execution path accuracy, and developing functionality to automatically detect a wider range of VEX `justification` reasons through analysis of project configuration files, among others. Furthermore, by applying this model to other ecosystems like Python and Java to verify its generalizability, we aim to contribute to building a more reliable software supply chain security framework.

Acknowledgment. This work was supported by the Korea Internet & Security Agency (KISA) grant funded by the Korea government (Ministry of Science and ICT, MSIT) through the 'Information Security Workforce Development (Information Security Specialized University Program)' in 2026 and by the Institute of Information & Communications Technology Planning & Evaluation (IITP) grant funded by the Korea government (MSIT) under the Innovative Human Resource Development for Local Intellectualization program (IITP-2026-RS-2023-00260267).

Appendix

Algorithm 1 Symbol Matching Logic

```
impD ← caller_import_details        ▷ Includes ImportedSymbolName, Alias, UsageType, UsageContext
expL ← callee_export_list   ▷ List of [ExportName, ExportType, ExportFilePath]
calleePkgExp ← callee_package_exports_field
subpath ← import_subpath
Output:
Matched Callee Export or null
procedure SymbolMatch(impD, expL, calleePkgExp, subpath)
    targetName ← DetermineTargetName(impD)
    potentialPaths ← ResolveExpPaths(subpath, calleePkgExp)
    candidates ← ∅
    for each expItem in expL do
        if expItem.Name = targetName then
            score ← 0
            if IsPathMatch(expItem.FilePath, potentialPaths) then
                score ← score + PRIORITY_PATH        ▷ Path match
            end if
            if IsTypeCompatible(impD.UsageType, expItem.Type) then
                score ← score + PRIORITY_TYPE        ▷ Type match
            end if
            if score > 0 then
                Add (expItem, score) to candidates
            end if
        end if
    end for
    if candidates ≠ ∅ then
        return item with highest score from candidates
    else
        return null
    end if
end procedure
```

References

1. Cybersecurity, Agency, I.S.: Vulnerability exploitability exchange (vex)-status justifications. Tech. rep., CISA (2022), https://www.cisa.gov/sites/default/files/publications/VEX_Status_Justification_Jun22.pdf
2. Cybersecurity, Agency, I.S.: Vulnerability exploitability exchange (vex)-use cases. Tech. rep., CISA (2022), https://www.cisa.gov/sites/default/files/publications/VEX_Use_Cases_Aprill2022.pdf

3. CycloneDX: cyclonedx-node-npm.: https://github.com/CycloneDX/cyclonedx-node-npm, gitHub repository (2022)
4. Koishybayev, I., Kapravelos, A.: Mininode: Reducing the attack surface of node. js applications. In: 23rd International Symposium on Research in Attacks, Intrusions and Defenses (RAID 2020). pp. 121–134 (2020)
5. Nielsen, B.B., Torp, M.T., Møller, A.: Modular call graph construction for security scanning of node. js applications. In: Proceedings of the 30th ACM SIGSOFT International Symposium on Software Testing and Analysis. pp. 29–41 (2021)
6. Node.js Foundation: Ecmascript modules. https://nodejs.org/api/esm.html (2024), node.js v24.2.0 Documentation
7. OWASP Foundation: CycloneDX Bill of Materials Standard. Web page (2024), https://cyclonedx.org/
8. Rabbi, M.F., Champa, A.I., Nachuma, C., Zibran, M.F.: Sbom generation tools under microscope: A focus on the npm ecosystem. In: Proceedings of the 39th ACM/SIGAPP Symposium on Applied Computing. pp. 1233–1241 (2024)
9. Rush, J.L., Ibrahim, J., Saul, K., Brodell, R.T.: Improving patient safety by combating alert fatigue (2016)
10. Szabó, T.: Incrementalizing production codeql analyses. In: Proceedings of the 31st ACM Joint European Software Engineering Conference and Symposium on the Foundations of Software Engineering. pp. 1716–1726 (2023)
11. Tariq, S., Baruwal Chhetri, M., Nepal, S., Paris, C.: Alert fatigue in security operations centres: Research challenges and opportunities. ACM Comput. Surv. **57**(9), 1–38 (2025)
12. Zhao, Y., Zhang, Y., Chacko, D., Cappos, J.: Covsbom: Enhancing software bill of materials with integrated code coverage analysis. In: 2024 IEEE 35th International Symposium on Software Reliability Engineering (ISSRE). pp. 228–237. IEEE (2024)
13. Zimmermann, M., Staicu, C.A., Tenny, C., Pradel, M.: Small world with high risks: A study of security threats in the npm ecosystem. In: 28th USENIX security symposium (USENIX Security 19). pp. 995–1010 (2019)

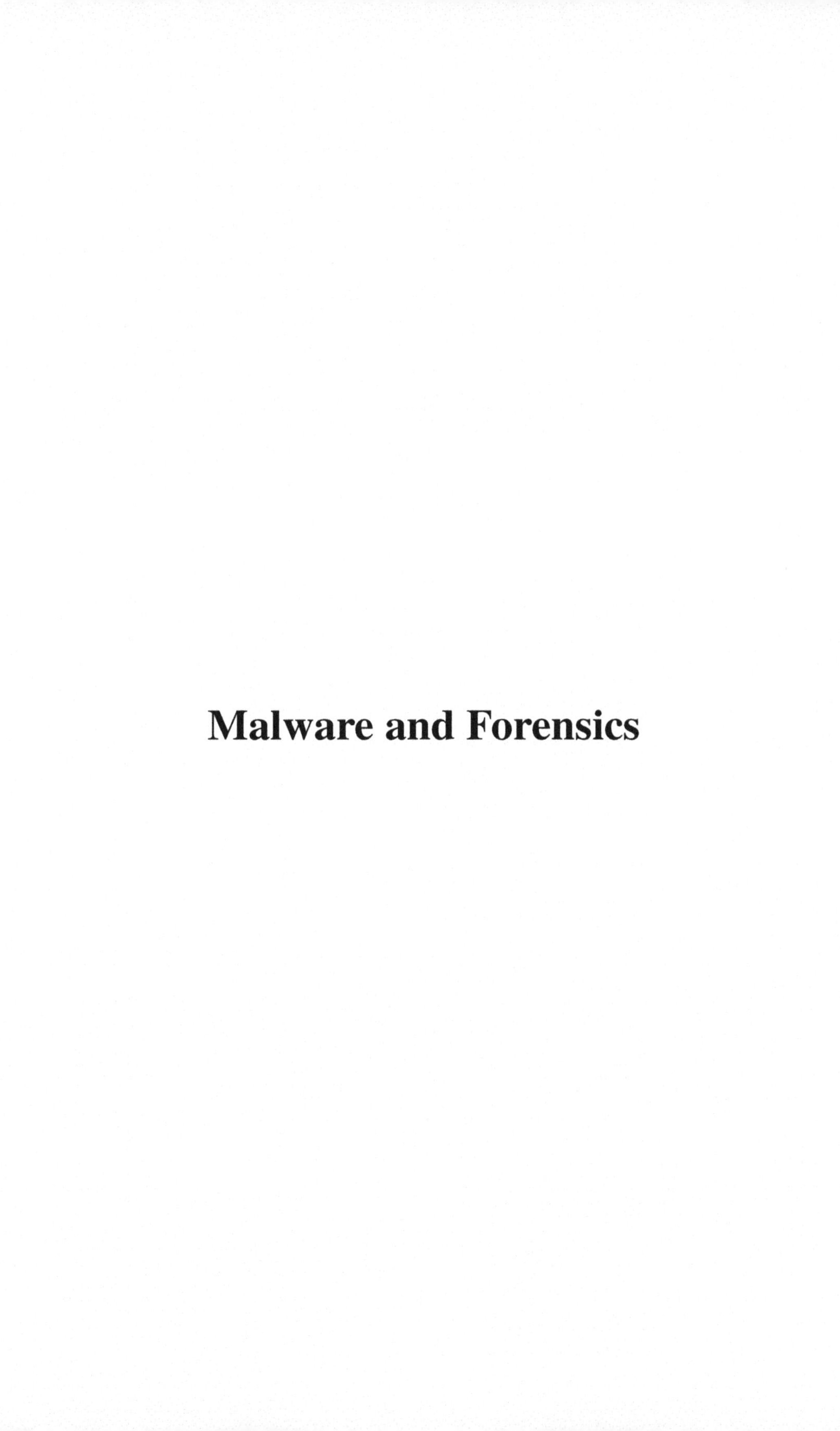

Malware and Forensics

User Conversation Recovery from ChatGPT Local Artifacts in Web Browsers for Digital Forensic Investigations

Minjung Yoo, Seunghyun Park, and Seongmin Kim(✉)

Sungshin Women's University, Seoul, Korea
{20211097,20211058,sm.kim}@sungshin.ac.kr

Abstract. Generative AI is a technology that automatically generates various forms of content, such as text, images, and code, and is rapidly spreading with the recent popularization of services such as ChatGPT. While these technologies have greatly improved productivity and convenience, they are also emerging as a security threat, with reports of them being used to commit cybercrime, such as ransomware creation and writing phishing emails. Nevertheless, digital forensic analysis of generative AI usage has been largely limited to mobile application environments, and there is a lack of research on Web browser-based usage traces, which are most commonly utilized by real-world users. This study aims to analyze digital artifacts generated in Web browser usage environments, with a focus on ChatGPT, and to present user activity data that can be utilized in investigations.

Keywords: Generative AI · Web browser artifacts · Digital forensic

1 Introduction

Generative artificial intelligence (Generative AI) has recently achieved significant advancements across various domains, including software development and education. Automatically creating diverse types of content- including text, images, and videos—based on user inputs enhances user convenience by enabling individuals and non-experts to produce professional-quality outputs easily. According to Netcraft, a cybersecurity company, the number of Websites containing AI-generated text increased nearly fourfold between March and August 2024 [1]. One prominent example of generative AI solution is ChatGPT, launched by OpenAI in 2022. Since its introduction, ChatGPT has garnered global attention and substantially contributed to the widespread adoption and popularization of generative AI.

However, generative AI has concurrently been exploited to advance cybercrime techniques, thereby emerging as a significant security threat. Recent reports highlight numerous instances where AI-based services like ChatGPT

K.-W. Park and J. Park (Eds.): WISA 2025 2025, LNCS 16434, pp. 143–155, 2026.
https://doi.org/10.1007/978-981-95-6857-4_11

were abused in various criminal activities, including ransomware creation, malicious software development, and scripts designed to bypass security measures [2–4]. For example, Check Point Research, a cybersecurity firm, demonstrated ChatGPT's potential misuse by employing it to generate phishing emails, Excel files embedded with malicious VBA code, and reverse shells [5]. Consequently, generative AI simultaneously enhances convenience and productivity while posing tangible security risks, emphasizing the urgent need for robust institutional and technical preparations to address these threats, which currently lag behind the rapid pace of technological advancement.

Given this context, a systematic analysis of generative AI misuse and the development of effective countermeasures are necessary. Previous studies primarily concentrated on analyzing forensic traces from generative AI services, with significant efforts directed toward log and cache data analysis in mobile application environments and their investigative potential [7,8]. However, browser-based environments—where most general users commonly interact with generative AI—have received relatively limited attention. This gap suggests a potential oversight of key forensic artifacts that could be crucial evidence in real-world investigations, marking an important research gap to be addressed.

This study aims to systematically analyze the forensic artifacts generated from using generative AI, specifically ChatGPT, in Web browser environments. By examining browser artifacts comprehensively, this research intends to uncover user activity data applicable to investigative scenarios. To achieve this, we analyzed foundational browser artifacts, including history and cache, to identify access patterns and browsing evidence related to ChatGPT, and further explored the IndexedDB structure to extract detailed conversational contents. These findings demonstrate that user activities, including conversation contents, can be reconstructed solely from local artifacts without relying on user account information or cooperation from the service provider, thereby enabling independent forensic investigations of generative AI services like ChatGPT.

2 Background and Literature Review

2.1 Usage Modes of Generative AI Services

Users typically access generative AI services such as ChatGPT through multiple channels, broadly categorized into Web browser-based access and dedicated application-based access. Web browser-based access enables users to interact with services directly through the official Website or via platforms integrated with this technology. This method is the most commonly adopted approach due to its ease of use and the absence of additional software installation. In contrast, dedicated application-based access involves installing applications on mobile devices or desktop computers. Recently, the availability of numerous third-party applications alongside the official mobile app has also significantly expanded the use of dedicated applications [13].

These variations in access methods consequently influence the type and distribution of data generated by user activities. In mobile application environments, user activity traces are typically stored in application logs, caches, and file storage. However, in Web browser environments, the residual data types and storage methods vary depending on the browser architecture. Thus, recognizing the distinct characteristics of each access method is essential for effective forensic artifact analysis.

2.2 Generative AI Artifact Analysis

Generative AI is capable of performing diverse tasks, including generating text and programming code. With the increasing availability of generative AI services through both Web browsers and dedicated applications, user convenience and accessibility have significantly improved. Along with this, research is actively underway to collect and analyze various types of artifacts generated during the use of generative AI, such as text, code, and logs, in order to explore the storage location, structure, and type of data.

Dragonas et al. [7] analyzed the data stored by the ChatGPT mobile application on Android and iOS to discover artifacts that could be utilized from a digital forensics perspective. Arsa et al. [8] analyzed the types of data accessed by each application in a mobile device environment, targeting ChatGPT, Gemini, and Copilot, and examined the potential security threats that could arise from this. Additionally, Cho et al. [14] analyzed forensic artifacts collected from real-world usage environments for major generative AI services including ChatGPT, Gemini, Copilot, and Claude, and proposed generalized analysis procedures and a forensic analysis framework based on open-source tools.

Previous studies have predominantly concentrated on collecting artifacts from generative AI-based conversational services within mobile environments, analyzing them from forensic and security perspectives. However, despite the widespread use of generative AI services via Web browsers in desktop environments, systematic analysis of artifacts generated in these contexts remains insufficient. Moreover, research exploring the collection of such data and evaluating its potential application to digital investigations and security practices is relatively limited, highlighting the need for further investigation.

3 Experimental Environment and Data Acquisition

To obtain forensic artifacts for investigating the misuse of ChatGPT, we conduct an empirical analysis covering multiple usage scenarios. The experimental environment was set up using a Windows 10 virtual machine, simulating typical user interactions with ChatGPT via the Chrome browser. The simulation consisted of the following steps: (1) launching the browser, (2) accessing the ChatGPT Website, (3) logging into a user account, (4) interacting with ChatGPT (through four distinct scenarios), and (5) subsequently logging out. All interactions were conducted using the same Google account to ensure consistency. To analyze variations in forensic artifacts associated with different user accounts, we repeated the experiment using two separate accounts. Detailed descriptions of each scenario are provided in Table 1. Note that Scenario 3 focuses on identifying artifacts generated during image-related interactions; thus, if ChatGPT generated an image, the simulation included downloading this image to the desktop. Scenario 4 examines artifacts generated when the "Search the Web" feature is enabled during the ChatGPT conversation.

Table 1. Detailed description of test scenarios

Category	Purpose	Detailed Scenarios
Scenario 1	Identify artifacts generated during default conversations	1. Hi 2. How's the weather today? 3. Apple 4. banana
Scenario 2	Identify artifacts generated during default conversations	1. Hi 2. tree 3. sea 4. mountain
Scenario 3	Identify artifacts generated during image-related conversation	1. Hi 2. Please draw a picture of a tree 3. Please draw a picture of an apple 4. What does a tomato look like?
Scenario 4	Identify artifacts generated when using the "Search the Web" feature	1. Hi 2. (Search the Web function enabled) I wonder what a tree looks like. 3. (Search the Web function enabled) What does an apple look like? 4. (Search the Web function enabled) What does a tomato look like?

Upon completion of user activity simulations, the VM disk image is acquired by copying the VM's disk file while it is powered off. The disk image is then extracted from the `.vmdk` file using FTK Imager, resulting in two separate images: one following the first simulation and another after the second. The Chrome browser stores installation-specific state and user profile data within the directory path `C:/Users/<username>/AppData/Local/Google/Chrome/User Data`. Forensic artifacts, such as Cache and History files, are located specifically in `C:/Users/ <username>/AppData/Local/Google/Chrome/User Data/Default`, and these artifact files are extracted for subsequent analysis of the user's Web activity. The History file, which is stored in SQLite format, is analyzed using SQLiteStudio, while the Cache data is examined using a HEX editor. In addition, the IndexedDB folder, located in the same Chrome directory, is extracted and converted into JSON format using publicly available tools to facilitate easier analysis [15]. The file paths of the extracted artifacts are listed in Table 2.

Table 2. Directory paths of Google Chrome Browser artifacts

Artifacts	Directory paths
History	AppData\Local \Google \Chrome \User Data \Default \History
Cache	AppData \Local \Google \Chrome \User Data \Default \Cache
IndexedDB	AppData \Local \Google \Chrome \User Data \Default \IndexedDB

4 ChatGPT Forensic Artifact Analysis

We aim to forensically acquire and analyze digital artifacts stored on disk that are associated with the use of generative AI services accessed through Web browsers. In this section, we present the results of our forensic analysis of the ChatGPT Web application.

4.1 Web Browser Default Artifacts

The History file contains a comprehensive record of the user's Web browsing activity. The `visits` table includes timestamps indicating when each page was accessed. Since the actual URLs are not directly stored in this table, correlation with the `urls` table using pointer references is necessary. The `urls` table provides the actual URL addresses along with their respective page types. The results from the `urls` table obtained during our analysis are shown in Fig. 1. The figure demonstrates that the user searched for ChatGPT using the search bar, accessed the service, and logged in by selecting the Google account option. The URL format of the chat window follows the structure "https://chatgpt.com/c/[UUID]", with the corresponding chat titles stored in the title field. For example, Fig. 1 illustrates two distinct UUID-based URLs and their associated titles, clearly indicating the creation of two separate conversations by the user. In addition, within the `content_annotations` table, the `password_state` value indicates the status of the login process. Typically, this field holds a value of 0, changes to 1 when a login attempt occurs, and is updated to 2 upon successful authentication.

Under typical conditions, the ChatGPT Web application does not store response content in the browser cache; however, metadata such as response headers or certificate details may be cached client-side. When analyzing the `data1` file within the browser cache for the keywords *conversation* and *ChatGPT*, we identified entries containing request URLs structured as "https://chatgpt.com/backend-api/conversation/[UUID]/textdocs", as illustrated in Fig. 2. Although the response body itself is not preserved, the existence of these API requests indicates conversation interactions. For further analysis, the cache address of the corresponding data stream entry is computed, locating the associated cache file (`data2`), which includes metadata like response headers and certificate chains, as shown in Fig. 3. These artifacts concretely demonstrate that conversation interactions took place.

In contrast, when the "Search the Web" feature is enabled within ChatGPT, certain portions of response data are locally cached. Visual elements such as

160	https://www.google.com/search?...	chat gpt - search
161	https://www.google.com/search?...	chat gpt - search
162	https://auth.openai.com/api/accounts/authorize?...	Login - ChatGPT
163	https://accounts.google.com/o/oauth2/v2/auth?response_type=code&client_id=799222349882-...	Login – Google Account
164	https://accounts.google.com/o/oauth2/v2/auth?response_type=code&client_id=799222349882-...	Login – Google Account
165	https://accounts.google.com/o/oauth2/v2/auth/oauthchooseaccount?...	Login – Google Account
166	https://accounts.google.com/v3/signin/identifier?response_type=code&client_id=799222349882-...	Login – Google Account
167	https://accounts.google.com/v3/signin/challenge/pwd?TL=ALgCv6wla7SJbl1dY_WU1ORokUSpvx_nUwle-...	Login – Google Account
168	https://accounts.google.com/CheckCookie?continue=https://accounts.google.com/signin/oauth/consent?...	Redirecting
169	https://accounts.youtube.com/accounts/SetSID?ssdc=1&sidt=ALWU2cuqU0xzWYZDvJAqUIUcnD2HOj1/...	Redirecting
170	https://accounts.google.co.kr/accounts/SetSID?ssdc=1&sidt=ALWU2ctT0dblYL8K4mbAH/...	Redirecting
171	https://accounts.google.co.kr/accounts/SetSID	ChatGPT
172	https://accounts.google.com/signin/oauth/consent?authuser=0&part=AJi8hANHDEdkYsXxhi0ZH0HySmrfpR...	ChatGPT
173	https://accounts.google.com/ServiceLogin?...	ChatGPT
174	https://accounts.google.com/InteractiveLogin?authuser=0&continue=https://accounts.google.com/signin/...	ChatGPT
175	https://accounts.google.com/signin/oauth/consent?authuser=0&part=AJi8hANHDEdkYsXxhi0ZH0HySmrfpR...	ChatGPT
176	https://auth.openai.com/api/accounts/callback/google?state=32ef0b9c-...	ChatGPT
177	https://auth.openai.com/api/oauth/oauth2/auth?...	ChatGPT
178	https://auth.openai.com/api/accounts/consent?consent_challenge=29rAQ--...	ChatGPT
179	https://auth.openai.com/api/oauth/oauth2/auth?...	ChatGPT
180	https://chatgpt.com/api/auth/callback/openai?...	ChatGPT
181	https://chatgpt.com/c/685050e9-8b3c-8002-9d15-681962299721	Today's Weather Forecast
182	https://chatgpt.com/c/6850515d-fa18-8002-8f0a-484fd6a73ba3	Tree Clarification

Fig. 1. URL records retrieved from the Chrome History file

```
001C0900  DD 5B 14 7A 00 00 00 00 9F 0D 00 90 00 00 00 00  Ý[.z....Ÿ.......
001C0910  00 00 00 00 00 00 00 00 E2 E2 78 16 7C 96 2F 00  ........ââx.|-/.
001C0920  8A 00 00 00 00 00 00 00 84 0B 00 00 02 00 00 00  Š.......„.......
001C0930  00 00 00 00 00 00 00 00 74 21 02 B2 EA 1B 01 A0  ........t!.²ê..
001C0940  00 00 00 00 00 00 00 00 00 00 00 00 00 00 00 00  ................
001C0950  00 00 00 00 00 00 00 00 00 00 00 00 CD E4 10 C8  ............Íä.È
001C0960  31 2F 30 2F 5F 64 6B 5F 68 74 74 70 73 3A 2F 2F  1/0/_dk_https://
001C0970  63 68 61 74 67 70 74 2E 63 6F 6D 20 68 74 74 70  chatgpt.com http
001C0980  73 3A 2F 2F 63 68 61 74 67 70 74 2E 63 6F 6D 20  s://chatgpt.com 
001C0990  68 74 74 70 73 3A 2F 2F 63 68 61 74 67 70 74 2E  https://chatgpt.
001C09A0  63 6F 6D 2F 62 61 63 6B 65 6E 64 2D 61 70 69 2F  com/backend-api/
001C09B0  63 6F 6E 76 65 72 73 61 74 69 6F 6E 2F 36 38 35  conversation/685
001C09C0  33 39 63 36 63 2D 66 39 61 63 2D 38 30 30 32 2D  39c6c-f9ac-8002-
001C09D0  62 39 63 33 2D 35 34 64 65 32 32 30 30 38 65 65  b9c3-54de22008ee
001C09E0  35 2F 74 65 78 74 64 6F 63 73 00 00 00 00 00 00  5/textdocs......
```

Fig. 2. ChatGPT API request URLs found in the data1 file of the cache

images or favicons hosted externally are stored in the cache, identifiable through URLs with `.jpg` formats. These cache entries indicate external content referenced during response generation, providing useful insights into third-party materials indirectly viewed by the user. Figure 4 illustrates cache data from Scenario 4, in which the "Search the Web" feature was activated. By computing the `data stream[1]` value of the entry and tracing it to the corresponding cache file, the cached image file can be examined.

4.2 IndexedDB Artifacts

When interacting with the ChatGPT Web application via Chrome, we observed that client-side IndexedDB captures information, such as conversation content and interface states resulting from interactions with the Web server. The Chrome browser creates one or more IndexedDB instances per origin and internally stores data locally using the LevelDB format. Specifically, accessing ChatGPT through the Web creates an IndexedDB instance named "https_chatgpt.com_0.indexeddb.leveldb" within Chrome's IndexedDB directory. This database is generated for each login session and structured according to the specific Google account

```
0085F000  80 0B 00 00 03 65 4F 8A 06 00 00 00 FD E5 78 16  €....eOŠ....ýåx.
0085F010  7C 96 2F 00 9A 63 82 16 7C 96 2F 00 9A 63 82 16  |-/.šc,.|-/.šc,.
0085F020  7C 96 2F 00 9D 02 00 00 48 54 54 50 2F 31 2E 31  |-/.....HTTP/1.1
0085F030  20 32 30 30 00 64 61 74 65 3A 54 68 75 2C 20 31   200.date:Thu, 1
0085F040  39 20 4A 75 6E 20 32 30 32 35 20 30 35 3A 31 33  9 Jun 2025 05:13
0085F050  3A 32 33 20 47 4D 54 00 63 6F 6E 74 65 6E 74 2D  :23 GMT.content-
0085F060  74 79 70 65 3A 61 70 70 6C 69 63 61 74 69 6F 6E  type:application
0085F070  2F 6A 73 6F 6E 00 63 6F 6E 74 65 6E 74 2D 6C 65  /json.content-le
0085F080  6E 67 74 68 3A 32 00 78 2D 65 6E 76 6F 79 2D 75  ngth:2.x-envoy-u
0085F090  70 73 74 72 65 61 6D 2D 73 65 72 76 69 63 65 2D  pstream-service-
0085F0A0  74 69 6D 65 3A 31 35 30 00 63 66 2D 63 61 63 68  time:150.cf-cach
0085F0B0  65 2D 73 74 61 74 75 73 3A 44 59 4E 41 4D 49 43  e-status:DYNAMIC
0085F0C0  00 72 65 70 6F 72 74 2D 74 6F 3A 7B 22 65 6E 64  .report-to:{"end
0085F0D0  70 6F 69 6E 74 73 22 3A 5B 7B 22 75 72 6C 22 3A  points":[{"url":
0085F0E0  22 68 74 74 70 73 3A 5C 2F 5C 2F 61 2E 6E 65 6C  "https:\/\/a.nel
0085F0F0  2E 63 6C 6F 75 64 66 6C 61 72 65 2E 63 6F 6D 5C  .cloudflare.com\
0085F100  2F 72 65 70 6F 72 74 5C 2F 76 34 3F 73 3D 71 76  /report\/v4?s=qv
```

Fig. 3. Metadata identified in cache file (data2)

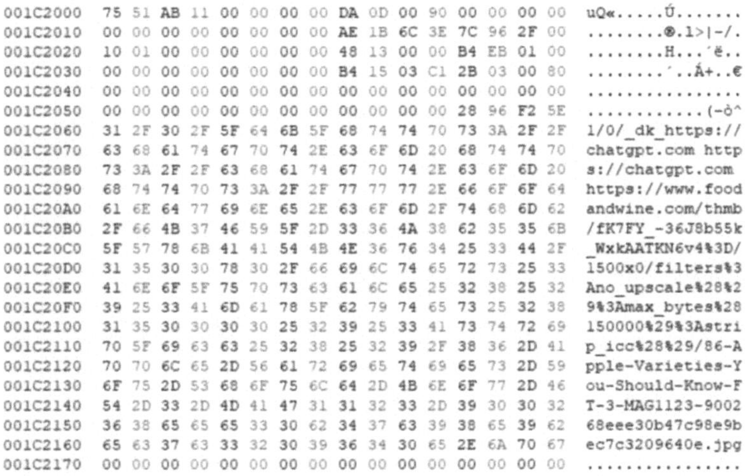

```
001C2000  75 51 AB 11 00 00 00 00 DA 0D 00 90 00 00 00 00  uQ«.....Ú.......
001C2010  00 00 00 00 00 00 00 00 AE 1B 6C 3E 7C 96 2F 00  ........®.l>|-/.
001C2020  10 01 00 00 00 00 00 00 48 13 00 00 B4 EB 01 00  ........H...´ë..
001C2030  00 00 00 00 00 00 00 00 B4 15 03 C1 2B 03 00 80  ........´..Á+..€
001C2040  00 00 00 00 00 00 00 00 00 00 00 00 00 00 00 00  ................
001C2050  00 00 00 00 00 00 00 00 00 00 00 00 28 96 F2 5E  ............(-ò^
001C2060  31 2F 30 2F 5F 64 6B 5F 68 74 74 70 73 3A 2F 2F  1/0/_dk_https://
001C2070  63 68 61 74 67 70 74 2E 63 6F 6D 20 68 74 74 70  chatgpt.com http
001C2080  73 3A 2F 2F 63 68 61 74 67 70 74 2E 63 6F 6D 20  s://chatgpt.com 
001C2090  68 74 74 70 73 3A 2F 2F 77 77 77 2E 66 6F 6F 64  https://www.food
001C20A0  61 6E 64 77 69 6E 65 2E 63 6F 6D 2F 74 68 6D 62  andwine.com/thmb
001C20B0  2F 66 4B 37 46 59 5F 2D 33 36 4A 38 62 35 35 6B  /fK7FY_-36J8b55k
001C20C0  5F 57 78 6B 41 41 54 4B 4E 36 76 34 25 33 44 2F  _WxkAATKN6v4%3D/
001C20D0  31 35 30 30 78 30 2F 66 69 6C 74 65 72 73 25 33  1500x0/filters%3
001C20E0  41 6E 6F 5F 75 70 73 63 61 6C 65 25 32 38 25 32  Ano_upscale%28%2
001C20F0  39 25 33 41 6D 61 78 5F 62 79 74 65 73 25 32 38  9%3Amax_bytes%28
001C2100  31 35 30 30 30 30 25 32 39 25 33 41 73 74 72 69  150000%29%3Astri
001C2110  70 5F 69 63 63 25 32 38 25 32 39 2F 38 36 2D 41  p_icc%28%29/86-A
001C2120  70 70 6C 65 2D 56 61 72 69 65 74 69 65 73 2D 59  pple-Varieties-Y
001C2130  6F 75 2D 53 68 6F 75 6C 64 2D 4B 6E 6F 77 2D 46  ou-Should-Know-F
001C2140  54 2D 33 2D 4D 41 47 31 31 32 33 2D 39 30 30 32  T-3-MAG1123-9002
001C2150  36 38 65 65 65 33 30 62 34 37 63 39 38 65 39 62  68eee30b47c98e9b
001C2160  65 63 37 63 33 32 30 39 36 34 30 65 2E 6A 70 67  ec7c3209640e.jpg
001C2170  00 00 00 00 00 00 00 00 00 00 00 00 00 00 00 00  ................
```

Fig. 4. Image URLs found in cache when using "Search the Web" feature

used. In our second test, logging in with a different Google account confirmed that data from the previous account was not retained but replaced entirely with information corresponding to the newly logged-in account. This indicates that IndexedDB data is session-specific rather than persistent across multiple user accounts. As depicted in Fig. 5, the database comprises multiple `.ldb` files along with additional associated files such as `.log` and `CURRENT`.

Figure 6 presents the contents of a `.ldb` file examined using a hex editor, highlighting the presence of the keyword *ConversationDatabase*, which indicates storage of conversation-related information at this location. This means that reconstructing and consolidating the LevelDB structure is necessary for a comprehensive analysis. To this end, the LevelDB data was converted into `.json` format and subsequently parsed to facilitate detailed investigation. As illustrated

Name	Size	Type
$I30	4,096 (4 KB)	NTFS Index Allocation
000022.ldb	29,062 (29 KB)	Regular File
000026.ldb	18,156 (18 KB)	Regular File
000028.log	46 (1 KB)	Regular File
000031.ldb	308 (1 KB)	Regular File
CURRENT	16 (1 KB)	Regular File
LOCK	0 (0 KB)	Regular File
LOG	3,067 (3 KB)	Regular File
LOG.old	142 (1 KB)	Regular File
MANIFEST-000025	1,417 (2 KB)	Regular File

Fig. 5. Structure of https_chatgpt.com_0.indexeddb.leveldb

in Fig. 7, the results confirm that the complete list of conversations associated with the logged-in ChatGPT account is stored within IndexedDB, with each conversation represented in a structured data format.


```
00000000  F0 29 08 00 0F 00 01 01 14 32 01 01 00 CD 03 01  ð).......2...Í..
00000010  0A 14 00 07 08 00 01 C4 09 0B 0C 08 07 33 BE 09  .......Ä.....3¾.
00000020  0A 88 0A 19 12 17 0A 15 43 6F 6E 76 65 72 73 61  .ˆ......Conversa
00000030  74 69 6F 6E 73 44 61 74 61 62 61 73 65 0A 16 08  tionsDatabase...
00000040  01 12 12 0A 10 05 3D 08 00 00 02 0D 08 18 01 06  ......=.........
00000050  09 00 02 00 DF 09 3F 01 54 00 D6 09 0B 0C 08 07  ....ß.?.T.Ö.....
00000060  33 D0 09 0A CA 54 00 1C 05 13 00 02 01 00 7F FF  3Ð..ÊT.........ÿ
00000070  05 01 08 FB 00 C8 09 49 14 10 08 DE 01 01 C7 09  ...û.È.I...Þ..Ç.
00000080  0C F0 65 0A DB 01 0A 8B 01 00 02 01 20 01 1D 00  .ðe.Û..‹.... ...
00000090  75 00 73 00 65 00 72 00 2D 00 74 00 53 00 57 00  u.s.e.r.-.t.S.W.
000000A0  43 00 57 00 4F 00 77 00 63 00 4C 00 78 00 59 00  C.W.O.w.c.L.x.Y.
000000B0  7A 00 36 00 72 00 4F 00 38 00 30 00 46 00 74 00  z.6.r.O.8.0.F.t.
```


Fig. 6. An .ldb file containing the ConversationDatabase keyword

The `id` field within the value object corresponds exactly to its associated key. By matching this identifier with the session identifier recorded in the browser's History file (i.e., /c/[UUID]), it becomes possible to trace conversation activities at specific points in time. Additionally, entries sharing the same key represent conversations created within a single session, enabling comprehensive analysis of the number of conversations and their query contents. The fields `accountUserId` and `authUserId` serve as unique identifiers associated with each ChatGPT login account. Our first and second test sessions confirmed these values differ when distinct accounts are used. The `title` field contains the conversation's title, while `updateTime` records the timestamp of the last data update. These fields facilitate constructing a timeline of user activity, helping pinpoint the most recent conversations. By correlating `updateTime` with browser History records, conversation initiation times and subsequent access patterns can be precisely reconstructed.

The `messages` field contains all text exchanged between the user and ChatGPT, structured as pairs of `id` and `text` content. Each `text` entry includes the actual message, while each `id` is a UUID uniquely assigned to that message. All conversation IDs consistently start with the prefix *client-created-root*.

```
{
  "key": "b'\\x01$\\x006\\x008\\x005\\x003\\x009\\x00c\\x004\\x005\\x00-\\x004\\x003\\x00c\\x00c\\x
  "value": {
      "id": "68539c45-43cc-8002-b9b4-0f93ef9618ae",
      "accountUserId": "user-dDpBljz4Al3v8JqLLIgJmrNI__4be6dbb7-e9ea-456e-90d5-76b84a957981",
      "authUserId": "user-dDpBljz4Al3v8JqLLIgJmrNI",
      "title": "Today's Weather Forecast",
      "isArchived": false,
      "updateTime": 1750309954.708,
      "messages": [
          {
```


Fig. 7. Internal structure of LevelDB data converted to JSON format

When identical or similar messages are sent repeatedly, the corresponding `id` values tend to be reused. Analysis of the `messages` field across different scenarios reveals that, in typical conversations (Scenarios 1 and 2), user and ChatGPT messages alternate sequentially, as shown in Fig. 8. Specifically, even-numbered entries represent user inputs, and odd-numbered entries correspond to ChatGPT responses.

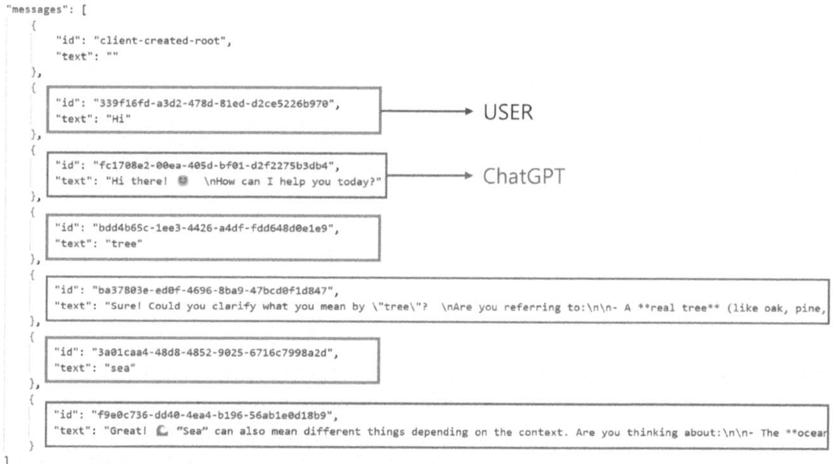

Fig. 8. IndexedDB entry from a standard conversation showing alternating user and ChatGPT messages

In Scenario 3, involving image generation, the user's request was recorded; however, as shown in Fig. 9, when ChatGPT's response consisted solely of an image without accompanying text, this response was not included in the `messages` field. This indicates that purely visual responses from ChatGPT without textual components are not stored in the dataset. In Scenario 4, with the "Search the Web" feature enabled, ChatGPT's responses included direct image links and URLs of the original websites hosting these images, as illustrated in

Fig. 10. These URLs allow viewing of the generated images, while linked websites provide valuable insights into the user's search behavior and intent.

In summary, the ChatGPT Web application systematically stores user activities in the local browser storage, enabling detailed forensic tracking of conversation histories, image generation requests, and external Web search interactions.

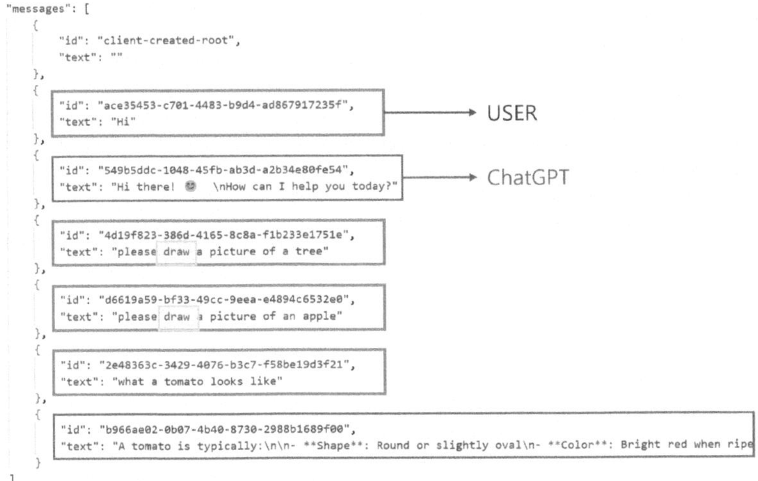

Fig. 9. No data recorded for visual-only responses generated by ChatGPT

5 Investigative Usage

The core contribution of this study lies in demonstrating that ChatGPT usage can be identified solely through forensic analysis of artifacts stored locally on disk, without requiring direct access to user account information or cooperation from the service provider. Typically, retrieving user account details or usage logs from Web-based generative AI services necessitates platform-level support. However, our analysis shows the potential to independently reconstruct user activities by examining data stored within the browser's IndexedDB. Specifically, the locally stored data enables investigators to determine conversation content, detect data generation or Web search activities, and reconstruct the sequence of actions involved in potential criminal behavior. Consequently, this forensic approach can be effectively utilized during the initial stages of criminal investigations, particularly when assessing the suspected planning or execution of crimes involving ChatGPT.

However, it is worth noting that IndexedDB stores data linked exclusively to a single login account, without recording activities from multiple users. Thus, for accurate forensic analysis, cross-validation with additional browser artifacts,

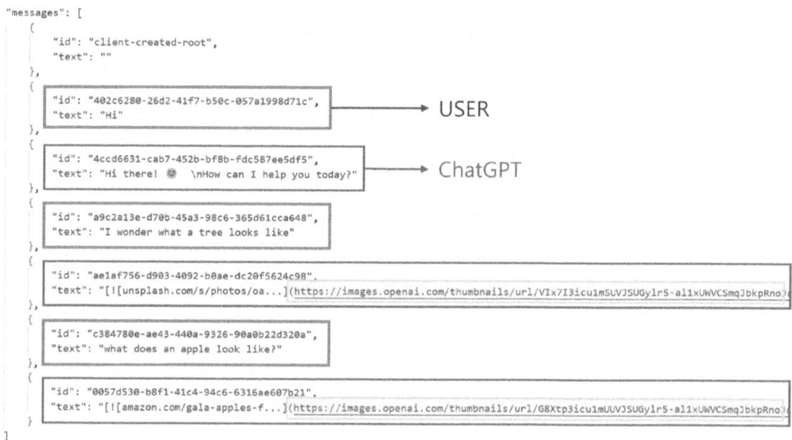

Fig. 10. Image links are embedded in responses when "Search the Web" is enabled

such as the History file, is required. The proposed investigative procedure consists of the following steps: First, the browser's History file is analyzed to verify account login status, timestamps of ChatGPT access, and session continuity. URLs recorded in the format "https://chatgpt.com/c/[UUID]" indicate active chat sessions, signifying either the initiation of new conversations or revisiting of previous ones. By correlating these UUID-based URLs with corresponding timestamps, user activity patterns (e.g., the number of sessions, creation time, and revisit frequency) can be accurately reconstructed.

Upon confirmation of ChatGPT-related activity, IndexedDB data is extracted and converted into a structured key-value JSON file for simplified analysis. Analysis of the `messages` field reveals conversation content, identifies potential malicious activities, and detects whether additional features—such as image generation or Web search—were employed. If such features are detected, external URLs referenced in the `messages` field can guide the retrieval of related files from the `Downloads` folder and cached copies of external Web resources. Finally, by integrating conversation content, timestamps, and associated artifacts (e.g., downloaded files, cached Web pages) based on UUID correlations, investigators can reconstruct a detailed sequence of user actions, generating robust forensic evidence suitable for criminal investigations.

6 Conclusion

This study confirmed that it is possible to perform forensic collection of a user's conversation history by analyzing artifacts left on the local disk after using ChatGPT in a Web browser environment. The findings demonstrate that, even without cooperation from the service provider or access to user account credentials, user activity patterns can be reconstructed solely from locally stored data. Given the widespread use of generative AI services like ChatGPT in the form of Web applications, this study offers a practical investigative approach that can be utilized to address the potential criminal misuse of such services. In particular, the proposed method is expected to contribute to quickly securing meaningful leads during the early stages of an investigation and systematically understanding the sequence of events in a case. Future research will focus on comparing and analyzing the artifacts generated when ChatGPT is used in different browser environments, such as Microsoft Edge and Firefox, to identify browser-specific characteristics.

Acknowledgments. This work is partly supported by the National Research Foundation of Korea(NRF) grant funded by the Korea government(MSIT) (No. RS-2024-00351898), the MOTIE under Training Industrial Security Specialist for High-Tech Industry (RS-2024-00415520) supervised by the Korea Institute for Advancement of Technology (KIAT), and the MSIT under the ICAN (ICT Challenge and Advanced Network of HRD) program (No. IITP-2022-RS-2022-00156310) supervised by the Institute of Information & Communication Technology Planning & Evaluation (IITP).

Disclosure of Interests. The authors have no competing interests to declare that are relevant to the content of this article.

References

1. Scam Sites at Scale: LLMs Fueling a GenAI Criminal Revolution. https://www.netcraft.com/blog/llms-fueling-gen-ai-criminal-revolution. Accessed from 2025/06/25
2. Chinese Hackers Allegedly Use ChatGPT to Write Ransomware. https://thehackernews.com/2024/01/chinese-hackers-allegedly-use-chatgpt.html. Accessed from 2025/06/25
3. Japanese teens arrested for using AI to create illegal phone contracts. https://www.straitstimes.com/asia/east-asia/japanese-teens-arrested-for-using-ai-to-create-illegal-phone-contracts. Accessed from 2025/06/26
4. Teens Arrested Over Rakuten ID Theft with Help from ChatGPT. https://japantoday.com/category/crime/teens-arrested-over-rakuten-id-theft-with-help-from-chatgpt. Accessed from 2025/06/25
5. OpenAI: AI That Can Save the Day or HACK it Away. https://research.checkpoint.com/2022/opwnai-ai-that-can-save-the-day-or-hack-it-away/. Accessed from 2025/06/25
6. Ministry of Science and ICT (MSIT): 2024 Cyber Threat Case Analysis and 2025 Outlook. Press release, MSIT (2024). https://www.msit.go.kr/bbs/view.do?bbsSeqNo=94&nttSeqNo=3185279. Accessed from 2025/06/25
7. Dragonas, E., Lambrinoudakis, C., Nakoutis, P.: Forensic analysis of OpenAI's ChatGPT mobile application. Forensic Sci. Int.: Digit. Investig. **50**, 301801 (2024). https://doi.org/10.1016/j.fsidi.2024.301801
8. Tyagi, S., Gong, Y., Karabiyik, U.: Forensic analysis and privacy implications of LLM apps: A case study of ChatGPT, Copilot, and Gemini. SSRN (2024). https://doi.org/10.2139/ssrn.5209937
9. Rathod, D.: Web browser forensics: Google Chrome. Int. J. Adv. Res. Comput. Sci. **8**(7), July–August (2017). https://doi.org/10.26483/ijarcs.v8i7.4433

10. Chand, R.R., Sharma, N.A., Kabir, M.A.: Advancing Web browser forensics: critical evaluation of emerging tools and techniques. SN Comput. Sci. **6**, 355 (2025). https://doi.org/10.1007/s42979-025-02562-y
11. Kim, H.G., Park, J.T., Moon, I.Y.: Analysis of Web caching techniques for efficient Web data loading. In: Proceedings of Korean Institutions and Information Communications Sciences Conference (KICS), pp. 497–500 (2018)
12. Kimak, S., Ellman, J.: The role of HTML5 IndexedDB, the past, present and future. In: Proceedings of the 10th International Conference on Internet Technology and Secured Transactions (ICITST), pp. 379–383. IEEE, London, UK (2015). https://doi.org/10.1109/ICITST.2015.7412126
13. Meta's largest AI competitors are fighting for users inside its most popular chatbot app: WhatsApp. https://www.businessinsider.nl/metas-largest-ai-competitors-are-fighting-for-users-inside-its-most-popular-chatbot-app-whatsapp/. Accessed from 2025/06/25
14. Cho, K., Park, Y., Kim, J., Kim, B., Jeong, D.: Conversational AI forensics: a case study on ChatGPT, Gemini, Copilot, and Claude. Forensic Sci. Int.: Digit. Investig. **52**, 301855 (2025). https://doi.org/10.1016/j.fsidi.2024.301855
15. Forensics.im Microsoft Teams Parser & Autopsy Plugin. https://github.com/lxndrblz/forensicsim. Accessed from 2025/06/27

Interaction-Aware System Call Sequence Analysis for Android Malware Classification

Jae-Min Choi[1], Sang-Hoon Choi[2], and Ki-Woong Park[3(✉)]

[1] SysCore Lab, Department of Information Security, and Convergence Engineering for Intelligent Drone, Sejong University, Seoul 05006, South Korea
c.jaem7532@gmail.com

[2] SysCore Lab, Sejong University, Seoul 05006, South Korea
csh0052@gmail.com

[3] Department of Information Security, and Convergence Engineering for Intelligent Drone, Sejong University, Seoul 05006, South Korea
woongbak@sejong.ac.kr

Abstract. The increasing number of mobile devices and the expansion of IoT (Internet of Things) and digital systems have made them targets for more sophisticated Android malicious apps. Existing detection techniques often use randomly generated events using 'monkey' tools, but this has limitations for apps that rely on user input for malicious behavior. In this paper, we extracted system calls and changed them to sequences to classify families of malicious apps by type with the DTW(Dynamic Time Warping) Algorithm. We evaluated using the AndroZoo dataset and found that family classification is possible for types of Trojan, Adware, and Exploit. In this study, we used view tree-based interaction for classification without using the 'monkey' tool to extract system call logs. We also extracted all logs through system call filtering to extract more malware behavior-focused system call logs. In the future, we plan to use more sophisticated interaction tools and ML and DL for classification and detection.

Keywords: Android malware · Malware family classification · Malware analysis

1 Introduction

The increasing of mobile devices and expansion IoT and digital systems, the information stored in mobile devices has become information that can cause direct or indirect damage to the user's life or company beyond personal information. To take this information, attackers are building and distributing more sophisticated and insidious malicious apps than ever before.

Attackers are not only distributing malicious apps through phishing and scams, but also by registering legitimate apps in official stores (such as Playstore

K.-W. Park and J. Park (Eds.): WISA 2025 2025, LNCS 16434, pp. 156–167, 2026.
https://doi.org/10.1007/978-981-95-6857-4_12

and Apple Store) and adding malicious behavior through subsequent updates [4]. Attackers are also taking advantage of the wide compatibility of mobile devices and the scalability of development tools to deploy malicious apps that are undetectable by traditional security technologies.

In March 2025, attackers used a C#-based Android and iOS app development tool Microsoft '.NET MAUI' to deploy malicious apps that bypassed detection that focuses on analyzing and detecting existing DEXs (Dalvik Executable) and native libraries [6]. In addition, another malicious app family called 'Crocodilus' appeared in March 2025, which used a dynamic code loading method through an external .dex file to bypass security solutions [9]. In June 2024, a malicious app called 'DroidBot' appeared [8]. This malicious app operated as a MaaS (Malware-as-a-Service), similar to RaaS (Ransomware-as-a-Service).

Malicious apps or malicious code, when distributed as XaaS (X-as-a-Service), tend to have similar code logic, attack methods, and penetration methods, and can be detected and blocked by similar detection and blocking technologies. Attackers are becoming more advanced and sophisticated in their attacks on mobile devices and deploying malicious apps.

Several static, dynamic, and hybrid analytics are being studied to detect and classify mobile malicious apps [2,5,7]. The above studies use 'monkey' tools to simulate user interactions to maximize the code coverage of malicious apps and collect system call logs for detection and classification. However, in the case of Trojan-type malicious apps, the focus is on taking user information. Therefore, Trojans usually have an input box that takes user input.

However, the 'monkey' tool has difficulty handling such inputs because it relies on random-based events (unless you write your own code). Also, collecting all system call logs for detection and classification is not enough to detect and classify actual malicious behavior, but if you use all of them as features, the resources used for Analysis will be considerable because all behaviors are recorded, including evasion logic intentionally planed by the attacker, internal storage for normal app activities, and access to external storage. In this research, we identify a number of those issues and present them as follows.

- *C01: Handling the attacker's intended victim's behavior:* In the case of Trojan Type, the purpose is to take the user's information. Therefore, in order for the user's input value to be sent to the C2 (Command & Control) server, the input value must be filled in according to the attacker's intention.

- *C02: Handling screen transitions from malicious apps:* Some malicious apps use automated tools like 'monkey' to perform screen transitions to evade analysis. In such cases, it is not possible to extract system calls correctly.

- *C03: Handling user behavior for maximum coverage:* Some malicious apps have malicious behavior that does not start immediately up on app launch, but rather after a specific button is touched.

- *C04: Handling non-malicious behavior logs from system calls:* If an attacker is intentionally planting evasion logic or collecting all legitimate app activity, the resources used for analysis will be very large.

To solve the above problem, we propose a framework that extracts system calls in changed sequence logs through preprocessing and filtering of user interactions and logs for more accurate classification.

This paper is organized as follows. Section 2 describes related work on system calls and describes the libraries used for our analysis. Section 3 describes the design of the framework proposed in this thesis and details its internal modules. Section 4 describes the results of classification using the framework. Section 5 presents conclusions, limitations, and future work.

2 Related Work

2.1 Android Malware Detection Based on System Call

Ahmed R. Nasser et al. proposed a DL-AMDet architecture for Android malicious apps based on static and dynamic features [5]. The study extracted permission request in the Manifest.XML file and API (Application Programming Interface) Calls through reverse engineering of the .dex file from static analysis, ran the malicious app for 15 min at 1-min intervals to extract system calls generated by the malicious app, and conducted dynamic analysis by generating events using 'monkey'. Based on the above three features, the CNN-BiLSTM method was used for training, and finally, 99.935% accuracy was achieved. In this study, the hybrid method effectively detected malicious apps.

Xiaojian Liu et al. extracted system calls for Android malicious apps and converted them into sequences to detect malicious apps using a CNN-LSTM model [2]. In this study, the system call is extracted and the frequency of occurrence is calculated to create a data dictionary. Then, based on the dictionary, it is converted into numerical information and trained with the CNN-LSTM model. At this time, 1000 random events were generated using 'monkey' to conduct dynamic analysis. In the end, 87.92% accuracy was achieved. In this study, system call was used to effectively detect malicious apps.

Christopher Jun Wen Chew et al. proposed a behavior-based ransomware detection technique based on extracting system calls generated by crypto ransomware [7]. The system calls generated by crypto ransomware are extracted, and the system calls are patterned to create behavior patterns. Then, based on regular expressions, we created an implementation that can detect crypto ransomware behavior in real time through FSM (Finite State Machine). In this study, presented the possibility of using it as part of a self-protection system on Android devices is explored.

2.2 Android View Client

The AndroidViewClient library by dtmilano is a Python library that helps automate and test the UI of Android apps [3]. The library extracts the UI (User Interface) structure based on the ADB (Android Debug Bridge) provided by Android and supports touch, text input, screen capture, structure analysis, etc., for each View. In this study, we used this library to identify touchable views and input boxes. Then, we utilized the identified views by touching them and typing text into the input box.

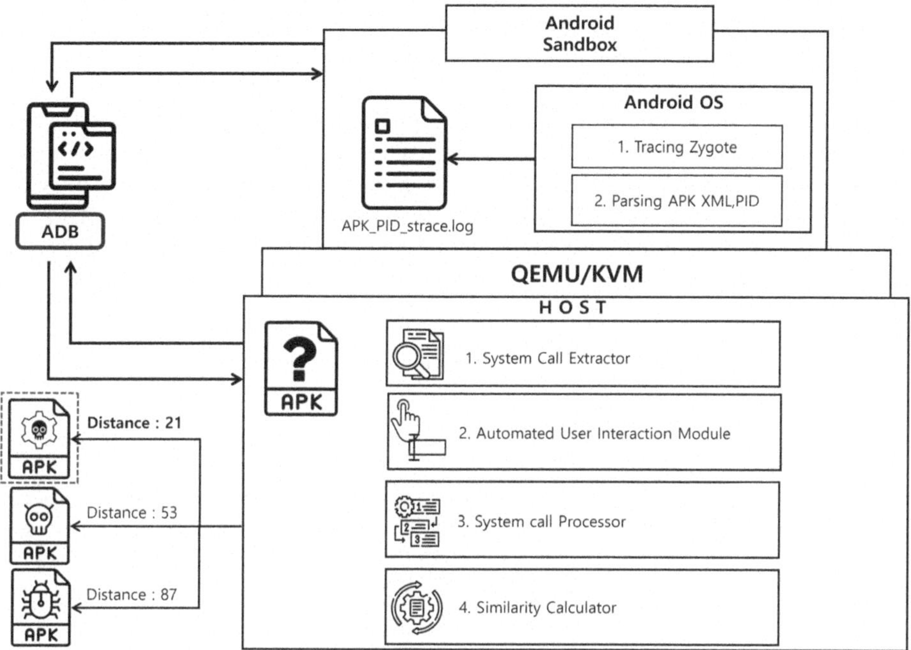

Fig. 1. Proposed Framework

3 Proposed Framework

This section describes the proposed framework and each module within the framework in detail. The structure of the proposed framework is shown in Fig. 1.

3.1 System Call Extractor

Install the malicious app using ADB on an Android virtual machine created with QEMU (Quick Emulator)+KVM (Kernel-based Virtual Machine). Then, extract the XML using the Android 'aapt' tool. Extract the 'android. intent.action.MAIN' value in the extracted XML to launch the Android app. If there is a loading splash in the form of 'android.intent.category.LAUNCHER', use that value. If the PID is extracted for the analysis app that is finally executed, it is impossible to extract the correct system call because it has already been executed.

To solve this problem, attach the 'strace' command to the 'zygote' or 'zygote64' process used by Android, including all child processes. This will allow to extract all system call logs from the moment the malicious app is executed. However, if we extract all system call functions, we will get a lot of noise. For example, functions such as 'ioctl' and 'get_clocktime' are not related to the actual malicious behavior. Excluding these functions, we extracted only the functions listed in Table 1 to extract only the functions listed in Table 1.

Android requires the 'minsdk' and 'maxsdk' versions to be specified when developing an app. Therefore, if the app to be analyzed does not match the current virtual machine and SDK (Software Development kit), it cannot be executed. Therefore, we saved the app with the error and extracted the Android SDK version 11. Through the above process, we extracted 'zygote' and all system calls generated by the malicious app.

Table 1. Filtering system call functions list

Category	System call functions
Process Control	clone, execve, fork, getuid, getuid32, geteuid, geteuid32
File I/O and Socket Connection	accept, bind, connect, getsockopt, mkdir, mkdirat, open, openat, pread64, read, readlinkat, recv, recvfrom, recvmsg, rename, renameat, rmdir, send, sendto, sendmsg, setsockopt, socket, stat, unlink, unlinkat, vfork, write, writev

3.2 Automated User Interaction Module

Some malicious app types may start malicious behavior depending on the user's input. As mentioned in C01 and C03, Trojan-type malicious apps require user input to send the value to the C2 server, and the user must press the final send button, not just fill in the input box. In addition, there are cases where the screen is switched when a specific button is touched to prevent an evade analysis by automated tools such as C02.

To solve C01, C02, and C03, we used the 'AndroidViewClient' library to extract the view tree for the current screen. Then, we extracted all the view IDs based on the view tree, and used a recursive function to navigate through the view tree. At this time, we categorized touch and input box types based on the view type.

The touch-type view simulates the user's input through the touch event, and the input box type view is divided into various cases.

For input boxes, you may want to validate input values when accepting certain forms, such as email. Also, there are cases where only numeric values, such as age, card number, and zip code, are accepted. To solve this problem, we created a set of input values in the form of a dictionary, extracted the screen using the ADB 'screencap' command, and entered a different type of input if the input values were not entered correctly. This way, we can simulate the user interaction correctly.

There are cases where the screen switches when the above touch event occurs. To prevent this, we used the 'dumpsys' command to extract the activity of the current foreground state. Using this command, we can find the current foreground activity, app, and compare it with the package name that was executed through it, and if the screen was switched, we solved it by using the 'back' command to return to the screen of the existing malicious app.

All of the above processes are recursive, meaning that we navigate from the parent view tree to the child view trees of the analysis app, and when the navigation is complete, we kill the process to end the analysis.

3.3 System Call Processor

The extracted system call logs contain all system calls made by 'zygote' and the malicious app. If all of these logs are used, the resources for analyzing them are considerable, as mentioned in C04 above, and there are difficulties in classifying them correctly. To solve this problem, the system call processor goes through the following steps.

From the extracted system call logs, we extract the system call logs of the app PID to be analysed and the child process that occurred in the app. Then, to extract the system call of the actual malicious behavior, we defined the parameter according to the system call function as shown in Table 2 and extracted the system call containing the parameter.

To apply the extracted system call logs to the DTW algorithm, we mapped each function to an integer as shown in Table 3.

Based on the above process, the final extracted system call log is much smaller in size than the full system call log, including 'zygote', and contains only malicious behavior due to noise removal. The data was reduced from a maximum of 140 MB to a minimum of 41 KB.

3.4 Similarity Calculator

To evaluate the similarity using the final extracted data, we used the DTW algorithm to evaluate the similarity. DTW algorithm is useful for evaluating the similarity of time series data regardless of the difference in data length through time base correction. In addition to the DTW algorithm, we also used Cosine Vector distance similarity and the SBD (Shape-based distance) algorithm, but the classification was not correct, so we finally evaluated the similarity with the DTW algorithm.

Before applying the DTW algorithm, the converted sequence logs extracted the maximum and minimum lengths within each type to select the maximum and max ratio values according to the distance difference. Even within the same family, we added a correction for the absolute length difference by calculating the case where the code changed according to the production time and adopted a new attack method.

Table 2. Filtering system call parameter list

Functions	System call parameters
openat()	base.apk, /storage/emulated/0, /data/user/0, /sdcard
Version 7 writev()	onCreate, onDestroy, onResume, LAUNCH_ACTIVITY, handlePauseActivity, destroy, handleRelaunchActivity, performPause
Version 9 writev()	MAIN_ACTIVITY, performCreate, performPause, performRestartActivity, performDestroy, handleStartActivity, RESUME_ACITIVTY, apache
write()	<?XML, getaddrinfo, Timeout, http, telnet
clone()	!zygote
mkdirat()	/storage/emulated/0, /data/user/0, /sdcard
renameat()	/storage/emulated/0, /data/user/0, /sdcard
connect()	AF_INET, AF_INET6
pread64()	table
socket()	!PF_LOCAL
recvmsg()	!-1
recvfrom()	!72, !232

Finally, the DTW algorithm was used to measure the distance value of each family within each type and normalise it to extract it.

4 Classification and Evaluation

This section details the classification results for the AndroZoo dataset [1] using our framework. We analyzed 282 samples with a VirusTotal Score over 30, divided into Adware (14 families), Exploit (2 families), and Trojan (39 families). The experimental setup is described in Table 4.

4.1 DTW Distance by Type

Proceed to extract the DTW Distance by malicious app type. At this time, representative values were extracted to create data within the same family. This process took about 20 times more time compared to the unfiltered data. The process of calculating DTW distance values using the filtered data in this experiment took about an hour. After extraction, the data that was labeled as 'family-n' was used to distinguish the different sequence patterns by version within the same family.

For example, in the case of the 'droidkungfu-1', 'droidkungfu-2' family of adware, depending on the version, the way of showing advertisements is divided into advertisement output through WebView and advertisement output through

Table 3. System call functions to integer for DTW algorithm

System Call Function	Integer	System call function	Integer
clone()	1	recv()	19
execve()	2	recvfrom()	20
fork()	3	recvmsg()	21
getuid()	4	rename()	22
getuid32()	5	renameat()	23
accept()	6	rmdir()	24
geteuid()	7	send()	25
geteuid32()	8	sendto()	26
accept()	9	sendmsg()	27
connect()	10	setsockopt()	28
getsockopt()	11	socket()	29
mkdir()	12	stat()	30
mkdirat()	13	unlink()	31
open()	14	unlinkat()	32
openat()	15	vfork()	33
pread64()	16	write()	34
read()	17	writev()	35
readlinkat()	18		

Table 4. An environment for framework

Environment	Environment Spec
Host OS	Ubuntu 64bit 22.04
Guest OS	Android-x86-11.0, Android-x86-9.0, Android-x86-7.1
CPU	Intel(R) Core i7-13700KF
Memory	DDR5 32GB

video output. In the case of Trojan type, it is divided into the case of sending user value (such as Gmail ID, phone number, phone model) to the C2 server after executing the malicious app and the case of send user input value to the C2 server by touching the button after receiving all user input value.

The above distinction was made to recognise cases where malicious behavior within the same family is different.

4.2 Classification Result

For evaluation, we randomly extracted 10 sequence logs from all datasets and compared the distance using DTW algorithm with the sequence logs of each

Table 5. Adware DTW with Sample1-5

Family	sample1	sample2	sample3	sample4	sample5
droidkungfu-1	999.0	157.8	999.0	999.0	406.1
droidkungfu-2	999.0	999.0	999.0	999.0	999.0
fakerun	**156.2**	999.0	999.0	999.0	999.0
gappusin	999.0	999.0	67.3	72.7	999.0
gingermaster	999.0	377.3	999.0	999.0	**0.0**
ginmaster	999.0	999.0	**8.3**	19.1	999.0
iadpush	999.0	999.0	55.3	56.4	999.0
ksapp	999.0	999.0	46.0	50.4	999.0
morepaks	999.0	999.0	38.1	41.0	999.0
nandrobox	999.0	999.0	999.0	999.0	999.0
plankton	999.0	**101.4**	999.0	999.0	383.5
utchi	999.0	999.0	21.9	**10.6**	999.0
wapsx	999.0	999.0	999.0	999.0	999.0
waps	999.0	125.5	999.0	999.0	392.6
youmi	999.0	999.0	32.3	35.7	999.0

Table 6. Exploit DTW with Sample6

Family	sample7
gingerbreak	**0.0**
lotoor	999.0

family. We assumed that the same family within the same type would show the same sequence behavior across versions. We conducted the experiment based on the hypothesis that 'malicious app families can be classified by comparing their similarity', and the final results are shown in Tables 5, 6, and 7.

At the data in Tables 5, 6, 7, for each family, there is a family that has the minimum number of distance. This means that sequence log belongs to that family. We compared the classified result with the labeled result to confirm that it belongs to the actual family. The data is different from the reference sequence logs, and we verified that the correct sequence logs can be classified into families.

4.3 Limitation

In our proposed study, the sequence logs generated by the framework were finally evaluated for similarity using the DTW algorithm. The dataset is relatively small to train ML (Machine Learning) and DL (Deep Learning) models, so we did not extend it to ML and DL. In addition, in the case of the interaction module,

Table 7. Trojan DTW with Sample7-10

Family	sample7	sample8	sample9	sample10
adrd	**0.0**	999.0	999.0	42.6
andcom	65.6	999.0	999.0	56.2
andup	999.0	69.7	61.0	999.0
artemis	999.0	65.9	62.5	999.0
ddlight	999.0	**43.7**	55.8	999.0
dougalek	63.9	999.0	999.0	6.4
fakedoc	999.0	72.2	57.2	999.0
fakelogo	42.5	999.0	999.0	22.0
fakerun	999.0	110.5	999.0	999.0
gamex	999.0	74.0	65.2	999.0
geinimi	33.0	999.0	999.0	34.7
gingermaster	999.0	999.0	999.0	999.0
ginmaster	999.0	77.7	76.5	999.0
golddream	999.0	109.1	91.3	999.0
gopf	50.1	999.0	999.0	999.0
iconosys	999.0	55.1	61.7	999.0
jifake	33.0	999.0	999.0	22.0
jsmshider	64.4	999.0	999.0	999.0
kmin	42.6	999.0	999.0	**0.0**
ksapp	999.0	78.4	63.7	999.0
lovetrap	999.0	96.1	89.5	999.0
morepaks	41.7	999.0	999.0	23.4
nandrobox	999.0	61.2	**31.3**	999.0
opfake	50.8	999.0	999.0	39.2
pjapps-1	999.0	999.0	80.1	999.0
pjapps-2	54.7	999.0	999.0	44.2
placms	32.5	999.0	999.0	21.1
ramnit	999.0	80.1	999.0	999.0
roguesppush	85.1	999.0	999.0	999.0
rufraud	59.8	999.0	999.0	17.4
smcc	999.0	82.9	60.9	999.0
smszombie	81.3	999.0	113.7	999.0
stiniter	26.9	999.0	999.0	33.5
uuserv-1	999.0	54.3	59.9	999.0
uuserv-2	77.1	999.0	82.6	999.0
vdloader	999.0	99.9	999.0	999.0
waps	50.9	999.0	999.0	28.0
winge	48.3	999.0	999.0	20.8
yzhc	33.0	999.0	999.0	22.0
zitmo	46.2	999.0	999.0	21.1
zsone	47.3	999.0	999.0	20.6

the process of verifying whether each data is entered correctly is based on the screencap, and if the data is entered, it is considered to be entered correctly. However, if the attacker did not write logic for input value validation in the input box, incorrect values may be recognized as correct values. As such, we think that interaction processing requires more accurate interaction processing than just view tree, screencap verification, and image comparison.

5 Conclusion

In this paper, we propose a framework to extract more accurate system calls by performing the attacker's intended interaction with malicious apps, pre-process and convert the system calls to generate sequence logs, and classify malicious app families based on them. Using the proposed framework, we verified that 14, 2, and 39 families of adware, exploit, and trojan types show the same sequence patterns. We also tested the DTW algorithm on 10 malicious apps based on the sequence logs to show that it is possible to classify them correctly. This shows that it is possible to classify malicious app families through system calls extracted through an accurate interaction process rather than interaction processing based on random events.

To date, system call logs have been proposed as a key feature in malicious app detection and classification research using various dynamic and hybrid analytics. Most of the proposed methods for extracting system calls in these studies use 'monkey' tools, which simulate interactions by generating events based on randomness. This makes it difficult for the attacker to perform their intended behavior. If a system call is extracted based on the interaction simulation method used in this framework, it is expected that it can be utilized as a better feature.

Acknowledgment. This work was supported by the Institute of Information & Communications Technology Planning & Evaluation (IITP) (2022-11220701, 40%), and the National Research Foundation of Korea (NRF) grant funded by the Korean Government (Project No. RS2023-00208460, 60%).

References

1. Allix, K., Bissyandé, T.F., Klein, J., Le Traon, Y.: Androzoo: collecting millions of android apps for the research community. In: 2016 IEEE/ACM 13th Working Conference on Mining Software Repositories (MSR). IEEE, pp. 468–471 (2016). https://doi.org/10.1109/MSR.2016.061
2. Chew, C.J.W., Kumar, V., Patros, P., et al.: Real-time system call-based ransomware detection. Int. J. Inf. Secur. **23**, 1839–1858 (2024). https://doi.org/10.1007/s10207-024-00819-x
3. dtmilano: Androidviewclient (2025). https://github.com/dtmilano/AndroidViewClient. Accessed from 2025-09-29
4. Kaspersky: It threat evolution q1 2024: Mobile statistics (2024). https://securelist.com/it-threat-evolution-q1-2024-mobile-statistics/112750/. Accessed from 2025-09-29

5. Liu, X., Zhang, Y., Duan, Y., Hou, B.: Android dynamic malware detection method based on system call sequences. In: 2024 9th International Conference on Intelligent Computing and Signal Processing (ICSP). IEEE, Xian, China, pp. 275–279 (2024). https://doi.org/10.1109/ICSP62122.2024.10744001
6. McAfee: New android malware campaigns evading detection using cross-platform framework .net maui (2024). https://www.mcafee.com/blogs/other-blogs/mcafee-labs/new-android-malware-campaigns-evading-detection-using-cross-platform-framework-net-maui/. Accessed from 2025-09-29
7. Nasser, A.R., Hasan, A.M., Humaidi, A.J.: Dl-amdet: Deep learning-based malware detector for android. Intell. Syst. Appl. **21**, 200318 (2024). https://doi.org/10.1016/j.iswa.2023.200318
8. SecurityWeek: Droidbot android trojan targets banking, cryptocurrency applications (2024). https://www.securityweek.com/droidbot-android-trojan-targets-banking-cryptocurrency-applications/. Accessed from 2025-09-29
9. Threatfabric: Exposing crocodilus: New device takeover malware targeting android devices (2024). https://www.threatfabric.com/blogs/exposing-crocodilus-new-device-takeover-malware-targeting-android-devices. Accessed from 2025-09-29

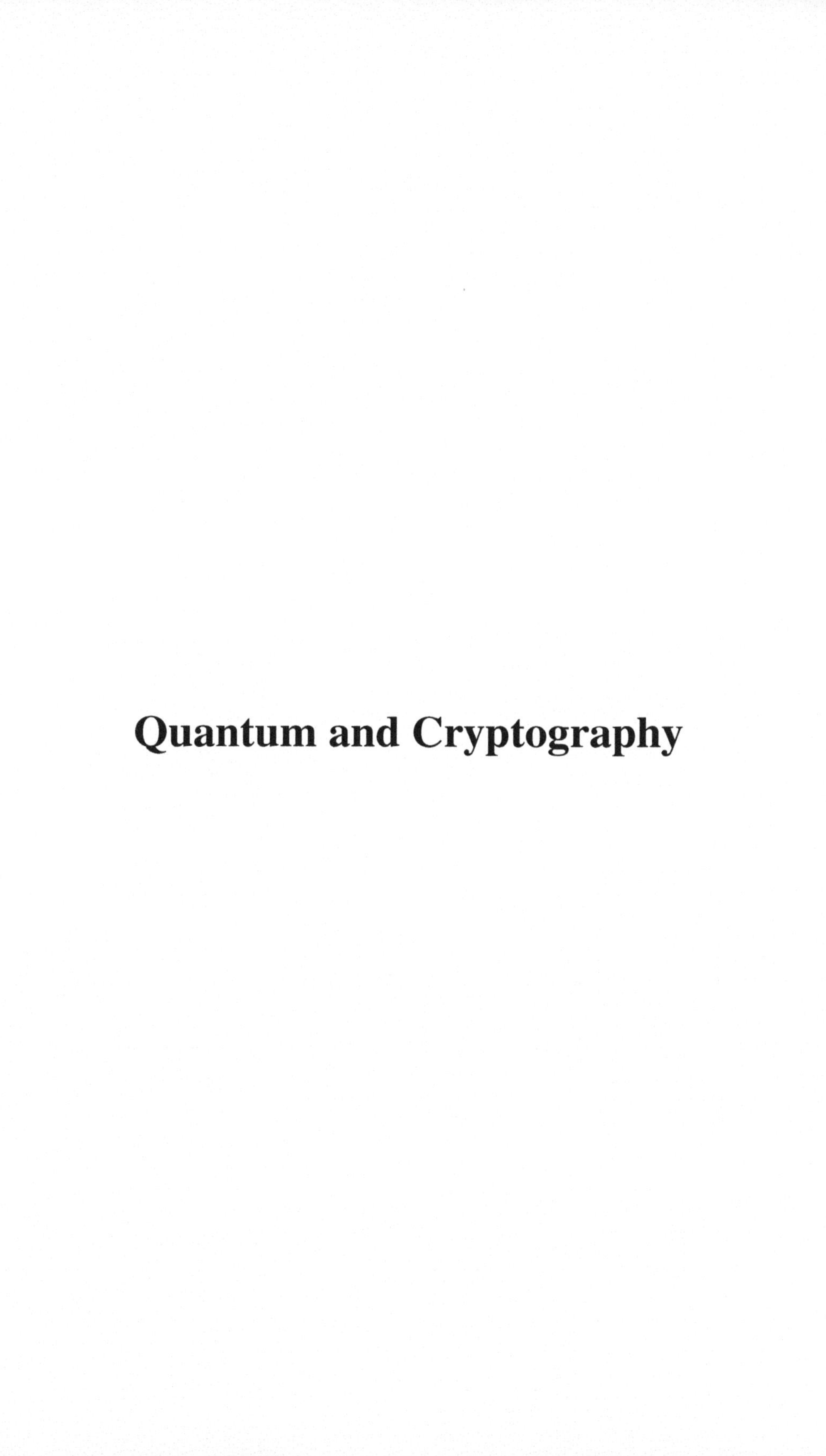

Quantum and Cryptography

Depth-Optimized Quantum Implementation of CHAM

Kyungbae Jang, Yujin Oh, and Hwajeong Seo(✉)

Hansung University, Seoul, South Korea
{starj1023,oyj0922,hwajeong84}@gmail.com

Abstract. Security weaknesses in the symmetric-key components of a cipher can compromise its overall security assurances. With the rapid progress in quantum computing in recent years, there is a growing focus on assessing the resilience of symmetric-key cryptography against possible quantum attacks. This paper is dedicated to examining the quantum attack resistance of CHAM, a family of lightweight block ciphers. We provide an optimized quantum circuit implementation of CHAM and evaluate its complexity metrics, such as the number of qubits, gate count, and circuit depth, within the context of Grover's search algorithm. For Grover's key search, minimizing the circuit depth is the key optimization goal, particularly when parallel search capabilities are taken into account. Our approach enhances parallelism for a low-depth quantum circuit of CHAM, aiming to reduce both the Toffoli depth and overall circuit depth.

Keywords: Quantum computing · Grover's search · CHAM

1 Introduction

Quantum computing poses a substantial threat to cryptography, especially to public key algorithms. Shor's algorithm, for instance, can reduce the complexity of attacking these algorithms to polynomial time. As a result, there has been significant research into the vulnerability of public key ciphers against quantum adversaries [2,7,17]. Generally, symmetric key ciphers are considered more resilient to quantum attacks than public key ciphers, as Grover's algorithm can find a k-bit key with approximately $\sqrt{2^k}$ operations, effectively reducing the attack complexity by a square root factor. This implies that to retain a comparable level of security in the face of quantum threats, symmetric key ciphers should double their key size.

It is important to note that quantum security considerations are often overlooked during the design phase of symmetric key ciphers. Although Grover's algorithm theoretically weakens key search security by a square root, in practice, quantum key recovery remains highly challenging due to the vast number of iterations required. Additionally, current quantum computers lack the capability to handle such complex, deep iterations.

K.-W. Park and J. Park (Eds.): WISA 2025 2025, LNCS 16434, pp. 171–181, 2026.
https://doi.org/10.1007/978-981-95-6857-4_13

Given these limitations, it is crucial to implement and evaluate new symmetric key ciphers in the context of adversaries equipped with quantum computing capabilities. If the quantum resources required to break a symmetric key cipher are substantial, the cipher may be considered quantum-resistant without needing to increase the key size.

In this context, the post-quantum security standards set by the National Institute of Standards and Technology (NIST) are essential [14,15]. NIST has established post-quantum security levels (from Level 1 to Level 5) to assess the strength of ciphers against quantum attacks, as further detailed in Sect. 2.2.

In this work, we implement quantum circuits for the lightweight block cipher CHAM [13]. We provide quantum implementations of CHAM that are optimized for circuit depth, with our design approach focusing on reducing depth rather than the number of qubits. This focus is motivated by the need to parallelize instances of Grover's search, which often becomes necessary due to the significant circuit depth involved in Grover's algorithm (as discussed in Sect. 2.3). We compare our results with previous works [10,21], which represent the most efficient quantum circuits for CHAM to date.

Using these depth-optimized quantum circuits for CHAM, we estimate the resource cost of Grover's key search and evaluate the post-quantum security level of CHAM according to the criteria set by NIST.

Contribution

1. **Depth-Optimized Quantum Circuits for CHAM**. We present the implementation of quantum circuits for different variants of CHAM. Our approach emphasizes minimizing circuit depth by employing additional ancilla qubits, enabling the inner quantum additions within the round functions to be executed in parallel.
2. **Post-Quantum Security Evaluation of CHAM**. We assess the post-quantum security of CHAM by estimating the cost of Grover's key search using the implemented quantum circuits. To conduct this security evaluation, we compare the estimated cost of Grover's key search for CHAM with that of AES, as determined by NIST [14,15].

2 Foundations

2.1 Grover's Key Search

Grover's search algorithm is a quantum algorithm that reduces the search complexity of ciphers compared to classical computers by a square root factor. For instance, a cipher using a k-bit key has an exhaustive key search complexity of $O(2^k)$ on a classical computer, but Grover's key search on a quantum computer reduces this complexity to $\sqrt{2^k}$. The Grover key search process for recovering a k-bit key, given a known plaintext-ciphertext pair, can be summarized as follows: $\textit{prepare} \rightarrow (\textit{Grover oracle} \text{ and } \textit{diffusion operator})^{\sqrt{2^k}} \rightarrow \textit{measure}$.

To begin, Hadamard (H) gates are applied to the k qubits to prepare the key in a superposition state. This operation creates a probability distribution over all possible key values (i.e., 2^k values), as represented in Eq. 1.

$$H^{\otimes k}|0\rangle^{\otimes k}(|\psi\rangle) = \left(\frac{|0\rangle + |1\rangle}{\sqrt{2}}\right) = \frac{1}{2^{k/2}}\sum_{x=0}^{2^k-1}|x\rangle \tag{1}$$

Next, qubits are initialized according to the known plaintext (P) by applying X gates based on its value. The core component, the Grover oracle, incorporates the quantum circuit of the target cipher. The known plaintext is encrypted using this quantum circuit along with the k-qubit key ($\psi(k)$), generating a superposition state of ciphertexts for all possible key values. The Grover oracle then compares this superposition of ciphertexts with the known ciphertext (C). If a match is found (Eq. 2), the oracle indicates the solution by flipping the sign of the corresponding key state (Eq. 3) as follows:

$$f(x) = \begin{cases} 1 \text{ if } Enc_{\psi(k)}(P) = C \\ 0 \text{ if } Enc_{\psi(k)}(P) \neq C \end{cases} \tag{2}$$

$$U_f(|\psi\rangle|-\rangle) = \frac{1}{2^{n/2}}\sum_{x=0}^{2^n-1}(-1)^{f(x)}|x\rangle|-\rangle \tag{3}$$

The diffusion operator, another critical module, amplifies the amplitude of the solution identified by the Grover oracle, thereby increasing the likelihood of recovering the correct key. Grover's key search involves iteratively applying the oracle and the diffusion operator $\sqrt{2^k}$ times to sufficiently amplify the amplitude of the solution, allowing the key to be recovered (measured) with high probability.

From a cost optimization perspective, minimizing the resources required for the encryption quantum circuit within the Grover oracle is essential to reducing the overall cost of Grover's key search.

2.2 NIST Post-Quantum Security

To assess the security of a cipher against quantum attacks, NIST has defined security bounds for various levels [14,15]:

- Level 1: The resource requirements for an attack are comparable to those needed to break AES-128 ($2^{170} \rightarrow \mathbf{2^{157}}$).
- Level 2: Resource requirements for the attack are similar to those for breaking SHA-256/SHA3-256.
- Level 3: The resource requirements for an attack are similar to those for breaking AES-192 ($2^{233} \rightarrow \mathbf{2^{221}}$).
- Level 4: Resource requirements for the attack are similar to those for breaking SHA-384/SHA3-384.

– Level 5: The resource requirements for an attack are equivalent to those for breaking AES-256 ($2^{298} \rightarrow \mathbf{2^{285}}$).

Based on the cost estimates for Grover's key search against AES variants as presented by Grassl et al. [6], NIST determined the quantum attack complexities for Levels 1, 3, and 5 (corresponding to different AES variants) as 2^{170}, 2^{233}, and 2^{298}, respectively (calculated as total gates multiplied by the depth of Grover's search). It is important to highlight that NIST's complexity estimates in [14] are derived from research results published in PQCrypto'16 [6]. Since that time, quantum circuits for AES have undergone continuous optimization, resulting in a significant decrease in the cost of attacks in recent years [8,9,11,22].

NIST also acknowledges that the attack complexities based on these levels are relative, given the ongoing optimizations in quantum circuits for AES (see p. 17 in [14]). Therefore, if a more efficient attack is proposed, the benchmarks may need to be updated.

Recently, NIST revised the security bounds for AES [15,16] following the findings presented at Eurocrypt 2020 [11]. In [11], the quantum attack costs for AES-128, -192, and -256 were significantly reduced to 2^{157}, 2^{221}, and 2^{285}, respectively, aligning with the updated values in [15,16].

2.3 NIST MAXDEPTH

Exhaustive key search using Grover's algorithm is still far beyond the current capabilities of quantum computing. Although Grover's key search theoretically reduces security by a square root factor, executing a successful attack requires managing an extremely deep quantum circuit. In practical scenarios, Grover's search may be performed in parallel by breaking it into smaller instances to reduce the lengthy sequential computations (as mentioned on p. 46 of [16]).

To address this, NIST defines a maximum allowable depth for quantum attacks, known as MAXDEPTH, which is set between 2^{40} and 2^{96}.

Thus, once the attacker reaches the MAXDEPTH limit, they must employ a parallel strategy for Grover's key search, as discussed in [12]. Parallel searches can be classified into outer and inner methods (for further details, see [12]).

It is crucial to understand that the efficiency of parallel searches is generally low due to the disproportionate trade-off between the reduction in depth and the success probability of key recovery. Usually, the depth-qubit count product is a primary metric for evaluating the performance of a quantum circuit. However, to reduce the depth of Grover's search by a factor of S, S^2 instances must be executed in parallel [11,12].

This means that the depth-qubit count product should be redefined as the depth^2-qubit count product when designing Grover's search for parallel execution to achieve successful key recovery. This is why minimizing the depth is more advantageous when considering the parallelization of Grover's search.

2.4 Quantum Gates

Various quantum gates are commonly used to implement ciphers within quantum circuits, including the X (NOT), CNOT, and Toffoli (CCNOT) gates. The X gate, equivalent to the classical NOT operation, flips the value of a qubit (i.e., $X(x) = \sim x$). The CNOT gate operates on two qubits, where the target qubit's value is modified based on the control qubit's value. Specifically, if the control qubit is 1, the target qubit is flipped; if it is 0, the target qubit remains unchanged (i.e., $\text{CNOT}(x, y) = (x, x \oplus y)$). Since this operation is equivalent to XORing the control qubit's value with that of the target qubit, the CNOT gate can serve as a quantum substitute for the classical XOR operation. The Toffoli gate, on the other hand, involves three qubits: two control qubits and one target qubit. The target qubit is flipped only when both control qubits are set to 1 (i.e., $\text{Toffoli}(x, y, z) = (x, y, z \oplus xy)$). This can be viewed as XORing the result of the AND operation between the control qubits with the target qubit's value, making the Toffoli gate a quantum analogue for the classical AND operation.

By leveraging these quantum gates, we can implement encryption algorithms in quantum computing, replacing classical NOT, XOR, and AND operations.

Optimizing quantum circuits requires minimizing the number of Toffoli gates, as they are particularly costly to implement. Toffoli gates require a combination of T gates (which impact the T-depth) and Clifford gates. Various decomposition techniques for Toffoli gates have been developed, where the "full depth" refers to the circuit depth after these gates have been decomposed. In this study, we estimate the resources needed for decomposition using a method that involves 7 T gates and 8 Clifford gates, resulting in a T-depth of 4 and a full depth of 8 for a single Toffoli gate, as detailed in [1].

2.5 CHAM

CHAM operates with either a 64-bit plaintext (16×4) or a 128-bit plaintext (32×4), denoted as X, and utilizes either a 128-bit or 256-bit key, denoted as K. In the key schedule of CHAM, the input key K is divided into segments as $K = K[0]||K[1]||\ldots||K[w]$, where $w = 8$ for CHAM-64/128 and CHAM-128/256, and $w = 4$ for CHAM-128/128. The key schedule is defined as follows:

$$\begin{aligned} RK[i] &= K[i] \oplus (K[i] \lll 1) \oplus (K[i] \lll 8), \\ RK[i+w] &= K[i] \oplus (K[i] \lll 1) \oplus (K[i] \lll 8) \end{aligned}$$

The round function of CHAM is dependent on the round number i. If the round number i is odd, the round function is defined by:

$$\begin{aligned} X_{i+1}[3] &= ((X_i[0] \oplus i) \boxplus (X_i[1] \lll 1) \oplus \ (RK[i \bmod w)) \lll 8 \\ X_{i+1}[j] &= X_i[j+1], (0 \leq j \leq 2) \end{aligned}$$

Otherwise, if $i = 0$ or is an even number, the round function is given by:

$$\begin{aligned} X_{i+1}[3] &= ((X_i[0] \oplus i) \boxplus (X_i[1] \lll 8) \oplus \ (RK[i \bmod w)) \lll 1 \\ X_{i+1}[j] &= X_i[j+1], (0 \leq j \leq 2) \end{aligned}$$

3 Quantum Circuit Implementation of CHAM

In this section, we describe how we reduce the circuit depth of CHAM compared to that in previous works [10,21]. Our goal in implementing the quantum circuit for CHAM is to minimize the circuit depth (suitable strategy for Grover's parallelization, see Sect. 2.3) while using additional ancilla qubits. It is worth noting that our approach is applicable to all variants of CHAM (i.e., CHAM-64, CHAM-128, and CHAM-256).

In previous quantum implementation of CHAM [10,21], full parallelism was not achieved. The difference between [10,21] lies in the quantum implementation of the linear layer in CHAM, which consists of XOR and rotation operations. In [10], an incomplete in-place implementation was presented for the linear layer. In contrast, [21] proposed complete in-place implementations using PLU factorization, along with an optimized method for the linear layer based on the approach in [20]. In their approach, the rounds are executed sequentially due to the reverse operation of the round key used in the round function. They initialize the round key (i.e., $|0\rangle$, using the reverse operation) to reduce the number of qubits required. However, the intermediate round state is required to initialize the round key, and this value is updated in subsequent rounds. In other words, the subsequent rounds cannot be performed until the reverse operation (to initialize the round key) is completed. As a result, although the number of qubits is reduced, the circuit depth increases.

In contrast, we allocate additional ancilla qubits to copy the round keys, and we do not reverse the operations to reverse them. This allows us to perform up to three rounds in parallel. After the use of the copied round keys, they are treated as garbage qubits since the intermediate round state is updated by the parallelization of three rounds. Note that these garbage qubits cannot be initialized. As a result, although additional ancilla qubits must be allocated for each round key, the circuit depth is significantly reduced, making this optimization well-suited for Grover's parallelization (see Sect. 2.3).

Algorithms 1 and 2 describe the quantum circuit implementations for CHAM-64/128 and CHAM-128/128, -128/256, respectively. We allocate additional ancilla qubits (RK_{temp} in Algorithms 1 and 2) for each round, and the round key is copied to these qubits using CNOT gates (16 CNOT gates for CHAM-64/128 and 32 CNOT gates for CHAM-128/128 and CHAM-128/256). Note that RK_{temp} is discarded after use (i.e., garbage qubits).

Table 1 shows the required quantum resources for the quantum circuits of the CHAM variants, along with a comparison to previous works [10,21]. We estimate the detailed quantum resources after decomposing the Toffoli gates. Among various decomposition methods, we adopt the one presented in [1], which uses 8 Clifford + 7 T gates, a T-depth of 4, and a full depth of 8. Note that this decomposition is the same as the one adopted in [10,21].

Algorithm 1 Quantum circuit for round function of CHAM-64/128 (i is *odd*).

Input: $X[0] \sim [3], RK, c$ (an ancilla qubit for quantum addition)
Output: $X[0] \sim [3]$
//Round constant addition
for $j = 0$ to 7 **do**
  if $(i \gg j)$ & 1 **then**
    $X[0] \leftarrow$X$(X[0][j])$
  end if
end for

//Store the round key in the ancilla qubits
$X[1] \leftarrow X[1] \lll 8$
$RK_{temp} \leftarrow$ Allocate 16 ancilla qubits for RK_{temp}
$RK_{temp} \leftarrow$ CNOT16$(X[1], RK_{temp})$
$RK_{temp} \leftarrow$ CNOT16(RK, RK_{temp})
$X[1] \leftarrow X[1] \ggg 8$

//Addition
$X[0] \leftarrow ADD(RK_{temp}, X[0], c)$

return $X[1], X[2], X[3], X[0] \lll 1$

Algorithm 2 Quantum circuit for round function of CHAM-128/128, -128/256 (i is *odd*).

Input: $X[0] \sim [3], RK, c$ (an ancilla qubit for quantum addition)
Output: $X[0] \sim [3]$
//Add round constant(i)
for $j = 0$ to 7 **do**
  if $(i \gg j)$ & 1 **then**
    $X[0] \leftarrow$X$(X[0][j])$
  end if
end for

//Store the round key in the ancilla qubits
$X[1] \leftarrow X[1] \lll 8$
$RK_{temp} \leftarrow$ Allocate 32 ancilla qubits for RK_{temp}
$RK_{temp} \leftarrow$ CNOT32$(X[1], RK_{temp})$
$RK_{temp} \leftarrow$ CNOT32(RK, RK_{temp})
$X[1] \leftarrow X[1] \ggg 8$

//Addition
$X[0] \leftarrow ADD(RK_{temp}, X[0], c)$

return $X[1], X[2], X[3], X[0] \lll 1$

Table 1. Quantum resources required for the CHAM quantum circuits.

Cipher	#CNOT	#1qCliff	#T	#Qubit (M)	Full depth (FD)
CHAM-64/128 [10]	27120	6960	16240	204	17034
CHAM-128/128 [10]	58040	14640	34160	292	37766
CHAM-128/256 [10]	70080	17584	40992	420	45252
CHAM-64/128 [21]	29960	6960	16240	195	17031
CHAM-128/128 [21]	58080	14640	34160	259	37768
CHAM-128/256 [21]	69696	17584	40992	387	44904
CHAM-64/128 (This work)	27120	6960	16240	1484	7105
CHAM-128/128 (This work)	58040	14640	34160	2852	14772
CHAM-128/256 (This work)	70080	17584	40992	3492	17712

4 Post-Quantum Security Evaluation of CHAM

In this section, we examine the post-quantum security of CHAM. Specifically, we estimate the cost of Grover's key search for CHAM and compare it with the costs of Grover's key search for various AES variants. The AES costs used for this post-quantum security evaluation are based on NIST estimates [14,15], which, in turn, rely on the findings of Grassl et al. [6] and Jaques et al. [11].

As detailed in Sect. 2.1, Grover's key search for a cipher using a k-bit key requires approximately $\sqrt{2^k}$ iterations of the Grover oracle and diffusion operator. A tighter analysis of Grover's algorithm [4] suggests that the optimal number of iterations is $\lfloor \frac{\pi}{4}\sqrt{2^k} \rfloor$, and our cost estimates are based on this calculation. When estimating the cost of Grover's key search, we exclude the diffusion operator, as its overhead is typically negligible (a common assumption in related studies [9,11]). Consequently, our cost estimation focuses only on the oracle.

The Grover oracle comprises the CHAM quantum circuit for encryption, an n-controlled NOT gate (where n represents the ciphertext size) to compare the ciphertext with the known ciphertext, and the reverse operation of the CHAM quantum circuit for the subsequent iteration. The n-controlled NOT gate is estimated to require $(32 \cdot n - 64)$ T gates, according to the decomposition method in [19]. Thus, the total cost of Grover's key search for CHAM is estimated as $\lfloor \frac{\pi}{4}\sqrt{2^k} \rfloor \times (32 \cdot 128 - 64)$ T gates $+ \lfloor \frac{\pi}{4}\sqrt{2^k} \rfloor \times$(Table 1 $\times$ 2). Since these iterations are executed sequentially, the number of qubits does not increase from what is indicated in Table 1, except for the addition of a single decision qubit used to compare the ciphertext against the known ciphertext. Table 2 summarizes the costs associated with Grover's key search for CHAM.

We also include the metrics $TD^2 \times M$ and $FD^2 \times M$ in Table 2. Grover's key search is characterized by a significant circuit depth, which makes it challenging to execute efficiently. Therefore, performing a parallelized search to reduce the circuit depth is more feasible in practice. However, the effectiveness of parallelizing Grover's search is notably limited (as discussed in Sect. 2.3). To reduce the depth by a factor of S, S^2 instances of Grover's algorithm must be run in parallel [11,12], which results in a qubit count increase by a factor of S. Hence, when considering a parallel search, the key metrics to optimize are $TD^2 \times M$ and $FD^2 \times M$. This explains why minimizing circuit depth is particularly advantageous for quantum circuits designed for Grover's key search.

To evaluate the post-quantum security of CHAM, we compare the costs of Grover's key search for AES variants. By comparing the updated Grover's key search costs from [15] with the costs for CHAM-64/128, -128/128, and -128/256, we find that these CHAM variants successfully achieve Levels 1, 3, and 5 (post-quantum security), as 2^{158}, 2^{159}, and 2^{289} exceed 2^{157}, 2^{157}, and 2^{285}, respectively.

Table 2. Costs of the Grover's key search for CHAM

Cipher	Total gates	Total depth	Cost (complexity)	#Qubit	$FD \times M$	$FD^2 \times M$
CHAM-I	$1.254 \cdot 2^{81}$	$1.362 \cdot 2^{77}$	$1.709 \cdot 2^{158}$	2841	$1.889 \cdot 2^{88}$	$1.287 \cdot 2^{166}$
CHAM-III	$1.304 \cdot 2^{81}$	$1.416 \cdot 2^{78}$	$1.847 \cdot 2^{159}$	2853	$1.973 \cdot 2^{89}$	$1.397 \cdot 2^{168}$
CHAM-V	$1.566 \cdot 2^{146}$	$1.698 \cdot 2^{142}$	$1.33 \cdot 2^{289}$	6729	$1.395 \cdot 2^{155}$	$1.395 \cdot 2^{297}$

5 Conclusion

This paper introduces the depth-optimized quantum circuit implementation of the lightweight block cipher CHAM. To minimize the cost of Grover's key search, developing an efficient quantum circuit for CHAM is crucial. Our approach achieves this by reducing circuit depth while maintaining a manageable number of qubits.

Using our depth-optimized quantum circuits for CHAM, we estimated the costs of Grover's key search for various CHAM variants. When comparing CHAM against several recent standards [14,15], we determined that CHAM-64/128, -128/128, and -128/256 consistently achieve post-quantum security Levels 1, 3, and 5, respectively.

Evaluating the post-quantum security of cryptographic systems against possible attacks by quantum computers, which present substantial threats, is vital for establishing a secure post-quantum framework. In this regard, our future work will focus on assessing post-quantum security across different scenarios for cryptographic algorithms. Approaches like Simon's algorithm [18] for period finding in ciphers or applying Grover's algorithm to other PQC algorithms, such as quantum sieving [5] for lattice-based cryptography and Quantum Information Set Decoding (QISD) [3] for code-based cryptography, could be prominent directions to explore.

Acknowledgment. This work was supported by the Institute of Information & Communications Technology Planning & Evaluation(IITP) grant funded by the Korea government(MIST) (No. RS-2019-II190033, Study on Quantum Security Evaluation of Cryptography based on Computational Quantum Complexity, 75%) and this work was supported by Institute for Information & communications Technology Promotion(IITP) grant funded by the Korea government(MSIT) (No.2018-0-00264, Research on Blockchain Security Technology for IoT Services, 25%).

References

1. Amy, M., Maslov, D., Mosca, M., Roetteler, M., Roetteler, M.: A meet-in-the-middle algorithm for fast synthesis of depth-optimal quantum circuits. IEEE Trans. Comput. Aided Des. Integr. Circuits Syst. **32**(6), 818–830 (2013). https://doi.org/10.1109/tcad.2013.2244643
2. Banegas, G., Bernstein, D.J., Van Hoof, I., Lange, T.: Concrete quantum cryptanalysis of binary elliptic curves. Cryptology ePrint Archive (2020)
3. Bernstein, D.J.: Grover vs. mceliece. In: Post-Quantum Cryptography: Third International Workshop, PQCrypto 2010, Darmstadt, Germany, May 25–28, 2010. Proceedings 3. Springer, pp. 73–80 (2010)
4. Boyer, M., Brassard, G., Høyer, P., Tapp, A.: Tight bounds on quantum searching. Fortschr. Phys. **46**(4–5), 493–505 (1998). 10.1002/(sici)1521-3978(199806)46:4/5<493::aid-prop493>3.0.co;2-p
5. Chailloux, A., Loyer, J.: Lattice sieving via quantum random walks. In: Advances in Cryptology–ASIACRYPT 2021: 27th International Conference on the Theory and Application of Cryptology and Information Security, Singapore, December 6–10, 2021, Proceedings, Part IV 27. Springer, pp. 63–91 (2021)
6. Grassl, M., Langenberg, B., Roetteler, M., Steinwandt, R.: Applying Grover's algorithm to AES: Quantum resource estimates. In: Takagi, T. (ed.) Post-Quantum Cryptography. Springer International Publishing, Cham, pp. 29–43 (2016)
7. Häner, T., Jaques, S., Naehrig, M., Roetteler, M., Soeken, M.: Improved quantum circuits for elliptic curve discrete logarithms. In: Post-Quantum Cryptography: 11th International Conference, PQCrypto 2020, Paris, France, April 15–17, 2020, Proceedings 11. Springer, pp. 425–444 (2020)
8. Huang, Z., Sun, S.: Synthesizing quantum circuits of AES with lower T-depth and less qubits. Cryptology ePrint Archive, Report 2022/620 (2022). https://eprint.iacr.org/2022/620
9. Jang, K., Baksi, A., Kim, H., Song, G., Seo, H., Chattopadhyay, A.: Quantum analysis of aes. Cryptology ePrint Archive, Paper 2022/683 (2022). https://eprint.iacr.org/2022/683,
10. Jang, K., Song, G., Kim, H., Kwon, H., Kim, H., Seo, H.: Parallel quantum addition for Korean block ciphers. Quantum Inf. Process. **21**(11), 373 (2022)
11. Jaques, S., Naehrig, M., Roetteler, M., Virdia, F.: Implementing grover oracles for quantum key search on AES and lowmc. In: Canteaut, A., Ishai, Y. (eds.) Advances in Cryptology - EUROCRYPT 2020 - 39th Annual International Conference on the Theory and Applications of Cryptographic Techniques, Zagreb, Croatia, May 10-14, 2020, Proceedings, Part II. Lecture Notes in Computer Science, vol. 12106. Springer, pp. 280–310 (2020). https://doi.org/10.1007/978-3-030-45724-2_10,

12. Kim, P., Han, D., Jeong, K.C.: Time-space complexity of quantum search algorithms in symmetric cryptanalysis: applying to aes and sha-2. Quantum Inf. Process. **17**, 1–39 (2018)
13. Koo, B., Roh, D., Kim, H., Jung, Y., Lee, D.G., Kwon, D.: Cham: A family of lightweight block ciphers for resource-constrained devices. In: International Conference on Information Security and Cryptology. Springer, pp. 3–25 (2017)
14. NIST.: Submission requirements and evaluation criteria for the post-quantum cryptography standardization process (2016). https://csrc.nist.gov/CSRC/media/Projects/Post-Quantum-Cryptography/documents/call-for-proposals-final-dec-2016.pdf
15. NIST.: Call for additional digital signature schemes for the post-quantum cryptography standardization process (2022). https://csrc.nist.gov/csrc/media/Projects/pqc-dig-sig/documents/call-for-proposals-dig-sig-sept-2022.pdf
16. NIST.: Stateless hash-based digital signature standard (2023). https://nvlpubs.nist.gov/nistpubs/FIPS/NIST.FIPS.205.ipd.pdf
17. Roetteler, M., Naehrig, M., Svore, K.M., Lauter, K.: Quantum resource estimates for computing elliptic curve discrete logarithms. In: Advances in Cryptology–ASIACRYPT 2017: 23rd International Conference on the Theory and Applications of Cryptology and Information Security, Hong Kong, China, December 3–7, 2017, Proceedings, Part II 23. Springer, pp. 241–270 (2017)
18. Simon, D.R.: On the power of quantum computation. SIAM J. Comput. **26**(5), 1474–1483 (1997)
19. Wiebe, N., Roetteler, M.: Quantum arithmetic and numerical analysis using repeat-until-success circuits (2014). arXiv:1406.2040
20. Xiang, Z., Zeng, X., Lin, D., Bao, Z., Zhang, S.: Optimizing implementations of linear layers. IACR Trans. Symmetric Cryptol. (2020)
21. Yang, Y., Jang, K., Baksi, A., Seo, H.: Optimized implementation and analysis of Cham in quantum computing. Appl. Sci. **13**(8), 5156 (2023)
22. Zou, J., Wei, Z., Sun, S., Liu, X., Wu, W.: Quantum circuit implementations of AES with fewer qubits. In: Moriai, S., Wang, H. (eds.) Advances in Cryptology - ASIACRYPT 2020. Springer International Publishing, Cham, pp. 697–726 (2020)

Quantum Implementation of SHA-1

Seyoung Yoon, Gyeongju Song, Kyungbae Jang, Sangmin Cha, and Hwajeong Seo(✉)

Hansung University, Seongbuk, South Korea
{sebbang99,thdrudwn98,starj1023,xhxhdwkdpsyentific,hwajeong84}@gmail.com

Abstract. As quantum computing technology rapidly advances, threats to existing symmetric-key and public-key cryptosystems are becoming increasingly real. In this study, we implement a SHA-1 quantum circuit that operates efficiently in a quantum computing environment. We optimize the quantum circuit, focusing on minimizing total circuit depth, a key performance indicator of quantum algorithms. The SHA-1 quantum circuit implementation used 985 qubits, resulting in a measured circuit depth of 9,026. Furthermore, by integrating this optimized circuit with the Grover algorithm, we establish the foundation for an efficient quantum attack on the SHA-1 algorithm. This research is significant not only because it presents a resource-efficient SHA-1 quantum implementation but also because it enables accelerated attacks in a quantum computing environment.

Keywords: Quantum computer · Grover's algorithm · Quantum collision search · SHA-1 · Post-quantum security

1 Introduction

Advances in quantum computing technology have revealed that the security of conventional symmetric-key cryptography and public-key cryptography algorithms is seriously threatened by quantum algorithms. Quantum algorithms are a major source of these threats. In particular, Shor's algorithm can compromise widely used public-key cryptosystems such as RSA and ECC by solving fundamental mathematical problems in polynomial time. Similarly, Grover's algorithm is known to be able to break symmetric-key cryptography by accelerating brute-force search operations by a square root. This ability stems from the unique properties of quantum computers. Quantum computers use qubits instead of classical bits (0 and 1). Leveraging the principles of superposition and entanglement, qubits can simultaneously represent states $|0\rangle$ and $|1\rangle$. This fundamental property allows quantum computers to perform parallel computations quickly. Therefore, in preparation for the era of quantum computing, active research is

K.-W. Park and J. Park (Eds.): WISA 2025 2025, LNCS 16434, pp. 182–197, 2026.
https://doi.org/10.1007/978-981-95-6857-4_14

underway to attack existing cryptographic systems using quantum computers and develop new quantum-resistant algorithms. Attacks on classical cryptosystems, such as symmetric key cryptography and hash functions, can be performed using Grover's algorithm, which is known to break n-bit hash functions with a complexity of $O(2^{n/2})$. To execute such an attack, the target algorithm must first be implemented as a quantum circuit composed of elementary quantum gates. The performance of a quantum circuit is primarily evaluated by the total circuit depth, which represents the number of qubits used and the number of sequential steps required for execution. When implementing a quantum circuit for the well-known hash function SHA-1, we focused on minimizing the circuit depth and took care not to waste qubits, contributing to the field of quantum circuit implementation.

This paper is organized as follows. Section 2 provides background information for this research. We first explain the Grover algorithm. Grover's algorithm is a quantum algorithm that can find a target solution with a high probability using approximately $\sqrt{2^n}$ queries in an n-qubit search space. Next, we describe the three main steps of the algorithm: state initialization, oracle, and diffusion operator. Finally, we describe the architecture and operation of the original SHA-1 algorithm. Section 3 presents our main contribution to a complete quantum circuit implementation of SHA-1, demonstrating how to reduce the circuit depth while using fewer qubits. Section 4 presents the results of a performance evaluation of two quantum adders that were at the core of the optimization process: a depth-optimized Draper adder and a qubit-optimized TTK adder. Finally, Sect. 5 concludes the paper by summarizing the research results and suggesting future directions.

1.1 Contribution

Our contributions are summarized as follows:

- **Complete Quantum Implementation of the SHA-1 Algorithm.** We present a full quantum circuit implementation of the SHA-1 hash function, designed to serve as a verifiable oracle for quantum cryptanalysis. This includes message padding and scheduling (W_t expansion), the 80-round compression function, and final hash computation. A key aspect of our design is the reversible logic construction of the non-linear round function (F_t), which changes across rounds, as well as the reuse of qubits for the message scheduling (W_t expansion).
- **Resource Optimization with Minimal Circuit Depth.** Our circuit achieves a low quantum circuit depth while using a minimal number of qubits. The depth of a quantum circuit is the time it takes to execute all the gates in the designed quantum circuit. Typically, minimizing the depth of a quantum circuit wastes significant qubit resources. Therefore, we addressed this issue by using the following methods: in-place computation to preserve ancilla qubits,

gate parallelization based on data dependencies, and a quantum adder optimized for circuit depth. Consequently, this study demonstrates a more realistic quantum threat to SHA-1 and sets a new standard for future research in quantum cryptography.

2 Background

2.1 Grover's Algorithm

For an n-qubit search space, Grover's search algorithm can find a target solution with high probability using approximately $\sqrt{2^n}$ queries. The algorithm consists of three main steps: *state initialization*, *oracle*, and *diffusion operator*.

1. *State initialization*: Apply Hadamard gates to each of the n input qubits to prepare a uniform superposition state $|\psi\rangle$, where all 2^n basis states are equally probable:

$$H^{\otimes n}|0\rangle^{\otimes n} = |\psi\rangle = \left(\frac{|0\rangle + |1\rangle}{\sqrt{2}}\right)^{\otimes n} = \frac{1}{2^{n/2}} \sum_{x=0}^{2^n-1} |x\rangle \tag{1}$$

2. *Oracle*: The oracle encodes the function to be searched (such as a hash function) as a quantum circuit. It evaluates the function on all inputs in superposition and flips the sign of the amplitude corresponding to a solution state (i.e., a pre-image x such that $\text{Hash}(x) = \text{target}$):

$$f(x) = \begin{cases} 1, & \text{if } \text{Hash}(x) = \text{target output} \\ 0, & \text{otherwise} \end{cases} \tag{2}$$

$$U_f(|\psi\rangle|-\rangle) = \frac{1}{2^{n/2}} \sum_{x=0}^{2^n-1} (-1)^{f(x)}|x\rangle|-\rangle \tag{3}$$

   The comparison between the computed and target hash outputs is typically omitted from quantum resource estimates [1–4].
3. *Diffusion operator*: This operator amplifies the amplitude of the marked solution states identified by the oracle, thereby increasing the probability of measuring the correct result. Due to its relatively low complexity compared to the oracle, the diffusion operator is often neglected in resource estimations for Grover's algorithm [1–4].

2.2 SHA-1

The Secure Hash Algorithm 1, commonly known as SHA-1, is a cryptographic hash function designed by the United States National Security Agency (NSA) as part of the U.S. Government's Capstone project. The original specification was first published by the National Institute of Standards and Technology (NIST) in 1993 as a Federal Information Processing Standard (FIPS) PUB 180 [5]. This initial version is now referred to as SHA-0. Shortly after its publication, the NSA withdrew this version to address a flaw that could reduce its cryptographic security. In 1995, a revised version was released as FIPS PUB 180-1, which became widely known as SHA-1 [6]. The primary purpose for its development was to be incorporated into the Digital Signature Standard (DSS) [7], making it a crucial component for ensuring data integrity and authenticity in various government and commercial applications. For years, SHA-1 was a foundational element in numerous security protocols, including TLS, SSL, PGP, SSH, and IPsec.

The SHA-1 algorithm works by taking a variable-length input message and producing a fixed-size 160-bit hash value, a message digest. This output is typically expressed as a 40-digit hexadecimal number. The computation begins with a preprocessing step that pads the input message so that its overall length is a multiple of 512 bits. The padded message is then processed sequentially in 512-bit chunks. The core of the algorithm is a compression function that utilizes the internal state of five 32-bit words initialized to a specific constant value. For each 512-bit chunk, the algorithm performs 80 rounds of computation. A key feature of this process is the use of a varying non-linear round function, F_t, whose logical operation changes throughout the rounds, along with round-specific constants and bitwise rotations. These operations iteratively update the internal state. After all message chunks have been processed, the final 160-bit hash value is produced by concatenating the five final internal state words. The complete specification of this process is detailed in the most recent standard, FIPS 180-4 [8]. The compression function of the SHA-1 algorithm, which forms the core of its iterative operation, is illustrated in Fig. 1.

Despite its widespread adoption, the security of SHA-1 began to face scrutiny in the early 2000s. In 2005, a research team led by Xiaoyun Wang presented a theoretical attack that could find collisions in SHA-1 with a complexity significantly lower than the brute-force benchmark of 2^{80} operations [9]. This discovery marked a turning point, after which SHA-1 was no longer considered secure against well-funded adversaries. Consequently, in 2011, NIST recommended against using SHA-1 for new digital signature generation and only use it when permitted by NIST protocol-specific guidelines [10]. Furthermore, NIST announced plans to deprecate SHA-1 for cryptographic applications by December 31, 2030. The need to transition to more secure alternatives, such as hash functions from the SHA-2 or SHA-3 family, has become even more pressing, especially for applications that require strong collision resistance.

The theoretical threat to SHA-1 became concrete and widely known in February 2017, when researchers at CWI Amsterdam and Google announced the first public collision attack, SHAttered ([11]). The researchers successfully generated two different PDF files that generated exactly the same SHA-1 hash, achieving a computational speed approximately 100,000 times faster than a brute-force attack. Subsequent research revealed vulnerabilities in SHA-1. In 2020, it was confirmed that chosen-prefix collisions compromise the signature schemes and handshake security of secure channel protocols (TLS, SSH), making chosen-prefix attacks against SHA-1 practical and enabling targeted attacks by sophisticated attackers. [12]. Although SHA-1 is currently considered cryptographically weak for mainstream use cases, particularly digital signatures, it has been widely used for some time in Keyed Hash Message Authentication Codes (HMACs), as specified in FIPS 198-1 [13]. Although the revised version, SP 800-224 [14], deprecated SHA-1 for HMAC.

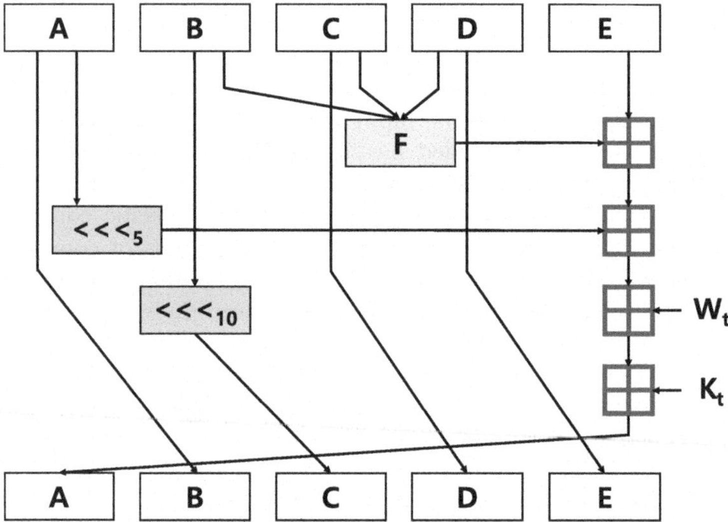

Fig. 1. An illustration of the compression function for a single round of the SHA-1 algorithm.

3 Quantum Circuit of SHA-1

This section describes a depth-optimized quantum circuit for the SHA-1 component. Since our primary goal is to minimize the depth of the quantum circuit, we employ a depth-optimized adder for our implementation. However, the number of qubits is just as important as the circuit depth. Therefore, we implement a SHA-1 quantum circuit that reduces the depth while reducing the number of qubits.

3.1 Message Padding and Round Word Computation

Classical Preprocessing The SHA-1 algorithm commences with a critical message preprocessing stage designed to transform a variable-length input into a standardized format. This process ensures the message length is congruent to 448 modulo 512 by padding it. The outcome of this stage is a message formatted into one or more sequential 512-bit blocks, which serve as the input for the subsequent computational steps.

Algorithm 1 Quantum SHA-1 Internal Functions

```
procedure FuncF1(result, x, y, z, temp)
for i ← 0 to 31 do
    CNOT — (y[i], temp[i])
    CNOT — (z[i], temp[i])
    Toffoli — (x[i], temp[i], result[i])
    CNOT — (y[i], temp[i])
    CNOT — (z[i], temp[i])
    CNOT — (z[i], result[i])
end for
end procedure

procedure FuncF2(result, x, y, z)
for i ← 0 to 31 do
    CNOT — (x[i], result[i])
    CNOT — (y[i], result[i])
    CNOT — (z[i], result[i])
end for
end procedure

procedure FuncF3(result, x, y, z, temp)
for i ← 0 to 31 do
    CNOT — (y[i], temp[i])
    CNOT — (z[i], temp[i])
    Toffoli — (x[i], temp[i], result[i])
    CNOT — (y[i], temp[i])
    CNOT — (z[i], temp[i])
    Toffoli — (y[i], z[i], result[i])
    CNOT — (temp[i], result[i])
    Toffoli — (y[i], z[i], temp[i])
end for
end procedure
```

Algorithm 2 Quantum SHA-1 Compression Function

```
procedure SHA1((H_0, ..., H_4), M_chunk)

    ▷ 1. Initialization
    a, b, c, d, e ← AllocateQubit(32)                         ▷ Working variables
    T, f, K_t ← AllocateQubit(32)                             ▷ Temporary registers
    (a, b, c, d, e) ← (H_0, H_1, H_2, H_3, H_4)
    W[0..15] ← LoadClassicalChunk(M_chunk)

    ▷ 2. Main loop: 80 rounds
    for t = 0 → 79 do                                         ▷ Round Logic
        if 0 ≤ t ≤ 19 then
            f ← FuncF1(b, c, d)                               ▷ Choose function
            K_t ← ClassicToQuantum(0x5A827999)
        else if 20 ≤ t ≤ 39 then
            f ← FuncF2(b, c, d)                               ▷ Parity function
            K_t ← ClassicToQuantum(0x6ED9EBA1)
        else if 40 ≤ t ≤ 59 then
            f ← FuncF3(b, c, d)                               ▷ Majority function
            K_t ← ClassicToQuantum(0x8F1BBCDC)
        else
            f ← FuncF2(b, c, d)
            K_t ← ClassicToQuantum(0xCA62C1D6)
        end if
                                        ▷ Compute round word W_t in-place for t ≥ 16
        if t ≥ 16 then
            W[t (mod 16)] ← ROTL(W[(t − 16) (mod 16)] ⊕ W[(t − 14) (mod 16)] ⊕ W[(t − 8)
    (mod 16)] ⊕ W[(t − 3) (mod 16)], 1)
        end if
                    ▷ Compute temporary value T using sequential quantum additions
        T ← ROTL(a, 5)
        T ← QuantumAdder(T, f, carry)
        T ← QuantumAdder(T, e, carry)
        T ← QuantumAdder(T, K_t, carry)
        T ← QuantumAdder(T, W[t (mod 16)], carry)

                    ▷ Update state variables (quantum register swaps)
        e ← d
        d ← c
        c ← ROTL(b, 30)
        b ← a
        a ← T
                    ▷ Uncompute this round's temporary values (f, K_t) to free qubits
    end for

    ▷ 3. Compute final hash value
    (H'_0, ..., H'_4) ← (H_0 + a, H_1 + b, H_2 + c, H_3 + d, H_4 + e)

    return (H'_0, ..., H'_4)
end procedure
```

Algorithm 3 Quantum Operators

```
procedure ClassicToQuantum(op1, op2)
    for i ← 0 to 31 do
        b ← (op2 ≫ i) ∧ 1
        if b = 1 then
            X — op1[i]
        end if
    end for
end procedure

procedure LeftCircularShift(op1, amount)
    n ← 32
    visited ← [False] × n
    cycles ← []
    for i ← 0 to n − 1 do
        if not visited[i] then
            cycle ← []
            j ← i
            while not visited[j] do
                append j to cycle
                visited[j] ← True
                j ← (j − amount) mod n
            end while
            if length(cycle) ¿ 1 then
                append cycle to cycles
            end if
        end if
    end for
    for all cycle ∈ cycles do
        for i ← 0 to length(cycle) - 2 do
            Swap(op1[cycle[i]], op1[cycle[i + 1]])
        end for
        Swap(op1[cycle[end]], op1[cycle[0]])
    end for
end procedure
```

Dynamic Qubit Allocation and Qubit Reuse After classical preprocessing, each 512-bit message block is loaded into the quantum circuit. This is achieved by allocating a 512-qubit register, organized into 16 blocks of 32 qubits, to store the initial words W_0 through W_{15}. The subsequent 64 words (W_{16} through W_{79}), required for the 80 compression rounds of the algorithm, are fully computed within the quantum circuit. A simple implementation would allocate new qubits for these additional words, resulting in significant resource overhead. To avoid this, this implementation utilizes a qubit reuse scheme. While the primary goal of this work is to optimize circuit depth, we introduce a crucial auxiliary optimization for qubit efficiency. The same initial 512-qubit register (organized into

16 blocks) is reused to sequentially compute and store the expanded words. This approach allows for a full 80-word message schedule expansion without allocating any additional qubits beyond the initial 512, significantly reducing overall resource requirements. A hint at qubit reuse lies in the SHA-1 message expansion algorithm (4). We implemented it to update the word corresponding to W_{i-16} (for example, store the value of W_{16} in W_0, and store the value of W_{32} in W_{16}, i.e., W_0) by taking advantage of the regularity of the index value corresponding to each word.

$$W_i = (W_{i-3} \oplus W_{i-8} \oplus W_{i-14} \oplus W_{i-16}) \lll 1 \tag{4}$$

A key advantage of this architecture is its resource efficiency for inputs larger than a single block. Since the compression function processes the message iteratively one 512-bit block at a time, the same quantum circuit and its 512-qubit register are reused for each block. Consequently, the total qubit count remains constant regardless of the message size. It is important to note that while the qubit requirement does not grow, the total circuit depth increases linearly with the number of message blocks, as the compression function is executed for each one.

3.2 Rounds (0-79)

SHA-1 Round Structure The core of the SHA-1 algorithm is its compression function, which iteratively processes the 80-word message schedule (W_t) through 80 rounds of computation. This process updates five 32-bit working variables, denoted A, B, C, D, and E, which collectively form the internal state of the hash. The 80 rounds are partitioned into four distinct stages of 20 rounds each. Each stage is characterized by two components that vary depending on the current round t: a non-linear logical function, F_t, and a unique additive round constant, K_t. The function F_t operates on three of the working variables, namely B, C, and D, to produce a 32-bit output based on a logical operation specific to that stage. The exact logical definition of $F_t(B, C, D)$ changes for each of the four stages, drawing from a set of three distinct underlying boolean functions. Concurrently, a unique constant K_t is assigned to each 20-round stage, beginning with $K_t =$ `0x5A827999` for the first stage and concluding with $K_t =$ `0xCA62C1D6` for the final stage. These two components, the output of the function F_t and the constant K_t, along with the message word W_t for the current round, provide the necessary parameters for the main state update operations that follow. The translation of these classical, non-linear logical operations into the quantum domain represents a critical aspect of our work. Thanks to these designs, we present resource-efficient quantum circuits for each of the distinct internal functions that constitute F_t. The detailed construction of these circuits from fundamental quantum gates is provided in Algorithm 1.

State Update Within a Round Once the round-specific function F_t and constant K_t are determined, the core state update takes place. First, a temporary

32-bit word, T, is computed by summing five values: the working variable a after a circular left shift of 5 bits ($a \lll 5$), the output of the logical function F_t, the working variable e, the round constant K_t, and the current message schedule word W_t. All additions are performed modulo 2^{32}. Following this calculation, the working variables are updated in a sequential cascade. The variable e takes the value of d, d takes the value of c, and c takes the value of b after it has been circularly shifted left by 30 bits ($b \lll 30$). Subsequently, b takes the value of the original a. Finally, the variable a is updated with the value of the newly computed temporary word, T. This entire sequence of operations ensures that the internal state is thoroughly mixed in each round, which is fundamental to the algorithm's security properties. The quantum implementation of this state update, with a focus on resource optimization, is presented in the following section.

Resource-Efficient Quantum Circuit Implementation We implement the aforementioned state update process as a quantum circuit, presented in Algorithm 2. As detailed in the algorithm, our implementation prioritizes qubit efficiency through two primary resource management strategies. Firstly, we employ the compute-uncompute paradigm for the temporary qubits that store the output of the non-linear function F_t (denoted as the 'result' variable). Instead of allocating new qubits for this calculation in every round, we compute the output of the function, use it, and then immediately uncompute the result. This procedure returns the ancillary qubits to their initial $|0\rangle$ state, allowing them to be cleanly reused in the subsequent round. Secondly, this optimization approach is extended to the management of the round constants, K_t. Rather than dedicating a permanent register for each of the four distinct constant values, we dynamically load the appropriate classical value into a single 32-qubit register. Once the constant is no longer needed for the round's computation, we uncompute this register to reset it. This just-in-time allocation strategy is crucial, as it prevents the redundant allocation of qubits and contributes significantly to minimizing the overall qubit footprint.

The two functions required to successfully build a complete quantum circuit are presented in the following Algorithm 3. The first function assigns classical bit strings to qubits. It is essential for initializing the quantum registers with appropriate values, using the input string and constants such as K_t. If the input value (classical bit) is 1, the X gate is used to flip the qubit value from 0 to 1. The second important subroutine is the quantum left rotation function, which implements the circular left shift ($\lll$) operation. The quantum analog of this function is implemented as an efficient network of SWAP gates that permutate the qubit states within the register. The definition of these basic functions also significantly impacts the performance of the main circuit. Therefore, it is important to keep the implementation simple so as not to waste circuit depth and the number of qubits.

Gate-Level Visualization of the Internal Functions Algorithm 1 provides the procedural description for the quantum implementation of the three distinct internal functions (F_t) used in SHA-1. To complement this, Figs. 2, 3, 4 offers a detailed visualization of the gate-level circuits corresponding to each of these procedures. The diagrams directly map each line of the pseudocode into its physical quantum gate operation, illustrating the flow of quantum information and the resource utilization for each function.

Figure 2 shows the quantum circuit of `FuncF1`. First, function F1 is an internal function of SHA-1, which means (5). As can be seen in the pseudocode, this circuit first computes the logical XOR of the inputs $y[i]$ and $z[i]$ using CNOT gates and stores the result in the auxiliary qubit $temp[i]$. Next, it performs the Toffoli (CCNOT) operation using $x[i]$ and $temp[i]$ as control qubits and stores the result in $result[i]$. Subsequent gates reset the auxiliary qubits to their initial states, demonstrating the compute-uncompute paradigm. Finally, the value of the result qubit $result[i]$ is modified using $z[i]$. In contrast, the `FuncF2` circuit shown in Fig. 3 is much more efficient because it does not require auxiliary qubits. Function F2 is an internal function of SHA-1, which means (6), and this algorithm implements a three-input XOR logic by applying a sequence of three CNOT gates. Each input qubit ($x[i]$, $y[i]$, $z[i]$) acts as a control for the target qubit ($result[i]$).

Finally, Fig. 4 shows the implementation of `FuncF3`, the most complex of the three. Function F3 stands for (7). Similar to `FuncF1`, this circuit also requires auxiliary *temp* qubits and uses a compute-uncompute paradigm. The simple explanation for F3 is as follows. First, y and z are XORed, and then the result is ANDed with x. This is equivalent to using the first CNOT gate twice, followed by a Toffoli gate. This stores the value $(x \wedge y) \oplus (x \wedge z)$ in *result*. After performing an operation to empty *temp*, the result of the AND operation of y and z is stored in *temp* using a Toffoli gate. Finally, *result* is modified using the CNOT gate and the value stored in *temp*. After storing the final result, we use Toffoli to reset *temp* to 0. These three schematics provide a complete and transparent blueprint of the core computational units of the SHA-1 implementation, clearly showing the complexity and resource requirements of each unit.

$$(x \wedge y) \vee (\bar{x} \wedge z) \tag{5}$$

$$x \oplus y \oplus z \tag{6}$$

$$(x \wedge y) \oplus (x \wedge z) \oplus (y \wedge z) \tag{7}$$

3.3 Final Hash Value Computation

The final stage of the SHA-1 algorithm commences after the 80 rounds of the main loop have been executed for each 512-bit message chunk. This concluding step is responsible for updating the internal state and, ultimately, producing the final message digest. The five working variables (a, b, c, d, e) that result from the main loop's computation for a given chunk are used to update the five 32-bit intermediate hash values, denoted as h_0 through h_4. Specifically, the new h_0 is the sum of the old h_0 and a, the new h_1 is the sum of the old h_1 and b, and so on for all five variables. These newly computed hash values then serve as the initial hash values for the processing of the next message chunk. It ensures that the entire message content sequentially influences the final output. Once the very last message chunk has been processed, the five final 32-bit hash values $(h_0, h_1, h_2, h_3, h_4)$ are concatenated in order to form the classical 160-bit message digest. In the context of quantum circuit implementation, this final 160-bit value would be encoded in the quantum state of the 160 qubits comprising five hash registers. To extract this result in the quantum domain, a standard computational measurement is applied to each of these 160 qubits. This measurement compresses the quantum state into a classical 160-bit string, representing the final output of SHA-1, typically expressed as a 40-digit hexadecimal number in big-endian format.

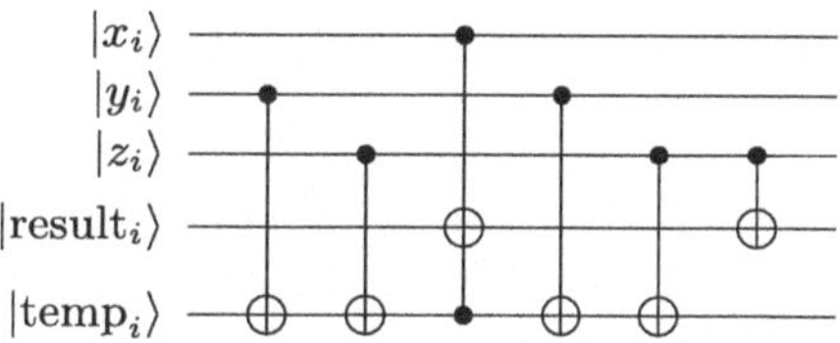

Fig. 2. The quantum circuit diagram for FuncF1.

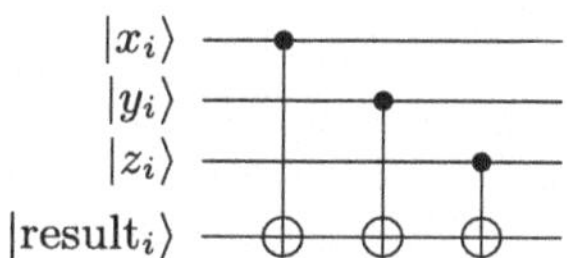

Fig. 3. The quantum circuit diagram for FuncF2.

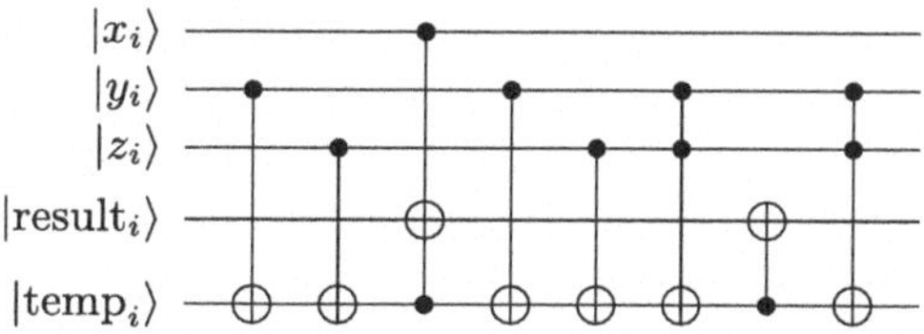

Fig. 4. The quantum circuit diagram for FuncF3.

4 Benchmark

4.1 SHA-1 Quantum Circuit with Draper Adder

The Draper adder, known as the Quantum Carry-Lookahead Adder (QCLA), is a widely recognized quantum arithmetic circuit notable for its logarithmic depth performance [15]. Drawing inspiration from classical carry-lookahead techniques, this adder contrasts sharply with earlier linear-depth ripple-carry adders. As detailed by Draper et al., the adder can sum two n-bit numbers in $O(\log n)$ depth using $O(n)$ ancillary qubits. This logarithmic depth provides a significant reduction in the required runtime for quantum algorithms that rely heavily on arithmetic, such as Shor's algorithm. For the implementation of our SHA-1 quantum circuit, we prioritized minimizing the overall circuit depth, as depth is a critical bottleneck on near-term quantum devices. Utilizing the Draper adder model allowed us to construct a circuit with a total depth of 9026, requiring 985 qubits for the complete implementation.

4.2 SHA-1 Quantum Circuit with TTK Adder

An alternative approach to quantum addition is presented by Takahashi, Tani, and Kunihiro (TTK), with a primary focus on minimizing the number of required qubits [16]. The foundational TTK adder design is remarkable for its ability to sum two n-bit numbers with no ancillary qubits, a significant achievement in qubit economy. However, this qubit efficiency comes at the cost of increased circuit depth, with the base model exhibiting a linear depth of $O(n)$. While the authors propose methods to reduce the depth, these often involve trade-offs or the use of specialized gates. To evaluate this trade-off in our context, we implemented the SHA-1 circuit using the TTK adder model. This configuration reduced the total qubit requirement to 929, but at the expense of a substantial increase in circuit depth, which measured 43232.

4.3 Comparative Resource Analysis

In selecting the optimal adder for our SHA-1 quantum circuit, we conducted a detailed comparison of the resource requirements for implementations based on the Draper and TTK models. A high-level summary of the qubit and depth trade-off is presented in Table 1. The implementation using the Draper adder resulted in a configuration of 985 qubits and a circuit depth of 9026, whereas the TTK-based implementation required 929 qubits but had a depth of 43232.

Although the TTK adder offered a savings of 56 qubits, this came with a nearly five-fold increase in total circuit depth. To understand the underlying reasons for this trade-off, we performed a detailed gate-level resource estimation, summarized in Table 1.

Fault-Tolerant Resource Metrics For a more holistic assessment of computational cost, especially in the context of fault-tolerant quantum computing, it is useful to consider metrics that capture both space (qubits) and time (depth) resources. One such metric is the Depth-Width (DW) Cost, which represents the overall space-time volume of the computation. As shown in Table 2, the Draper-based implementation demonstrates superior efficiency. Its DW-Cost of 8.89×10^6 is more than four times lower than the 4.02×10^7 cost of the TTK model. This significant difference highlights the practical advantage of the Draper adder's architecture.

In the era of Noisy Intermediate-Scale Quantum (NISQ) computers and beyond, circuit depth is often a more critical limiting factor than the absolute qubit count. The substantial performance gain and lower overall computational cost, as evidenced by the DW-Cost, offered by the much shallower Draper adder were determined to far outweigh its modest additional qubit cost. Consequently, we selected the Draper adder as the foundational arithmetic component for our final, optimized SHA-1 circuit.

Table 1. Detailed Gate-Level Resource Estimation for the two SHA-1 circuit implementations. All gate counts are obtained using the ProjectQ [17] resource counter. (***Input size $\leq$ 512bits**)

Metric	Draper Adder	TTK Adder
Qubits	985	929
Toffoli (CCX) Gates	90,940	24,315
CNOT (CX) Gates	67,879	78,279
X Gates	20,339	189
Circuit Depth	**9,026**	**43,232**

Table 2. Fault-Tolerant Resource Estimation and Costs. The DW-Cost is calculated as (Qubits × Circuit Depth). (* **Input size $\leq$ 512bits**)

Metric	Draper Adder	TTK Adder
Full Depth	9,026	43,232
DW-Cost	8.89×10^6	4.02×10^7

5 Conclusion

Quantum computing advancements pose a significant threat to the security of ubiquitous cryptographic algorithms, including classical hash functions such as SHA-1. Although the theoretical susceptibility of SHA-1 to quantum attacks like Grover's algorithm is well-established, a precise assessment of the danger requires a detailed understanding of the practical resources involved. Our study aimed to fill this knowledge gap by creating a comprehensive and resource-optimized quantum circuit for SHA-1. We placed a special emphasis on reducing the circuit's depth, as this is a primary performance limitation for current and near-future quantum hardware.

This paper presents a depth-optimized quantum circuit design for SHA-1, including gate-level implementations of all core components. Key optimizations, such as just-in-time qubit allocation and extensive compute-uncompute recycling, significantly reduce qubit overhead. We also compare two quantum adders, finding that although the TTK adder saves some qubits, the Draper adder's nearly five-fold depth reduction makes it the clear choice for minimizing decoherence on Noisy Intermediate-Scale Quantum (NISQ) hardware.

First, it provides a concrete blueprint and accurate resource estimates for the quantum implementation of SHA-1, offering a solid baseline for quantum pre-image attacks using Grover's algorithm. Second, our modular design and optimization strategies—especially dynamic resource management and systematic compute-uncompute—offer a practical framework for implementing other complex cryptographic algorithms on quantum computers. The presented algorithms and circuit diagrams form a transparent foundation for future quantum cryptanalysis research.

Our subsequent research will investigate better depth-qubit tradeoffs for SHA-1 quantum circuits and accurate resource estimation for Grover's algorithm. We will also focus on quantum circuit implementations for other cryptographic algorithms. We are confident that the circuit implementation methodology proposed in this study can be applied to quantum circuit optimization for various cryptographic functions, including other hash functions, which will advance quantum threat research for modern cryptography.

Acknowledgment. This work was supported by the Institute of Information & Communications Technology Planning & Evaluation(IITP) grant funded by the Korea government(MIST) (No. RS-2019-II190033, Study on Quantum Security Evaluation of Cryptography based on Computational Quantum Complexity, 75%) and this work was supported by Institute for Information & communications Technology Promotion(IITP) grant funded by the Korea government(MSIT) (No.2018-0-00264, Research on Blockchain Security Technology for IoT Services, 25%).

References

1. Grassl, M., Langenberg, B., Roetteler, M., Steinwandt, R.: Applying Grover's algorithm to AES: quantum resource estimates. In: Takagi, T. (ed.) Post-Quantum Cryptography, pp. 29–43. Springer International Publishing, Cham (2016)
2. Jaques, S., Naehrig, M., Roetteler, M., Virdia, F.: Implementing grover oracles for quantum key search on AES and LowMC. In: Canteaut, A., Ishai, Y. (eds.) EUROCRYPT 2020, Zagreb, Croatia, May 10-14, 2020, Proceedings, Part II, Lecture Notes in Computer Science, vol. 12106, pp. 280–310. Springer (2020)
3. Jang, K., Baksi, A., Kim, H., Song, G., Seo, H., Chattopadhyay, A.: Quantum analysis of AES. Cryptology ePrint Archive, Paper 2022/683 (2022). https://eprint.iacr.org/2022/683

4. Liu, Q., Preneel, B., Zhao, Z., Wang, M.: Improved quantum circuits for AES: Reducing the depth and the number of qubits. Cryptology ePrint Archive, Paper 2023/1417 (2023). https://eprint.iacr.org/2023/1417
5. National Institute of Standards and Technology, "Secure Hash Standard," Tech. Rep. FIPS PUB 180, Fips pub (1993)
6. National Institute of Standards and Technology, "Secure Hash Standard," Tech. Rep. FIPS PUB 180-1, Fips pub (1995)
7. National Institute of Standards and Technology, "Digital Signature Standard (DSS)," Tech. Rep. FIPS PUB 186-5, Fips pub (2023)
8. National Institute of Standards and Technology, "Secure Hash Standard (SHS)," Tech. Rep. FIPS PUB 180-4, Fips pub (2015)
9. Wang, X., Yin, Y.L., Yu, H.: Finding collisions in the full sha-1. In: Advances in Cryptology – CRYPTO 2005: 25th Annual International Cryptology Conference, Santa Barbara, California, USA, August 14-18, 2005, Proceedings, vol. Proceedings 25, pp. 17–36 (2005)
10. Barker, E., Roginsky, A.: Transitioning the Use of Cryptographic Algorithms and Key Lengths, Tech. Rep. SP 800-131A Revision 2, National Institute of Standards and Technology (2019)
11. Stevens, M., Bursztein, E., Karpman, P., Albertini, A., Markov, Y.: The first collision for full sha-1. Advances in Cryptology - CRYPTO **2017**, 570–596 (2017)
12. Leurent, G., Peyrin,T.: SHA-1 is a Shambles: First Chosen-Prefix Collision on SHA-1 and application to the PGP web of trust. In: 29th USENIX Security Symposium (USENIX Security 20), pp. 271–288, USENIX Association (2020)
13. Turner, J.M.: The Keyed-Hash Message Authentication Code (HMAC), Tech. Rep. FIPS 198-1, Federal Information Processing Standards Publication (2008)
14. Sönmez Turan, M., TAN Brandão, L.: Keyed-Hash Message Authentication Code (HMAC): Specification of HMAC and Recommendations for Message Authentication, Tech. Rep. NIST SP 800-224(Draft), National Institute of Standards and Technology (2024)
15. Draper, T.G., Kutin, S.A., Rains, E.M., Svore, K.M.: A logarithmic-depth quantum carry-lookahead adder (2004). arXiv preprint quant-ph/0406142
16. Takahashi, Y., Tani, S., Kunihiro, N.: Auantum addition circuits and unbounded fan-out (2009). arXiv preprint arXiv:0910.2530
17. Steiger, D.S., Häner, T., Troyer, M.: ProjectQ: an open source software framework for quantum computing. Quantum **2**, 49 (2018)

PoC Hash: A Power-of-Commutators Hash over Hamiltonian Quaternions

Hyungrok Jo[1(✉)] and Junji Shikata[1,2]

[1] Institute of Advanced Sciences, Yokohama National University, Yokohama, Japan
[2] Graduate School of Environment and Information Sciences, Yokohama National University, Yokohama, Japan
{jo-hyungrok-x,shikata-junji-rb}@ynu.ac.jp

Abstract. In this paper, we propose PoC Hash, a post-quantum cryptographic hash function that operates natively in Hamilton's quaternion algebra over a finite field, with security based on the hardness of the Multivariate Cubic (MC) problem. Each compression step takes two input quaternions, forms their non-abelian commutator, multiplies the result by the conjugate of a third quaternion, raises the product to the third power, and finally adds a fixed non-central offset. This procedure costs only five quaternion multiplications (roughly 80 finite-field multiplies), so software performance is expected to be comparable to the SHA-2 family while scaling efficiently on SIMD and GPU hardware. Finding a pre-image for a t-block message reduces to solving an $(n, m, q) = (6t, 4t, q \approx 2^{128})$ multivariate cubic system. PoC Hash thus combines prime-field efficiency with a non-commutative hardness foundation and meets the 256-bit security goal.

Keywords: Quaternion algebra · Power of commutator hash · Multivariate cubic hardness · Provable security · Post-quantum cryptography

1 Introduction

One of cryptographic hash functions grounded in algebraic structures typically regard a message as a walk in a Cayley graph: a collision would reveal a short non-trivial relation and is therefore as hard as the group word problem. The idea originated with Zémor and the TillichZémor scheme [14,17] after the advent of Merkle-Damgård transform. Especially, TillichZémor scheme resisted the many attacks for a decade, which is totally analyzed by Petit et al. Charles, Lauter, and Goren later applied the paradigm to supersingular-isogeny expanders and proved collision resistance by reducing it to the isogeny path problem [5]. Subsequent work extended the isogeny approach to genus-2 Richelot and superspecial curves [4,13], while LeGrow et al. analysed the supersingular non-superspecial abelian surfaces [8], which mitigates existing meet-in-the-middle attacks.

Charles, Lauter, and Goren also introduced Cayley hash function based on LPS Ramanujan graph [5], parallelly one based on supersingular-isogeny

K.-W. Park and J. Park (Eds.): WISA 2025 2025, LNCS 16434, pp. 198–211, 2026.
https://doi.org/10.1007/978-981-95-6857-4_15

expanders mentioned above. It became directions which are considerable of hash functions based on matrix groups over finite fields with algebraic provable mixing property. However, most of these suggestions based on several explicit constructions of Ramanujan graphs including LPS hash function above, are fully cryptanalyzed because of well-known their mathematical backgrounds. Several graphs with high girth (mainly over Cayley graphs with $SL_2(\mathbb{F}_q)$) supplied yet provable secure cryptographic hash functions: Mullan and Tsaban gave homomorphic hashes in $SL_2(\mathbb{F}_q)$ with a worst-casetoaverage-case reduction and showed that any collision forces a long random walk [9]. Tomkins et al. built free-subgroup hashes in $GL_2(\mathbb{F}_{p^n})$ using Tits' ping-pong lemma, eliminating short relations by design [15].

Satake and Jo used arc-transitive automorphisms to link collision resistance to the graph's word problem [11]. Aikawa et al. introduced left-right walks on Cayley complexes to obtain non-backtracking hashes with formal universality bounds [1], while ShpilrainSosnovski added stateful "cookies" to strengthen preimage resistance with 3 generators in $SL_2(\mathbb{F}_q)$. [12]. Across these lines the common theme is a standard-model security reduction to a well-studied algebraic problem, avoiding the random-oracle heuristic. Most existing constructions, however, rely either on abelian or near-abelian groups (where hidden-subgroup quantum algorithms apply) or on arithmetic in large field extensions.

Quaternion algebras provide a contrasting platform: they are inherently noncommutative sidestepping known quantum algorithms and yet their arithmetic is as efficient as prime-field matrix multiplication, making them a natural next trials for algebraic hashing. Unlike traditional hash functions (SHA-family) that are treated as black-box random oracles in security proofs, Cayley-graph-based hashes come with standard-model security arguments: their collision resistance is usually reduced to a well-established hard problem such as finding a short relation in a large group (*group word problem*), or computing an isogeny between distant nodes in an expander graph (*supersingular isogeny path finding problem*). Among the algebraic frameworks explored for provable hashing (matrix groups, isogeny expanders, leftright Cayley complexes, etc.), only a handful combine noncommutativity with prime-field arithmetic. The inherent non-commutativity of quaternion algebras makes them an attractive platform: it situates the resulting hash outside the abelian hidden-subgroup framework where sub-exponential quantum algorithms are known, while the underlying field arithmetic remains as fast as that required by competing algebraic constructions. Quaternion algebras in particular have been fruitful in this context: they provide groups with efficient arithmetic properties [16].

Quaternion algebras as a hashing substrate. Over a finite field $\mathbb{F}_q$, the Hamiltonian quaternion algebra $\mathbb{B} = \left(\frac{-1,-1}{\mathbb{F}_q}\right)$ supports constant-time arithmetic and, being non-commutative, frustrates low-degree algebraic shortcuts. Message blocks are mapped to pure quaternions and combined by the algebra's own multiplication.

Our construction. We propose the *Power-of-Commutators (PoC) hash.* Its compression function

$$G(a,b,c) = ([a,b]\bar{c})^3 - \lambda_*, \qquad a,b,c \in \mathbb{B},$$

uses the quaternion commutator $[a,b] = ab - ba$, a round-dependent "rotation" by $\bar{c}$, and a cube exponentiation, followed by a fixed non-central offset λ_*. One call to G needs five quaternion multiplications (roughly $5 \times 16 = 80$ field multiplications), making PoC comparable in speed to SHA-2 on modern CPUs and highly parallelisable on SIMD and GPUs. PoC Hash offers a new, quaternion-native point in the design space of post-quantum hash functions, as we detail below.

Hamiltonian parameters. Although one could instantiate $\mathbb{B}$ with any pair of non-square parameters $(-1,-p)$, we argue in Sect. 3.1 that the Hamiltonian choice $(-1,-1)$ is safest and fastest: it guarantees a division algebra whenever $q \equiv 3 \pmod 4$, avoids accidental splits that would enable rank attacks, and removes two constant multiplications per quaternion product (since all structure constants are ± 1).

Provable security. A single PoC compression round translates a collision or second pre-image into four cubic equations in six block variables; after the standard cubic-lifting (Sect. 4) this becomes an $(n,m,d) = (10,8,3)$ as MC (multivariate cubic) instance. For a full message of t blocks the algebraic system grows linearly to $(10t, 8t, 3)$. Under the semi-regular heuristic a Gröbner or hybrid attack on such a system requires about $q^{\omega d_{\text{reg}}}$ field operations with $d_{\text{reg}} \approx 5t$ and $\omega \simeq 2.3$; even $t = 4$ already pushes the cost beyond 2^{256} for $q \approx 2^{128}$. Rank-defect and hidden-field shortcuts are excluded because the coefficients vary with the state and stay full-rank, avoiding the weaknesses exploited by BaenaCabarcasEscudero [2]. Thus, with the recommended parameters (128-bit prime field and a minimum of four real blocks), every known classical or quantum technique remains exponentially far from breaking PoC Hash's 256-bit security goal.

2 Preliminaries

2.1 Cryptographic Notation

Definition 1. (*Negligible function*) A function negl : $\mathbb{N} \to \mathbb{R}_{>0}$ is called *negligible* if, for every positive polynomial $p(\cdot)$, there exists a constant N such that $\text{negl}(\lambda) < \frac{1}{p(\lambda)}$. Equivalently, $\text{negl}(\lambda)$ decreases faster than the inverse of any polynomial in the security parameter λ.

Definition 2. (*Probabilistic Polynomial Time, PPT*) An algorithm $\mathcal{A}$ is said to run in *probabilistic polynomial time* if, on input the unary security parameter 1^λ (and any auxiliary data), it halts in time $\text{poly}(\lambda)$ while making unrestricted use of internal random bits. In the sequel we refer to such algorithms simply as **PPT** algorithms.

Cryptographic hash functions and security notions A *hash function* is a deterministic, polynomial-time algorithm

$$\mathcal{H} : \{0,1\}^* \longrightarrow \{0,1\}^n,$$

where the output length n is fixed and publicly known. We require that $\mathcal{H}$ is *efficiently computable* and *non-invertable* satisfying with the following security properties.

Definition 3. (*Pre-image resistance*) $\mathcal{H}$ is *pre-image resistant* if, for every probabilistic polynomial-time (PPT) adversary $\mathcal{A}$,

$$\Pr\big[\,\mathcal{A}(1^\lambda, y) \in \mathcal{H}^{-1}(y)\big] \;\le\; \mathrm{negl}(\lambda),$$

where the probability is over the randomly chosen $y \xleftarrow{\$} \{0,1\}^n$ and the randomness of $\mathcal{A}$. In other words, given a random digest y, it is computationally infeasible to find *any* input that hashes to y.

Definition 4. (*Second pre-image resistance*) $\mathcal{H}$ is *second pre-image resistant* if, for every PPT adversary $\mathcal{A}$,

$$\Pr\big[\mathcal{A}(1^\lambda, x) = x' \;\wedge\; x' \neq x \;\wedge\; \mathcal{H}(x') = \mathcal{H}(x)\big] \;\le\; \mathrm{negl}(\lambda),$$

where the probability is over a randomly chosen $x \xleftarrow{\$} \{0,1\}^*$ and the randomness of $\mathcal{A}$. In other words, given an input x, it is computationally infeasible to find a distinct input x' that collides with it (i.e. $\mathcal{H}(x') = \mathcal{H}(x)$).

Definition 5. (*Collision resistance*) $\mathcal{H}$ is *collision resistant* if, for every PPT adversary $\mathcal{A}$,

$$\Pr\big[\mathcal{A}(1^\lambda) = (x, x') \;\wedge\; x \neq x' \;\wedge\; \mathcal{H}(x) = \mathcal{H}(x')\big] \;\le\; \mathrm{negl}(\lambda).$$

In other word, is is computationally infeasible to find *any* pair of distinct inputs hashing to the same output.

The negligible function $\mathrm{negl}(\lambda)$ decreases faster than any inverse polynomial in the security parameter λ. Collision resistance implies second pre-image resistance, but the converse is not known to hold; pre-image resistance is logically independent of the other two properties.

2.2 Mathematical Notation

We provide some mathematical notations for constructing our desired hash function. We mainly refer to [16].

Quaternion Algebras over $\mathbb{F}_q$. Given $a, b \in \mathbb{F}_q^{\times}$, we denote by

$$\mathbb{B} = \left(\frac{a,b}{\mathbb{F}_q}\right) \stackrel{\text{def}}{=} \mathbb{F}_q\langle i,j\rangle \Big/ \left(i^2 = a,\ j^2 = b,\ k = ij = -ji\right)$$

the (generalized) quaternion algebra over $\mathbb{F}_q$. It is a central simple $\mathbb{F}_q$-algebra of dimension 4. The algebra $\mathbb{B}$ is a *division algebra.* Throughout this paper we deal with the *Hamiltonian algebra*

$$\mathbb{B} = \left(\frac{-1,-1}{\mathbb{F}_q}\right),$$

which is division whenever -1 is a non-square in $\mathbb{F}_q$ (i.e. whenever $q \equiv 3 \pmod 4$). When $q \equiv 1 \pmod 4$ we instead choose arbitrary independent non-squares u, v and set $\mathbb{B} = \left(\frac{u,v}{\mathbb{F}_q}\right)$; all subsequent arguments remain valid because any two such division quaternion algebras are mutually isomorphic.

Basic Operations in $\mathbb{B}$. For $x = x_0 + x_1 i + x_2 j + x_3 k \in \mathbb{B}$ we write:

- **Conjugation:** $\bar{x} = x_0 - x_1 i - x_2 j - x_3 k$.
- **Trace:** $\mathrm{Tr}(x) = x + \bar{x} = 2x_0 \in \mathbb{F}_q$.
- **Norm:** $\mathrm{N}(x) = x\,\bar{x} = \bar{x}\,x = x_0^2 - ax_1^2 - bx_2^2 + ab\,x_3^2 \in \mathbb{F}_q$.

For $x, y \in B$ the *commutator* is defined as $[x, y] = xy - yx$. When u, v are *pure* quaternions (i.e. $\mathrm{Tr}(u) = \mathrm{Tr}(v) = 0$), one has $[u, v] = 2(u \times v)$, where $\times$ denotes the usual 3dimensional vector crossproduct.

Pure Quaternions, Dot Product, and Cross Product. In the Hamiltonian algebra $\mathbb{B}_{-1,-1}$ every element splits into a scalar and a *pure* part:

$$x = x_0 + \boldsymbol{x}, \qquad \boldsymbol{x} = x_1 i + x_2 j + x_3 k.$$

Via the isomorphism

$$\boldsymbol{x} \longleftrightarrow (x_1, x_2, x_3) \in \mathbb{F}_q^3,$$

we freely identify pure quaternions with 3-dimensional vectors. This allows the usual *dot* and *cross* products to be imported verbatim:

$$\langle \boldsymbol{u}, \boldsymbol{v} \rangle = u_1 v_1 + u_2 v_2 + u_3 v_3 \quad \in \mathbb{F}_q,$$

$$\boldsymbol{u} \times \boldsymbol{v} = \big(u_2 v_3 - u_3 v_2\big) i + \big(u_3 v_1 - u_1 v_3\big) j + \big(u_1 v_2 - u_2 v_1\big) k \quad \in \mathrm{Im}(\mathbb{B}).$$

Here, we write

$$\mathrm{Im}(\mathbb{B}) = \big\{ x \in B \bigm| \mathrm{Tr}(x) = 0 \big\},$$

i.e. the subspace of *pure quaternions* whose scalar part vanishes. Equivalently, if $x = x_0 + x_1 i + x_2 j + x_3 k$ with $x_0, x_1, x_2, x_3 \in \mathbb{F}_q$, then $x \in \mathrm{Im}(\mathbb{B})$ precisely when $x_0 = 0$.

Key identity. For two pure quaternions $\boldsymbol{u}, \boldsymbol{v} \in \mathrm{Im}(\mathbb{B})$, the quaternion product expands as

$$\boldsymbol{u}\boldsymbol{v} = -\langle \boldsymbol{u}, \boldsymbol{v} \rangle + \boldsymbol{u} \times \boldsymbol{v},$$

so the *commutator* simplifies to

$$[\boldsymbol{u}, \boldsymbol{v}] = \boldsymbol{u}\,\boldsymbol{v} - \boldsymbol{v}\,\boldsymbol{u} = 2\,(\boldsymbol{u} \times \boldsymbol{v}).$$

Quadratic Non-Residues. Let q be an odd prime power. For $x \in \mathbb{F}_q^\times$ the *Legendre symbol* (quadratic character) is defined as

$$\left(\frac{x}{q}\right) = x^{(q-1)/2} \in \{\pm 1\}.$$

We call x a *square* (resp. a *non-square*) in $\mathbb{F}_q$ if this value is $+1$ (resp. -1).

Definition 6. (*MC system*) Let $n, m \in \mathbb{N}$ and let $\mathbb{F}_q$ be a finite field. An *MC system* is a system of multivariate polynomials

$$F = (f_1, \ldots, f_m) \in \mathrm{MC}(n, m, q),$$

where m numbers of $f_\ell(x_1, \ldots, x_n)$ with n variables for each f_ℓ has total degree at most 3:

$$f_\ell(x) = \sum_{i,j,k} a_{\ell,i,j,k}\, x_i x_j x_k + \sum_{i,j} b_{\ell,i,j}\, x_i x_j + \sum_i c_{\ell,i}\, x_i, \qquad a_{\ell,i,j,k}, b_{\ell,i,j}, c_{\ell,i} \in \mathbb{F}_q.$$

Definition 7. (*MC Problem*) Given an MC system $F \in \mathrm{MC}(n, m, \mathbb{F}_q)$ and a target vector $v \in \mathbb{F}_q^m$, the *MC problem* asks for a vector $x \in \mathbb{F}_q^n$ such that

$$F(x) = v, \quad \text{i.e.} \quad (f_1(x), \ldots, f_m(x)) = v.$$

When $v = 0$ the task is to find a common root of the cubic system; otherwise it is to solve an inhomogeneous cubic system.

The MC problem generalises the well-known MQ (Multivariate Quadratic) problem and is believed to be at least as hard, with no efficient classical or quantum algorithms known.

3 Our Proposal

Let λ denote the security parameter (in bits), and we assume $\log_2 q \geq \lambda$. In what follows we focus on the 128-field-bit (256-bit security) setting. Specifically, we choose:

- Security parameter $\lambda = 256$.
- A prime q (or prime power) with $\log_2 q \approx 128$ and $q \equiv 3 \pmod 4$ (so that -1 is a quadratic non-residue in $\mathbb{F}_q$).
- The Hamiltonian quaternion algebra

$$\mathbb{B} = \left(\frac{-1,-1}{\mathbb{F}_q}\right) = \mathbb{F}_q\langle i, j\rangle / \left(i^2 = j^2 = -1,\ ij = -ji\right).$$

- A fixed pure-quaternion constant $\lambda_* \in \mathrm{Im}(\mathbb{B}) \setminus \{0\}$, e.g. $\lambda_* = i + j + 2k$ (which has $\mathrm{Tr}(\lambda_*) = 0$).

The hash operates by repeatedly applying a compression function G defined as:

$$G(a,b,c) = \big([a,b]\,\bar{c}\big)^3 - \lambda_*, \qquad (a,b,c \in \mathbb{B}), \tag{1}$$

where $[a,b] = ab - ba$ is the quaternion commutator and $\bar{c}$ denotes the quaternion conjugate of c. We now describe the hashing process, following a MerkleDamgård domain extender.

Hashing process (MerkleDamgård variant). Let $M = (m_1, \dots, m_\ell) \in \mathbb{F}_q^\ell$ be the message, represented as a sequence of field elements.

1. **Padding:** Append a bit "1" to the message, and then append the minimum number of "0" bits so that the final total length (in bits) is a multiple of $3\log_2 q$.
2. **Initial value:** $h_0 := 1 + i + j + k \in \mathbb{B}$ (a fixed non-zero initial state).
3. **Block processing:** Parse the padded message into $\lceil \ell/3 \rceil$ blocks of three field elements each. For each block index $r = 0, \dots, \lceil \ell/3 \rceil - 1$, interpret the r-th block as two pure quaternions:

   $$B_r = m_{3r+1}\, i + m_{3r+2}\, j + m_{3r+3}\, k, \qquad C_r = m_{3r+4}\, i + m_{3r+5}\, j + m_{3r+6}\, k,$$

   and update the state as

   $$h_{r+1} = G\big(h_r,\ B_r,\ C_r\big).$$

4. **Digest output:** Output h_t (with $t = \lceil \ell/3 \rceil$) as the hash value in $\mathbb{B}$ (this can be represented as a $4\log_2 q$-bit string). If a longer digest is required, one can continue applying G (with e.g. $B = C = 0$ for additional blank rounds) and concatenate the outputs.

PoC_Hash(M)

1. *Parameters:* $q \equiv 3 \pmod 4$, $\mathbb{B} = \left(\frac{-1,-1}{\mathbb{F}_q}\right)$, $\lambda_* \in \mathrm{Im}(\mathbb{B}) \setminus \{0\}$.
2. *Pad and split:* Represent M as $(m_1, \dots, m_\ell) \in \mathbb{F}_q^\ell$. Append a 1-bit then 0-bits until the length is a multiple of 6 field elements.
3. *Initial state:* $h \leftarrow 1 + i + j + k$.
4. *Process blocks:* For $r = 0$ to $\lceil \ell/3 \rceil - 1$:
   (a) $B \leftarrow m_{3r+1}\, i + m_{3r+2}\, j + m_{3r+3}\, k$.
   $C \leftarrow m_{3r+4}\, i + m_{3r+5}\, j + m_{3r+6}\, k$.
   (b) $h \leftarrow \big([\,h,\ B\,]\,\overline{C}\big)^3 - \lambda_*$.
5. *Return:* digest h.

Remark 1. (*Omission of scalar input component*) At first glance one might consider encoding every 4-tuple $(s,x,y,z) \in \mathbb{F}_q^4$ as the quaternion $s + xi + yj + zk \in \mathbb{B}$ and feeding such elements into the compression function. Our design deliberately *omits* the scalar part and restricts each message block to the pure quaternion subspace $\mathrm{Im}(\mathbb{B})$:

$$x\,i + y\,j + z\,k \;\in\; \mathrm{Im}(\mathbb{B}).$$

This has three advantages:

1. **Avoiding trivial commutator collapses.** Any scalar element lies in the *center* of $\mathbb{B}$. If an attacker could inject a block whose quaternion representation is purely central (i.e. of the form $s + 0i + 0j + 0k$), then the commutator with the current state h_j would vanish: $[h_j,\ s] = 0$. In that case the left factor of Eq. (1) becomes zero and the entire round output simplifies to the constant $-\lambda_*$. Two identical such blocks in different positions would yield an immediate collision (the state would reset to $-\lambda_*$ each time), an obviously undesirable situation.
2. **Guaranteeing noncommutativity.** With a pure quaternion input B_j, the commutator $[h_j,\ B_j]$ is generally non-zero (indeed it vanishes only in the special case that the two 3dimensional vectors $\boldsymbol{h_j}$ and $\boldsymbol{B_j}$ are parallel). Thus every round is forced to exercise the non-commutative part of the algebra, and differences in the state cannot commute away. This ensures that the full cubic map is applied and small input differences propagate thoroughly.
3. **Entropy utilization.** Using three field elements per block instead of four reduces the hashing *rate* from $4\log_2 q$ to $3\log_2 q$ bits per compression. This loss is marginal relative to the algebraic security gained by avoiding central inputs. In practice the throughput is dominated by quaternion multiplication count (which is unchanged), not by the slightly shorter block length.

3.1 Choice of Hamiltonian Parameters $(-1, -1)$

Let $\mathbb{B}_{(a,b)} = \left(\frac{a,b}{\mathbb{F}_q}\right)$ with $a, b \in \mathbb{F}_q^\times$ denote an *arbitrary* quaternion algebra over $\mathbb{F}_q$. Our proposal instantiates

$$\mathbb{B} \;=\; \mathbb{B}_{(-1,-1)}$$

(the *Hamiltonian algebra*) whenever $q \equiv 3 \pmod 4$, and falls back to an equivalent choice (u, v) of independent nonsquares if $q \equiv 1 \pmod 4$. For comparison, one could consider a more general instantiation such as $(-1, -p)$. Table 1 contrasts our choice with this generic $(-1, -p)$ approach. We retain the parameters $(-1, -1)$ throughout this work for three mutually reinforcing reasons. First, they guarantee that the quaternion algebra $\mathbb{B}$ is a *division algebra* whenever $q \equiv 3 \pmod 4$. If $\mathbb{B}$ were to split isomorphic to $M_2(\mathbb{F}_q)$, the commutator would degenerate to a 2×2 matrix commutator of rank at most one—exactly the rank-deficient configuration exploited by Baena et al. [2]. Fixing $(-1, -1)$ therefore precludes that entire class of attacks. Second, arithmetic becomes measurably simpler: every structure constant is ± 1, so one quaternion product costs exactly 16 field additions and 16 field multiplications; choosing $(-1, -p)$ would insert two extra constant-p multiplications per product, slowing 64-bit software by roughly 10 to

15% (the effect is smaller, though still noticeable, in wide-vector AVX2 or on GPUs). Third, $(-1, -1)$ aligns with widely used Mersenne and Solinas primes such as $2^{127} - 1$ and $2^{61} - 1$ (both congruent to 3 mod 4), so no per-prime tuning is required in practice. If an application must operate over a prime with $q \equiv 1 \bmod 4$ (for instance $2^{255} - 19$), one should *not* hard-wire a single value of p.

Table 1. Hamiltonian parameters versus a generic $(-1, -p)$ choice

	Hamiltonian $(-1, -1)$	Generic $(-1, -p)$
Division criterion	$q \equiv 3 \pmod 4$	Requires $\left(\frac{-p}{q}\right) = -1$. Choose a *square* p, causing $B \simeq M_2(\mathbb{F}_q)$ (which contains zero divisors)
Multiplication cost	Only *sign flips* (± 1) appear in the multiplication rules	$i^2 = -1$, but $j^2 = -p$ (cost $\approx$ 12 field multiplications each time)
Cryptanalytic surface	Most-studied quaternion instance; no hidden parameters for an attacker to exploit	Exotic p may in theory embed exploitable structure (e.g. a hidden subfield or special algebraic relation), albeit none is currently known
Portability to $q \equiv 1 \pmod 4$	*Not* a division algebra in this case (splits into matrices)	Can choose a suitable non-square p, hence portable to **all** primes by appropriate parameter selection

Instead, any fixed pair of independent non-squares (u, v) can be selected at design time, preserving full-rank security and arithmetic simplicity while avoiding the risk of a split algebra. In short, the Hamiltonian choice $(-1, -1)$ is both the safest and the fastest default, and alternative non-square pairs (u, v) remain a sound fallback whenever -1 fails to be a quadratic non-residue modulo the chosen prime.

Finite-field caveat. For odd characteristic q, every quaternion algebra over $\mathbb{F}_q$ splits: $\left(\frac{a,b}{\mathbb{F}_q}\right) \cong M_2(\mathbb{F}_q)$. Accordingly, the choice of parameters (a, b) should be viewed as a *computational basis choice* rather than a structural distinction between division and split cases; over finite fields, the algebra is always split.

Implementation note (basis vs. matrices). There are two natural implementation routes: (i) expand products in the quaternion basis $\{1, i, j, k\}$, or (ii) fix an explicit isomorphism to $M_2(\mathbb{F}_q)$ and use 2×2 matrix multiplication. A naive quaternion-basis product costs about 16 field multiplications and 16 additions when all structure constants are ± 1 (as with $(-1, -1)$), whereas a standard 2×2 matrix product needs 8 multiplications and 4 additions (Strassen reduces multiplications to 7 at the expense of extra additions). Hence, for multiplication-dominated kernels, the matrix representation is typically faster. The only practical advantage of $(-1,-1)$ over $(-1,-p)$ appears when one insists on the quaternion basis: the former avoids constant-p multiplications in each product, yielding a small constant-factor speedup; under a matrix implementation this difference essentially disappears.

4 Security Analysis

This section evaluates the security of PoC Hash through the aspect of multivariate polynomial cryptanalysis. We begin by formalizing the underlying hardness assumption in terms of a *non-commutative cubic root* problem and *multivariate cubic system* problem (Sect. 4.1). We then relate these to known attacks on multivariate polynomial systems (Sect. 4.2), and derive parameter guidelines (Sect. 4.3). In particular, our modeling of the multivariate cubic setting is aligned with prior MC-based formulations in identification schemes, notably Sakumoto et al. [10].

4.1 Hardness Assumption: The NC–CubeRoot Problem

Recall that the compression map is defined by

$$G(a,b,c) = \left([a,b]\,\bar{c}\right)^3 - \lambda_*,$$

operating in the Hamiltonian quaternion algebra $\mathbb{B} = \left(\frac{-1,-1}{\mathbb{F}_q}\right)$.

Related to Collision Resistance for One Block. Finding a hash collision essentially reduces to solving a certain equation in $\mathbb{B}$. We formalize this core problem as follows:

Definition 8. (*NC–CubeRoot problem*) Given an element $z \in \mathbb{B}$ (with $z \neq 0$), find *two distinct* elements $x, x' \in \mathbb{B}$ such that

$$x^3 = x'^3 = z.$$

(That is, find two distinct "cubic roots" of z in the non-commutative algebra $\mathbb{B}$.)

Expanding the equation $x^3 = z$ in coordinates provides a system of multivariate cubic polynomial equations. Writing an unknown $x \in \mathbb{B}$ as $x = x_0 + x_1 i + x_2 j + x_3 k$, the single quaternion equation $x^3 = z_0 + z_1 i + z_2 j + z_3 k$ is equivalent to a system of four cubic equations in the four unknowns $x_0, x_1, x_2, x_3 \in \mathbb{F}_q$. In other words, NC–CubeRoot is a special case of a multivariate cubic (MC) system of size $(n, m, q) = (4, 4, q)$.

Related to Pre-Image Resistance for One Block.

Theorem 1. (Reduction to MC problem) *Let $\mathcal{H}(M)$ denote the PoC hash of a message M, and suppose M consists of t compression blocks. For any fixed target hash value $y \in \mathbb{B}$, finding a preimage M such that $\mathcal{H}(M) = y$ (or finding a second preimage for a given M) is at least as hard as solving a system of multivariate cubic equations in $\mathcal{O}(t)$ variables over $\mathbb{F}_q$.*

Proof. It is enough to argue about a single compression round (one message block); the general t-round case is a straightforward extension. Let the internal state before the round be $a \in \mathbb{B}$, and suppose we are given a target output $z \in \mathbb{B}$ for the state after the round. We treat the message block as two pure quaternion inputs b and c, writing

$$b = x_1 i + x_2 j + x_3 k, \qquad c = x_4 i + x_5 j + x_6 k,$$

with unknown coefficients $x_1, \ldots, x_6 \in \mathbb{F}_q$. The goal is to solve $G(a, b, c) = z$ for these unknowns.

1. *Quadratic stage:* Compute the intermediate value

   $$u = [a, b]\, \bar{c}.$$

   Expanding u yields $u = y_0 + y_1 i + y_2 j + y_3 k$, where each coordinate y_k is a quadratic polynomial in the variables $x_1, \ldots, x_6$. (This follows since $[a, b]$ is linear in (x_1, x_2, x_3) and multiplying by $\bar{c}$ is linear in (x_4, x_5, x_6), so each component of u is bilinear in the two groups of variables.)
2. *Cubic stage:* The compression function output is $u^3 - \lambda_*$. Setting this equal to the target $z = z_0 + z_1 i + z_2 j + z_3 k$ yields four scalar equations:

   $$(u^3)_0 = z_0 + \lambda_*^{(0)}, \quad (u^3)_1 = z_1 + \lambda_*^{(1)}, \quad (u^3)_2 = z_2 + \lambda_*^{(2)}, \quad (u^3)_3 = z_3 + \lambda_*^{(3)},$$

   where $-\lambda_* = \lambda_*^{(0)} + \lambda_*^{(1)} + \lambda_*^{(2)} + \lambda_*^{(3)}$. Each equation is a degree-3 polynomial equation in the unknowns $x_1, \ldots, x_6$ (because the coordinates of u^3 are cubic functions of the coordinates of u, which were quadratic in the x_i). We thus obtain a system of four cubic equations:

   $$\begin{cases} f_0(x_1, \ldots, x_6) = 0, \\ f_1(x_1, \ldots, x_6) = 0, \\ f_2(x_1, \ldots, x_6) = 0, \\ f_3(x_1, \ldots, x_6) = 0, \end{cases}$$

   over $\mathbb{F}_q$.

One round of the hash yields a system of four equations in six unknowns (a special $(6, 4, q)$-MC system). For a full t-block message, similar equations arise from each round's output matching the next round's input; the overall system will have $4t$ equations in roughly $6t$ unknowns (the exact count depends on whether we consider intermediate chaining values $h_1, \ldots, h_{t-1}$ as additional unknowns).

4.2 Hardness of the Global (6t,4t,q) (6t,4t,q) MC System

Oneblock versus multiblock perspective. For a *single* compression round the attacker faces a $(6, 4, q)$ MC Problem: six unknown field elements (the three coordinates of each pure-quaternion block b and c) and four cubic equations (from the four coordinates of $G(a, b, c) = z$). Such small systems are routinely solved in milliseconds with Faugére's F4 [6]/F5 [7] algorithms or with resultant elimination; they therefore do not by themselves confer 256-bit security.

Growth of the algebraic system. Without lifting, one round supplies four cubic equations in the six block variables, so a t-block message produces

$$n = 6t, \qquad m = 4t,$$

i.e. a $(6t, 4t, q)$ MC system.

Semi-regular estimate. For a random cubic system the expected degree of regularity is $d_{\text{reg}} \approx \frac{3}{2}n - m$ [3]; here $d_{\text{reg}} \approx 9t - 4t = 5t$. The F4/F5 complexity is dominated by solving a $d_{\text{reg}} \times d_{\text{reg}}$ Macaulay matrix, costing $\tilde{\mathcal{O}}(q^{\omega d_{\text{reg}}})$ row operations with $\omega \simeq 2.3$. Taking $q \simeq 2^{128}$,

$$\log_2(\text{time}) \approx \omega\, d_{\text{reg}} \log_2 \text{q} = 2.3 \times 5t \times 128 \approx 1472\,t.$$

Thus even $t = 1$ already gives $\gtrsim 2^{1472}$ operations—well above the 256-bit target. Allowing for large hidden constants and hybrid refinements, a safety margin of is ample.

$$t_{\min} = 4 \implies n = 24,\ m = 16,\ \log_2(\text{time}) \approx 5900$$

Hybrid (guess—determine) check. Fixing k variables costs a factor q^k and lowers the Gröbner stage to $n - k$ variables whose degree of regularity is $\approx 5t - \frac{5}{2}k$. The total cost $q^k \cdot q^{\omega(5t - \frac{5}{2}k)}$ is minimised at $k \approx (\omega - 1)\frac{5}{2}t$; substituting $t = 4$ and $q = 2^{128}$ still exceeds 2^{256}. Hence a minimum of four real blocks is enough to retain the 256-bit margin under all known Gröbner and hybrid attacks.

Any valid preimage or second preimage must correspond to a solution of this global multivariate system. Conversely, any solution to the system immediately gives a valid (second) pre-image M producing the target hash y. Solving this system directly is therefore as hard as finding a preimage or collision. The best known algorithms (e.g. Gröbner basis methods, brute-force search, or specialized algebraic attacks) for such random-looking multivariate systems all have exponential complexity in the number of variables or the degree, which for our parameters yields the desired 256-bit security level.

Intuitively, Theorem 1 shows that the task of an attacker is equivalent to solving a set of coupled cubic equations. This problem is believed to be intractable in general. Indeed, solving arbitrary systems of polynomial equations (even quadratic ones) over a finite field is known to be NP-hard. In our setting, the hardness is amplified by the large field size (making brute force over each variable infeasible) and by the absence of any obvious algebraic structure or symmetry that could simplify the equations.

4.3 Recommended Parameters and Security Margin

We target a classical 2^{256} (and quantum 2^{128}) security level. The analysis in Sect. 4.2 shows that the global multivariate system arising from at least $t_{\min} = 4$ compression blocks already forces every known Gröbner, hybrid and quantum search attack above this threshold. Concretely we recommend:

- **Field size.** Choose a prime $q \equiv 3 \pmod 4$ with $\log_2 q \geq 128$. The Mersenne prime $q = 2^{127} - 1$ is a convenient instantiation, giving a 508-bit digest and a birthday bound of 2^{254}. Selecting a slightly larger prime (e.g. $2^{131} - 1$) widens the margin but is not strictly necessary.
- **Offset.** Fix any non-zero pure quaternion $\lambda_* \in \mathrm{Im}(\mathbb{B})$. Its sole purpose is to prevent the compression output from ever being 0; performance is insensitive to the exact value.
- **Minimum blocks.** Ensure every message is processed through $t \geq t_{\min} = 4$ calls to G. (It can be remedied by appending deterministic *non-central* constants as padding.)

5 Further Discussions

A convincing security argument for PoC Hash ultimately requires a rigorous, high-dimensional description of how the commutator, conjugation and cubic map propagate algebraic structure across rounds. Our heuristic discussion suggests that a single compression already mixes all three imaginary coordinates and raises the total degree, but this falls short of a proof. In particular we lack: (i) a quantitative bound on the rank of the Jacobian of the full t-round map, (ii) a precise description of the growth of the degree of regularity for the associated ideal, (iii) an analysis of whether any lower-dimensional algebraic varieties remain invariant under the round function, and (iv) a characterisation of diffusion when some inputs are drawn from structured subfields or sublattices.

Addressing these points will likely require tools from non-commutative algebraic geometry, representation theory of quaternion orders, and the theory of semi-regular sequences over large fields. We therefore leave a full algebraic-diffusion proof or a counter-example as an open research problem.

Acknowledgment. This work was supported by JST K Program Grant Number JPMJKP24U2, Japan. This work was in part supported by JSPS KAKENHI Grant Number JP23K24846.

References

1. Aikawa, Y., Jo, H., Satake, S.: Left-right cayley hashing: a new framework for provably secure hash functions. Math. Cryptol. **3**(2), 53–65 (2023)
2. Baena, J., Cabarcas, D., Escudero, D.E., Khathuria, K., Verbel, J.: Rank analysis of cubic multivariate cryptosystems. In: Post-Quantum Cryptography: 9th International Conference, PQCrypto 2018, Fort Lauderdale, FL, USA, April 9–11, 2018, Proceedings 9, pp. 355–374. Springer (2018)
3. Bardet, M., Faugere, J.C., Salvy, B., Yang, B.Y.: Asymptotic behaviour of the degree of regularity of semi-regular polynomial systems. In: Proceedings of MEGA. vol. 5, pp. 2–2 (2005)
4. Castryck, W., Decru, T., Smith, B.: Hash functions from superspecial genus-2 curves using richelot isogenies. J. Math. Cryptol. **14**(1), 268–292 (2020)
5. Charles, D.X., Lauter, K.E., Goren, E.Z.: Cryptographic hash functions from expander graphs. J. Cryptol. **22**(1), 93–113 (2009)
6. Faugere, J.C.: A new efficient algorithm for computing gröbner bases (f4). J. Pure Appl. Algebra **139**(1–3), 61–88 (1999)
7. Faugere, J.C.: A new efficient algorithm for computing gröbner bases without reduction to zero (f 5). In: Proceedings of the 2002 International Symposium on Symbolic And Algebraic Computation, pp. 75–83 (2002)
8. LeGrow, J., Ti, Y.B., Zobernig, L.: Supersingular non-superspecial abelian surfaces in cryptography. Math. Cryptol. **3**(2), 11–23 (2023)
9. Mullan, C., Tsaban, B.: Sl _2 sl 2 homomorphic hash functions: worst case to average case reduction and short collision search. Des. Codes Crypt. **81**, 83–107 (2016)
10. Sakumoto, K.: Public-key identification schemes based on multivariate cubic polynomials. In: International Workshop on Public Key Cryptography, pp. 172–189. Springer (2012)
11. Satake, S., Jo, H.: On cryptographic hash functions from arc-transitive graphs. Math. Cryptol. **2**(1), 2–20 (2022)
12. Shpilrain, V., Sosnovski, B.: Cayley hashing with cookies. In: Future of Information and Communication Conference, pp. 706–718. Springer (2025)
13. Takashima, K.: Efficient algorithms for isogeny sequences and their cryptographic applications. In: Mathematical Modelling for Next-Generation Cryptography: CREST Crypto-Math Project, pp. 97–114. Springer (2017)
14. Tillich, J.P., Zémor, G.: Hashing with sl 2. In: Advances in Cryptology—CRYPTO'94: 14th Annual International Cryptology Conference Santa Barbara, California, USA August 21–25, 1994 Proceedings 14, pp. 40–49. Springer (1994)
15. Tomkins, H., Nevins, M., Salmasian, H.: New zémor-tillich type hash functions over $GL_2(\mathbb{F}_2)$. J. Math. Cryptol. **14**(1), 236–253 (2020)
16. Voight, J.: Quaternion Algebras. Springer Nature (2021)
17. Zémor, G.: Hash functions and Cayley graphs. Des. Codes Crypt. **4**(3), 381–394 (1994)

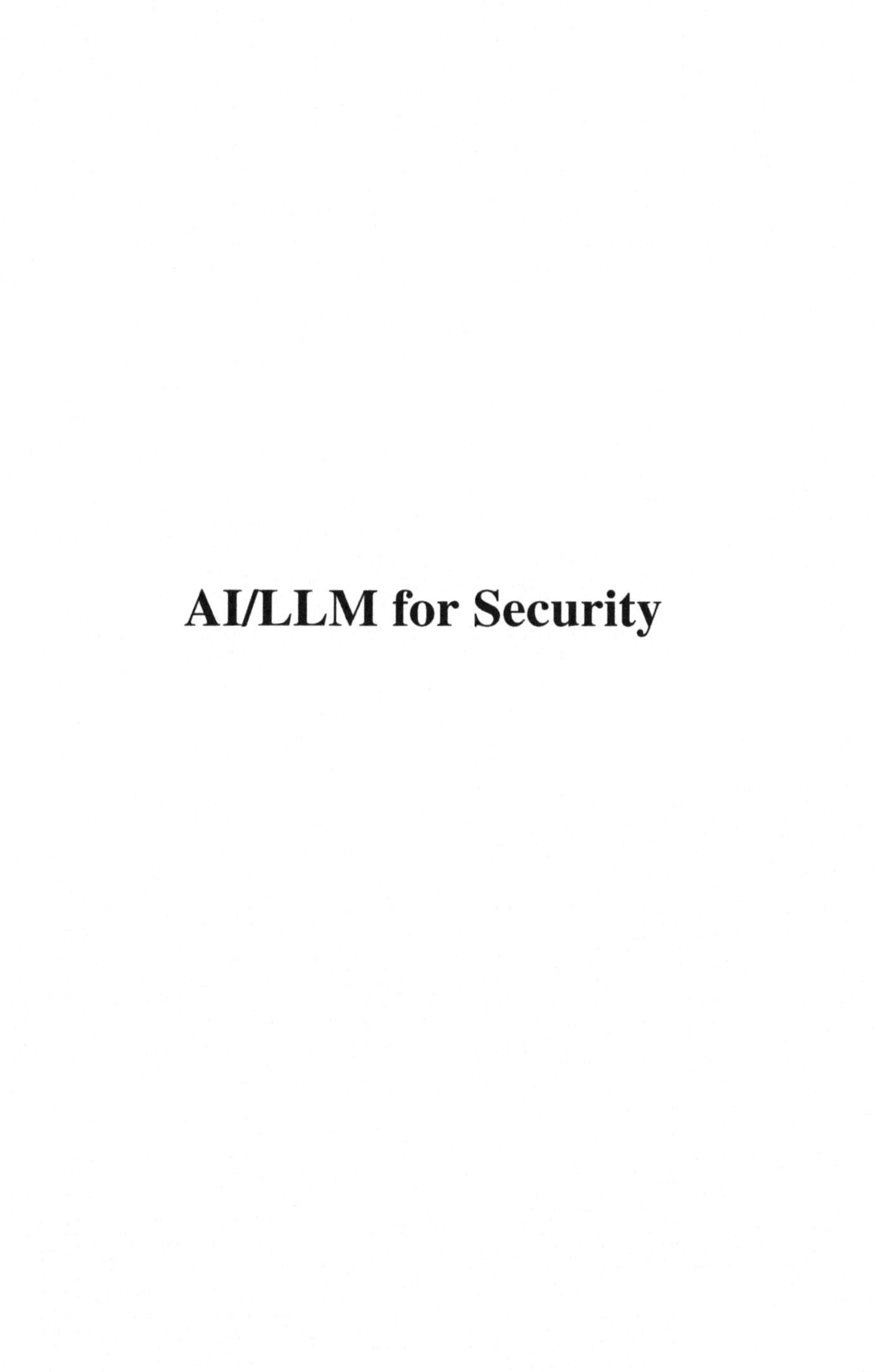

AI/LLM for Security

Detecting Malicious JavaScript Code by Code-Specialized LLM

Keiichi Kinoshita and Mamoru Mimura(✉)

National Defense Academy, 1-10-20 Hashirimizu, Yokosuka, Kanagawa, Japan
{em63021,mim}@nda.ac.jp

Abstract. Malicious JavaScript remains a significant cybersecurity threat. The challenge is that the detection rate of unknown malicious JavaScript is low. On the other hand, large language models (LLMs), which excel in the ability to explain codes, are expected to be effective in the detection field. However, quantitative evaluation and detailed analysis in the detection of malicious JavaScript using LLMs is still insufficient. This study proposes an offline-based LLMs approach for malicious JavaScript detection, specifically evaluating LLaMA2, LLaMA3, and the code-specialized CodeLLaMA. Our results show CodeLLaMA achieved a high F-measure of 0.89. Furthermore, we thoroughly analyzed the impact of individual tokens on detection using both gradient-based and attention-based methods. This analysis revealed that the gradient-based approach offers more explainable features for malicious tokens. These findings highlight the strong potential of LLMs, particularly code-specialized models, for effective malicious JavaScript detection and improve the interpretability of their decisions.

Keywords: Large language model · Malicious Javascript · XAI

1 Introduction

JavaScript plays a crucial role in modern web applications, yet its widespread use makes it a prime target for cyberattacks, notably drive-by downloads, where users unwittingly obtain malicious code [1]. The persistent threat of malicious JavaScript necessitates robust detection mechanisms. Various static analysis methods have been proposed to address this problem, including approaches that transform JavaScript into Abstract Syntax Trees (ASTs) [2], and those that combine semantic tokenization with AST features [5,13]. Furthermore, neural network-based techniques, such as Convolutional Neural Networks (CNNs) [7] attention mechanisms, and Long Short Term Memory (LSTM) networks, have also been explored [4]. These non-execution-based methods offer efficiency by avoiding the overhead of code execution. However, these methods are fast because they do not execute JavaScript, but they have a low detection rate of unknown malicious JavaScript.

K.-W. Park and J. Park (Eds.): WISA 2025 2025, LNCS 16434, pp. 215–227, 2026.
https://doi.org/10.1007/978-981-95-6857-4_16

In recent years, Large Language Models (LLMs) have reveal as powerful tools and have demonstrated remarkable capabilities in a variety of domains, including cybersecurity LLMs have been studied for general malicious code detection and code analysis, but malicious comprehensive quantitative evaluation for JavaScript behavior detection is still largely lacking. To overcome these limitations and address the existing gaps, we propose a novel detection method leveraging Large Language Models (LLMs). Our approach utilizes advanced LLMs such as LLaMA2, CodeLLaMA, and the more recent LLaMA3 of Meta. These models can be specifically optimized for malicious pattern detection through fine-tuning. We specifically evaluate detection performance on imbalanced datasets that more accurately simulate real-world threat environments. Building on existing knowledge, we focus specifically on malicious JavaScript and perform rigorous quantitative evaluation on real-world datasets.

Furthermore, we analyzed the impact of individual tokens on the detection precess. While a common approach in conventional Bidirectional Encoder Representations from Transformers (BERT) based classification involves quantifying Multi-Head Attention weights related to the ([CLS]) token to identify tokens of interest for the detector [9]. Therefore, We propose a gradient-based aggregation method. This approach involves obtaining gradients for each token with respect to the model's malicious/benign classification decision, specifically from the layers contributing to this classification. By aggregating these gradients, we can then identify tokens that are considered important for the model's final determination. Furthermore, this proposed gradient-based method will be compared and analyzed against an attention-based aggregation technique, which is adapted from conventional methods that quantify Multi-Head Attention weights often associated with the start-of-sequence token (<s>).

This study seeks to answer the following research questions(RQs):

(RQ1) How effective are LLMs compared to existing detection models in detecting malicious JavaScript?
(RQ2) Is a code-specialized LLM more effective than its original model in detecting malicious JavaScript?
(RQ3) Which approach, gradient-based or attention-based, is more effective for interpretability when analyzing the tokens that LLMs consider important?

Experimental results demonstrate that our proposed LLM-based method consistently improves detection accuracy, achieving the highest F-measure of 0.89. Notably, CodeLLaMA outperformed LLaMA2 in detection accuracy, highlighting the benefits of code-specialized models. Our key contributions are summarized as follows:

1. We propose a method for detecting malicious JavaScript using LLMs.
2. We verify that the code-specialized LLM, Code LLaMA, detects malicious JavaScript more accurately compared to the original LLaMA2.
3. We reveal how individual tokens influence the judgment of LLMs by analyzing token-level gradients, providing insights into its decision-making process.

The remainder of this paper is organized as follows. Section 2 reviews related works on malicious JavaScript detection. Section 3 introduces related technologies regarding LLMs. Section 4 describes the proposed method. Section 5 explains the experimental methods and results. Section 6 discusses the experimental results. Finally, Sect. 7 concludes the study.

2 Related Work

This section reviews prior studies on malicious JavaScript detection and LLM-based malware classification. While dynamic analysis methods, such as sandbox, have been explored, our study focuses on static detection based on linguistic features.

2.1 Methods for Detecting Malicious JavaScript

Early approaches employed traditional machine learning models with feature extraction techniques. Curtsinger et al. converted JavaScript into ASTs and applied a Naive Bayes classifier [2]. Fass et al. combined semantic tokenization with AST features using a Random Forest(RF) model [5].

Later studies introduced neural network-based techniques. Ndichu et al. utilized Doc2Vec embeddings with Support Vector Machines(SVMs) and neural networks [11]. Fang et al. proposed a Bi-LSTM model with attention mechanisms [4], while Huang et al. applied TextCNN with Word2Vec for syntactic unit sequences [7]. Kunlun et al. developed JSRevealer, which combines ASTs with data flow analysis and attention [13]. Ngoc et al. addressed class imbalance using oversampling with Doc2Vec and LSTM [12].

Thus, various feature extraction methods and methods for detecting malicious JavaScript using neural networks have been proposed. However, these studies have the problem that the detection rate of unknown malicious JavaScript is low, although the time required for detection is fast. To the best of the authors' knowledge, there is no method for quantitatively evaluating the detection of malicious JavaScript using LLMs.

2.2 Malware Detection Using LLMs

Research using LLMs for malware detection includes studies on detecting malicious applications. Stein et al. proposed a Deep Packet Inspection (DPI) algorithm utilizing Transformer models to detect malicious network traffic [14]. Natsos et al. also proposed a Transformer-based malware detection approach using process resource utilization metrics [10], achieving superior performance over LSTM models in accuracy, precision, recall, and scalability.

For JavaScript malware detection, Hwang et al. proposed a method using variant of Stacked Denoising Autoencoders (SDA) with logistic regression to identify obfuscated malicious JavaScript [8]. Their model learned robust features from ASTs by injecting synthetic obfuscation, achieving high accuracy and strong generalization. Fang et al. investigated source code analysis capability of LLMs [3]. The understanding of LLMs with respect to obfuscation and code vulnerabilities has been quantitatively evaluated using manually generated correct data and metrics such as cosine similarity and BERT-based semantic similarity. However, an exhaustive quantitative evaluation and detailed analysis of LLMs capabilities in the specific domain of malicious JavaScript detection is still lacking.

Building upon these findings, our study specifically focuses on malicious JavaScript, providing a quantitative evaluation on real-world datasets and investigating which features LLMs classify based on by analyzing token-level sensitivity.

3 Related Technologies

This section describes the LLMs and fine-tuning technologies utilized in this study. Specifically, we employ LLaMA, a pre-trained Transformer-based model, for classification tasks, using Low-Rank Adaptation (LoRA) for efficient fine-tuning. This approach allows us to quantitatively evaluate the LLMs and investigate its impact on token-level classification decisions.

3.1 LLaMA

Developed by Meta, LLaMA2 is a pre-trained model that leverages the Transformer architecture. Its advanced design and training on a wide range of datasets allows it to perform a variety of natural language processing tasks, including text generation and classification. It can be used offline and implemented with relatively low parameters. It also offers derivatives such as CodeLLaMA, which is an extension of LLaMA2 specifically for programming-related datasets.

In this study, LLaMA2, CodeLLaMA, and LLaMA3 are used. 7B parameter configurations were chosen for LLaMA2 and CodeLLaMA in the experiments to optimize computational efficiency and balance the trade-off between performance and processing time. configurations available, but the 8B model was chosen for the same reason.

3.2 LoRA

LoRA is a technique designed to efficiently fine-tune LLMs by leveraging low-rank matrices. This approach aims to reduce the computational resources and time required to adapt a model to specific tasks or domains [6]. The weight matrix update in LoRA can be expressed as Eq. 1:

$$W_{new}x = W_0x + \delta Wx = W_0x + L_2L_1x \tag{1}$$

Into a product of low-rank matrices, only the updated weights need to be stored, which significantly reduces storage requirements. This method enables selective tuning of specific parameters, thereby achieving efficient performance improvements with minimal computational overhead. We use that technology in fine-tuning.

3.3 Sequence Classification

Sequence Classification categorizes an entire input sequence into a single class, used in tasks like malicious code detection. Transformer models excel at Sequence Classification due to their ability to capture complex token relationships via attention mechanisms, processing the entire sequence to grasp its overall meaning. In this study, we configured the LLMs for a sequence classification task and analyzed the classification results along with token-level insights.

4 Proposed Method

This section details the proposed method for detecting malicious JavaScript using LLMs.

4.1 Overview

Figure 1 illustrates an overview of the proposed method.

The proposed method primarily consists of preprocessing the dataset and fine-tuning the LLMs. The following steps describe the proposed approach:

1. Perform data cleansing on JavaScript and convert it into tokens.
2. Use the preprocessed training dataset to fine-tune the LLMs using LoRA.
3. Classify JavaScript using the fine-tuned LLMs.
4. Aggregation of Tokens Prioritized by LLMs for judgment

In this study, the LLMs are configured for a binary classification task using the LlamaForSequenceClassification module from the Transformers library. LoRA is then employed to enhance the parameter efficiency of the model.

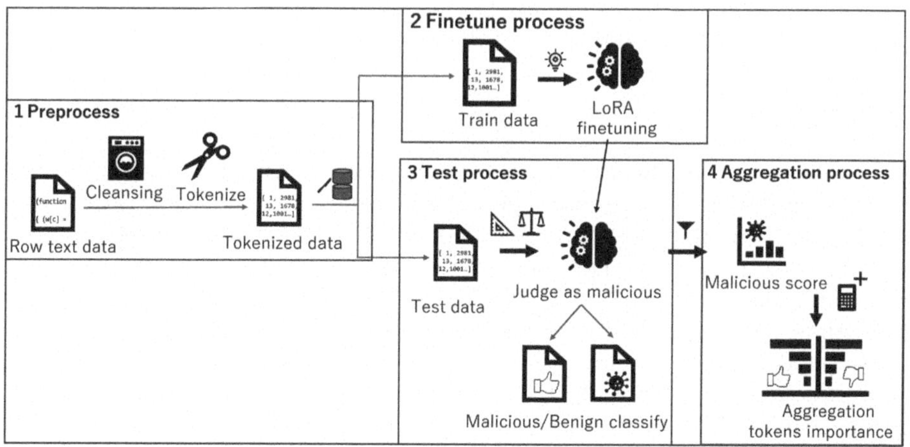

Fig. 1. Proposed method

4.2 Preprocessing

The preprocessing stage involves performing data cleansing for all samples, followed by converting them into tokens.

Data Cleaning During data cleansing, specific long strings unique to obfuscated JavaScript are replaced with two-letter alphabetic strings. The objective is to replace meaningless long strings with two-character alphabetic strings to efficiently perform subword tokenization. This is an example of the replacement process.

Token Conversion For token conversion, the LLaMATokenizer from the Transformers [16] library is used to convert JavaScript into tokens. The tokenizer uses Byte-Pair Encoding (BPE) [15]. BPE is a technique that merges frequent character pairs and splits words into subwords, converting them into tokens. This enables the flexible handling of unknown tokens.

4.3 Fine-Tuning

During training, some layers of the LLMs are transformed into low-rank parameters using LoRA, and fine-tuning is executed with the Trainer module from the Transformers library. Based on prior research, we specify the layers to be tuned as q_proj and v_proj. The loss function used is cross-entropy loss, defined as follows:

$$L = -\frac{1}{N} \sum_{i=1}^{N} [y_i \log(P_i) + (1 - y_i) \log(1 - P_i)] \tag{2}$$

where N represents the total number of samples, y_i is the true label (1 for malicious), and P_i is the predicted probability.

4.4 Classification

In the Sequence Classification task, the final layer of an LLM outputs a logit vector as a prediction for the entire input sequence. For binary classification, such as malicious/benign, this logit vector consists of two elements, representing raw scores for each respective class. Since these logits are not specifically optimized for a particular task (e.g., malicious code detection) during the pre-training phase, they generally require fine-tuning for optimal performance.

The model directly utilizes these logits for making classification decisions. These raw logits are typically transformed into probabilities using a softmax function, and the class with the highest probability is then predicted.

4.5 Aggregation of Tokens Prioritized by LLMs for Judgment

We employ an aggregation technique to prioritize LLM tokens in the classification of malicious/benign JavaScript code. This method is based on the principle that the higher a token's priority, the greater its influence on the final decision of LLMs. By applying this technique, we can analyze whether LLMs are primarily focusing on specific code elements or recognizing more complex contextual patterns within the code. This analysis also provides crucial clues for understanding and mitigating false positives. Ultimately, this approach offers valuable insights into the explainability (XAI) of LLMs, significantly enhancing their trustworthiness in cybersecurity applications.

To systematically identify which tokens the LLMs prioritizes in its judgments, we follow these steps:

1. **Obtain Logits**: Execute the forward pass of the model to acquire raw, unnormalized scores (logits) from the final prediction layer. For binary classification tasks, this typically results in a two-element vector.
2. **Define Loss**: Define the loss function as the logit value corresponding to the target class (e.g., malicious class) itself. This allows for the calculation of influence on that specific logit during backpropagation.
3. **Clear Model Gradients**: Invoke `model.zero_grad()` to clear any accumulated gradients from previous computations for all trainable parameters of the model (weights and biases), ensuring accurate gradient calculation for the current loss.
4. **Calculate Importance per Sample**: Perform `L.backward()` on the defined loss L to obtain gradients with respect to the input embeddings. The sum of the absolute values of these gradients is computed as the importance score for each token, quantifying its influence on the malicious/benign judgment for each JavaScript code snippet.
5. **Aggregate and Rank Top 10**: After computing importance scores for all test samples, scores for identical tokens are aggregated and averaged per class (e.g., malicious, benign). Tokens are then ranked by their average importance, and the top 10 tokens are extracted to identify token characteristics prioritized by the model across the entire class.

5 Evaluation

5.1 Datasets

We used two different datasets. Benign samples were sourced from Alexa's website ranking, specifically the top 50 URLs from 178 countries and 762 categories, totaling 21,745 samples collected on December 19, 2018. Malicious samples were drawn from two distinct collections: The first, from PhishTank, comprised 15,000 URLs with duplicates removed based on hash values, and samples were labeled as malicious if at least one VirusTotal detector identified them as such. This dataset was collected from February to March 2016, with the first half used for training and the second for testing. The second malicious dataset came from

GitHub, providing pre-labeled samples; 4,000 were collected from September to October 2016 for training, and another 4,000 from November to December 2016 for testing.

In the experimental evaluation, benign samples from Alexa were used in combination with malicious samples from PhishTank to create dataset A, and with malicious samples from GitHub to create dataset B. These datasets are henceforth referred to as dataset A and dataset B. The datasets are shown in Table 1.

Table 1. Number of samples in each datasets

	Benign (Alexa)	Malicious A (Phishtank)	Malicious B (Github)
Training data	10,872	106	4,000
Test data	10,873	108	4,000

5.2 Experimental Setup

The environment used in the experiment is shown below.

Implementation The proposed method was implemented using Python 3.8.9. The machine learning model was implemented using Transformers4.41.1 and TensorFlow2.13.0, while the fine-tuning library used was peft0.10.0, with the rank for matrix r = 16, lora alpha = 16, and lora dropout = 0.05.

These parameters were chosen on the basis of four iterations to achieve the best accuracy.

Model for Comparison To evaluate the performance of the proposed LLM-based detection method, we compared it with six baseline models commonly used in malware detection. These include RF, DNN, CNN, LSTM+Attention, SVM, and Extreme Gradient Boosting (XGBoost).

5.3 Experimental Results

The precision for each dataset is shown in Table 2. Additionaly, The gradiant-based aggregation results are shown in Table 3a and the Attention-based aggregation results are shown in Table 3b.

Across all datasets, it was confirmed that the proposed method generally outperformed existing methods [12] and models in terms of accuracy. Notably, CodeLLaMA, a model specialized for code, demonstrated higher accuracy overall compared to LLaMA2.

Table 2. Evaluation

	DatasetA			DatasetB		
	Presision	Recall	F-measure	Presision	Recall	F-measure
Ngoc et al. [12]	0.69	0.38	0.49	0.99	0.53	0.70
RF	0.92	0.75	0.83	0.99	0.08	0.16
SVM	0.89	**0.83**	**0.86**	**1.00**	0.30	0.46
XGBoost	**1.00**	0.00	0.00	0.99	0.51	0.67
DNN	0.91	0.09	0.17	0.99	0.60	0.75
CNN	0.88	0.78	0.83	0.99	0.47	0.64
LSTM+Attention	0.80	**0.83**	0.81	0.99	0.66	0.79
Code LLaMA	0.95	0.70	0.81	0.99	**0.80**	**0.89**
LLaMA2	0.88	0.64	0.74	0.98	0.64	0.77
LLaMA3	0.82	0.69	0.74	0.99	0.79	0.88

Table 3. Top 10 important tokens

Top 10 gradiant base tokens

True Label	Benign		Malicious	
Tendency	N	P	N	P
1	_Process	istiques	bra	iste
2	_Trust	_PATH	ensor	assa
3	_eval	_registration	ria	mania
4	_DDR	_Syntax	able	ler
5	_String	aco	rant	inv
6	estra	_estad	yal	assign
7	_gg	enti	loc	are
8	_cm	_qual	cent	_T
9	rc	_vs	doc	look
10	See	_vb	immer	ran

Top 10 attention base tokens

True Label	Negative		Positive	
Predict Label	N	P	N	P
1	<0x0A>	,	0	,
2	.	2	7	<0x0A>
3	<s>	<s>	x	_=
4	_	(	_=	var
5	_=	9	var	0
6	0	1	3	x
7	-	_	<0x0A>	_
8	1	a	1	<s>
9	(	.	2	7
10	:	%	5	_'

Tokens beginning with an underscore (_) are the second half of a token that was cut off in the middle of a word segmentation, indicating that there is some string of characters before this token.The gray background color indicates that more than three tokens are found in the same table.

6 Discussion

6.1 Detection Accuracy of LLMs

The validation experiments confirmed that the proposed LLM-based method generally exceeded the detection accuracy of existing methods and models. For Dataset B, it outperformed baselines across all metrics: precision, recall, and F-measure.

For Dataset A, the proposed method showed higher precision (excluding XGBoost) but had relatively low recall, resulting in a slightly lower F-measure. This discrepancy is likely due to Dataset A, small sample size and potential inaccuracies in its labels. Specifically, 87 samples, accounting for over 40% of the total, were labeled as malicious because at least one antivirus software in VirusTotal identified them as such, even if only two out of 58 VirusTotal detectors marked them as positive and they exhibited no inherently malicious behavior. Consequently, Dataset A may be less suitable for accurate evaluation due to its limited sample size and the potential inaccuracy of its labels.

In conclusion, the proposed LLM-based detection method generally surpasses the accuracy of existing approaches.

6.2 Effectiveness of Code-Specialized LLMs Models

Code-specialized LLMs are effective in detecting malicious JavaScript. CodeLLaMA consistently demonstrated superior performance over LLaMA2 in terms of F-measure across both Data Set A and Data Set B. Specifically, CodeLLaMA achieved an F-measure of 0.81 on Data Set A (Compared to 0.74 for LLaMA2) and 0.89 on Data Set B (Compared to 0.77 for LLaMA2). Furthermore, CodeLLaMA even slightly surpassed the latest general-purpose model, LLaMA3, by 0.02 points, indicating that specialized models offer superior learning accuracy compared to general-purpose models, even with more training data.

6.3 Evaluation of LLM Context Understanding and Important Token Analysis

Table 3 presents two tables comparing token prioritization methods for LLM-based malicious/benign JavaScript classification.

Table 3a suggests that LLMs heavily rely on **superficial code patterns and specific keyword presence** for malicious JavaScript detection. For **malicious tokens**, malicious-positive ones include clear JavaScript operation fragments (e.g., `assign`) and short, obfuscated string fragments (e.g., `iste`, `assa`), implying that despite obfuscation, critical operational traces remain. Malicious-negative tokens also frequently appear as nonsensical fragments. Conversely, for **benign tokens**, benign-positive ones are typically distinct keywords related to program structure (e.g., `_PATH`, `_Syntax`). Benign-negative tokens include JavaScript built-in objects or security-related keywords (e.g., `_eval`, `_String`), indicating the model learns the **contextual tendency of tokens** rather than just their presence. These findings suggest LLMs learn token tendencies within specific code types. While malicious code relies on obfuscated fragments, benign code is characterized by meaningful structural keywords.

On the other hand, Table 3b primarily shows generic syntactic elements and special characters for both negative (benign) and positive (malicious) classes (e.g., `<0x0A>`, `_`, `()`). These tokens reflect general code structure or tokenizer artifacts rather than specific indicators of malicious intent or benign functionality. This suggests attention may focus on broader contextual relevance rather than direct decision-making influence.

In summary, the gradient-based approach offers superior interpretability, providing clearer insights into how the LLMs distinguishes between malicious and benign JavaScript by identifying specific, indicative token characteristics, particularly those related to obfuscation. This contrast validates the effectiveness of gradient-based methods for LLMs explainability in code analysis.

6.4 Research Ethics

This study employs LLMs using an offline-based approach. Related research often involves sending malicious JavaScript code to external servers using online LLMs like GPT, but the risks associated with uploading such malicious files to external servers are not sufficiently discussed. Transmitting malicious code inherently carries risks of data privacy breaches and can potentially serve as an attack vector against external LLMs services.

Our offline approach significantly mitigates these potential security risks. By eliminating the need to transmit sensitive code data to external servers, it removes the risk of data leakage and reduces vulnerability to malicious prompt injection attacks.

6.5 Limitations of the Study

The malicious samples used in this study were collected from PhishTank and GitHub, and they may not fully represent the population of real-world malicious JavaScript. Therefore, it is necessary to analyze the sample content to ensure a diverse range of malicious samples is included.

Furthermore, the labels assigned to these samples might not always reflect their actual behavior. In the case of JavaScript, the code itself may not exhibit explicitly malicious behavior, making it challenging to definitively classify a single script as malicious. Thus, the reliability of the labelling warrants further investigation.

7 Conclusion

In this study, we proposed a method for detecting malicious JavaScript based on linguistic features using LLMs. Validation experiments using practical datasets demonstrated that the proposed method achieved improved accuracy compared to existing detection models. Furthermore, it was confirmed that code-specialized LLMs could detect malicious JavaScript with higher accuracy compared to their original models. We also analyzed the influence of individual tokens on the judgment of LLMs.

Future challenges include optimizing the sequence length of the models and improving information extraction for better judgment. Additionally, the comprehensiveness of the samples in the datasets and the reliability of their labels require continued investigation.

References

1. Tusk: unraveling a complex infostealer campaign (2024). https://securelist.com/tusk-infostealers-campaign/113367/. Accessed 15 Aug 2024
2. Curtsinger, C., et al.: ZOZZLE: fast and precise in-browser javascript malware detection. In: 20th USENIX Security Symposium, San Francisco, CA, USA, August 8–12, 2011, Proceedings. USENIX Association (2011). http://static.usenix.org/events/sec11/tech/full_papers/Curtsinger.pdf
3. Fang, C., et al.: Large language models for code analysis: Do llms really do their job? CoRR (2023). arxiv:abs/2310.12357, https://doi.org/10.48550/ARXIV.2310.12357
4. Fang, Y., et al.: Detecting malicious javascript code based on semantic analysis. Comput. Secur. **93**, 101764 (2020). https://doi.org/10.1016/J.COSE.2020.101764
5. Fass, A., et al.: Jast: Fully syntactic detection of malicious (obfuscated) javascript. In: Giuffrida, C., Bardin, S., Blanc, G. (eds.) Detection of Intrusions and Malware, and Vulnerability Assessment—15th International Conference, DIMVA 2018, Saclay, France, June 28-29, 2018, Proceedings. Lecture Notes in Computer Science, vol. 10885, pp. 303–325. Springer (2018). https://doi.org/10.1007/978-3-319-93411-2_14
6. Hu, E.J., et al.: Lora: Low-rank adaptation of large language models. In: The Tenth International Conference on Learning Representations, ICLR 2022, Virtual Event, April 25–29, 2022. OpenReview.net (2022). https://openreview.net/forum?id=nZeVKeeFYf9
7. Huang, Y., et al.: Jscontana: Malicious javascript detection using adaptable context analysis and key feature extraction. Comput. Secur. **104**, 102218 (2021). https://doi.org/10.1016/J.COSE.2021.102218
8. Hwang, S., et al.: A detector using variant stacked denoising autoencoders with logistic regression for malicious javascript with obfuscations. In: New Trends in Computer Technologies and Applications—25th International Computer Symposium, ICS 2022, Taoyuan, Taiwan, December 15-17, 2022, Proceedings. Communications in Computer and Information Science, vol. 1723, pp. 374–386. Springer (2022). https://doi.org/10.1007/978-981-19-9582-8_33
9. Kumar, A., others Gupta, S.: Leveraging transfer learning: Fine-tuning methodology for enhanced text classification using bert. In: 2024 IEEE Pune Section International Conference (PuneCon), pp. 1–5 (2024). https://doi.org/10.1109/PuneCon63413.2024.10895448
10. Natsos, D., et al.: Transformer-based malware detection using process resource utilization metrics. Results Eng. **25**, 104250 (2025)
11. Ndichu, S., et al.: A machine learning approach to malicious javascript detection using fixed length vector representation. In: 2018 International Joint Conference on Neural Networks, IJCNN 2018, Rio de Janeiro, Brazil, July 8-13, 2018. pp. 1–8. IEEE (2018). https://doi.org/10.1109/IJCNN.2018.8489414
12. Ngoc, P.M., et al.: Detection of malicious javascript on an imbalanced dataset. Internet Things **13**, 100357 (2021). https://doi.org/10.1016/J.IOT.2021.100357
13. Ren, K., et al.: Jsrevealer: A robust malicious javascript detector against obfuscation. In: 53rd Annual IEEE/IFIP International Conference on Dependable Systems and Network, DSN 2023, Porto, Portugal, June 27-30, 2023, pp. 339–351. IEEE (2023). https://doi.org/10.1109/DSN58367.2023.00041
14. Stein, K., et al.: A transformer-based framework for payload malware detection and classification. In: 2024 IEEE World AI IoT Congress (AIIoT), pp. 105–111 (2024). https://doi.org/10.1109/AIIoT61789.2024.10579000

15. Touvron, H., et al.: Llama: Open and efficient foundation language models (2023). https://arxiv.org/abs/2302.13971
16. Wolf, T., et al.: Transformers: State-of-the-Art Natural Language Processing, pp. 38–45. Association for Computational Linguistics (2020). https://www.aclweb.org/anthology/2020.emnlp-demos.6

A Framework for Assessing Nation-State Cyber Attack Capabilities Using MITRE ATT&CK and Large Language Models

HyungKwan Kim(✉), HyungGyu Lee, and Wook Shin

The Attached Institute of ETRI, Daejeon, South Korea
{james,hglee88,wshin}@nsr.re.kr

Abstract. This study presents a framework for assessing nation-state cyber attack capabilities by integrating MITRE ATT&CK with Large Language Models. We developed a multidimensional assessment framework comprising operational capabilities, technical capabilities, and tactical maturity, enhanced by LLM-based sophistication evaluation and synergy effect models. We conducted validation using five models (GPT-4.1-nano, GPT-4o-mini, o3, o3-mini, o4-mini) with three repeated measurements per model, selecting o3 based on statistical consistency. The framework was validated using 36 versions of ATT&CK data from 2018 to 2025, tracking 89 APT groups across 9 nations. This research provides security professionals and policymakers a practical tool for systematic cyber capability assessment.

Keywords: Assessment framework · MITRE ATT&CK · Large language models · Cyber capabilities · Nation-state actors

1 Introduction

1.1 Research Background

As cyberspace becomes central to national security, objective frameworks for assessing nation-state cyber attack capabilities are increasingly needed. Existing methodologies rely on qualitative approaches [1] or conceptual analysis [2]. Current indices like national cyber power indices fail to reflect actual attack data [3], while NCSI focuses on policies rather than capabilities [4], and the Cyber Power Index depends heavily on subjective expert surveys [5].

MITRE ATT&CK systematically classifies observed cyber attacks and has become the global standard [6]. However, research applying ATT&CK to nation-state capability assessment remains limited [7]. Most studies focus on individual APT groups or specific techniques [8,9], with comprehensive nation-state assessments being rare.

K.-W. Park and J. Park (Eds.): WISA 2025 2025, LNCS 16434, pp. 228–240, 2026.
https://doi.org/10.1007/978-981-95-6857-4_17

1.2 Research Objectives

Our core objective is to **develop a reproducible framework for assessing nation-state cyber attack capabilities**. We pursue three goals: building a systematic framework combining MITRE ATT&CK with LLMs, developing validation methodology for LLM reproducibility, and creating hybrid weight determination combining expert judgment with data-driven approaches.

1.3 Research Differentiation and Contribution

This research provides the first cyber capability assessment to systematically address LLM reproducibility. We performed three repeated measurements on 5 LLM models, selecting the optimal model through statistical validation, addressing consistency issues raised by [10,11]. Our framework-centered approach focuses on developing and validating the assessment framework itself.

2 Assessment Framework Design

2.1 Framework Overview

The framework comprises four modules: data collection from MITRE ATT&CK, LLM evaluation for group-country associations and sophistication, indicator calculation and normalization, and integrated assessment with weights and synergy effects (Fig. 1).

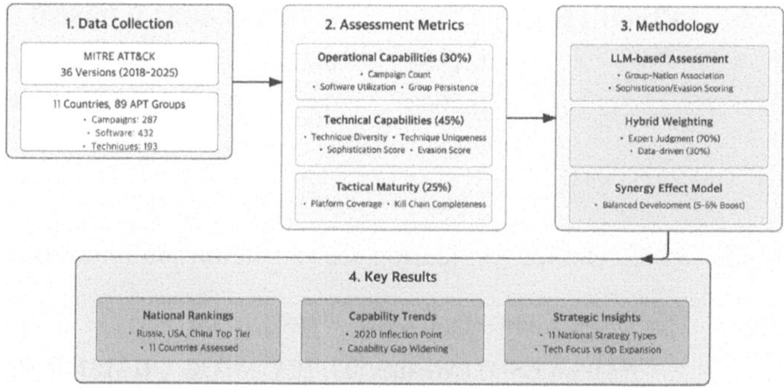

Fig. 1. Structure of the proposed cyber capability assessment framework

2.2 Assessment Indicator System

The framework defines 9 detailed indicators across three dimensions: operational capability (campaign count, software utilization, persistence), technical capability (technique diversity, uniqueness, sophistication, evasion), and tactical maturity (platform coverage, kill chain completeness).

Operational Capability Dimension Evaluates cyber operation execution with OC1 measuring weighted campaigns, OC2 calculating software diversity ratio, and OC3 assessing temporal persistence.

Technical Capability Dimension Measures technical sophistication through TC1–TC2 for technique breadth and exclusivity, TC3–TC4 for LLM-evaluated sophistication and evasion scores.

Tactical Maturity Dimension Assesses tactical scope via TM1 platform coverage and TM2 kill chain completeness across ATT&CK tactics.

2.3 LLM-Based Evaluation Components

Multi-Model Validation for Ensuring Reproducibility We selected 5 LLM models representing different architectures: general task models (GPT-4.1-nano, GPT-4o-mini), reasoning-specialized models (o3, o3-mini), and experimental model (o4-mini). Each model underwent 3 repeated measurements with controlled temperature settings (Fig. 2 and Tables 1, 2).

Table 1. Model-wise group-country association evaluation reproducibility indicators

Model	Temperature	Correlation	ICC	CV	RMSE	Max Diff
GPT-4.1-nano	0.2	0.9213	0.9204	0.1542	0.1003	0.7061
GPT-4o-mini	0.2	0.8843	0.8840	0.2444	0.0953	0.5455
o3	**Fixed (High)**	**0.7998**	**0.7920**	**0.4631**	**0.0386**	**0.2873**
o3-mini	–	0.7855	0.7757	0.0345	0.0764	0.7061
o4-mini	–	0.7063	0.6951	0.0542	0.0989	0.8030

Table 2. Model-wise technique evaluation score distribution and reproducibility

Model	Tech score	Det score	Tech	Det	Tech	Det
	(Mean±SD)	(Mean±SD)	ICC	ICC	RMSE	RMSE
GPT-4.1-nano	6.38±1.52	6.22±2.10	0.773	0.538	1.023	1.245
GPT-4o-mini	5.74±1.55	6.65±1.30	0.976	0.902	0.339	0.412
o3	**5.12±1.66**	**6.33±1.41**	**0.906**	**0.790**	**0.719**	**0.856**
O3-mini	3.98±1.63	5.42±2.41	0.885	0.783	0.783	0.923
O4-mini	4.41±2.06	6.85±1.54	0.891	0.729	0.963	1.087

The o3 model demonstrated optimal performance with lowest RMSE (0.0386) despite high temperature constraints, balanced evaluation characteristics, and actual logical reasoning capabilities aligned with expert assessments (Fig. 3).

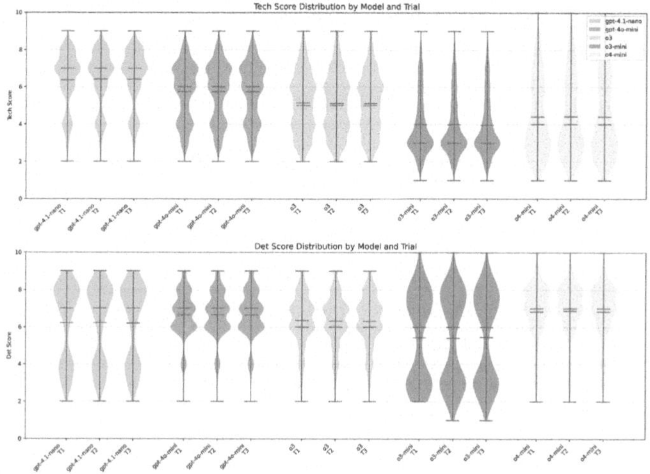

Fig. 2. Model-wise tech score and det score distributions (3 measurements per model)

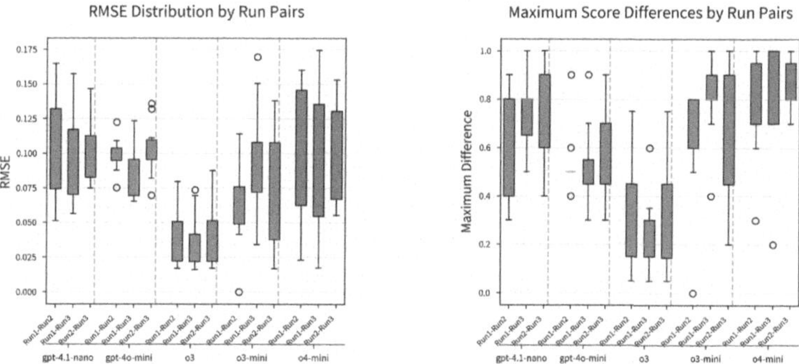

Fig. 3. Comparison of RMSE and maximum score difference by LLM model (5 types)

Prompt Engineering Strategy Carefully designed prompts ensure reproducibility through clear role definitions, evidence-based evaluation emphasis, structured JSON output formats, and explicit constraints.

2.4 Weight Determination Framework

Hybrid Weight Methodology The framework provides three weight methods: expert-based using Delphi technique, data-based combining PCA and entropy methods 50:50, and hybrid combining both approaches with $\alpha = 0.7$ favoring expert knowledge.

Weight Determination Results See Table 3.

Table 3. Comparison of assessment indicator weights (Expert vs. Data-Based)

Category	Detailed indicator	Expert-based	Data-based
		Weight	Weight
Operational capability	Campaign count	0.120	0.095
	Software utilization	0.105	0.118
	Persistence indicator	0.075	0.087
Technical capability	Technique diversity	0.135	0.142
	Technique uniqueness	0.090	0.078
	Sophistication score	0.113	0.125
	Evasion score	0.113	0.105
Tactical maturity	Platform coverage	0.113	0.098
	Kill chain completeness	0.138	0.152

2.5 Synergy Effect Model

Synergy Calculation Model The framework models dimension interactions through Balance Score measuring variance across dimensions and Integration Score calculating min/max ratios, with adjustable synergy coefficient $\alpha = 0.15$.

Theoretical Basis for Synergy Effects Synergy effects reflect operational-technical synergy where campaign experience promotes innovation, technical-tactical synergy enabling new tactics, and tactical-operational synergy supporting efficient operations.

3 Framework Validation and Application

3.1 Experimental Design

The validation utilized 36 ATT&CK versions from January 2018 to May 2025, covering 9 countries and 89 APT groups with 193 techniques, 412 software, and 187 campaigns.

Dataset Configuration The validation utilized 36 ATTCK versions (v1.0–v17.1) covering 9 LLM-evaluated nations with $\geq$1.0 APT group attributions, encompassing 89 APT groups, 193 techniques, 412 software, and 187 campaigns.

Validation Methodology Framework validation examined internal consistency, temporal stability, convergent validity, and discriminant validity through comprehensive statistical analyses.

3.2 LLM Reproducibility Validation Results

Model Consistency Analysis Detailed analysis confirmed o3 model's superior consistency with average CV of 0.06 across major APT group attributions, significantly outperforming other models (Table 4).

Table 4. Model-wise Consistency of Major APT Group-Country Attribution Evaluation

Evaluation target	GPT-4o-mini	GPT-4.1-nano	o3	o3-mini	o4-mini
APT1 (Nation G)	0.85±0.12	0.78±0.18	0.92±0.03	0.89±0.05	0.87±0.08
APT28 (Nation A)	0.91±0.09	0.83±0.15	0.95±0.02	0.93±0.04	0.90±0.06
Lazarus (Nation B)	0.88±0.11	0.80±0.17	0.94±0.03	0.91±0.05	0.89±0.07
APT29 (Nation A)	0.89±0.10	0.82±0.16	0.93±0.03	0.92±0.04	0.88±0.07
Average CV	**0.18**	**0.22**	**0.06**	**0.09**	**0.11**

Temperature Effects Analysis High temperature settings in o3 resulted in logical reasoning rather than pattern matching, maintaining low RMSE (0.039) and 100% Top-K consistency for core threats (Table 5).

Table 5. Model-wise Reproducibility Characteristics by Temperature Settings

Characteristic	Low Temperature (0.2)	High Temperature (o3)
Inter-run Correlation	0.88–0.92	0.80 (Actual: 0.98*)
Rank Consistency	High	Medium (Top-K: 100%)
RMSE	0.095–0.100	0.039
Reasoning Depth	Pattern matching centered	Logical reasoning centered

Technique Evaluation Reproducibility Analysis of 193 ATT&CK techniques showed consistent reproducibility across all categories with ICC > 0.78 (Table 6).

3.3 Framework Validity Validation

Internal Consistency Validation Cronbach's alpha confirmed excellent internal consistency across all dimensions with overall $\alpha = 0.85$ (Table 7).

Table 6. o3 Model evaluation consistency by technique category

Technique category	Number of Techniques	Tech score ICC	Det score ICC	Average CV
Initial Access	9	0.912	0.805	0.065
Execution	13	0.903	0.792	0.068
Persistence	19	0.908	0.788	0.071
Privilege Escalation	13	0.911	0.795	0.069
Defense Evasion	42	0.905	0.791	0.072
Credential Access	17	0.907	0.789	0.070
Discovery	31	0.904	0.787	0.073
Lateral Movement	9	0.909	0.793	0.067
Collection	17	0.906	0.790	0.071
Command and Control	16	0.902	0.786	0.074
Exfiltration	9	0.910	0.794	0.066
Impact	14	0.913	0.796	0.064
Total	**193**	**0.906**	**0.790**	**0.070**

Table 7. Internal consistency by assessment dimension

Dimension	Cronbach's α	Interpretation
Operational Capability	0.82	Excellent
Technical Capability	0.87	Excellent
Tactical Maturity	0.79	Good
Total	**0.85**	**Excellent**

Temporal Stability Validation Strong temporal stability demonstrated with correlations of 0.96, 0.91, and 0.84 for 3, 6, and 12 month intervals respectively (Table 8).

Convergent Validity Validation High intra-dimension correlations (0.68–0.73) confirmed indicators within each dimension measure consistent constructs (Table 9).

Discriminant Validity Validation Lower inter-dimension correlations (0.38–0.45) compared to intra-dimension values confirmed distinct construct measurement (Table 10).

Table 8. Temporal stability analysis (Spearman's ρ)

Period	Correlation Coefficient	p-value
3-month interval	0.96	<0.001
6-month interval	0.91	<0.001
12-month interval	0.84	<0.001

Table 9. Inter-indicator correlations within assessment dimensions

Dimension	Average inter-indicator Correlation	Range
Operational Capability	0.68	0.62–0.74
Technical Capability	0.71	0.65–0.78
Tactical Maturity	0.73	0.71–0.75

Expert Validation Results Five cybersecurity experts validated framework outputs with high agreement rates across all assessment dimensions (Table 11).

3.4 Framework Application Cases

Sensitivity Analysis Weight modifications of ±20% resulted in minimal rank changes, demonstrating framework robustness (Table 12).

3.5 Limitations and Considerations

Framework Limitations Key limitations include dependency on public ATT&CK data, attribution uncertainty from LLM public information training, temporal gaps between activities and registration, and focus solely on attack capabilities.

Table 10. Inter-dimension correlations

	Operational Capability	Technical Capability	Tactical Maturity
Operational Capability	1.00		
Technical Capability	0.42	1.00	
Tactical Maturity	0.38	0.45	1.00

Table 11. Expert validation results

Assessment Item	Average score (out of 5)	Agreement (%)
Appropriateness of Technique Scores	4.6	92
Validity of Country Attribution	4.2	84
Reasonableness of Relative Rankings	4.4	88
Realism of Temporal Changes	4.5	90

Table 12. Rank changes with ±20% weight modification

Change Scenario	Countries with Rank Changes	Maximum Rank Change
Operational Capability +20%	3/9	2 positions
Technical Capability +20%	2/9	1 position
Tactical Maturity +20%	2/9	1 position
Random ±20%	4/9	2 positions

4 Framework Application Results and Analysis

4.1 Data Overview

The analysis encompasses 36 versions of MITRE ATT&CK data spanning from January 17, 2018 (v1.0) to May 6, 2025 (v17.1). Country selection was determined through LLM evaluation, identifying 9 nations that were assessed to have 1.0 or more APT group attributions based on the highest attribution counts. This methodological approach enhances framework objectivity and reproducibility by eliminating subjective country selection bias.

The framework employs a hybrid weighting method combining expert-based (70%) and data-based (30%) approaches, where the data-based component equally integrates PCA and entropy methods. This 70:30 ratio reflects the importance of domain expertise while incorporating data-driven patterns. Synergy effects were applied to capture interaction benefits between capability dimensions.

4.2 Comprehensive Assessment Results of National Cyber Capabilities

Rankings Based on Latest Version (v17.1) Analysis of the latest version reveals a multi-tier structure. Nation A maintains its top position with a score of 65.70, followed closely by Nation B (63.81) and Nation C (61.88), forming a clear leading group with significant APT group presence. The middle tier comprises Nations D, E, F, G, and H with scores ranging from 59.67 to 61.78, showing diverse capability profiles (Table 13).

Table 13. Comprehensive national cyber capability rankings (v17.1, May 2025)

Rank	Nation	Total Score	Base Score	Synergy Bonus	APT Group Count
1	A	65.70	62.11	3.59	40.0
2	B	63.81	60.47	3.34	8.0
3	C	61.88	58.76	3.12	24.0
4	D	61.78	58.42	3.36	5.0
5	E	61.59	58.24	3.35	5.0
6	F	61.20	57.89	3.31	1.0
7	G	59.69	56.38	3.31	62.0
8	H	59.67	56.54	3.13	2.0
9	I	56.26	53.71	2.55	1.0

Time Series Change Analysis All nations showed capability improvements with average scores rising from low 50s to 60s, with 2020 marking an inflection point likely due to pandemic-driven digital transformation (Fig. 4).

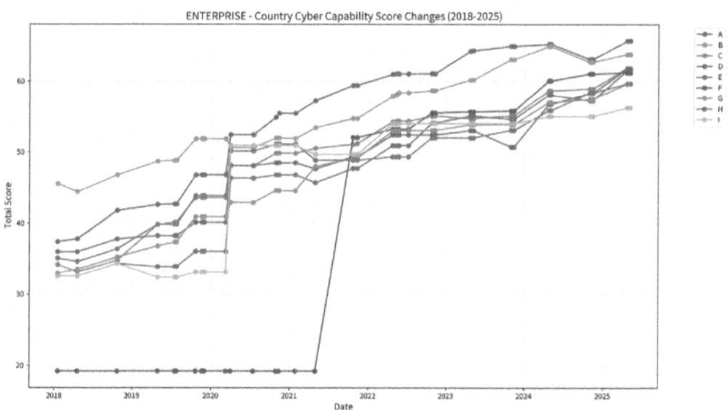

Fig. 4. National cyber capability score time series changes (2018–2025)

Rank Change Analysis Significant rank changes included Nation B's rise to second position (+1), Nation C's advancement to third (+2), Nation E's improvement to fifth (+2), and Nation G's decline to seventh (–1) (Fig. 5 and Table 14).

4.3 APT Group Activity Analysis

Changes in Number of APT Groups by Nation Nation A showed highest absolute growth (13→40 groups), while Nation G maintained largest total with 62 groups, suggesting different threat visibility patterns (Table 15).

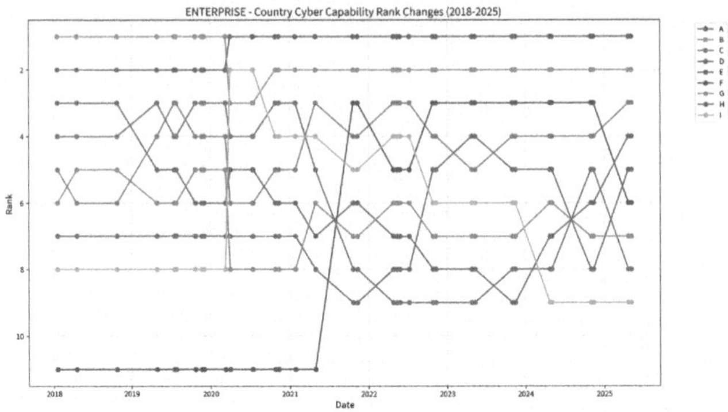

Fig. 5. National cyber capability rank changes (2018–2025)

Table 14. Major rank change cases

Nation	2018 Rank	2025 Rank	Change	Major Change Period
B	1	2	–1	Consistent high rank
C	5	3	+2	Rise after 2021
E	7	5	+2	Recovery after 2023
G	6	7	–1	Gradual decline
D	3	4	–1	Recent decline

Qualitative Changes in Group Activities Beyond quantitative increases, qualitative improvements included 45% increase in technique diversity, sophistication scores rising from 5.8 to 7.2, and evasion scores improving from 6.1 to 7.8.

5 Conclusion

5.1 Key Achievements and Contributions

This study established new standards for LLM reproducibility validation, demonstrating o3 model's superior performance with lowest RMSE and excellent ICC values. The practical framework with 9 indicators and synergy effects systematically quantifies complex cyber capabilities while maintaining high temporal consistency. Balanced capability development across dimensions yields 5–6% additional improvement through synergy effects.

5.2 Significance and Impact

Academically, this pioneering research applies MITRE ATT&CK to nation-state assessment while demonstrating reasoning models' unique value. Practically, it

Table 15. Changes in APT group numbers for major nations (Selected Versions)

Nation	v1.0 (2018)	v9.0 (2021)	v17.1 (2025)	Growth Rate (%)
G	27.0	46.0	62.0	129.6
A	13.0	24.0	40.0	207.7
C	5.0	16.0	24.0	380.0
B	1.0	6.0	8.0	700.0
D	2.0	4.0	5.0	150.0
E	1.0	3.0	5.0	400.0

provides an immediately deployable tool at $1,200 annual cost with balanced expert-data hybrid weights. Strategically, it captures critical trends including the 2020 inflection point and emerging cyber powers' rise.

5.3 Limitations and Future Tasks

Limitations include reliance on public ATT&CK data, attack-only focus, attribution uncertainty from public-information-trained LLMs, and Western data bias in models. Future research should integrate multiple threat intelligence sources, expand to defense capabilities, utilize diverse regional models like DeepSeek, and continuously evaluate emerging models.

5.4 Closing Remarks

This framework provides a common language for understanding cyber capabilities rather than determining superiority. Its key contribution lies in systematically solving LLM reproducibility challenges and demonstrating reasoning models' value. The o3 model's low RMSE and high evaluation quality present new possibilities for AI-based cybersecurity assessment, contributing to safer cyberspace through reproducible, objective evaluation methodologies.

References

1. Klimburg, A.: Mobilising cyber power. Survival **53**(1), 41–60 (2011)
2. Lewis, J.A.: Assessing the Risks of Cyber Terrorism. Cyber War and Other Cyber Threats, Center for Strategic and International Studies (CSIS) Report (2002)
3. Voo, J., Hemani, I., Jones, S., DeSombre, W., Cassidy, D., Schwarzenbach, A.: National cyber power index 2020. Belfer Center for Science and International Affairs (2020)
4. e-Governance Academy: National Cyber Security Index (2024). https://ncsi.ega.ee
5. International Institute for Strategic Studies: Cyber capabilities and national power: A net assessment. IISS Research Papers (2021)

6. MITRE Corporation: MITRE ATT & CK R : Design and Philosophy (2024). https://attack.mitre.org/docs/ATTACK_philosophy_March_2020.pdf
7. Al-Sada, B., Sadighian, A., Oligeri, G.: MITRE ATT&CK: state of the art and way forward. ACM Comput. Surv. **56**(9), 1–38 (2024)
8. Maymí, F., Bixler, R., Jones, R., Lathrop, S.: Towards a definition of cyberspace tactics, techniques and procedures. In: 2017 IEEE International Conference on Big Data, pp. 4674–4679 (2017)
9. Pennington, A., Shenoi, P., Campbell, P.: An empirical study of MITRE ATT&CK techniques. In: Proceedings of the 15th International Conference on Cyber Warfare and Security, pp. 387–396 (2020)
10. Yao, Y., Duan, J., Xu, K., Cai, Y., Sun, Z., Zhang, Y.: A survey on Large Language Model (LLM) security and privacy: the good, the bad, and the ugly. High-Confidence Comput. **4**(2), 100150 (2024)
11. Xu, H., Shawn, S., Benjamin, T., Hassan, T.: Large Language Models for Cyber Security: A Systematic Literature Review (2024). arXiv:2405.04760

Understanding Encrypted Network Anomalies with LLMs: A Post-Hoc Cognitive Framework

Seon-Woo Lee[1], Hyeon-Woo Park[2], and Tae-Jin Lee[3](✉)

[1] Department of Information Security, Gachon University, Seongnam, Republic of Korea

[2] Department of Computer Engineering, Hoseo University, Asan, Republic of Korea

[3] Department of Smart Security, Gachon University, Seongnam, Republic of Korea
kinjecs0@gmail.com

Abstract. The widespread use of encrypted traffic poses challenges for traditional anomaly detection systems that rely on payload inspection. While unsupervised learning methods offer scalable solutions by detecting statistical deviations in NetFlow-like data, they often suffer from high false positive rates due to their lack of interpretability. In this paper, we propose an LLM-assisted reinterpretation framework that augments anomaly detection outputs with natural language explanations. These explanations are designed to help human analysts, particularly junior-level security operators, to re-evaluate detection outcomes and correct misclassifications. Notably, our approach is detection-model-agnostic and can complement various anomaly detection backends. An empirical study with junior participants shows that LLM-guided interpretation reduces false positives significantly and increases confidence in the detection process. This demonstrates the potential of LLMs to serve as a cognitive aid in SOC environments where expert resources are limited.

Keywords: Anomaly detection · Encrypted traffic · Unsupervised learning · Large language model · False positive reduction · Soc operations

1 Introduction

The widespread deployment of encryption protocols such as TLS 1.3 and HTTPS has rendered traditional deep packet inspection (DPI) ineffective for network anomaly detection [1]. In encrypted environments, where payloads are inaccessible, security systems must rely instead on flow-level metadata–such as packet counts, duration, and byte volume–for behavioral analysis.

Unsupervised learning has emerged as a promising solution in this context, enabling anomaly detection by modeling statistical regularities in unlabeled NetFlow-like data [2,3]. However, despite their scalability, these models often

K.-W. Park and J. Park (Eds.): WISA 2025 2025, LNCS 16434, pp. 241–252, 2026.
https://doi.org/10.1007/978-981-95-6857-4_18

operate as black boxes and generate excessive false positives–especially when benign deviations are incorrectly flagged as malicious due to model opacity [4]. Such outcomes burden Security Operations Center (SOC) personnel with alert fatigue and wasted triage effort.

Industry reports estimate that up to 60% of SOC alerts are ultimately classified as false positives [5–7], exacerbating operational inefficiencies. This is further intensified by the global shortage of cybersecurity professionals, which is estimated to exceed 4 million unfilled roles [8–10]. Many SOCs consequently rely on junior analysts who may lack the expertise to confidently interpret ambiguous alerts.

To address these challenges, we propose a model-agnostic **Cognitive-Aid Framework for Alert Reinterpretation** that sits atop existing anomaly detection systems. Our framework leverages Large Language Models (LLMs) to convert opaque alert outputs into natural language explanations derived from flow-level features. These cognitively-accessible summaries aim to support junior analysts in reassessing alerts, filtering out false positives, and increasing triage accuracy. Our empirical study demonstrates that this reinterpretation layer significantly improves both precision and analyst confidence, highlighting the potential of LLMs as cognitive aids in SOC workflows.

2 Related Work

2.1 Unsupervised Anomaly Detection for Encrypted Traffic

The transition toward encrypted communications has necessitated metadata-centric detection strategies. Surveys such as [2,3] catalogue a range of unsupervised approaches—including autoencoders, clustering methods, one-class SVMs, and graph-based techniques—tailored to flow-level telemetry. These methods aim to learn baseline distributions of benign behavior and identify statistical deviations that signal anomalies.

However, such models frequently suffer from excessive false positive rates due to benign but unusual activity patterns [4]. Techniques like SVM-based filtering [11] and open-set recognition [12] have been proposed to enhance tolerance for unknown yet legitimate deviations. Nonetheless, these approaches often require regular retraining and delicate threshold calibration, hindering their practical deployment in dynamic SOC environments.

2.2 Interpretability and False-Positive Mitigation

The opacity of unsupervised models has emerged as a major barrier to SOC adoption. Explainable AI (XAI) techniques offer post-hoc interpretability by attributing decisions to salient input features. Prior surveys [13,14] cover representative methods such as LIME, SHAP, and rule-based abstraction. For example, DeepEAD [15] applies attention-based models over system logs to extract key contributors to anomalies, thus providing operational transparency.

Recent work has explored the use of LLMs for interpretability. Lin et al. [16] demonstrated that LLM-generated rationales can reduce analyst review time without altering the underlying detector. Such language-based interfaces present a cognitive bridge between statistical models and human users, making them particularly useful for junior analysts with limited experience.

While LLM-based explanations represent a promising direction, current implementations are often tightly integrated with specific detection models or remain experimental in nature. Despite these advances, a persistent gap remains between statistical detection outputs and actionable human understanding—particularly in environments where alert triage is performed by junior-level analysts. Existing solutions either require modifications to the detection pipeline or lack adaptability across diverse SOC deployments. This highlights the need for a decoupled interpretability layer that can operate independently of the underlying anomaly detector while providing cognitively accessible summaries of alerts.

Our proposed framework aims to fill this gap by leveraging large language models to reinterpret flow-level anomalies in natural language, thus serving as a cognitive aid that enhances both interpretability and operational efficiency in SOC environments.

3 Proposed Approach

The proposed framework is composed of two decoupled yet complementary components: an unsupervised anomaly detector and a post-hoc reinterpretation module powered by a Large Language Model (LLM). As depicted in Fig. 1, the system ingests raw NetFlow or IPFIX logs and transforms them through a structured pipeline that enables both accurate detection and interpretable explanation.

Flow Preprocessing. Raw flow logs are first segmented into 2 min sliding windows. Each window is then aggregated based on unique source-destination IP-pair tuples. This aggregation forms the basic unit of analysis for both detection and interpretation.

Feature Extraction and Branching. For each IP-pair within a window, we extract statistical features that fall into two categories: (1) Aggregated Features—such as flow density, SYN ratio, and connection failure rate—are used by the anomaly detection model, and (2) Interpretation Features—such as hubness score, pattern consistency, and malicious peer ratios—are reserved for the explanation stage.

Anomaly Detection via Autoencoder. The aggregated features are passed to an Autoencoder model trained to reconstruct normal traffic patterns. A high reconstruction error signals behavioral deviation, and the corresponding IP-pair in that window is flagged as anomalous.

Post-hoc Reinterpretation with LLM. Once an anomaly is detected, both aggregated and interpretation features are passed to a Feature-to-Prompt Translation module. This module encodes semantic knowledge of known attack patterns (e.g., Brute Force, PortScan, DDoS) into structured prompts. These prompts are then passed to the LLM, which generates a human-readable explanation of the anomaly's behavioral characteristics.

Natural Language Output. The output is a natural language rationale that justifies the anomaly label in terms of measurable traffic behaviors. This explanation can be used to assist human analysts or to enrich automated alert triage systems.

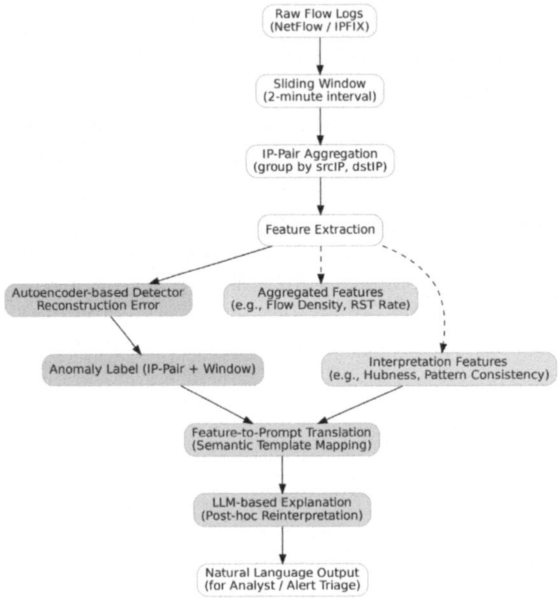

Fig. 1. Overall architecture of the proposed framework. Detection is performed via flow-level feature aggregation and Autoencoder scoring. Post-hoc reinterpretation is conducted using structured prompt generation and an LLM-based explanation layer

3.1 Unsupervised Anomaly Detection Pipeline

At the core of our detection pipeline is an unsupervised Autoencoder model trained to learn baseline behaviors from benign traffic. As shown in Fig. 1, the system processes flow logs in a 2 min sliding window and aggregates records by IP-pair. From these windows, statistical features are extracted to represent each pairs communication behavior.

The extracted features serve two roles: a subset is fed into the Autoencoder to compute reconstruction errors, and the rest are preserved for downstream interpretation. If the reconstruction error exceeds a predefined threshold, the corresponding IP-pair and time window are flagged as anomalous.

This approach enables lightweight, label-free detection that captures deviations in behavioral patterns. By operating on IP-level windows rather than individual flows, the system is robust to noise and better aligned with real-world operational visibility.

Feature Design The feature set summarized in Table 1 is designed to support both detection accuracy and post-hoc interpretability. Aggregated traffic metrics (e.g., flow density, short-flow ratio, packet imbalance) characterize volumetric and temporal aspects of communication, while interpretation-specific metrics (e.g., hubness, malicious peer ratios) enrich semantic understanding of network roles and behavior patterns.

These two feature paths form the foundation of our decoupled architecture: the Autoencoder identifies potential anomalies based on statistical deviations, and the LLM component later explains those anomalies using feature-informed narrative prompts.

Table 1. Feature set for anomaly detection and post-hoc interpretation

Feature Group	Feature Name (Src/Dst)	Description
	Aggregated Features (per IP-Pair, 2 min window)	
Traffic Volume	Flow Density	Number of flows between the IP-pair per 120 s
	Total Packet Count	Total number of forward and backward packets exchanged
Connection Indicators	Directional Imbalance Ratio	Proportion of packets in one direction (Fwd / Total)
	Connection Failure Rate	Ratio of flows with TCP RST flags to total flows
	SYN Packet Ratio	Proportion of SYN packets in total packet count
	Short Flow Ratio	Fraction of flows with duration under 1 s
Port and Timing Patterns	Unique Port Count	Number of distinct destination ports within a window
	IAT Std Dev	Standard deviation of inter-arrival times (IAT)
	Time Burstiness	Max-to-Mean ratio of flow counts in 10 s bins
Flow Similarity	Flow Pattern Similarity	Cosine similarity among flows in the window
Post-hoc Interpretation Features		
Behavioral Roles	Hubness Score (Src/Dst)	Squared degree divided by total links; high values suggest central relay-like behavior (e.g., C&C node)
	Unique Peer Count (Src/Dst)	Number of distinct IPs communicating with the source/destination IP
Malicious Communication	Malicious Peer Ratio (Src/Dst)	Fraction of communication peers previously flagged as anomalous when interacting with this IP
	Malicious Peer Count (Src/Dst)	Count of such anomalous peers
Pattern Consistency	Pattern Consistency (Src/Dst)	Cosine similarity among flows sent to (or received from) multiple peers—high values indicate repetitive or templated behavior
	Target Concentration (Src)	Degree to which source IP concentrates communication on a few destination IPs
	Sender Dispersion (Dst)	Degree to which destination IP receives flows from many different sources

As summarized in Table 1, the features are organized into two groups. The first group captures flow-level traffic statistics over 2 min windowssuch as volume, connection failures, burstiness, and similarityand serves as input to the Autoencoder for anomaly detection.

The second group is designed for semantic reinterpretation, quantifying behavioral cues like peer diversity, malicious exposure, and communication consistency. These enable the LLM to contextualize alerts in analyst-friendly language.

This dual-path structure decouples detection and interpretation, while ensuring that statistical anomalies are paired with semantically grounded explanations.

3.2 Post-Hoc Reinterpretation via LLM

To bridge the interpretability gap in unsupervised anomaly detection, we introduce a post-hoc LLM module that converts statistical alerts into analyst-friendly narratives. Acting as a cognitive aid, this component helps junior analysts understand and validate alerts without deep domain expertise.

Decoupled and Modular Explanation. The LLM module operates independently of the detector, receiving only the flagged IP-pair and its feature vector. This decoupling ensures that explanations are reproducible and can evolve separately from the detection model.

Feature-to-Prompt Translation. We employ structured prompts based on pre-defined behavioral templates rather than free-form generation. Each anomaly is matched against known feature patterns associated with attack types, such as:

- **Brute Force**: high short-flow ratio, frequent connection failures, and destination focus.
- **Port Scan**: wide port diversity, short durations, and low packet volume.
- **DDoS**: high flow density, strong directional imbalance, and uniform traffic patterns.

Structured Prompts Grounded in Feature Semantics. Drawing from recent advances in prompt engineering–such as Chain-of-Thought and zero-shot reasoning [17,18]–we generate explanations using structured templates that embed feature values into semantically meaningful scaffolds. This constrains the LLMs output space, guiding it to produce consistent and actionable interpretations while minimizing hallucinations.

An example prompt fragment is shown below:

> (Brute Force) The source IP (10.0.0.5) generated 92% of its flows toward a single destination (192.168.1.2), with an average duration of 0.4 seconds. The short flow ratio was 0.89 and the connection failure rate was 0.67, indicating repeated failed attempts.

Cognitive-Aid over Prediction. Importantly, the LLM is not used to infer or predict maliciousness but to articulate the rationale behind a detection decision made by the Autoencoder. This separation of concerns enhances interpretability while preserving trust in the underlying detection model. Similar architectures–where LLMs serve as explanatory overlays rather than predictors–have demonstrated value in structured security analysis and model auditing [16].

By anchoring LLM output in interpretable statistical patterns, the proposed framework empowers analysts with concise, behavior-based justifications, helping reduce false positives and improve triage efficiency.

4 Experimental Setup

4.1 Dataset and Preprocessing

We base our evaluation on CIC-IDS2017, which is known to suffer from flow reconstruction errors and TCP mislabeling [19,20]. To address these issues, we adopt the corrected version proposed by Engelen et al. [20], which restores proper TCP semantics and labeling consistency.

Training/Test Split: Monday's benign-only traffic is used to train the Autoencoder, while the remaining days are reserved for evaluation.

Table 2. Window-level sample distribution after 2 min aggregation (with Downsampled BENIGN)

Day (File)	Label	2 min Windows
Monday	BENIGN (All)	67,335
Tuesday	BENIGN (All)	55,519
	BENIGN (Sampled)	300
	FTP-Patator	32
	SSH-Patator	33
Wednesday	BENIGN (All)	54,891
	BENIGN (Sampled)	300
	Fast DoS	15
	Slow DoS	15
	Heartbleed	11
Friday-Botnet	BENIGN (All)	23,590
	BENIGN (Sampled)	318
	Botnet	106
Friday-Portscan	BENIGN (All)	18,857
	BENIGN (Sampled)	300
	Portscan	17
Friday-DDoS	BENIGN (All)	8,202
	BENIGN (Sampled)	300
	DDoS	11

Preprocessing: Flows are segmented into 2 min sliding windows and grouped by `srcIP-dstIP`. Each group is converted into a statistical feature vector (Sect. 3.1) using only flow metadata, assuming encrypted payloads.

Benign Downsampling: To emphasize high-value triage cases in LLM evaluation, benign flows in the test set are downsampled while preserving attack variety. Table 2 summarizes the result.

4.2 Evaluation Metrics

To evaluate our unsupervised anomaly detection pipeline, we use both threshold-dependent and independent metrics to ensure robust and fair assessment.

Precision, Recall, F1-Score: We report standard classification metrics to measure the correctness and completeness of anomaly detection. Precision reflects the accuracy of positive predictions, Recall captures detection coverage, and F1-Score balances both.

TPR and FPR: We also report True Positive Rate (TPR) and False Positive Rate (FPR) to assess detection sensitivity and specificity across thresholds.
Threshold Selection: Thresholds are selected using Youdens J statistic [21], which identifies the ROC point that best balances TPR and FPR:

$$J = \text{Sensitivity} + \text{Specificity} - 1$$

This principled method avoids manual tuning and supports reproducible evaluation.

4.3 Detection and False Positive Reduction via LLM-Based Reinterpretation

While the initial anomaly detection pipeline demonstrates strong recall across multiple attack scenarios, it still suffers from a notable rate of false positivesparticularly in patterns resembling benign anomalies. To address this, we applied our LLM-based reinterpretation layer as a post-hoc filter, generating structured explanations for each alert and discarding cases lacking behavioral alignment with known attack patterns.

Effectiveness of LLM-Based Filtering Table 3 shows that the LLM reinterpretation layer significantly improves detection precision across all datasets, raising the average from 0.88 to 0.96. The most notable gain appears in the Friday-PortScan case, where precision improved from 0.3902 to 0.7619, demonstrating the LLMs effectiveness in filtering benign-looking anomalies lacking attack-specific feature patterns.

Confusion Matrix Perspective. Table 4 presents detailed confusion matrix statistics, with a notable reduction in false positivesfrom 65 down to 12. Consequently, the overall False Positive Rate (FPR) dropped significantly from 4.0% to 0.79%. These results suggest that the LLM-based reinterpretation process effectively filters out statistical anomalies that do not align with known attack behaviors, contributing directly to improved alert reliability.

Table 3. Precision, Recall, and F1-Score Before and After LLM-based Reinterpretation

Dataset	Before Interpretation			After Interpretation		
	Precision	**Recall**	**F1-Score**	**Precision**	**Recall**	**F1-Score**
Tuesday	0.7805	0.9846	0.8696	0.9697	0.9846	0.9771
Wednesday	0.8125	0.9512	0.8767	0.9512	0.9512	0.9512
Friday-Botnet	0.8974	0.9906	0.9418	0.9722	0.9906	0.9813
Friday-PortScan	0.3902	0.9412	0.5517	0.7619	0.9412	0.8421
Friday-DDoS	0.9091	0.9091	0.9091	1.0000	0.9091	0.9524
ALL	**0.7826**	**0.9750**	**0.8690**	**0.9512**	**0.9750**	**0.9630**

Table 4. Confusion Matrix and TPR/FPR Before and After LLM-based Reinterpretation

Dataset	Before Interpretation						After Interpretation					
	TP	FP	TN	FN	TPR	FPR	TP	FP	TN	FN	TPR	FPR
Tuesday	64	18	282	1	0.9846	0.0600	64	2	298	1	0.9846	0.0067
Wednesday	39	9	291	2	0.9512	0.0300	39	2	298	2	0.9512	0.0067
Friday-Botnet	105	12	306	1	0.9906	0.0377	105	3	315	1	0.9906	0.0094
Friday-PortScan	16	25	275	1	0.9412	0.0833	16	5	295	1	0.9412	0.0167
Friday-DDoS	10	1	299	1	0.9091	0.0033	10	0	300	1	0.9091	0.0000
ALL	**234**	**65**	**1453**	**6**	**0.9750**	**0.0428**	**234**	**12**	**1506**	**6**	**0.9750**	**0.0079**

Interpretation-Driven Triage. These results validate our hypothesis that cognitively structured, feature-based explanations can assist in refining raw anomaly detection outputs. Alerts that fail to exhibit alignment with any known behavioral templates such as lacking port scan signatures or automated timing patterns are re-labeled as benign (i.e., "no suspicious behavior detected") by the LLM. This reinterpretation effectively filters out false positives that stem from statistical deviations unrelated to attack behavior. By embedding domain-specific behavior templates into LLM prompts, our framework enables more reliable triage transforming a purely statistical detector into a practical decision-support tool.

Figure 2 demonstrates reinterpretation cases where high connection failure rates and traffic concentration toward a single destination indicate possible brute force or fast-paced DoS behaviors. The structured explanation outlines feature values such as RST ratio, destination focus, and packet asymmetry to support the interpretation.

As shown in Fig. 3, port scanning behavior is captured through the combination of high port diversity and low session durations. The LLM articulates this in the context of enumeration behavior aimed at identifying exploitable services.

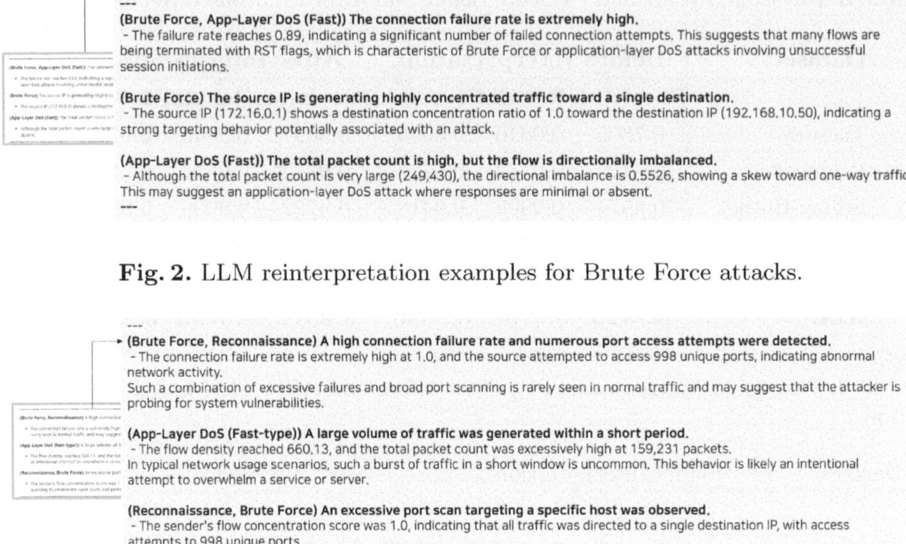

Fig. 2. LLM reinterpretation examples for Brute Force attacks.

Fig. 3. LLM reinterpretation examples for Port Scan.

Figure 4 presents LLM reinterpretation examples for Botnet (C&C) behavior, where the destination IP receives coordinated traffic from multiple sources. The structured explanation highlights three key features: pattern consistency across senders, strict temporal regularity, and high anomaly rates among the involved sources. The LLM interprets these signals as evidence of automated, synchronized communication likely driven by bot-infected hosts interacting with a C&C server. This form of behavior often evades traditional threshold-based detectors due to its low volume but high coordination.

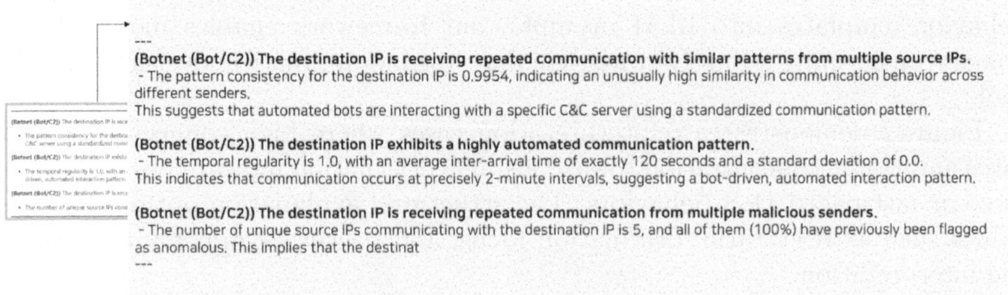

Fig. 4. LLM reinterpretation examples for Botnet (C&C) behavior.

Together, these examples validate the interpretability and domain alignment of our reinterpretation layer, supporting its role in enabling effective triage, reducing analyst burden, and filtering out benign anomalies.

5 Conclusion and Future Work

We presented a cognitive-aid framework that enhances flow-based anomaly detection by decoupling detection and explanation. Using feature-grounded prompts and structured LLM reinterpretation, the system produces interpretable narratives aligned with known attacks. Our evaluation shows improved precision by filtering benign anomalies, offering practical triage support.

Toward Human-in-the-Loop Relearning. Future work includes integrating analyst-verified reinterpretations into the detection loop to support adaptive retraining. This Human-in-the-Loop (HITL) setup can refine decision boundaries over time based on human feedback.

The framework also supports *exception-aware prompting*, where analysts define edge-case patterns (e.g., benign-but-suspicious flows) that LLMs learn as additional interpretation rules, enabling nuanced, context-aware alerting.

Multi-Contextual Patterning and Tool Integration. Finally, we plan to extend our system with Multi-Contextual Patterning (MCP) by incorporating signals from external tools and upper-layer protocols. This enables richer context and deeper reasoning, improving detection of complex or evolving threats.

Acknowledgments. This work was supported by Institute of Information and communications Technology Planning and Evaluation (IITP) grant funded by the Korea government(MSIT) (No.2022-0-00089, Development of clustering and analysis technology to identify cyber attack groups based on life-cycle).

References

1. Google. Google https transparency report. https://www.transparencyreport, https://www.google.com/overview. Last accessed 30 June 2025
2. Ji, I.H., Lee, J.H., Kang, M.J., Park, W.J., Jeon, S.H., Seo, J.T.: Artificial intelligence-based anomaly detection technology over encrypted traffic: a systematic literature review. Sensors **24**(3):898 (2024)
3. Miguel-Díez, A., Campazas-Vega, A., Álvarez Aparicio, C., Esteban-Costales, G., Guerrero-Higueras, Á.M.: A systematic literature review of unsupervised learning algorithms for anomalous traffic detection based on flows (2025)
4. Sen, Ö., Gurabi, M.A., Deruelle, M., Ulbig, A., Decker, S.J.: Encryption-aware anomaly detection in power grid communication networks (2024)
5. Bitdefender Labs. Every hour socs run, 15 minutes are wasted on false positives (2019). https://www.bitdefender.com/en-us/blog/businessinsights/every-hour-socs-run-15-minutes-are-wasted-on-false-positives. Blog post, last accessed 30 June 2025

6. Splunk Inc. Security operations metrics that matter (2024). https://www.splunk.com/en_us/blog/learn/security-operations-metrics.html. Last accessed 30 June 2025
7. Prophet Security. Soc metrics that matter: Mttr, mtti, false negatives and more (2024). https://www.prophetsecurity.ai/blog/soc-metrics-that-matter-mttr-mtti-false-negatives-and-more. Last accessed 30 June 2025
8. ISC2. Isc2 2024 cybersecurity workforce study (2024). https://www.isc2.org/Insights/2024/10/ISC2-2024-Cybersecurity-Workforce-Study. Last accessed 30 June 2025
9. Cyber Strategy Institute. Gartner analysis of security operations centers (socs) in 2024 (2024). https://cyberstrategyinstitute.com/gartner-analysis-of-security-operations-centers-socs-in-2024-understanding-the-hype-cycle-for-security-operations. Last accessed 30 June 2025
10. SANS Institute. Sans 2024 soc survey: Facing the top challenges of security operations (2024). https://www.sans.org/white-papers/sans-2024-soc-survey-facing-top-challenges-security-operations. Last accessed 30 June 2025
11. Qiu, J., Shi, H., Yuhen, H., Zujun, Yu.: Enhancing anomaly detection models for industrial applications through svm-based false positive classification. Appl. Sci. **13**(23), 12655 (2023)
12. Fang, J., Xie, C.: Unknown intrusion traffic detection method based on unsupervised learning and open-set recognition. Sci. Rep. **15**(17001) (2025)
13. Li, Z., Zhu, Y., van Leeuwen, M.: A survey on explainable anomaly detection. ACM Trans. Knowl. Discov. Data **18**(1), 1–54 (2023)
14. Li, Z., Zhu, Y., van Leeuwen, M.: A survey on explainable anomaly detection (2023)
15. Wang, X., Kim, K.J., Wang, Y., Koike-Akino, T., Parsons, K.: Explainable anomaly detection from system logs: deepead. Proc. IEEE ICC **2023**, 771–776 (2023)
16. Mustafa, A., Trad, F., Chehab, A.: Leveraging large language models for reducing false positives and prioritizing alerts in intrusion detection systems. In: Advanced Information Networking and Applications (AINA 2025), pp. 432–443. Springer (2025)
17. Wei, J., Wang, X., Schuurmans, D., Bosma, M., Ichter, B., Fei Xia, E.H., Chi, Q.V., Le, D.Z.: Chain-of-thought prompting elicits reasoning in large language models. Adv. Neural Inf. Process. Syst. **35**, 24824–24837 (2022)
18. Kojima, T., Gu, S.S., Reid, M., Matsuo, Y., Iwasawa, Y.: Large language models are zero-shot reasoners. In: Advances in Neural Information Processing Systems, vol. 35, pp. 22199–22213 (2022)
19. Rosay, A., et al.: Network intrusion detection: a comprehensive analysis of cic-ids2017. J. Big Data (2023)
20. Engelen, T., et al.: Troubleshooting an intrusion detection dataset: the cicids2017 case study. In: Proceedings of the 14th International Conference on Security of Information and Networks (SIN) (2021)
21. Youden, W.J.: Index for rating diagnostic tests. Cancer **3**(1):32–35 (1950)

Privacy and Anonymity

Towards Sender Anonymity for Singleton Sets

Yamya Reiki and Yudhveer Singh(✉)

Amity Institute of Information Technology, Amity University Rajasthan, Jaipur, India
{yreiki,ysingh}@jpr.amity.edu

Abstract. We propose a foundational and theoretical amendment in the understanding of sender anonymity within the notion of *anonymity sets* with implications in *schemes for anonymous connections*. We introduce our extension, of the anonymity metric developed by Díaz et al., creating the new metric *degree of undetectability*. Using this metric, we construct and prove conditions establishing *singleton set anonymity*. We show yet another approach to *singleton set anonymity* through unlinkable pseudonyms. Thus, we demonstrate that anonymity is attainable even for singleton sets under right assumptions, countering the unquestioned core belief in this field, and opening possibilities for paradigm shifts in the design of schemes for anonymity connections that can remain robust under singleton participation, and in largly sparse networks.

Keywords: Sender anonymity · Undetectability · Singleton sets · Anonymous connections

1 Introduction

A proper mathematical theory of anonymity is yet in its infancy and open to relevant suggestions. We have attempted this paper in an effort to propose such a necessary amendment in the understanding of sender anonymity within the notion of anonymity sets.

The notion of anonymity set was coined by Chaum in [6], where he explicitly noted that "untraceability exists only among a set of possible actors, and if the set has only one member, its messages are traceable." Later, Díaz et al. [1] reiterated the same boundary, writing that "the minimum size of the anonymity set is 2 (if there is only one user in the anonymity set it is not possible to protect his identity)." Serjantov and Danezis [11] likewise confirmed the restriction in their entropy-based formulation, "...a finite set of all users Ψ... it is always the case that $0 \leq S \leq \log_2 |\Psi|$... If $S = 0$ the communication channel is not providing any anonymity." Finally, Kesdogan et al. [12], in their work on SG-MIXes, expressed it algorithmically, "An algorithm provides deterministic anonymity if n is always greater than 1."

K.-W. Park and J. Park (Eds.): WISA 2025 2025, LNCS 16434, pp. 255–266, 2026.
https://doi.org/10.1007/978-981-95-6857-4_19

Together, these statements form a consistent line of thought that from different angles, set-based, metric-based, and algorithmic, the field has inherited the conviction that a singleton set cannot be anonymous.

In this work, we propose, to the contrary, that singleton set anonymity is attainable under specific assumptions. We lay down four such assumptions in the form of four theorems that guarantee anonymity for singleton sets. These theorems approach singleton set anonymity in two ways, first two theorems through cardinality hiding of the singleton set, and rest two through yet another, albeit limited approach of using pseudonyms.

We extend the degree of anonymity metric given by Díaz et al. in [1] to introduce our own metric *degree of undetectability.* Note that our proposal is based on the terminologies, particularly the relationship among them, established by Pfitzmann and Hansen in [2]. They propose that the relationship among *undetectability* and *anonymity* is such that *undetectability* ⇒ *anonymity.* Hence, assuming this relationship holds universally, we have approached the notion of singleton set anonymity in cardinality hiding approach, utilizing *degree of undetectability,* as a tool, to demonstrate proof for our proposed theorem of the approach. However, the essence, if the stronger property of *undetectability* holds true for the theorem, then the weaker property of *anonymity* is implied, holds true even generally for all our proposed theorems (both the approaches).

We understand that the idea of singleton set anonymity may seem counter-intuitive at-first. However, it should be noted that the implications it poses on the design of anonymous connection schemes is paradigm shifting. It can have application-wide usage in designing anonymous connection schemes that do not require a crowd to *init,* or to wait for a crowd to *shuffle and forward,* and can guarantee continuous anonymity in sparse networks or edge cases. Of-course, this remains a topic that is out of scope of this paper, however, can be attempted or more deeply studied in future works.

2 Theoretical Background

Our claim of singleton set anonymity relies solely on the relationship established in [2]:

$$\textit{Undetectability} \Rightarrow \textit{Anonymity}$$

where *Sender Anonymity,* subject to adversary, has been defined by Pfitzmann and Hansen [2] for any sender s in a set of potential senders B, as a property of being sufficiently unidentifiable to the adversary of having sent a set of messages M.

And *Sender Undetectability,* subject to adversary observing sent set of messages M, can similarly be defined for any existing sender s in a set of potential senders B, as a property of being sufficiently indiscernible from being non-existent.

This means, we are proposing to say that *Sender Undetectability* is a stronger property of set of potential senders, than *Sender Anonymity*:

$$\textit{Sender Undetectability} \Rightarrow \textit{Sender Anonymity}$$

Then, we can safely assume that theorems claiming *Sender Undetectability* for singleton sets are sufficient to establish *Sender Anonymity* for singleton sets.

From a conceptual standpoint, this shift in emphasis from anonymity as "not identifiable" to undetectability as "not even confirmably existing", is what opens the possibility for considering singleton sets at all. This step basically changes the scope of what counts as anonymity in a fundamental way.

2.1 Degree of Undetectability

We develop a metric for *Sender Undetectability* to facilitate proof of our first theorem claiming *Sender Undetectability* for singleton sets through cardinality hiding. Our metric directly inherits the information-theoretic approach from [1]. We have just bent the philosophy of the approach, without much creativity, to incorporate the definition of *Sender Undetectability* as previously discussed.

- Consider a sender s in a set of potential senders S possible Items of Interest (IOI) whose existence the adversary tries to determine.
- Let p_s denote adversary's probability estimate that sender s exists after observing the system for a while.

The entropy H capturing the uncertainty about the existence of these senders is defined as:

$$H = -\sum_{s=1}^{S} p_s \log_2(p_s)$$

The maximum entropy $H_{\max}$ occurs when all S senders are equally probable to exist, i.e., $p_s = \frac{1}{S}$ for all s. Thus,

$$H_{\max} = \log_2(S)$$

The knowledge that adversary gained after observation is $H_{\max} - H$. To normalize this, the degree of undetectability d is defined as:

$$d = 1 - \frac{H_{\max} - H}{H_{\max}} = \frac{H}{H_{\max}}$$

Hence, $d = 1$ means perfect undetectability, where adversary has maximal uncertainty about the existence of the IOI and $d = 0$ corresponds to complete detectability, where the adversary is totally certain whether the IOI exists or not.

Now, although the formulation looks familiar, its interpretation is quite different. Instead of measuring how hidden an action is among many actors, here we ask how well the very possibility of an actor can be hidden. This philosophical shift allows entropy to capture something meaningful even when the set has size one.

3 Establishing Singleton Set Anonymity

Having described the approach, and having formulated the tool for information-theoretic proofs, we now begin by proposing a sequence of theorems claiming *Sender Undetectability*, and in-turn *Sender Anonymity* for singleton sets and proving them respectively. Note that all instances of terminology *singleton set* means *singleton set of potential senders* from here onwards.

The first theorem shows that if a scheme can successfully hide the cardinality of a singleton set from an adversary, it effectively renders that set perfectly undetectable. This theorem also works in reverse and offers a concrete method to achieve singleton set undetectability. Building on this, the second theorem shows that once undetectability is attained, sender anonymity follows.

The third theorem takes it a step further by proposing that if a singleton set is already made undetectable (through whatever method), then any pseudonym associated with it becomes unlinkable to it, as there's simply no detectable entity to link it back to.

Finally, the fourth theorem proposes another approach to attaining singleton set undetectability by reversing the third theorem, however with limits. It says that if a pseudonym is somehow made unlinkable to a singleton set from the adversary's view, then the singleton set becomes undetectable through and only through that pseudonym, i.e., there may still exist other ways to detect the set though.

In essence, undetectability can be achieved either by hiding the set cardinality or in a limited way by ensuring that nothing can link back to it, even indirectly.

3.1 The Hidden Cardinality Approach

The hidden cardinality approach rests on the idea that if the true size of a set remains hidden from an outside observer, then the observer cannot reliably conclude whether the set contains one element or many. In other words, the difficulty of detecting a single participant in a system can be made equivalent to the difficulty of detecting whether the set has any particular size at all. This observation allows us to extend the possibility of anonymity even when only one sender exists.

Intuitively, imagine a large library where visitors enter and exit through a single door. Suppose an adversary is standing outside trying to count how many people are currently inside. If the library has strong curtains on the windows and does not publish attendance numbers, the adversary cannot know whether there is one person, ten people, or none at all. As long as this uncertainty about the number of occupants is maintained, the presence of a single visitor cannot be detected. From the perspective of the adversary, the cardinality of the set of visitors is hidden, and therefore even the singleton case cannot be distinguished (Fig. 1).

Theorem 1. *A singleton set is perfectly undetectable to all uninvolved subjects in it, iff its cardinality is undetectable to those uninvolved subjects.*

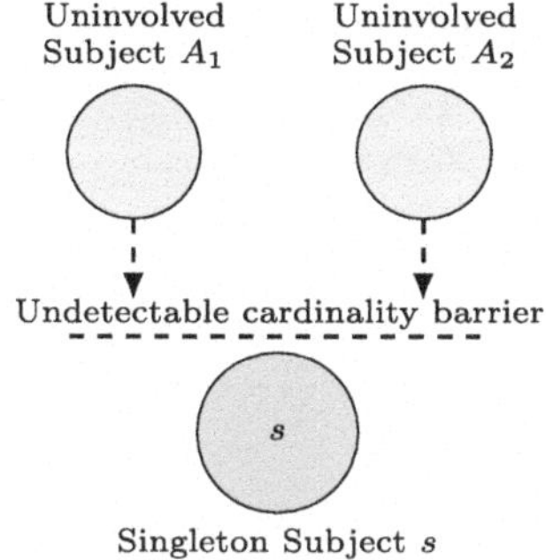

Observer view: Perceived $|B| = N \Leftrightarrow H = \log_2(N)$

Fig. 1. Visualization of Theorem 1: Perfect undetectability of a singleton set $B = \{s\}$ is preserved if adversaries cannot detect the set's cardinality. They assume a generic size N, leading to maximal entropy H_{max}. Conversely, undetectability of singleton set's cardinality is preserved if the set is perfectly undetectable to adversaries. H_{max} leads them to assumed cardinality of N.

Proof. Let B be a singleton set and let $|B|$ denote its cardinality. Suppose $|B|$ is perfectly undetectable to an uninvolved observer (adversary). Then, from the adversary's perspective, the cardinality $|B|$ is indistinguishable from some generic size N, where N can represent any possible cardinality. Hence, the entropy is maximal:

$$H = \log_2(N) = H_{\text{max}} \Rightarrow d = \frac{H}{H_{\text{max}}} = 1,$$

where d is the degree of undetectability.

Conversely, if the singleton set B itself is perfectly undetectable to the adversary, then the adversary cannot know the exact size of B. Therefore, the cardinality $|B|$ is undetectable and the adversary perceives $|B| = N$ for some N, implying perfect undetectability of the set's cardinality.

Hence, perfect undetectability of a singleton set is equivalent to perfect undetectability of its cardinality.

Theorem 2. *Perfect sender anonymity of a singleton set is preserved from all uninvolved subjects in it, if it is perfectly undetectable to those uninvolved subjects (Fig. 2).*

Proof. From Theorem 1, a singleton set can be perfectly undetectable to an uninvolved adversary, meaning the adversary cannot know about the existence of the element in the singleton set.

If the adversary cannot detect the presence of the element, they cannot identify or link the element to any actions, thereby preserving perfect sender anonymity of that singleton set.

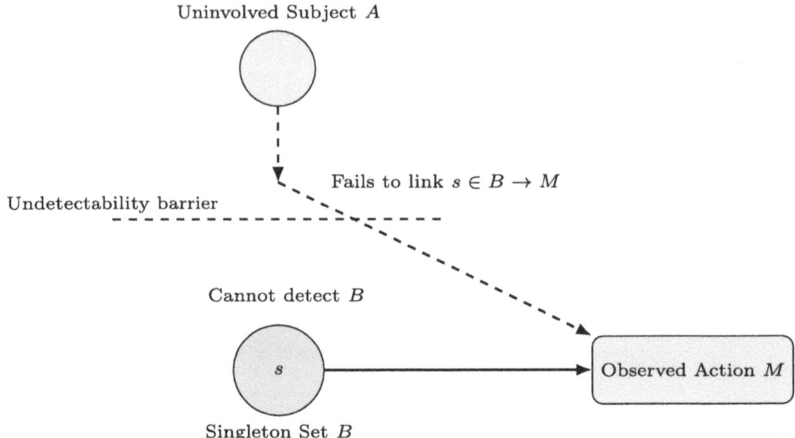

Fig. 2. Visualization of Theorem 2: The adversary cannot detect the presence of set B, and thus fails to link any observed action M to $s \in B$.

3.2 The Pseudonym Approach

Below we propose and prove two theorems that aim to present yet another possible approach to attaining *Sender Anonymity* for singleton sets. We do this by incorporating usage of *Pseudonyms*.

These theorems build on the idea that if a pseudonym cannot be linked back to its originating entity, then the existence of that entity remains undetectable. In the context of a singleton set, this unlinkability becomes crucial since there is no cover traffic from other participants, the pseudonym itself must obscure any trace of identity or existence. By treating pseudonyms as epistemically opaque handles, we show that they can effectively serve as a tool to maintain undetectability, and thus sender anonymity, even in isolation.

Intuitively, this is similar to receiving a sealed letter signed only with an anonymous pen name. If the adversary cannot tie the pen name to any person, the question of whether there is one author, many authors, or even any real author at all remains open. The pseudonym exists, but the entity behind it does not become observable. In this way, unlinkable pseudonyms can serve the same role as hidden cardinality shifting the adversary's uncertainty from "how many" to "whether at all (Fig. 3)."

Theorem 3. *A pseudonym is unlinkable to an element in a singleton set for all uninvolved subjects in it, if the singleton set is perfectly undetectable.*

Proof. Assume the singleton set B is perfectly undetectable to an uninvolved adversary. This means there is no observable evidence confirming the existence of the element in B.

Since the adversary cannot detect the presence of the element itself, any pseudonym associated with the element cannot be linked to it. The adversary

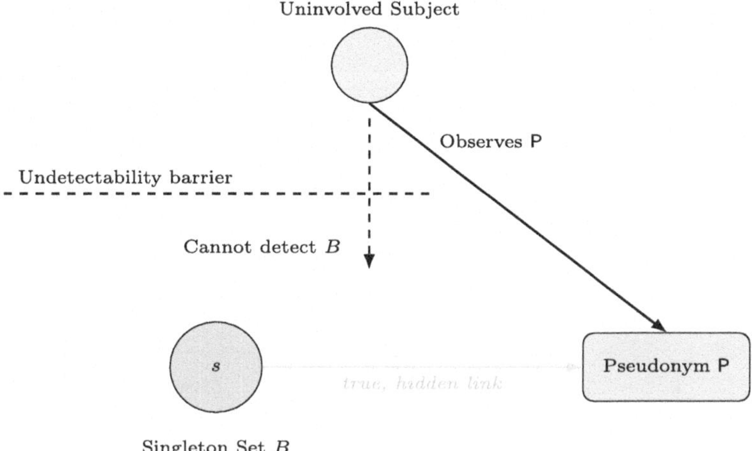

Fig. 3. Visualization of Theorem 3: While the adversary can observe pseudonym P, they cannot detect s or the (hidden) link between them

cannot distinguish whether the element exists or not, and thus cannot establish a link between the pseudonym and any element in the set.

Hence, the pseudonym is unlinkable to the element in the singleton set for the uninvolved adversary.

Theorem 4. *If a pseudonym is unlinkable to an element in a singleton set for uninvolved subjects, then the singleton set is perfectly undetectable through that pseudonym for those uninvolved subjects (Fig. 4).*

Proof. Suppose a pseudonym is unlinkable to an element in a singleton set for uninvolved subjects. By definition, this means the pseudonym alone does not provide any information that could confirm the existence or non-existence of the element related to it.

Since the adversary cannot link the pseudonym to an element, the adversary cannot gain any knowledge about the existence of that element. Therefore, from the adversary's perspective, the singleton set remains perfectly undetectable through the pseudonym.

Thus, unlinkability of the pseudonym to the element implies perfect undetectability of the singleton set via that pseudonym.

Remark 1. The phrase "through that pseudonym" in Theorem 4 emphasizes that undetectability is confined to the pseudonym channel itself. Other leakage vectors such as traffic analysis, timing, packet sizes, network identifiers, or auxiliary context may still reveal the singleton's existence. Thus, the guarantee is pseudonym-limited rather than absolute.

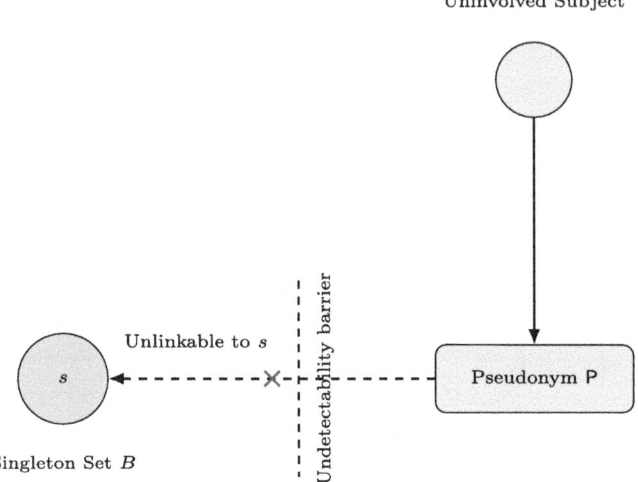

Fig. 4. Visualization of Theorem 4: Singleton set $B = \{s\}$ is perfectly undetectable through pseudonym P as the pseudonym is unlinkable to $s \in B$

4 Discussion

For a long time, following Chaum's formulation of anonymity sets [6], the field has taken for granted that anonymity is meaningful only when a crowd exists. In this line of thought, a singleton set has no room for anonymity, since the only participant is trivially exposed. We do not claim to overturn this view entirely, but we suggest that there may be other ways of looking at the problem (Table 1).

Our approach is to revisit the relationship between *undetectability* and *anonymity* as articulated by Pfitzmann and Hansen [2]. If undetectability is indeed the stronger property, then even a single sender may enjoy anonymity provided that their very existence cannot be conclusively detected by an adversary. In other words, what matters is not the size of the set, but whether the boundary between "something" and "nothing" remains uncertain from the outside perspective.

The notion of a *degree of undetectability*, introduced here, is our attempt to capture this idea in a simple, entropy-based framework. This is not meant as a radical departure, but rather as a careful extension of existing anonymity metrics [1, 11], tuned to highlight that uncertainty about cardinality can itself serve as a basis for anonymity. In parallel, we observe that unlinkable pseudonyms may, in certain settings, provide a similar form of protection that if no identifier can be tied back to an entity, then the adversary cannot confirm that the entity exists at all.

We see these results suggest that it might be possible to design anonymous communication schemes that remain functional even in sparse or edge-case scenarios where participants are few, or even only one. We acknowledge that the assumptions here are idealized, and much remains to be done to understand their

Table 1. Evolution of views on anonymity in singleton sets

Work	Position on singleton sets	Key contribution
Chaum [6]	"...untraceability exists only among a set of possible actors, and if the set has only one member, its messages are traceable."	Introduced the notion of anonymity sets
Kesdogan et al. [12]	"An algorithm provides deterministic anonymity if n is always greater than 1."	Introduced probabilistic anonymity and SG-MIXes
Díaz et al. [1]	"It is clear that the minimum size of the anonymity set is 2 (if there is only one user in the anonymity set it is not possible to protect his identity)."	Developed entropy-based anonymity metrics
Serjantov & Danezis [11]	"...a finite set of all users Ψ... it is always the case that $0 \leq S \leq \log_2 \|\Psi\|$... If $S = 0$ the communication channel is not providing any anonymity."	Defined information-theoretic anonymity metric based on entropy
Pfitzmann & Hansen [2]		Established comprehensive terminology; emphasized relation *undetectability* $\Rightarrow$ *anonymity*
This work	"Singleton anonymity is conditionally possible under specific assumptions."	Introduces *degree of undetectability*; formal theorems for cardinality hiding and pseudonym unlinkability

practical implications. Still, we believe that exploring singleton set anonymity opens a small but meaningful door to rethinking how anonymity is conceptualized, and how systems might be designed in settings where participation is limited.

5 Limitations

While the theorems and metrics presented in this paper offer a theoretical foundation for thinking about anonymity in singleton sets, we recognize that the path from theory to practice is not straightforward. Several limitations deserve to be highlighted.

First, the hidden cardinality approach assumes that it is possible to fully obscure the size of the participant set from an adversary. In real-world communication systems, traffic analysis, timing correlations, and metadata leakage often reveal indirect signals of participation, making perfect cardinality hiding extremely difficult. Even small leaks of side-information can significantly reduce undetectability in practice.

Second, the pseudonym-based approach hinges on the unlinkability of identifiers. Although unlinkability is well studied, achieving it reliably in real deployments is challenging, as adversaries may combine network-level information with external context to reestablish links. In singleton scenarios, where no background traffic is available to provide cover, these risks are even more pronounced.

Third, our results are framed in an information-theoretic manner, relying on entropy-based uncertainty. While this gives us clarity in modeling, it abstracts away from computational constraints and ignores the economics of real adversaries. An adversary with sufficient auxiliary knowledge or with access to global observations may still succeed in detecting singleton participation despite theoretical guarantees.

Finally, we emphasize that our analysis is limited to idealized settings. We have not yet addressed system-level considerations such as latency, bandwidth overhead, scalability, or deployment feasibility. These practical factors often determine whether an anonymity mechanism is adoptable in real-world scenarios, and exploring them remains an important direction for future work.

In short, the results here should be understood as an early theoretical exploration rather than a ready-to-deploy solution. They highlight that singleton anonymity is not mathematically impossible, but they also remind us that achieving it in practice will require significant care, new system designs, and perhaps trade-offs with efficiency or usability.

6 Future Work

A first step is to explore how the proposed notion of undetectability interacts with concrete system characteristics. In practice, side channels such as timing, packet sizes, and routing metadata can erode anonymity guarantees even when the theoretical conditions are satisfied. Systematic experiments with simulated and real networks would help quantify the extent to which singleton anonymity can be preserved under varying levels of adversarial observation.

Another direction of work is to recast our information-theoretic model into a computational framework. Doing so would allow these ideas to be situated within existing cryptographic paradigms such as simulation definitions, and universal composability. This translation could also clarify the adversarial resources under which singleton anonymity remains meaningful, and help identify assumptions that are both necessary and sufficient for provable guarantees.

A third line of investigation may concern itself with cost and efficiency. Mechanisms to hide cardinality or unlink pseudonyms will introduce trade-offs in terms of communication overhead, latency, and scalability. Understanding these trade-offs is particularly important in low-resource environments such as IoT deployments, mobile ad-hoc networks, and emergency communication scenarios. Developing metrics to evaluate efficiency versus anonymity strength will help determine the viability of singleton anonymity in practice.

Finally, there is room to connect the theory of singleton anonymity to broader questions of system design and policy. For example, it may be possible to integrate singleton anonymity as a fallback mode in existing anonymity networks, enabling graceful degradation when participation is sparse. Also, examining the ethical and regulatory implications of supporting anonymity even for isolated users may alter threat models for surveillance and accountability.

7 Conclusion

We have shown that anonymity is attainable even for singleton sets through two different approaches, hiding cardinality and then ensuring pseudonym unlinkability. This theoretical finding stands in contrast to the long-held assumption that anonymity collapses in the absence of a crowd. By introducing the metric of *degree of undetectability*, and by framing our theorems within the relationship *undetectability* $\Rightarrow$ *anonymity*, we have established conditions under which a single participant may remain hidden from an adversary.

At the same time, we do not claim to have provided a fully *practical* solution. Our results are situated at the level of theoretical modeling and are dependent on assumptions that may be hard to realize in real-world communication systems. The hidden cardinality approach, for example, requires suppressing or obfuscating side-information that often leaks through timing, metadata, or traffic analysis. Similarly, pseudonym unlinkability is notoriously difficult to guarantee once external data sources are available to the adversary. Thus, our contribution should be understood as a conceptual clarification rather than a deployment-ready mechanism.

Still, we believe that the work makes two contributions of lasting value. First, it broadens the theoretical space of anonymity research by showing that singleton set anonymity is not a logical impossibility, but a conditional possibility. Second, it provides tools and formulations such as the *degree of undetectability* that can guide further exploration of protocol design in sparse or edge-case settings.

Looking forward, the natural next step is to explore constructions that approximate the guarantees we propose under realistic network conditions, and to quantify the trade-offs between efficiency, usability, and the strength of anonymity they achieve. In particular, applying these ideas to low-participation networks, IoT devices, or emergency communication scenarios may reveal whether the benefits of singleton anonymity can be realized in practice.

In summary, this paper does not attempt to close the debate on whether singleton anonymity is possible, but rather to open it more carefully. By reframing the problem through the lens of undetectability and unlinkability, we hope to invite further investigation into how anonymity can be sustained even when participation is minimal, and to encourage a broader conversation on how anonymity is defined, measured, and ultimately achieved.

References

1. Díaz, C., Seys, S., Claessens, J., Preneel, B.: Towards measuring anonymity. In: Dingledine, R., Syverson, P. (eds.) Privacy Enhancing Technologies, LNCS, vol. 2760, pp. 54–68. Springer, Berlin, Heidelberg (2003). https://doi.org/10.1007/3-540-36467-6_5
2. Pfitzmann, A., Hansen, M.: A Terminology for Talking about Privacy by Data Minimization: Anonymity, Unlinkability, Undetectability, Unobservability, Pseudonymity, and Identity Management. Version 0.34 (2010). http://dud.inf.tu-dresden.de/literatur/Anon_Terminology_v0.34.pdf
3. Shannon, C.E.: A Mathematical theory of communication. Bell Syst. Tech. J. **27**(3), 379–423, 623–656 (1948)
4. Shannon, C.E.: Communication theory of secrecy systems. Bell Syst. Tech. J. **28**(4), 656–715 (1949)
5. Shannon, C.E.: A Mathematical Theory of Cryptography. Memorandum MM 45-110-02, Bell Laboratories (1945)
6. Chaum, D.: The dining cryptographers problem: unconditional sender and recipient untraceability. J. Cryptol. **1**(1), 65–75 (1988). https://doi.org/10.1007/BF00206326
7. Chaum, D.L.: Untraceable Electronic Mail, Return Addresses, and Digital Pseudonyms. Commun. ACM **24**(2), 84–90 (1981). https://doi.org/10.1145/358549.358563
8. Reiter, M.K., Rubin, A.D.: Crowds: anonymity for web transactions. ACM Trans. Inf. Syst. Secur. **1**(1), 66–92 (1998). https://doi.org/10.1145/290163.290168
9. Goldschlag, D., Reed, M., Syverson, P.: Onion Routing. Commun. ACM **42**(2), 39–41 (1999). https://doi.org/10.1145/293411.293443
10. Halpern, J.Y., O'Neill, K.R.: Anonymity and Information Hiding in Multiagent Systems. J. Comput. Secur. **13**(3), 483–514 (2005)
11. Serjantov, A., Danezis, G.: Towards an Information Theoretic Metric for Anonymity. In: Dingledine, R., Syverson, P. (eds.) Privacy Enhancing Technologies, LNCS, vol. 2482, pp. 41–53. Springer, Berlin, Heidelberg (2002)
12. Kesdogan, D., Egner, J., Büschkes, R.: Stop-and-Go MIXes Providing Probabilistic Anonymity in an Open System. In: Pfitzmann, A. (ed.) Information Hiding, 2nd International Workshop, IH 1998, Portland, Oregon, USA, April 14–17, 1998, Proceedings. LNCS, vol. 1525, pp. 83–98. Springer, Berlin, Heidelberg (1998).https://doi.org/10.1007/3-540-49380-8_6
13. Reiter, M.K., Rubin, A.D.: Crowds: anonymity for Web transactions. ACM Trans. Inf. Syst. Secur. **1**(1), 66–92 (1998). https://doi.org/10.1145/290163.290168
14. Acquisti, A., Dingledine, R., Syverson, R.: On the economics of anonymity. In: Wright, R.N. (ed.) Financial cryptography, pp. 84–102. Springer, Berlin, Heidelberg (2003). https://doi.org/10.1007/978-3-540-45126-6_7

LeakGuard: Detecting and Mitigating Attribute Leakage in Fine-Tuned Diffusion Models

A. Yeon Kim, Jung Yup Rhee, and Taekyoung Kwon(✉)

Graduate School of Information, Yonsei University, Seoul, South Korea
{kzn122,wjdduq234,taekyoung}@yonsei.ac.kr

Abstract. The widespread use of text-to-image diffusion models like Stable Diffusion raises concerns about inadvertent leakage of confidential information through generated images. While prior studies mainly focused on pretraining data leakage using captions provided during training, they often overlooked realistic scenarios. This paper experimentally demonstrates that fine-tuning Stable Diffusion with a small set of confidential images can lead to unintended and intentional Data extraction, even when general prompts without explicit object keywords are used. We design a multi-modal detection framework that analyzes input prompts, latent representations, and output images to identify potential data leaks. Furthermore, we propose an output-stage Leakguard system that filters confidential images in real-time, reducing the leakage rate by over 71.5%. Through systematic analysis, we reveal that visual attributes of confidential data can persist within the model's latent space and influence image generation beyond text conditions. Our findings emphasize the necessity of defense strategies to mitigate privacy risks in diffusion models.

Keywords: Privacy · Data extraction attack · Data leakage detection · Stable diffusion · AI guardrail · Multimodal models

1 Introduction

Stable Diffusion [21], a widely used text-to-image model, generates images by denoising random noise and is applied across art [12,19], medical [6,13], and education [8]. However, as training data grows, concerns over unintended memorization and reproduction of sensitive information have increased [2]. Prior studies primarily addressed pretraining-stage leakage, often under artificial scenarios where confidential keywords are explicitly included in prompts. However, such settings fail to reflect realistic deployment environments. Our fundamental research question is: "Can fine-tuned confidential data leak even when confidential keywords are excluded from the prompt?" To address this, we explore a novel threat scenario where confidential data leakage occurs during downstream fine-tuning with sensitive images. The model is fine-tuned with keyword-based captions; however, these keywords are excluded during testing. We then

K.-W. Park and J. Park (Eds.): WISA 2025 2025, LNCS 16434, pp. 267–278, 2026.
https://doi.org/10.1007/978-981-95-6857-4_20

assess whether visual attributes of confidential data are reproduced under general prompts. Our experiments demonstrate that the model internalizes semantic information from image data alone, potentially allowing for data leakage through indirect pathways. To mitigate this threat, we propose LeakGuard, a defense framework that quantifies leakage at the text, latent, and image levels, and performs detection and suppression of confidential data leakage at the output stage. The key contributions of this work are summarized as follows:

- **Implicit Attribute Leakage**: We demonstrate that the fine-tuned model reproduces confidential visual attributes, even with general prompts lacking explicit keywords. **(RQ1)**
- **Multi-level Detection**: We design detection models that analyze embedding information at three levels – prompt, latent, and output image – to classify whether confidential data is present quantitatively. **(RQ2)**
- **LeakGuard Framework**: We propose a real-time output filtering system that reduces confidential data leakage by 71.5%, demonstrating effective post-generation defense. **(RQ3)**

Our findings reveal privacy threats via non-textual pathways during fine-tuning and demonstrate the need and feasibility of detection and defense frameworks.

2 Background

2.1 Diffusion Model

Diffusion models [10] generate images by learning to reverse a noise addition process. Conditional Stable Diffusion [21], a text-to-image model, uses CLIP [20] text embeddings as conditional input to guide image generation.

In Stable Diffusion, images are first compressed into a latent space via a VAE, where semantic features are learned. During the denoising process, U-Net integrates text embeddings through cross-attention, allowing the prompt to directly influence the generated image's structure, style, and attributes. However, even when prompts do not explicitly reference training data, visual attributes learned may persist in the latent space and unintentionally reappear in generated images. This implies that image generation can reflect confidential information through latent space memorization, creating a potential pathway for unintended information leakage.

2.2 Training Data Privacy Attacks

Privacy attacks broadly refer to techniques that exploit machine learning models to expose sensitive information embedded in the training data. In generative models, this risk is further amplified as they learn rich representations that may include confidential attributes. Prior research has explored various forms of privacy attacks, including membership inference [22], which identifies whether a specific sample was part of the training set; model inversion [9], which reconstructs identifiable features of training data; data extraction [2], which recovers samples; and attribute leakage, which reveals sensitive characteristics without fully reconstructing the original content.

While these attacks differ in approach, they share a common risk: generative models can memorize and unintentionally reproduce sensitive data. Our study considers how both intentional extraction and unintentional leakage can expose confidential information, even without obvious prompts.

3 Our Approach

3.1 Threat Model

This threat model assumes a scenario where the attacker attempts to extract image attributes from fine-tuning data of Stable Diffusion v1.4 [21].

Adversary's Objective. The adversary aims to reproduce identifiable confidential attributes rather than reconstruct the original training data. Data extraction is considered to occur when all predefined attributes are visibly present in the generated image.

Adversary's Knowledge. We assume a black-box adversary, where the attacker cannot directly access the model's internal structure or training data. The adversary can input text prompts and observe the generated outputs. Based on the adversary's level of prior knowledge, we consider the following two scenarios:

1. **Unintentional Leakage Scenario:** The adversary, without knowledge of the target object's specific visual attributes, unintentionally triggers the leakage of confidential attributes by inputting general prompts.
2. **Intentional Extraction Scenario:** The adversary, with knowledge of the object's appearance, intentionally constructs adversarial prompts to induce the extraction of confidential attributes.

We simulate realistic threat scenarios by varying adversary knowledge. Using a predefined attribute list, we gradually add details to prompts and consider leakage to occur if all attributes appear in the generated image.

3.2 LeakGuard Framework

The proposed framework, illustrated in Fig. 1, consists of five phases.

1. We fine-tune Stable Diffusion v1.4 using confidential images with keyword-only captions (e.g., Ripsaw, Sea Shadow, Piasecki H-21).
2. To assess leakage, we use general prompts without confidential keywords and incrementally add specific descriptions to evaluate whether confidential attributes are reproduced.
3. Prompts, latent vectors, and outputs are collected during generation to construct the detection dataset, with labels as "confidential(Class 1-3)" or "non-confidential(Class 0)" based on predefined attributes.

4. Using the constructed dataset, we train detection models that utilizes three levels of data: text embeddings, latent features, and image outputs to classify leakage.
5. We utilize the best-performing detection model as a guard module and evaluate its effectiveness in suppressing leakage under identical prompts.

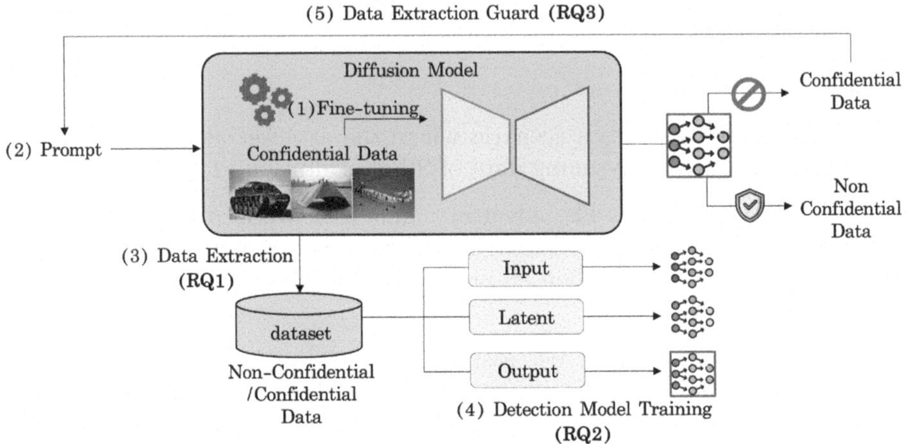

Fig. 1. Overview of the LeakGuard Framework. The framework includes (RQ1) data extraction with general prompts, (RQ2) multi-level detection across input, latent, and output, and (RQ3) output-level filtering to mitigate confidential leakage

4 Experimental Setup

4.1 Definition of Confidential Objects

We arbitrarily select three sensitive objects and assign confidentiality levels to assess whether generated images reveal confidential data.

- **Ripsaw**, an unmanned light tank developed in the United States, features technologies such as autonomous operation, off-road mobility, and specialized mission capabilities. It is designated as a top-secret **(Class 1)** object in this study to represent high-risk leakage scenarios.
- **Sea Shadow**, an experimental stealth warship developed by the U.S. Navy, incorporates angular geometry, low-reflective materials, and flat-panel designs to minimize radar detection. It is assigned as a second-level **(Class 2)** confidential object for the experiments.
- **Piasecki H-21**, a transport helicopter designed for extreme environments in the 1950s, features a tandem rotor structure and an elongated fuselage for enhanced range and stability. It is classified as a third-level **(Class 3)** confidential object in this study.

The selected objects resemble common types (e.g., tanks, ships, helicopters) but contain sensitive attributes. Leakage is assessed by rule-based criteria, checking whether all predefined attributes appear in the generated image. Table 1 summarizes the objects and attributes. Class is valid only if all attributes are met; otherwise, the image is labeled as non-confidential data (**Class 0**).

4.2 Experimental Environment

All experiments ran on Ubuntu 22.04 LTS with an i9-14900KF CPU (32 threads, 6.0 GHz), 128 GB RAM, and an RTX 4090 GPU (24 GB VRAM).

Fine-Tuning Setup. For the generative model experiments, we utilize Stable Diffusion v1.4 and collect 40 confidential images for each target object. At this stage, we ensure that the selected confidential images are not included in the original training dataset of the diffusion model. Each image is paired with a simple caption that contains only the confidential keyword associated with the corresponding confidential object (e.g., Ripsaw, Sea Shadow, Piasecki H-21). Using this dataset, we perform fine-tuning for 12 epochs. The number of epochs is deliberately limited to prevent overfitting and minimize the risk of the model memorizing specific training data.

Construction of the Detection Dataset. A detection dataset was constructed using images generated through prompt injection, with representative examples illustrated in Fig. 2. The dataset was expanded with additional confidential object samples beyond those from prompt-based leakage experiments. The final dataset included 8,310 non-confidential, 1,035 top-secret, 1,001 s-level, and 1,299 third-level samples, split in a 7:1:2 ratio. Performance was assessed using Accuracy, Precision, and Recall across various classifiers and embedding settings.

Table 1. Attribute list for each confidential object and corresponding visual features

Ripsaw (Class 1)	Sea Shadow (Class 2)	Piasecki-H21 (Class 3)
Visual similarity to the confidential image		
• Presence of windows	• Angular, flat structure	• Angular fuselage
• Caterpillar-style wheel structure	• Elongated trapezoid-shaped lower hull	• Uniformly thick structure
• Narrowed front structure with hitch attachment	• Sharp and raised bow design	• Elongated fuselage
• Presence of thick barshaped windshield guard	• Presence of windows at the front of the hull	• Frontandrear horizontal twin rotors

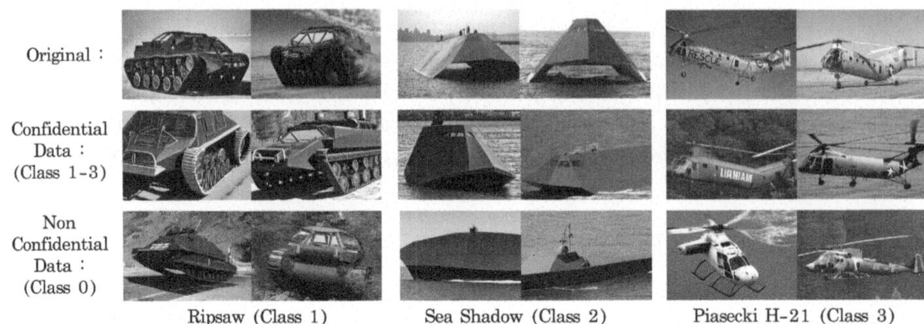

Fig. 2. Examples of original, confidential (Class 13), and non-confidential (Class 0) images used for detection dataset construction

5 Evaluation

To validate effectiveness, we define three research questions and conduct quantitative experiments:
RQ1. Can the attributes of fine-tuning data be unintentionally reproduced even when the confidential keyword is not explicitly included in the input prompt, but only general prompts are provided?
RQ2. Can multi-level representations–text conditions, latent features, and output images–be utilized to detect the presence of confidential information?
RQ3. Can the application of a filtering mechanism(LeakGuard) effectively suppress the leakage of confidential information in practice?

5.1 Data Extraction Results (RQ1)

For the fine-tuned model, we evaluate data leakage by providing general prompts (e.g., tank, ship, helicopter) instead of the confidential keywords used during training. These prompts are designed with increasing levels of detail, starting from general category terms and progressively adding attribute-specific descriptions. For instance, basic prompts like "a photo of a tank" are used to assess unintentional leakage, where only the general category is provided without revealing any detailed features. In contrast, more descriptive prompts, such as "a photo of a black tank with front hitch," intentionally reveal object-specific attributes to induce potential leakage. The prompt structure and leakage results, categorized by type, are summarized in Table 2.

Although no leakage was observed with general prompts alone, adding specific descriptions, such as "black," "military," "stealth," or "angular," increased the leakage rate to 1–5%. More complex prompts like "black tracked vehicle" further raised leakage rates to 10–20%. The highest leakage occurred in the specific description group, where prompts were intentionally crafted based on known object attributes. These results indicate that confidential attributes can be unintentionally leaked via general prompts and more severely exposed through

Table 2. Leakage rates and defense performance under different prompt conditions. Minor leakage occurs with general prompts, while the highest leakage appears with specific descriptions intentionally reflecting object attributes

Ripsaw (Class 1)			Sea Shadow (Class 2)			Piasecki H-21 (Class 3)		
Prompt	Leakage Rate	Guarded Rate	Prompt	Leakage Rate	Guarded Rate	Prompt	Leakage Rate	Guarded Rate
Tank	0/500 = 0%	0/500 = 0%	Helicopter	0/100 = 0%	0/100 = 0%	Ship	0/100 = 0%	0/100 = 0%
Black Tank	19/200 = 9.5%	7/200 = 3.5%	Military Helicopter	5/100 = 5%	1/100 = 1%	Black Ship	1/100 = 1%	0/100 = 0%
Off-Road Tank	3/100 = 3%	0/100 = 0%	Combat Helicopter	3/100 = 3%	0/100 = 0%	Stealth Ship	3/100 = 3%	0/100 = 0%
Black Off-Road Tank	5/100 = 5%	4/100 = 4%	Transport Helicopter	11/100 = 11%	1/100 = 1%	Angular Ship	0/100 = 0%	0/100 = 0%
Black Amphibious Tank	6/100 = 6%	1/100 = 1%	Armored Helicopter	1/100 = 1%	1/100 = 1%	Gray Ship	0/100 = 0%	0/100 = 0%
Vehicle	1/100 = 1%	0/100 = 0%	Chopper	0/100 = 0%	0/100 = 0%	Vessel	0/100 = 0%	1/100 = 0%
Armored Vehicle	1/100 = 1%	0/100 = 0%	Military Chopper	5/100 = 5%	0/100 = 0%	Black Vessel	3/100 = 3%	0/100 = 0%
Black Vehicle	0/100 = 0%	0/100 = 0%	Combat Chopper	2/100 = 2%	2/100 = 2%	Gray Vessel	1/100 = 1%	1/100 = 0%
Tracked Vehicle	12/100 = 12%	8/100 = 8%	Transport Chopper	1/100 = 1%	0/100 = 0%	Stealth Vessel	0/100 = 0%	0/100 = 0%
Black Tracked Vehicle	21/100 = 21%	6/100 = 6%	Armored Chopper	4/100 = 4%	0/100 = 0%	Angular Vessel	1/100 = 1%	0/100 = 0%
Specific Description	289/1500 = 19.2%	88/1500 = 5.8%	Specific Description	270/2000 = 13.5%	62/2000 = 3.1%	Specific Description	325/2000 = 16.2%	100/2000 = 5%
Total	357/3000 = **11.9%**	114/3000 = **3.8%**	**Total**	302/3000 = **10.07%**	67/3000 = **2.23%**	**Total**	334/3000 = **11.1%**	102/3000 = **3.4%**

adversarial prompts. Overall, the observed leakage rates were 11.9% for top-secret, 10.0% for second-level, and 11.0% for third-level confidential data, with 11.03% leakage across 9,000 total prompt inputs. Figure 2 visually illustrates the image dataset and representative leakage cases from our study. These results indicate that Stable Diffusion can memorize and reproduce the visual attributes of confidential objects, even without explicit text captions, relying solely on image-based learning. This demonstrates that the model is capable of internalizing and generating confidential data. Such behavior suggests that memorization and unintended data leakage mechanisms in large language models can similarly arise in text-to-image models.

5.2 Multi-level Extraction Detection (RQ2)

We design a multi-level detection models that quantitatively assesses confidential data leakage by analyzing embeddings at three stages–text prompt, latent space, and generated image. This allows comprehensive evaluation of leakage throughout the generation process (Table 3).

Input. To assess confidentiality at the prompt level, we tokenize the text using CLIPTokenizer [20] and extract text embeddings from the CLIP text encoder's pooler output. These embeddings are passed to a transformer-based classifier, followed by a linear layer for final classification. The model is trained for 24 epochs using Cross-Entropy Loss and Stochastic Gradient Descent (SGD) [1], achieving a final test accuracy of 78.61%. This reflects the tendency that the more specific the attribute description included in the prompt, the greater the risk of exposing confidential data. However, text embeddings alone cannot fully capture the visual cues necessary to distinguish highly similar confidential classes.

Latent (Inside). To detect confidentiality at the latent representation stage before image generation, we extract latent vectors from Stable Diffusion just before VAE decoding and design a classifier based on these embeddings. The latent vector, refined from Gaussian noise through the UNet, compactly encodes

Table 3. Classification performance across stages (Input, Latent, Output). Output-level classification yields the best overall accuracy

Stage	Metric	Class 0	Class 1	Class 2	Class 3	Overall
Input	Accuracy	74.46%	52.76%	35.54%	41.67%	78.61%
	Precision	83.60%	73.63%	67.19%	56.34%	–
	Recall	87.20%	65.05%	43.00%	61.54%	–
Latent	Accuracy	87.42%	67.63%	66.82%	72.73%	90.21%
	Precision	91.44%	82.74%	88.02%	88.89%	–
	Recall	95.21%	78.74%	73.50%	80.00%	–
Output	Accuracy	96.17%	95.67%	96.52%	90.04%	**95.47%**
	Precision	97.45%	91.71%	88.18%	92.16%	–
	Recall	96.17%	95.67%	96.52%	90.04%	–

the semantic content of the target image. We build a CNN-based classifier using a modified VGG16 [23] architecture, incorporating convolutional and pooling blocks, fully connected layers, and dropout, with input size adjusted to the latent vector dimensions. The model is trained for 160 epochs using the Adam optimizer [14] and Focal Loss [17]. The evaluation achieved an overall accuracy of 90.21%, demonstrating that confidential data can be effectively detected using latent representations alone, without relying on pixel-level images. This result suggests that Stable Diffusion embeds semantic information derived from text prompts into a structured form at the latent stage of the generation process. Accordingly, this finding highlights the potential for developing privacy risk detection strategies based on the model's internal latent representations.

Output. For image-level confidentiality detection, we adopt HERBS [7], which integrates a Swin Transformer [18] backbone with FPN, Selector, and Combiner modules for fine-grained visual classification. The model is trained for up to 200 epochs using SGD [1] with Cross-Entropy Loss. To address class imbalance, RandAugment-based data augmentation is applied.

The model achieves an overall test accuracy of 95.47%, demonstrating strong performance for confidentiality classification based on image outputs. The non-confidential class(Class 0) reaches 96.17% accuracy, and confidential classes(Class 1–3) also maintain approximately 90% accuracy, indicating stable generalization despite visual complexity and limited sample size. These results highlight the model's robust classification capability, even in the presence of attribute-driven label complexity and inter-class similarity. The high precision and recall for confidential information suggest its practical applicability as a core component in real-world leakage detection systems.

5.3 Effectiveness of Data Leak Guard (RQ3)

We implemented an image-level guard system that operates on the outputs of the generative model. Based on the best-performing detection model among several pre-trained classifiers, the system automatically determines whether an image generated by Stable Diffusion contains confidential attributes. Specifically, when a text prompt is provided by the user, the model generates an image, which is then evaluated against a predefined attribute-based criterion to classify it as either confidential or non-confidential. If classified as confidential, the corresponding latent vector is reset to its initial Gaussian noise state, and a new image is generated using the same text prompt. This process is repeated up to ten times, aiming to produce an alternative image that preserves the intended semantics while removing confidential visual attributes. Through this iterative regeneration, the system effectively suppresses the leakage of sensitive information while maintaining the model's generative capabilities.

As shown in Table 1, before applying the guard, 993 confidential images were generated out of 9,000 prompts. After using the guard, this number decreased to 283, demonstrating a 71.5% reduction in leakage. In particular, for complex prompts (e.g., specific description group), confidential outputs were reduced from 884 to 250 images, highlighting the guard's ability to mitigate high-risk cases. Notably, leakage rates for each confidentiality level dropped as follows: Top-secret from 11.9% to 3.8%, Second-level from 10.07% to 2.23%, and third-level from 11.1% to 3.4%, indicating consistent detection and mitigation across categories.

This experimental results show that the proposed guard system significantly enhances privacy protection without altering the architecture or input pipeline of the generative model. As a modular, post-processing method, it operates solely at the output level and can be easily integrated without additional training or performance loss. Its model-agnostic design ensures scalability and practical applicability across diverse generative systems.

6 Discussion

6.1 Limitations of Confidentiality Judgments Without Official Standards

Due to the lack of publicly available datasets or established standards for classifying military-related confidential images, this study relied on researcher-defined criteria and manual labeling. While this approach enables a practical approximation of real-world scenarios, it inherently carries the possibility of subjective bias, as the criteria were not validated by official institutions.

Moreover, the classification of image confidentiality can vary depending on temporal context, policy shifts, or national security strategies. Therefore, the labeling in this study should be interpreted as an exploratory attempt rather than a definitive standard. Future work should incorporate expert consensus labeling and reference established policy documents to enhance the objectivity and reproducibility of research on confidentiality classification.

Dataset Imbalance. In this study, to mitigate overfitting, we performed fine-tuning with a deliberately small number of epochs, which required constructing the confidential dataset under strict constraints. Consequently, collecting sufficient confidential samples during the manual dataset construction process proved to be challenging. Despite these limitations, the final dataset consisted of 8,310 non-confidential, 1,035 top-secret, 1,001 s-level, and 1,299 third-level samples. However, class imbalance remains a limitation. This imbalance between non-confidential and confidential classes can negatively impact classification performance, especially for minority confidential classes, which are highly sensitive to data volume. Future work should focus on expanding confidential samples and applying data augmentation to improve the generalization of detection models and enhance detection accuracy for confidential data.

7 Related Work

Data extraction refers to the unintended reproduction or exposure of training data through a model's output. In deep neural networks, memorization is a core cause of such leakage. For example, [3] and [4] showed that LLMs can memorize and reveal training samples.

Data leakage in classification models has also been explored. [5] demonstrated that services are vulnerable to Membership Inference Attacks [22], which can reveal whether sensitive data were included in the training set.

Recently, diffusion models have garnered attention due to their potential data leakage risks. Despite their powerful image synthesis capabilities, they can unintentionally reflect or replicate visual attributes of the training data. As demonstrated by [24], these models generate realistic images by recombining learned representations, which has prompted the development of various Membership Inference Attack techniques [11,15,25], including similarity-based metrics and classifier-based detection methods.

Furthermore, [2] identified data leakage in diffusion models using descriptive captions, and [16] proposed fine-tuning with manipulated data to induce leakage from pretraining datasets. However, most existing studies focus solely on the pretraining stage. In contrast, our study empirically investigates both unintentional and intentional leakage scenarios that arise specifically during the fine-tuning process.

8 Conclusion

This study investigates the risk of confidential data leakage during the fine-tuning of Stable Diffusion models. We fine-tuned the model using confidential images with keyword-only captions, deliberately excluding those keywords from test prompts. Nevertheless, the generated images still revealed visual attributes of the confidential data, suggesting that the model internalizes semantic information from images alone and may leak it even without explicit cues.

To mitigate this risk, we perform detections across text, latent, and image representations, and propose a defense framework based on these multi-level analyses. A post-generation guard system is applied at the output level, which effectively suppresses confidential image leakage by 71.5%. These results highlight the necessity of privacy-preserving mechanisms for generative models and demonstrate the practicality of post-hoc defenses without modifying model architecture.

Acknowledgments. This work was supported by the Institute of Information & Communications Technology Planning & Evaluation (IITP) grants funded by the Korea government (MSIT) (No. RS-2024-00439762), (No. RS-2023-00230337), and (No. RS-2024-00436936).

References

1. Bottou, L.: Stochastic gradient descent tricks. In: Montavon, G., Orr, G., Müller, K. (eds.) Neural Networks: Tricks of the Trade, LNCS, vol. 7700, pp. 421–436. Springer, Berlin, Heidelberg, 2 edn. (2012)
2. Carlini, N., Hayes, J., Nasr, M., Jagielski, M., Sehwag, V., Tramer, F., Wallace, E.: Extracting training data from diffusion models. In: 32nd USENIX Security Symposium (USENIX Security 23), pp. 5253–5270. USENIX Association, Anaheim (2023)
3. Carlini, N., Ippolito, D., Jagielski, M., Lee, K., Tramer, F., Zhang, C.: Quantifying memorization across neural language models. In: The 11th International Conference on Learning Representations (ICLR) (2022)
4. Carlini, N., Tramer, F., Wallace, E., Jagielski, M., Herbert-Voss, A., Lee, K., Raffel, C.: Extracting training data from large language models. In: 30th USENIX Security Symposium (USENIX Security 21), pp. 2633–2650. USENIX Association, Vancouver (2021)
5. Carlini, N., Tramer, F., Wallace, E., Jagielski, M., Herbert-Voss, A., Lee, K., Raffel, C.: Extracting training data from large language models. In: 30th USENIX Security Symposium (USENIX Security 21), pp. 2633–2650. USENIX Association, Vancouver (2021)
6. Cho, J., Zakka, C., Shad, R., Wightman, R., Chaudhari, A., Hiesinger, W.: Medisyn: Text-guided diffusion models for broad medical 2d and 3d image synthesis (2024). arXiv:2405.09806
7. Chou, P., Kao, Y., Lin, C.: Fine-grained visual classification with high-temperature refinement and background suppression (2023). arXiv:2303.06442
8. Dehouche, N., Dehouche, K.: What's in a text-to-image prompt? the potential of stable diffusion in visual arts education. Heliyon **9**(6), e16944 (2023)
9. Fredrikson, M., Jha, S., Ristenpart, T.: Model inversion attacks that exploit confidence information and basic countermeasures. In: Proceedings of the 22nd ACM SIGSAC Conference on Computer and Communications Security (CCS), pp. 1322–1333. ACM, Denver (2015)
10. Ho, J., Jain, A., Abbeel, P.: Denoising diffusion probabilistic models. Adv. Neural. Inf. Process. Syst. **33**, 6840–6851 (2020)
11. Hu, H., Pang, J.: Membership inference of diffusion models (2023). arXiv:2301.09956

12. Huang, N., Tang, F., Dong, W., Xu, C.: Draw your art dream: Diverse digital art synthesis with multimodal guided diffusion. In: Proceedings of the 30th ACM International Conference on Multimedia. ACM, New York, pp. 1085–1094 (2022)
13. Huang, P., Gao, X., Huang, L., Jiao, J., Li, X., Wang, Y., Guo, Y.: Chest-diffusion: a light-weight text-to-image model for report-to-cxr generation. In: 2024 IEEE International Symposium on Biomedical Imaging (ISBI). IEEE, San Diego, pp. 1–5 (2024)
14. Kingma, D., Ba, J.: Adam: A method for stochastic optimization. In: 3rd International Conference on Learning Representations (ICLR) (2015)
15. Li, Z., He, X., Yu, N., Zhang, Y.: Membership inference attack against masked image modeling (2024). arXiv:2408.06825
16. Li, Z., Hong, J., Li, B., Wang, Z.: Shake to leak: Fine-tuning diffusion models can amplify the generative privacy risk. In: 2024 IEEE Conference on Secure and Trustworthy Machine Learning (SaTML). IEEE, San Jose, pp. 18–32 (2024)
17. Lin, T., Goyal, P., Girshick, R., He, K., Dollár, P.: Focal loss for dense object detection. In: Proceedings of the IEEE International Conference on Computer Vision (ICCV). IEEE, Venice, pp. 2980–2988 (2017). https://doi.org/10.1109/ICCV.2017.324
18. Liu, Z., Lin, Y., Cao, Y., Hu, H., Wei, Y., Zhang, Z., Lin, S., Guo, B.: Swin transformer: Hierarchical vision transformer using shifted windows. In: Proceedings of the IEEE/CVF International Conference on Computer Vision (ICCV). IEEE, pp. 10012–10022 (2021)
19. Po, R., Wang, Y., Golyanik, V., Aberman, K., Barron, J., Bermano, A., Wetzstein, G.: State of the art on diffusion models for visual computing. Comput. Graph. Forum **43**(2), e15063 (2024)
20. Radford, A., Kim, J., Hallacy, C., Ramesh, A., Goh, G., Agarwal, S., Sutskever, I.: Learning transferable visual models from natural language supervision. In: International Conference on Machine Learning (ICML). PMLR, Virtual Event, pp. 8748–8763 (2021)
21. Rombach, R., Blattmann, A., Lorenz, D., Esser, P., Ommer, B.: High-resolution image synthesis with latent diffusion models. In: Proceedings of the IEEE/CVF Conference on Computer Vision and Pattern Recognition (CVPR). IEEE, New Orleans, pp. 10684–10695 (2022)
22. Shokri, R., Stronati, M., Song, C., Shmatikov, V.: Membership inference attacks against machine learning models. In: 2017 IEEE Symposium on Security and Privacy (SP). IEEE, San Jose, pp. 3–18 (2017)
23. Simonyan, K., Zisserman, A.: Very deep convolutional networks for large-scale image recognition. In: 3rd International Conference on Learning Representations (ICLR) (2015)
24. Somepalli, G., Singla, V., Goldblum, M., Geiping, J., Goldstein, T.: Diffusion art or digital forgery? investigating data replication in diffusion models. In: Proceedings of the IEEE/CVF Conference on Computer Vision and Pattern Recognition (CVPR). IEEE, Vancouver, pp. 6048–6058 (2023)
25. Wu, Y., Yu, N., Li, Z., Backes, M., Zhang, Y.: Membership inference attacks against text-to-image generation models (2022). arXiv:2210.00968

Privacy-Preserving Logistic Regression Using Homomorphic Encryption: An Adaptive Optimization Approach

Hye-Yeon Shim, Yeon-Ji Lee, and Il-Gu Lee(✉)

Sungshin Women's University, Seoul 02844, Korea
{220237062,220247018,iglee}@sungshin.ac.kr

Abstract. With the advancement of artificial intelligence, the risk of personal information breaches has become a significant concern, underscoring the importance of technologies that ensure data privacy. This study proposes an adaptive logistic regression method to enhance the performance of privacy-preserving machine learning using homomorphic encryption. The proposed technique simultaneously performs model training and training parameter optimization, enabling higher accuracy even when operating on encrypted data. Experimental results demonstrate that the adaptive homomorphic encryption logistic regression method achieves 55.92% higher prediction accuracy compared to models trained with random parameters. Although the proposed approach significantly mitigates the noise-induced performance degradation common in conventional homomorphic encryption methods, it requires longer training times owing to the overhead of multi-round optimization.

Keywords: Homomorphic Encryption · Logistic Regression · Machine Learning · Adaptive Optimization · Training Parameter

1 Introduction

The advent of the Internet of Things (IoT) and industrial artificial intelligence (AI) technology is precipitating a paradigm shift in various industries, including the medical field [1]. AI is being applied in various industries, including real-time monitoring using intelligent surveillance cameras and medical information processing using deep learning models. The advent of machine learning as a service (MLaaS) has significantly impacted the field of AI, particularly in terms of accessibility. The ability for individuals to use AI without constructing models has been a notable development [2,3]. However, as the economic and industrial importance of datasets used for AI model training increases, the risk of personal information breaches owing to data leaks and attacks is also growing [4].

K.-W. Park and J. Park (Eds.): WISA 2025 2025, LNCS 16434, pp. 279–290, 2026.
https://doi.org/10.1007/978-981-95-6857-4_21

To address the privacy concerns, a range of technologies has been proposed to protect the training datasets used in AI learning. The most used are differential privacy and homomorphic encryption [5]. Differential privacy is a technology that protects personal information by introducing random noise into datasets. This makes it difficult to infer the original data. However, this process is accompanied by a trade-off in terms of performance degradation [6]. As the strength of personal information protection increases, model performance may decrease, and the possibility of errors caused by noise replacing the original data also increases, making the practical application challenging.

Homomorphic encryption allows operations such as addition and multiplication to be performed on encrypted data, thereby enabling data to be processed while preserving privacy [7]. Studies have demonstrated that homomorphic encryption offers superior performance preservation compared to differential privacy. Furthermore, it is highly secure because it performs operations and learns on encrypted data. However, the process has certain limitations, including an increase in the size of encrypted data compared to the original, high computational overhead, and increased latency [8]. Furthermore, it has been demonstrated that minor noise elements introduced during the homomorphic encryption process undergo accumulation during computation. The ciphertext resulting from homomorphic encryption displays divergent characteristics from plaintext data, thereby hindering the applicability of conventional data preprocessing or parameter tuning techniques [9,10]. Consequently, techniques such as parameter tuning, which are employed to enhance the performance of existing AI learning models, may have a negligible effect or even result in a decline in model performance within a homomorphic encryption learning environment. For example, in general machine learning (ML), increasing the number of training epochs typically improves performance or leads to convergence. However, in ML models that use homomorphic encryption, the accumulation of homomorphic encryption noise can lead to a degradation in performance once the number of epochs exceeds a certain threshold.

To address these limitations, this study proposes an adaptive optimization technique for improving ML performance using homomorphic encryption. The core of the proposed technique is to dynamically adjust the epoch, learning rate, and feature selection during the learning process when optimizing performance.

The contributions of this study are as follows.

- To surmount the limitations of extant homomorphic encryption-based ML models that learn with fixed parameter values, we propose an adaptive learning approach that links learning and parameter optimization and adjusts parameters according to performance changes.
- The proposed optimization technique is adaptable to any type of dataset and ML model, as it performs adaptive learning.
- The simultaneous execution of learning and parameter optimization has resulted in high-performance, high-efficiency learning, reducing computational latency and enhancing performance.

The remainder of this study is organized as follows. Section 2 analyses previous research on optimizing homomorphic encryption logistic regression models. Section 3 describes the structure and operation of the proposed adaptive logistic regression model learning technique. Section 4 examines the experimental results, and Sect. 5 concludes the paper.

2 Related Work

Various approaches have been proposed to improve the performance and efficiency of homomorphic encryption-based ML models, and several optimization techniques have been developed to enable smooth computation and learning even in an encrypted state.

Table 1. Summary of related works on homomorphic encryption in ML

Reference	Methodology	Advantages	Limitations
Qipeng et al. [5]	Optimizing encryption parameters(key size, noise level, and batch size) in homomorphic encryption-based privacy-preserving federated learning through techniques such as minimizing unnecessary encryption operations and compressing model parameters	Improving training efficiency in homomorphic encryption-based federated learning	Lowered security level of the overall system, increased system complexity
Aftab et al. [11]	Adjusting training parameters to protect input data privacy in MLaaS encrypted with homomorphic encryption	Improving the balance between security, efficiency, and performance	Improving efficiency compromises security, fundamental performance trade-offs remain
Yao et al. [12]	Applying FedAvg to CKKS-based federated learning and optimizing encryption parameters such as polynomial degree and coefficient size in homomorphic encryption	Achieving high performance and security in CKKS-based federated learning	To improve efficiency, some security parameters need adjustment; security-performance trade-off issues exist
Junyi et al. [13]	Homomorphic encryption-based key feature extraction technique for improving ML performance while preserving medical image privacy	Security through homomorphic encryption, performance enhancement through feature extraction	Processing speed reduced by approximately 75 times compared to before feature extraction application; limitations in real-world implementation

Qipeng et al. [5] adjusted encryption parameters such as key size, noise level, and batch size to improve the efficiency of homomorphic encryption-based privacy-preserving federated learning. It also applies various optimization techniques, such as minimizing unnecessary cryptographic operations and compressing model parameters. However, this method exhibits limitations by optimizing efficiency at the expense of security, reducing in overall system protection. To compensate for this, it is necessary to combine additional privacy protection techniques, which increase the system's complexity.

Aftab et al. [11] applied homomorphic encryption to protect the privacy of input data in an MLaaS environment and sought to implement more efficient and secure classification through various parameter adjustments. This study adjusted the parameters of homomorphic encryption to enhance the trade-off between security, efficiency, and performance. Nevertheless, the approach involved reducing certain security-related parameters to optimize efficiency. Consequently, computational efficiency was improved; however, the fundamental trade-off issue of reduced security remained unresolved.

Yao et al. [12] proposed FedSHE, a CKKS-based federated learning model to achieve both high performance and security. This method adapts CKKS to FedAvg to improve the trade-off between performance, security, and efficiency, and optimizes security parameters such as polynomial degree and coefficient size to ensure efficiency. However, the fundamental trade-off between security and efficiency remains unresolved because of the adoption of a method that lowers security parameters to improve efficiency.

Junyi et al. [13] proposed a feature extraction technique that extracts key features from homomorphic encrypted data to improve the performance of ML-based diagnostic models while protecting the privacy of medical image data. This method is significant in that it improves performance while maintaining security by extracting key features within the encrypted domain. However, there is a limitation in that the processing speed is reduced by approximately 75 times compared to before applying feature extraction; hence, there are still constraints on achieving practical efficiency.

Table 1 summarizes previous research on homomorphic encryption-based ML. Previous studies have mainly focused on reducing the latency of homomorphic encryption, and many have adopted the method of lowering security parameters to achieve this. However, this approach has the limitation of compromising security despite the introduction of homomorphic encryption to protect privacy. Nevertheless, studies applying homomorphic encryption-based feature extraction to improve performance while maintaining security have been reported. However, the problem of a maximum 75-fold decrease in computational speed remains, and the trade-off between security and efficiency has not yet been completely resolved.

3 Proposed Technique

Homomorphic encryption-based logistic regression learning consists of encrypting data using homomorphic encryption, repeatedly performing learning, and updating the model. Owing to the characteristics of homomorphic encryption, the results of operations involving ciphertexts are also produced as ciphertexts. Therefore, certain variables used in logistic regression model training, such as weight and bias, are structured in homomorphic encryption form. Consequently, numerous homomorphic encryption operations are inevitably performed during the model update process, leading to increased model training time. To improve and optimize the performance of logistic regression models, parameters such as epoch and learning rate should be optimized according to the training dataset and environment, which requires iterative training. However, owing to the high computational complexity of homomorphic encryption operations included in the training process, even single model training takes a long time, resulting in excessive time required for searching optimal parameters.

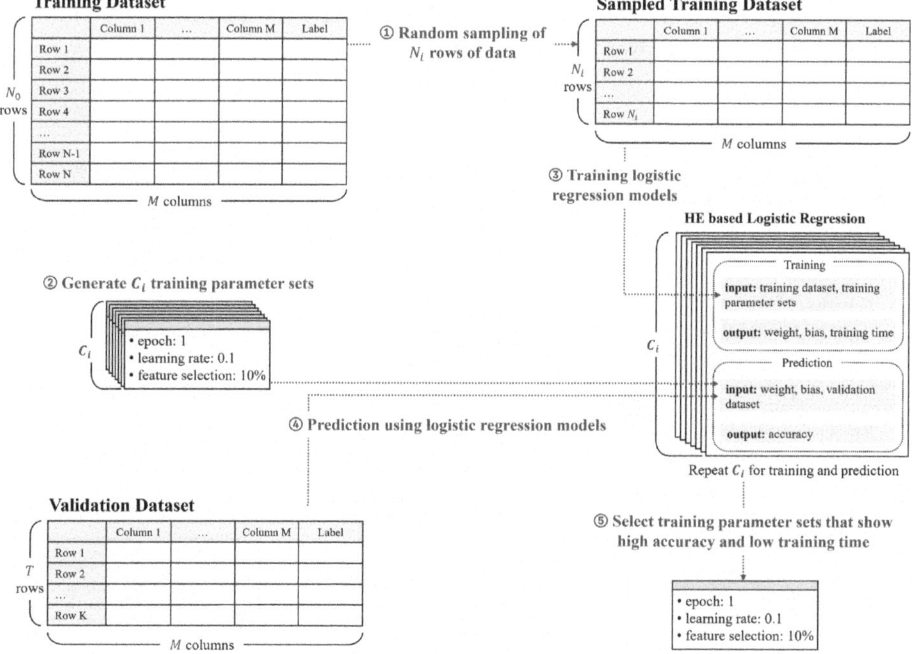

Fig. 1. Flowchart of i-th round operation of an adaptive logistic regression technique.

Accordingly, this study proposes an adaptive logistic regression learning technique for deriving optimized parameter values and effective learning. The adaptive homomorphic encryption logistic regression technique trains the model over

R rounds, and the i-th round of the proposed technique operates as shown in Fig. 1. First, to construct the training dataset to be input to the i-th round training, N_i rows are randomly sampled from the entire training dataset of N rows. At this point, the sampled dataset is not used in the next training. Next, C_i sets of logistic regression training parameters are generated. In this study, the following parameters were adjusted: epoch, learning rate, and feature selection percentile. The generated C_i sets of training parameters were then sequentially applied to the sampled training dataset N_i to generate the model, and the number of models generated in the i-th round was equal to the number of generated parameters.

In the performance evaluation for parameter updating, the efficiency is evaluated by measuring the training time of each model, and the performance is evaluated by the prediction accuracy of the model. Then, one parameter set with the highest efficiency is selected from the C_i training parameter sets applied in that round. First, the training parameter set with the highest prediction accuracy is selected, and other sets with similar accuracy are also considered as candidates. In this study, training parameters with a difference of less than 2% from the highest prediction accuracy were selected as candidates. Subsequently, the training parameter set with the lowest training time among the candidate training parameter sets was finally selected.

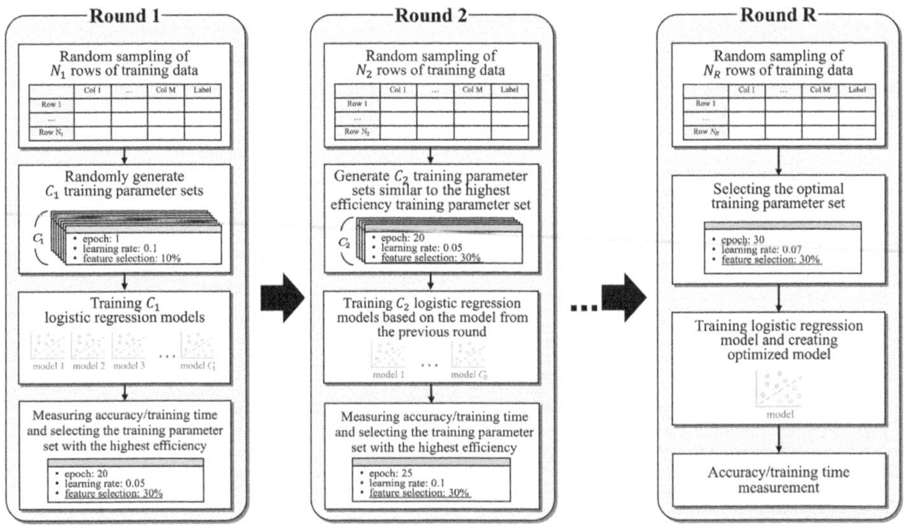

Fig. 2. Flow of operations for the entire round of the adaptive logistic regression technique.

The overall round operation flow of the proposed adaptive homomorphic encryption logistic regression learning technique is shown in Fig. 2. Closer to the initial round, a small learning dataset was sampled, and the logistic model was trained with many training parameters to derive the results. This allowed us to quickly identify the range of training parameters that show high efficiency in the dataset. Conversely, as the round progressed toward the final round, a vast amount of training data was sampled, and the model was trained with high efficiency using parameters with values similar to the parameters optimized in the previous round. At this point, the weights and biases of the logistic regression model generated by the training results of the previous round were used as the initial weights and biases for the next round of training. Therefore, the model was updated after each round.

Training dataset sampling. The sampling rate of the training dataset gradually increases with each round. In the initial rounds, a small percentage of the training dataset is randomly sampled. A higher percentage of the training dataset is randomly sampled in subsequent rounds than in the initial rounds. At this point, data that has been sampled once in a previous round is excluded in the next round. Therefore, in each round, the logistic regression model is trained with non-overlapping data, and at the end of the last round, the model is trained with the entire data.

Table 2. Range of each training parameter generated in the first round

Training parameter	Range of values
Epoch	1–50
Learning rate	0.05–1
Feature selection percentile	1–100

Generate a set of training parameters. The number of training parameter set gradually decreases with each round. In the first round, the training parameter epochs, iteration rate, and feature selection percentile are generated as random values. The range of each training parameter generated in the first round is summarized in Table 2; the range of each training parameter was determined based on the characteristics of homomorphic encryption and logistic regression training. From the second round to the $(R-1)$-th round, a parameter set similar to the training parameter set that showed the highest efficiency in the previous round is generated. The generated training parameters include the optimal training parameters derived from the previous round. The other $C_i - 1$ training parameter sets are generated as random values similar to the optimal training parameter set. Because the weight and bias from the previous round are used, the feature selection percentile is fixed and used as the optimal value derived from the first round. The epoch is generated by adding a random value in the range of $-\frac{C_i}{2}$ to $+\frac{C_i}{2}$ to the optimal epoch value derived from the previous round. The learning rate is generated by adding a random value in the range of $-\left(0.01 \times \frac{C_i}{2}\right)$ to $\left(0.01 \times \frac{C_i}{2}\right)$ to the optimal learning rate value derived from the previous round. In the last R-th round, the optimal training parameter set derived in the $(R-1)$-th round is used.

Model training and performance measurement. The training model is generated as many times as the number of training parameter sets C_i in the corresponding round. The model is trained with all training parameter sets in the corresponding round, and a total of C_i trained models are derived. Subsequently, the prediction accuracy and training time for all models generated in this round are measured, and the training model with the highest efficiency is selected. The selected training parameter set and the logistic regression model trained with the selected training parameter set are then passed on to the next round. In the next round, the initial weight and bias are configured with the weight and bias of the logistic regression model that was passed on. Therefore, the model trained in the previous round is further trained based on the data from the subsequent round.

4 Experiments and Analysis

4.1 Experimental Environment

The dataset used in the experiment is the synthetic mobile money transaction dataset for financial fraud detection ML. The synthetic mobile money transaction dataset comprises synthetic mobile money transaction records generated to resemble actual transaction data and has nine features [14]. Because this study addresses model improvement through feature selection, the features of the dataset are expanded for use. The features are expanded using the PolynomialFeatures technique from scikit-learn. When PolynomialFeatures is applied, the total number of features in the dataset increases to 44. Homomorphic encryption was performed using TenSEAL homomorphic encryption, a library that enables homomorphic encryption operations on tensors based on Microsoft's SEAL [15]. Homomorphic encryption was implemented using the CKKS scheme in a Python 3.8 environment. The ML technique used in the experiment was logistic regression, which performs binary classification.

The comparison groups in this experiment were Plain, HE, and the proposed technique. Plain is the result of training a logistic regression model with random training parameter values using plaintext data as input. HE represents the result of training a logistic regression model with random training parameter values using a dataset encrypted with homomorphic encryption as input. The proposed model represents the result of training a model using the proposed adaptive logistic regression technique. The proposed method consists of four rounds, and the number of training parameter sets used in each round is 45, 21, 9, and 1, respectively. In other words, in the first round, the logistic regression model is optimized and trained with 45 training parameter sets, and in the last round, the model is trained with one optimized training parameter set.

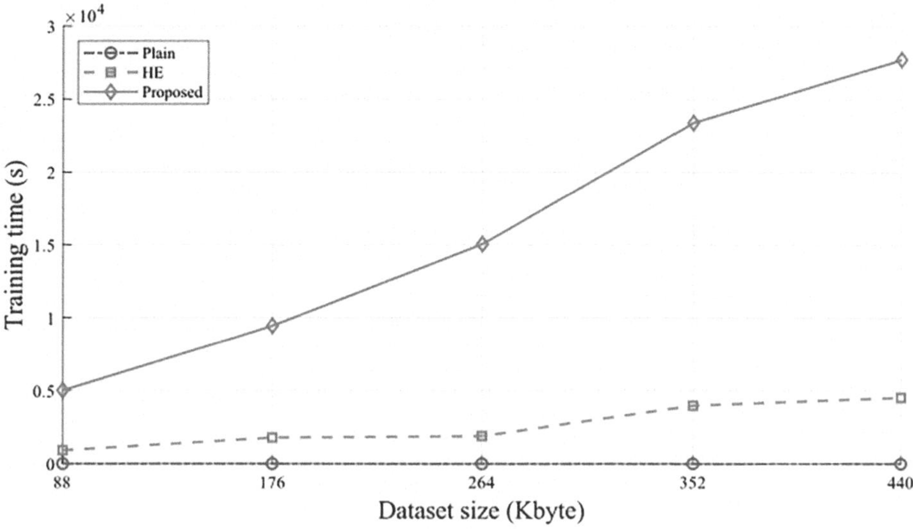

Fig. 3. Prediction accuracy of logistic regression as the dataset size increases.

4.2 Experimental Results

Figure 3 illustrates the prediction accuracy of logistic regression models across three comparison groups relative to dataset size. Conventional models, Plain and HE, exhibit lower prediction accuracy because they train logistic regression models using fixed training parameters without optimization. Notably, HE experiences severe performance degradation owing to homomorphic encryption characteristics when parameters are unoptimized, as it operates on homomorphically encrypted datasets. However, the proposed method achieves 20.21% higher accuracy than Plain and 55.92% higher than HE by optimizing training parameters in each round, despite using homomorphically encrypted data for training.

Figure 4 depicts the training time of logistic regression models as the number of dataset size increases. Plain completes training in under 1 s on average when using unencrypted datasets. HE requires significantly longer training times than Plain because of the homomorphic encryption/decryption overhead and computational latency. The proposed method shows the longest training time among all groups, as it iterates training across four rounds to identify optimal training parameters.

The proposed technique substantially improves performance while maintaining homomorphic encryption security, effectively addressing conventional HE's noise-induced degradation. However, it fails to fully resolve the trade-off between security, efficiency, and performance, as accuracy gains incur increased training time.

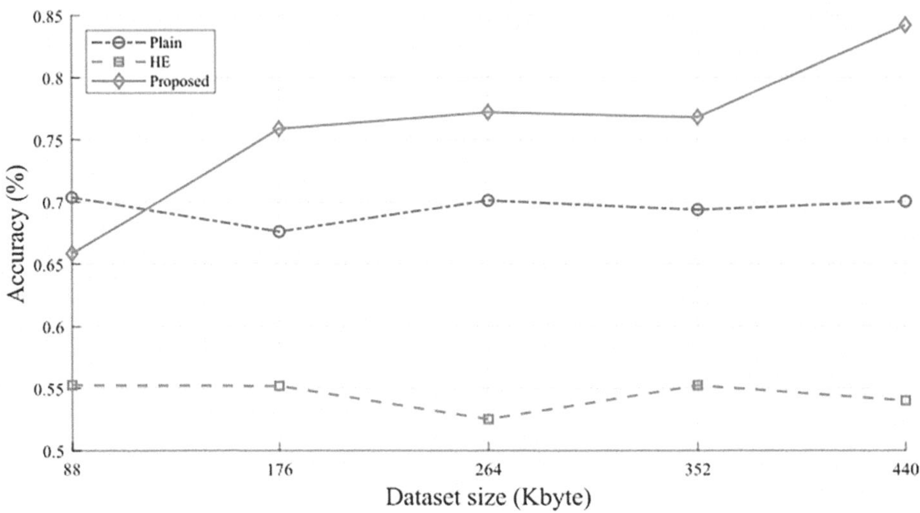

Fig. 4. Training time of logistic regression as the dataset size increases.

5 Conclusion

Homomorphic encryption enables computation on encrypted data such as addition and multiplication, while preserving confidentiality. Applying it to ML allows privacy-preserving model training. However, limitations include increased model training latency owing to computational overhead and reduced prediction accuracy caused by encryption noise. To address these constraints, this study proposes a training parameter optimization technique for homomorphic encryption-based ML. The adaptive homomorphic encryption logistic regression method trains models over multiple rounds, deriving optimized parameter values in each round to refine the learning model.

Experimental results demonstrate that the proposed adaptive homomorphic encryption logistic regression achieves 55.92% higher prediction accuracy than homomorphic encryption logistic regression trained with random parameters. Nevertheless, the overhead from identifying optimized parameters through multiple rounds results in longer training times than conventional homomorphic encryption logistic regression. Future work will validate practical applicability by accelerating the proposed technique using hardware accelerators such as GPUs and FPGAs.

Disclosure of Interests. The authors have no competing interests to declare that are relevant to the content of this article.

Acknowledgments. This work was supported by the Korea Foundation for Women In Science, Engineering and Technology (WISET-2025-164) grant, funded by the Ministry of Science and ICT(MSIT) under the Team Research Program for female engineering students, and the Ministry of Trade, Industry and Energy (MOTIE) under Training

Industrial Security Specialist for High-Tech Industry (RS-2024-00415520) supervised by the Korea Institute for Advancement of Technology (KIAT), and the Ministry of Science and ICT (MSIT) under the ICAN (ICT Challenge and Advanced Network of HRD) program (No. IITP-2022-RS-2022-00156310) supervised by the Institute of Information & Communication Technology Planning & Evaluation (IITP).

References

1. Zehui, Z., Ningxin, H., Qingdan, L., Kunshu, W., Hang, G., Tiegang, G.: DetectPMFL: privacy-preserving momentum federated learning considering unreliable industrial agents. IEEE Trans. **18**(11), 7696–7706 (2022)
2. Francesco, C., Donato, I., Giuseppe, P.: An efficient and privacy-preserving federated learning approach based on homomorphic encryption. IEEE Open J. Comput. Soc. **6**, 336–347 (2025)
3. Jiangjun, Y., Weinan, L., Jiawen, S., Qingqing, L.: Approximate homomorphic encryption-based privacy-preserving machine learning: a survey. Artif. Intell. Rev. **58**(3), 82 (2025)
4. Yunlong, L., Xiaohong, H., Yueyue, D., Sabita, M., Yan, Z.: Blockchain and federated learning for privacy-preserved data sharing in industrial IoT. IEEE Trans. Ind. Inform. **16**(6), 4177–4186 (2019)
5. Qipeng, X., Siyang, J., Linshan, J., Yongzhi, H., Zhihe, Z., Salabat, K.: Efficiency optimization techniques in privacy-preserving federated learning with homomorphic encryption: a brief survey. IEEE Internet Things J. **11**(14), 24569–24580 (2024)
6. Ahmed, E.O., Ahmed, A.: Differential privacy for deep and federated learning: a survey. IEEE Access **10**, 22359–22380 (2022)
7. Eugene, F., Khoa, N., Mindaugas, B., Tanveer, K., Antonis, M.: GuardML: efficient privacy-preserving machine learning services through hybrid homomorphic encryption. In: SAC'24: Proceedings of the 39th ACM/SIGAPP Symposium on Applied Computing, pp. 953–962. Association for Computing Machinery, New York, United States (2024)
8. Takumi, I., Takuya, S., Hayato, Y.: Latency-aware inference on convolutional neural network over homomorphic encryption. In: International Conference on Information Integration and Web Intelligence (iiWAS 2022). Lecture Notes in Computer Science (LNCS), vol. 13635, pp. 324–337. Springer, Virtual Event (2022)
9. Andrey, K., Yuriy, P., Vincent, Z.: Revisiting homomorphic encryption schemes for finite fields. In: 27th International Conference on the Theory and Application of Cryptology and Information Security. Lecture Notes in Computer Science (LNCS), vol. 13092, pp. 608–639. Springer, Singapore (2021)
10. Seungwan, H., Jaihyun, P., Wonhee, C., Hyeongmin, C., Junghee, C.: Secure tumor classification by shallow neural network using homomorphic encryption. BMC Genomics **23**(284), 1–19 (2022)
11. Aftab, A., Fawad, K., Shahzaib, T., Asif, I., Syed, A.S., Abdullah, B.: Privacy preserving inference for deep neural networks: optimizing homomorphic encryption for efficient and secure classification. IEEE Access **12**, 15684–15695 (2024)
12. Yao, P., Zheng, C., Wang, H., Yang, J., Li, H., Wang, L.: FedSHE: privacy preserving and efficient federated learning with adaptive segmented CKKS homomorphic encryption. Cybersecurity **7**(40), 1–21 (2024)

13. Junyi, Z., Xingpeng, X., Wenkun, R., Yaomin, Z.: Privacy-preserving feature extraction for medical images based on fully homomorphic encryption. J. Adv. Comput. Syst. **4**(2), 15–28 (2024)
14. Denish, A., Marriette, K., Engineer, B.: A labeled synthetic mobile money transaction dataset. Data Brief **60**, 111534 (2025)
15. Ayoub, B., Bilal, R., Bogdan, C., Alaa Eddine, B.: TenSEAL: A library for encrypted tensor operations using homomorphic encryption (2021). arXiv:2104.03152

IoT and Traffic Analysis

IoT Botnet Detection Based on the Behaviors of DNS over TLS Queries

Cheng-Han Shie[1], Yu-Chun Tseng[1], and Chun-I Fan[1,2,3](✉)

[1] Department of Computer Science and Engineering, National Sun Yat-sen University, 804201 Kaohsiung, Taiwan
cifan@mail.cse.nsysu.edu.tw

[2] Information Security Research Center, National Sun Yat-sen University, 804201 Kaohsiung, Taiwan

[3] Intelligent Electronic Commerce Research Center, National Sun Yat-sen University, 804201 Kaohsiung, Taiwan

Abstract. This work demonstrates that IoT botnets evade detection through covert channels and proposes a botnet detection scheme based on DoT queries. The results indicate that this scheme effectively distinguishes between website domain names, IoT domain names, and DGA-generated domain names. This approach enables network administrators to identify botnet traffic and devices within encrypted DNS traffic in real-time, helping to prevent related attacks and the spread of infection.

Keywords: Internet of Things (IoT) · Botnet · Domain Name System (DNS) Privacy · DNS over TLS (DoT) · Machine learning · Domain Generation Algorithm (DGA)

1 Introduction

Many botnets leverage domain name system (DNS) for command-and-control (C2) communications. A notable example is Mirai, a DNS-based IoT botnet that emerged in 2016. Mirai compromises IoT devices via brute-force attacks and uses domain generation algorithms (DGA) to create random domains, bypassing traditional firewall blocklists. Once connected, the botnet receives commands from the C2 server and can launch DNS-based attacks.

As DGA techniques become more sophisticated, detection becomes increasingly difficult. This work aims to prevent encrypted DNS queries from being used for DNS-based IoT botnets. Although existing methods such as frequency analysis, entropy, and co-word analysis can detect pseudo-random domains, future botnets may continue to evade intrusion detection and prevention systems (IDS/IPS) by hiding within encrypted DNS traffic, posing ongoing challenges for security analysis.

K.-W. Park and J. Park (Eds.): WISA 2025 2025, LNCS 16434, pp. 293–304, 2026.
https://doi.org/10.1007/978-981-95-6857-4_22

While packet padding can help defend against encrypted DNS-based threats, it adds overhead—particularly problematic for low-power IoT devices—and fails to fully mask the number of resource loads or reduce traffic visibility. To support network administrators, we propose a method to detect malicious DNS traffic generated by DGAs, helping mitigate future encrypted connection threats. This work focuses specifically on DNS over TLS (DoT) and explores its potential vulnerabilities.

The following summarizes the main contributions of our work.

- The proposed scheme can swiftly distinguish between any two encrypted DNS packets with different domain names, as subtle differences remain in the features of each encrypted DNS traffic.
- The proposed scheme demonstrates that in an IoT environment with unpadded DoT, malicious traffic struggles to blend into regular network traffic. Even when DGA and encrypted DNS are used to access the C2 server, traffic analysis can still identify and block suspicious packets.

1.1 Organization

The remainder of the paper is structured as follows: Sect. 2 covers the technical preliminaries of the proposed method. Section 3 provides a brief overview of related work. Our proposed DoT query-based botnet detection scheme is detailed in Sect. 4. Finally, the evaluation and conclusion are presented in Sects. 5 and 6, respectively.

2 Preliminaries

In this section, we present an overview of some preliminary backgrounds that are helpful in an unambiguous presentation of the paper.

2.1 DNS-Based Website Fingerprinting

Website fingerprinting refers to patterns in resource sequences (e.g., images, fonts, JavaScript) automatically loaded by browsers, which reflect user behavior and are widely used to analyze encrypted traffic such as Tor, DoT, and DoH [11–18]. Inspired by prior work, we apply DNS-based website fingerprinting to detect IoT botnets in DoT traffic.

While DNS encryption hides content, metadata like packet size and timing remains exposed. Most existing research focuses on website identification rather than IoT traffic. Using the IoT dataset from Sivanathan et al. [22], we observe that only 20% of DNS queries are fingerprintable, significantly lower than in typical office traffic.

Although fingerprint composition can vary over time due to ads, CDN support, or location, we argue that IoT-related fingerprints are more static and thus more exploitable. Our approach leverages these DNS-based fingerprints to identify IoT botnet behavior.

2.2 DNS Query Based IoT Botnet Behavior

The botnet is a network of devices infected with botnet viruses and other hijacked devices, allowing attackers to control remotely. The botnet is often used for phishing, sending spam, downloading malware, or launching DDoS attacks against organizations. It can even be rented to other users for profit. In addition to its versatility and cross-platform features, the botnet can also serve as a carrier and delivery platform for various information security threats. For instance, to help attackers carry out malicious activities such as targeting threats, data stealing, redirection, and hiding their tracks.

3 Related Works

Recent research has explored encrypted DNS traffic, but most studies focus on general network environments, with limited attention to IoT contexts. This section reviews related works and compares them with our experimental results in Sect. 5.

Siby et al. [8] examine encrypted DNS from monitoring and censorship perspectives, emphasizing DoH privacy. They accessed 1,500 domains from Alexa's top sites and captured the corresponding DoH traffic. Using directional website fingerprinting encoded as bi-grams, they trained a Random Forest model to identify visited web pages with 94.

Houser et al. [9] focused on DoT privacy, extracting features such as packet length, traffic direction, and timestamp. These were used to calculate statistics like query counts, response sizes, and inter-arrival times. They built classification models using Random Forest and Adaptive Boosting to infer visited websites.

Patsakis et al. [10] studied encrypted DNS in the context of DGA-based botnets. Their dataset includes Alexa's top 1,000 websites and ten DGA families totaling 11,000 domains. Using the Hodrick-Prescott filter and ARIMA, they analyzed traffic trends to identify DGA behavior. Their work aims to build IoCs for rapid detection, classification, and prediction of botnet activity.

Bushart et al. [23] addressed the limitations of DNS padding (RFC8467), showing that padding alone is insufficient to prevent website inference. They analyzed traffic burst patterns and inter-load intervals using Tranco Ranking domains and applied k-NN with Damerau-Levenshtein distance, achieving 86.1% accuracy. They also proposed constant-rate and adaptive padding schemes to better conceal timing information.

4 DoT Query Based Botnet Detection Scheme

In this section, we present DoT query based botnet detection scheme.

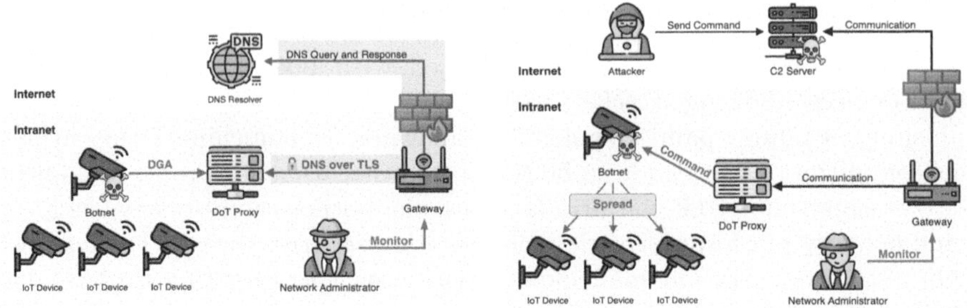

(a) Phase 1: DNS Queries Based on DGA. (b) Phase 2: C2 Server Connection.

Fig. 1. Botnet using DGA Though DNS over TLS Scenario.

4.1 Threat Model

The proposed work considers the scenario illustrated in Fig. 1, where IoT devices within an organization use DoT as a covert channel for DNS queries. It assumes that an attacker has compromised IoT devices through methods such as social engineering or exploiting network vulnerabilities, and installed malware to convert them into bots.

As shown in Fig. 1a (Phase 1), the bot uses a DGA to generate random domain names and performs DNS queries via DoT to evade IDS/IPS detection. In Fig. 1b (Phase 2), once a valid C2 domain is resolved, the bot connects to the C2 server, allowing the attacker to confirm its status and issue commands or exfiltrate data. Encrypted DNS traffic thus becomes a barrier for network monitoring. This study focuses on Phase 1 traffic, specifically monitoring port 853 (used by DoT) for abnormal DNS query patterns.

Most existing encrypted DNS research adopts the attacker's viewpoint, collecting encrypted traffic traces from victims and using classifiers to infer the websites they access. In contrast, this research takes the defender's (blue team) perspective, targeting IoT traffic. It assumes the attacker does not tamper with or decrypt TLS messages but merely sends commands via the C2 server. From the defender's side, encrypted DNS traffic can still be monitored in real-time. Administrators can infer network behavior using features such as HTTP status codes and website fingerprinting. For example, a legitimate connection to "www.aws.amazon.com" would also trigger resolutions of related domains like "www.cdn.a-mazonaws.com" and "www.thumbs.amazonaws.com", helping distinguish benign traffic from malicious DGA-generated domains.

4.2 Data Collection

In our research on encrypted DNS, most of the datasets generate encrypted packets by themselves using the public domain names without encryption and encrypted packets [8–10,23]. The average number of domain names in each classification is about 1,000 to 1,500. Table 1 shows the proposed data collection and statistical properties.

Table 1. The proposed data collection and statistical properties

Dataset	Amount	Min length	Max Length	Average Length
Pochat et al. Tranco Ranking [21]	2,000	4	23	11.23
Sivanathan et al. IoT trances [22]	2,000	21	74	28.00
Tinba DGA family [27,28]	1,000	15	18	15.76
Ramnit DGA family [27,28]	1,000	11	25	17.66
Necurs DGA family [27,28]	1,000	10	25	17.30
Cryptolocker DGA family [27,28]	1,000	15	21	17.76
Emotet DGA family [27,28]	1,000	19	19	19.00

In order to verify the authenticity of the data for website domain names, the proposed scheme utilizes `curl` to check the HTTP status code for inaccessible websites.

4.3 Experimental Design

Figure 2a shows the experiment process. The proposed scheme uses the computer specification of Intel i7-8700, the kernel of Linux 5.10.0-13-amd64 (x86-64), and Docker with Ubuntu 20.04 TLS to build a experimental environment. Then, encrypted DNS packets are collected using the Stubby DNS Privacy stub resolver (with DNS over TLS) [26] and the domain name dataset without encryption from the Sect. 4.2 with the `tcpdump` command to capture the encrypted DNS packets via port 853.

The proposed scheme uses Selenium in headless Chrome mode to simulate user visits to domain names in the dataset. Unlike traditional command-line tools such as `curl` or `wget`, Selenium performs full DNS lookups and loads additional resources from multiple origins, enabling website fingerprinting. Alternative tools like the `dig` command can also retrieve DNS information, but do not simulate user browsing behavior.

During experimentation, several challenges arose. Issues such as "Encrypted alert" disconnections, interference from system-level DNS queries, and DNS retransmissions complicate packet collection and analysis. Encrypted content further obscures critical information, and diagnosing these problems proved time-consuming.

To analyze the data, we used Wireshark to inspect 9,000 PCAP files and then parsed the packets with Python's Scapy. We extracted relevant fields including source/destination IPs and encrypted DNS message lengths. TLS handshake packets were excluded, as they contain no DNS data beyond connection setup.

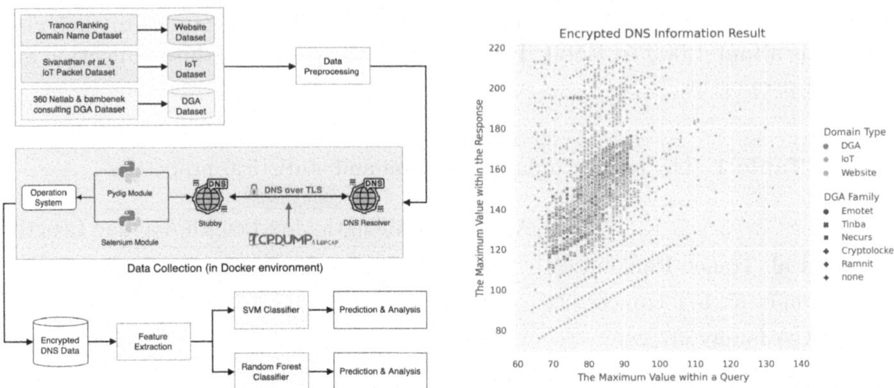

(a) Schematic Diagram of the Experimental Environment

(b) Encrypted DNS Information Result

Fig. 2. Overview of the Experimental Setup and Encrypted DNS Data Output

4.4 Feature Extraction

Most previous studies on DGA classification have focused on analyzing domain names directly. However, these methods are ineffective against encrypted DNS traffic. In contrast, the proposed scheme extracts features from encrypted DNS by leveraging DNS-based website fingerprinting as the primary characteristic, supplemented with encrypted DNS information gathered using Python pydig. These features are further categorized into queries and responses based on connection direction for processing.

Feature Processing The first step in feature processing is to fill the null values, which is a common approach in machine learning. The length of the DNS-based website fingerprinting collected by different domain names varies. Each length is noteworthy so that the balance between the values cannot be destroyed by the average or maximum value. Therefore, we use zero to fill the null values to normalize the length of the website fingerprint. In addition, retransmission often occurs for encrypted DNS information generated by Python pydig as a feature. Thus, we take the maximum value as the length of the encrypted DNS information for the domain name.

In addition to filling the null values, we try another feature processing method to eliminate the order of DNS-based website fingerprinting generated by each domain name, called website fingerprinting vector. We use the following equation for feature conversion.

The transformation converts the list $WFP_i = \{w_{i,1}, w_{i,2}, \ldots, w_{i,L}\}$, where each $w_{i,j} \in \mathbb{Z}_{p+1}$, into a binary vector $VEC_i = (v_{i,1}, v_{i,2}, \ldots, v_{i,p})$, such that $v_{i,k} = 1$ if $k \in WFP_i$, and $v_{i,k} = 0$ otherwise.

Let WFP_i denote the i-th data list collected from DNS-based website fingerprinting, including both queries and responses. VEC_i represents the corresponding binary vector, with $w_{i,j}$ and $v_{i,k}$ denoting the j-th and k-th components of WFP_i and VEC_i, respectively. The objective is to convert WFP_i into VEC_i, the expected binary representation. Let p be the maximum value among all WFP_i entries.

The length of DNS queries and responses correlates with ciphertext length. Using Python pydig, this scheme queries domain names and treats the results as assets. Figure 2b shows ciphertext length distributions from 9,000 DNS lookups. Multiple query methods were tested to analyze encrypted traffic patterns, and the data also helps identify NXDOMAIN responses in encrypted DNS. Due to frequent retransmissions, the maximum and average number of queries per domain were recorded.

Related work, such as Anderson et al. [24], used Windows TLS handshake behavior for traffic analysis. Based on this, we evaluated JA3 TLS fingerprinting [25], which includes TLS version, cipher suites, and extensions. However, due to the uniform behavior of typical resolvers and inconsistent TLS use in IoT communications, TLS fingerprinting showed minimal variation and was excluded from feature extraction.

While some botnet studies use time-based features like query frequency or timestamps [20], such patterns remain visible even when encrypted. This work instead targets identifying encrypted domain names directly within ciphertext during transmission.

4.5 Algorithm Selection

We note that many studies use Random Forest as the primary choice of the classification algorithm. Since it is a holistic learning application that combines multiple Decision Trees to build a robust model, the more trees in the forest, the more robust the prediction would be and thus higher accuracy. Also, Random Forest is well known in the face of the case of multi-collinearity and unbalanced data.

Considering Random Forest as the primary classifier, we also choose SVM from the linear classifier as the object for experimental evaluation and comparison. SVM is an algorithm that uses optimization to balance model accuracy and generalization ability. It is famous for small, non-linear, and multidimensional data.

5 Evaluation

In this section, we analyze and discuss the results of our proposed scheme and compare with other related works. As mentioned in Sect. 4, the goal is to identify the encrypted DGA traffic that occurs in the IoT environment. We set up attack scenarios and restrictions and propose different feature extraction for the dataset generated by the data collection.

5.1 Experiment Results

This work aims to identify the DoT traffic of DGA that occurs in the IoT environment and discuss the domain names of IoT and the website. Since IoT domain name is easily confused with DGA domain name in ciphertext length, we combine the features generated in Sect. 4.4 and analyze them by two machine learning models, namely SVM and Random Forest, with 10-fold cross-validation.

The proposed feature contains DNS-based website fingerprinting, encrypted DNS information generated by Python pydig, and a transformed website fingerprinting vector. Each feature is split into a query and a response, fed into the model by the following five combinations.

- **Combination A**: Pad the encrypted DNS information list with zeros.
- **Combination B**: Pad the DNS-based website fingerprinting list with zeros.
- **Combination C**: Pad both encrypted DNS information list and DNS-based website fingerprinting list to the same length with zeros.
- **Combination D**: Use the website fingerprinting vector.
- **Combination E**: Use the website fingerprinting vector and the maximum length of encrypted DNS information.

Table 2 shows parameter settings for SVM and Random Forest.

Table 2. Parameter Settings for SVM and Random Forest

Method	Parameter	Setting	Validation
SVM	Kernel	RBF	10-fold cross-validation
	Gamma	Auto	
	C	125	
Random Forest	n_estimators	100	10-fold cross-validation
	Criterion	Gini	

Table 3 shows that Random Forest outperforms SVM in identification precision, achieving a maximum precision of 97.81%. Other classification accuracies for IoT and websites average around 96%, with most feature combinations correctly classified.

The website fingerprinting vector is designed to eliminate resource load order by representing presence with binary values rather than frequency. Our experiments found that including frequency reduced precision and increased the SVM model's FPR to 9.95%. Combination D's lower precision compared to Combination B further suggests that resource load order affects model performance, with an average accuracy near 95%.

Identifying IoT domain names in encrypted DNS traffic is challenging. Many IoT domains lack web-like behavior and may not generate fingerprints through Selenium. In SVM results, Combination B shows a 7.46% FPR, with many IoT

Table 3. Performance comparison of SVM and random forest on different domain types and feature combinations

Combination	Target	Model	Accuracy (%)	Precision (%)	Recall (%)	F1-Score (%)	FPR (%)
A	DGA	SVM	96.11	96.95	95.98	96.46	3.73
		RF	96.88	96.62	97.79	97.20	4.22
	IoT	SVM	96.66	89.49	96.55	92.89	3.29
		RF	98.33	97.00	95.56	96.27	0.86
	Website	SVM	96.77	95.21	89.94	92.50	1.28
		RF	97.88	95.91	94.47	95.18	1.14
B	DGA	SVM	96.66	94.31	100.00	97.07	7.46
		RF	98.00	97.43	98.99	98.20	3.23
	IoT	SVM	95.55	98.22	81.77	81.77	0.43
		RF	98.00	96.95	94.08	95.50	0.86
	Website	SVM	96.88	92.11	93.96	93.96	2.28
		RF	98.44	96.95	95.97	96.46	0.85
C	DGA	SVM	97.44	96.11	99.39	97.72	4.97
		RF	98.22	**97.81**	98.99	98.40	2.73
	IoT	SVM	95.11	98.18	79.80	88.04	0.43
		RF	98.22	97.46	94.58	96.00	0.71
	Website	SVM	95.44	85.90	94.97	90.21	4.42
		RF	98.44	96.48	96.48	96.48	0.99
D	DGA	SVM	95.00	94.49	96.58	95.53	6.96
		RF	97.66	96.85	98.99	97.91	3.98
	IoT	SVM	94.00	85.64	88.17	86.89	4.30
		RF	96.55	95.74	88.66	92.07	1.14
	Website	SVM	95.88	94.50	86.43	90.28	1.42
		RF	96.88	92.11	93.96	93.03	2.28
E	DGA	SVM	96.33	94.79	98.79	96.75	6.71
		RF	98.11	97.62	98.99	98.30	2.98
	IoT	SVM	97.00	95.36	91.13	93.19	1.29
		RF	97.66	95.95	93.59	94.76	1.14
	Website	SVM	97.33	96.79	90.95	93.78	0.85
		RF	97.77	95.43	94.47	94.94	1.28

and website domains misclassified as DGA. IoT domain names are typically longer, designed for device management rather than memorability, making their encrypted lengths more easily confused with DGAs under DoT.

5.2 Comparison and Discussion

Table 4 summarizes recent research on encrypted DNS. Most studies focus on website environments, aiming to distinguish specific sites using features like website fingerprinting, traffic direction, and timing. Some also target website and DGA domain names, achieving high accuracy by leveraging DNS-related features. In contrast, our work targets DGA detection in IoT environments, a more challenging task. Differences from prior research, in addition to the challenges discussed in Sect. 5.1, are outlined below.

Table 4. Comparison with other works based on encrypted DNS traffic

Work	Dataset	Protocol	Algorithm	Feature Selection	Precision
[8]	Alexa Ranking	DoH	Random Forest	Website Fingerprinting, Traffic Direction	94.0%
[9]	Alexa Ranking, Sensitive Websites	DoT	Random Forest, Adaptive Boosting	Packet Length, Traffic Direction, Timestamp	96.12%
[10]	Alexa Ranking, 10 DGA Families	DoT, DoH	Hodrick-Prescott Filter	DNS Information	99.99%
[23]	Tranco Ranking	DoT, DoH	k-NN Classifier	Website Fingerprinting, Time Interval	92.20%
Ours	Tranco Ranking, **IoT Domain Names, 5 DGA Families**	DoT	Random Forest, Support Vector Machine	Website Fingerprinting, Traffic Direction, DNS Information	97.81%

Dataset. Most studies use Alexa's top-ranked websites. However, we argue that a single dataset is vulnerable to SEO manipulation, which can skew rankings. To ensure reliability, we adopt the same dataset used by Bushart et al. [23]. Additionally, there is no standardized public list of IoT domain names, making domain collection inherently inconsistent. Although we use the public IoT dataset from Sivanathan et al. [22], concerns about fairness and representativeness remain.

Protocol. DoT and DoH were introduced to secure DNS queries. Siby et al. [8] found DoT harder to classify than DoH. Hounsel et al. [19] noted DoT performs nearly as fast as traditional DNS. To align with prior work, we emphasize distinguishing DGA over DoT in IoT environments with over 90% accuracy using SVM or Random Forest.

Lastly, our research focuses on the IoT context, considering real-time connections and the limited computational power of IoT devices. We specifically examine unpadded DoT traffic, anticipating its use in future IoT deployments. Our results demonstrate effective identification of encrypted domain name traffic across websites, IoT, and DGA.

6 Conclusion

DNS often faces "last mile" security issues—network addresses remain exposed even when sensitive data is securely transmitted. While DNSSEC ensures resolver authentication and data integrity, it does not secure the final segment between applications and DNS.

This work emphasizes the need to analyze IoT traffic within encrypted DNS packets. We assess IoT security and propose methods to detect potential DGA threats over DoT. In addition to website fingerprinting for domain classification, we use DNS features to identify DGA activity. Our approach strengthens defenses against threats hidden in encrypted traffic, enhancing IDS, IPS, and other security systems as IoT increasingly adopts DoT.

Acknowledgments. This work was supported in part by the National Science and Technology Council of Taiwan under Grants NSTC 114-2634-F-110-001-MBK and 114-2221-E-110-040, in part by the Information Security Research Center at National Sun Yat-sen University, and in part by the Intelligent Electronic Commerce Research Center from the Featured Areas Research Center Program through the Framework of the Higher Education Sprout Project by the Ministry of Education in Taiwan.

References

1. Mockapetris, P.: Domain names: Concepts and facilities (RFC Editor, 1987, 11). https://www.rfc-editor.org/rfc/rfc1034.txt
2. Mockapetris, P.: Domain names: Implementation and specification (RFC Editor, 1987, 11). https://www.rfc-editor.org/rfc/rfc1035.txt
3. Hu, Z., Zhu, L., Heidemann, J., Mankin, A., Wessels, D., Hoffman, P.: Specification for DNS over Transport Layer Security (TLS) (RFC Editor, 2016, 5). https://www.rfc-editor.org/rfc/rfc7858.txt
4. Hoffman, P., McManus, P.: DNS queries over HTTPS (DoH) (RFC Editor, 2018, 10). https://www.rfc-editor.org/rfc/rfc8484.txt
5. Damas, J., Graff, M., Vixie, P.: Extension mechanisms for DNS (EDNS(0)) (RFC Editor, 2013, 4). https://www.rfc-editor.org/rfc/rfc6891.txt
6. Mayrhofer, A.: The EDNS(0) padding option (RFC Editor, 2016, 5). https://www.rfc-editor.org/rfc/rfc7830.txt
7. Mayrhofer, A. Padding policies for extension mechanisms for DNS (EDNS(0)) (RFC Editor, 2018, 10)
8. Siby, S., Juarez, M., Diaz, C., Vallina-Rodriguez, N., Troncoso, C.: Encrypted DNS ⇒ privacy? A traffic analysis perspective. In: Network And Distributed System Security Symposium (NDSS) (2019)
9. Houser, R., Li, Z., Cotton, C., Wang, H.: An investigation on information leakage of DNS over TLS. In: Proceedings Of The 15th International Conference On Emerging Networking Experiments And Technologies, pp. 123–137 (2019)
10. Patsakis, C., Casino, F., Katos, V.: Encrypted and covert DNS queries for botnets: challenges and countermeasures. Comput. Secur. **88**, 101614 (2020)
11. Herrmann, D., Wendolsky, R., Federrath, H.: Website fingerprinting: attacking popular privacy enhancing technologies with the multinomial naïve-bayes classifier. In: Proceedings of the 2009 ACM Workshop on Cloud Computing Security, pp. 31–42 (2009)
12. Wagner, D., Schneier, B.: Analysis of the SSL 3.0 protocol. Second USENIX Workshop Electron. Commerce Proc. **1**, 29–40 (1996)
13. Panchenko, A., Niessen, L., Zinnen, A., Engel, T.: Website fingerprinting in onion routing based anonymization networks. In: Proceedings of the 10th Annual ACM Workshop on Privacy in the Electronic Society, pp. 103–114 (2011)

14. Juarez, M., Afroz, S., Acar, G., Diaz, C., Greenstadt, R.: A critical evaluation of website fingerprinting attacks. In: Proceedings of the 2014 ACM SIGSAC Conference on Computer and Communications Security, pp. 263–274 (2014)
15. Panchenko, A., Lanze, F., Pennekamp, J., Engel, T., Zinnen, A., Henze, M., Wehrle, K.: Website fingerprinting at Internet scale. In: Network and Distributed System Security Symposium (NDSS) (2016)
16. Sirinam, P., Imani, M., Juarez, M., Wright, M.: Deep fingerprinting: undermining website fingerprinting defenses with deep learning. In: Proceedings of the 2018 ACM SIGSAC Conference on Computer and Communications Security, pp. 1928–1943 (2018)
17. Luo, X., Zhou, P., Chan, E., Lee, W., Chang, R., Perdisci, R.: HTTPOS: sealing information leaks with browser-side obfuscation of encrypted flows. In: Network and Distributed System Security Symposium (NDSS), vol. 11 (2011)
18. Dyer, K., Coull, S., Ristenpart, T., Shrimpton, T.: Peek-a-boo, I still see you: why efficient traffic analysis countermeasures fail. In: 2012 IEEE Symposium on Security and Privacy, pp. 332–346 (2012)
19. Hounsel, A., Schmitt, P., Borgolte, K., Feamster, N.: Can encrypted DNS be fast? In: International Conference on Passive and Active Network Measurement, pp. 444–459 (2021)
20. MontazeriShatoori, M., Davidson, L., Kaur, G., Lashkari, A.: Detection of DoH tunnels using time-series classification of encrypted traffic. In: The 5th IEEE Cyber Science and Technology Congress, pp. 63–70 (2020)
21. Pochat, V., Van Goethem, T., Tajalizadehkhoob, S., Korczyński, M., Joosen, W.: Tranco: a research-oriented top sites ranking hardened against manipulation. In: Network And Distributed System Security Symposium (NDSS) (2019)
22. Sivanathan, A., Gharakheili, H., Loi, F., Radford, A., Wijenayake, C., Vishwanath, A., Sivaraman, V.: Classifying IoT devices in smart environments using network traffic characteristics. IEEE Trans. Mob. Comput. **18**, 1745–1759 (2018)
23. Bushart, J., Rossow, C.: Padding ain't enough: assessing the privacy guarantees of encrypted DNS. In: 10th USENIX Workshop on Free and Open Communications on the Internet (FOCI 20) (2020)
24. Anderson, B., Paul, S., McGrew, D.: Deciphering malware's use of TLS (without decryption). J. Comput. Virol. Hacking Tech. **14**, 195–211 (2018)
25. Deri, L., Sartiano, D.: Monitoring IoT encrypted traffic with deep packet inspection and statistical analysis. In: 2020 15th International Conference for Internet Technology and Secured Transactions (ICITST), pp. 1–6 (2020)
26. Team Stubby. *GitHub Repository*. https://github.com/getdnsapi/stubby
27. DGA. *360 Netlab*. https://data.netlab.360.com/dga/
28. DGA. *Bambenek Consulting*. https://osint.bambenekconsulting.com/feeds/

Bootstrap-Based Evaluation of Clustering Suitability Across TCP Payload Dataset Structures

Dung Ta Anh, Yasuhiro Nakamura, and Hidema Tanaka(✉)

National Defense Academy of Japan, 1-10-20 Hashirimizu, Yokosuka, Kanagawa 239-8686, Japan
{somovn422,nda.cs.yas}@gmail.com, hidema@nda.ac.jp

Abstract. Our study presents a bootstrap-based framework for evaluating the clustering suitability of TCP payload-derived datasets constructed under different configurations. Specifically, we investigate whether combining the first payload with packet header information offers a more effective proxy for client behavior than header-centric or all-payload-centric approaches. Utilizing the UNSW-NB15 dataset, we extract payload features using BIGBIRD and apply UMAP for dimensionality reduction. Using these features, we construct three types of datasets: HeaderOnly (HO), HeaderWithFirstPayload (HFP) and HeaderWithAllPayload (HAP). Clustering is performed using HDBSCAN and clustering suitability is evaluated by observing the stability of clustering results across bootstrap replicas using the Adjusted Rand Index. Our results show that HFP consistently achieves the highest clustering stability across a broad range of configurations. Interestingly, while HAP contains more information, it performs worse than HFP due to noise and overly complex features. HO, though lightweight, lacks representational capacity unless paired with specialized analysis techniques. These findings suggest that first-payload features strike the balance between information richness and resource friendliness. In addition, our work emphasizes the value of bootstrap-based approach in statistical analysis under scarce-data operating conditions. Future work will investigate the generalizability of our pipeline to real-world traffic and explore its use in designing lightweight intrusion detection systems.

Keywords: TCP payload analysis · Bootstrap method · Clustering

1 Introduction

As network attacks are on the rise, the demand for more effective and adaptive network traffic analysis methods has become increasingly urgent. While traditional signature-based methods often fail to detect novel or obfuscated malware, behavior-based methods offer an alternative by analyzing deviations from normal activity. Among them, clustering-based packet analysis is a promising approach

K.-W. Park and J. Park (Eds.): WISA 2025 2025, LNCS 16434, pp. 305–316, 2026.
https://doi.org/10.1007/978-981-95-6857-4_23

for studying data structure as well as detecting behavioral anomalies and potential attack patterns without requiring labeled data. Existing clustering-based approaches to packet analysis typically fall into two categories:

Header-centric approaches: These methods are often used in darknet monitoring or stepping stone detection [1,2], relying on IP addresses, port numbers and timestamps to find out anomaly patterns. Working with lightweight data makes them resource-efficient, thus suitable for large-scale and real-time environments. However, they lack semantic depth and have not yet exploited critical attack-relevant information contained within the payloads.

All-payload-centric approaches: These methods capture all payloads from the session using deep packet inspection (DPI) and other content-aware techniques. These data are then clustered to study network traffic patterns such as in [3,4]. Although offering a detailed picture of client and server behavior, they often suffer from noise, overly complex data, and high resource usage.

Each approach has its own strengths and limitations. Header-only analysis is efficient but shallow, while clustering all-payload data is expressive but costly. Hence, we focus on an intermediate method that could balance information richness and resource friendliness: Using the first payload from the sender combined with the packet header as data for clustering.

Research Question

Is the dataset created by combining first payload and packet header more suitable for clustering than header-only and all-payload-based datasets?

To answer this question, we compare the stability of the clustering result produced by each dataset using a bootstrap-based approach inspired by [5,6]. Specifically, we apply the bootstrap method detailed in Sect. 3 to generate multiple replicas of each dataset. By observing the repetition rate of the original clustering result across these replicas, we quantitatively assess the stability mentioned.

2 Network Monitoring and Dataset Construction

2.1 Network Monitoring

In this study, we focus on TCP network traffic due to its dominance in various domains of network communication and its rich yet clear structure. As is well known, a TCP connection begins with a three-way handshake: A client first sends a SYN packet asking for synchronization, the server responds with a SYN+ACK packet if it agrees to communicate, and the client then completes the handshake by sending an ACK packet, after which data transmission truly begins. Here we define:

Response time: The delay between the first SYN+ACK packet sent by the server and the first ACK packet sent by the client. This is the main index for detecting the abnormal client behavior in previous work [2].

First payload: The payload in the first packet sent by the client after completing the handshake by sending the ACK packet.

All payload: The combined payloads of all packets sent by the client from the moment the handshake is completed until the session is terminated.

2.2 Datasets Construction

For each TCP connection stream, we extract the following fields:

1. srcip: Source IP address (string)
2. dstip: Destination IP address (string)
3. srcport: Source port (integer)
4. dstport: Destination port (integer)
5. restime: Response time (float)
6. All payload data sent by the source (hexadecimal string)

We define the header vector as (srcip, dstip, srcport, dstport, restime). For constructing datasets, we focus on three configurations: **HeaderOnly(HO)**, **HeaderWithFirstPayload(HFP)** and **HeaderWithAllPayload(HAP)**. We define them as follows:

HO: Contains only header vectors
HFP: Header vector features + first payload features
HAP: Header vector features + all payload features

3 Methodology

3.1 Bootstrap Resampling [5,6]

To evaluate the clustering stability of each dataset, we apply column bootstrap resampling as follows. Let $\mathbf{X} \in \mathbb{R}^{m \times n}$ be a dataset with m samples and n features. Let $x_j \in \mathbb{R}^m$ be the j-th column vector of $\mathbf{X}$. Then,

$$\mathbf{X} = [x_1, x_2, \ldots, x_n].$$

We generate B bootstrap replicas $\mathbf{X}_1^*, \mathbf{X}_2^*, \ldots, \mathbf{X}_B^*$ by sampling columns with replacement:

$$\mathbf{X}_b^* = [x_{t_1}, x_{t_2}, \ldots, x_{t_n}],$$

for $b = 1, 2, \ldots, B$, with each t_k is randomly chosen from $\{1, 2, \ldots, n\}$. Each resampled matrix preserves the number of rows (number of samples) but may include repeated or omitted columns (components of sample vectors).

3.2 Stability Evaluation via Adjusted Rand Index

Assume that we apply a clustering algorithm to the dataset $\mathbf{X}$ and derive the clustering result $\mathbf{L}$. For each bootstrap replica $\mathbf{X}_b^*$, we apply the same clustering algorithm to obtain a new result $\mathbf{L}_b^*$. We then compute the Adjusted Rand Index [7] (ARI) between $\mathbf{L}$ and $\mathbf{L}_b^*$:

$$\mathrm{ARI}(\mathbf{L}, \mathbf{L}_b^*) = \frac{\text{Index} - \text{Expected Index}}{\text{Max Index} - \text{Expected Index}},$$

where Index, Expected Index and Max Index are defined as follows:

Index denotes the total number of pairwise agreements between $\mathbf{L}$ and $\mathbf{L}_b^*$, which include both:
- The number of pairs of samples belonged to the same cluster in both $\mathbf{L}$ and $\mathbf{L}_b^*$.
- The number of pairs of samples belonged to the different clusters in both $\mathbf{L}$ and $\mathbf{L}_b^*$.

Expected Index denotes the expected value of **Index** over the statistic where cluster assignments are done randomly, while preserving the number and size of clusters in $\mathbf{L}$ and $\mathbf{L}_b^*$.

Max Index denotes the maximum value of Index in the mentioned statistic.

Let $\mathbf{L}$ be the set of clusters $[\mathbf{l}_1, \mathbf{l}_2, \ldots, \mathbf{l}_u]$ and $\mathbf{L}_b^*$ be the set of clusters $[\mathbf{l}_1^*, \mathbf{l}_2^*, \ldots, \mathbf{l}_v^*]$. To give a more specific formula of ARI, for $1 \leq i \leq u$; $1 \leq j \leq v$, we denote:

$$n_{ij} = \#(\mathbf{l}_i \cap \mathbf{l}_j^*),\ a_i = \sum_{j=1}^{v} n_{ij},\ b_j = \sum_{i=1}^{u} n_{ij},$$

where $\#(\cdot)$ denotes the cardinality function. Then:

$$\mathrm{ARI}(\mathbf{L}, \mathbf{L}_b^*) = \frac{\sum_{i=1}^{u}\sum_{j=1}^{v}\binom{n_{ij}}{2} - \left[\sum_{i=1}^{u}\binom{a_i}{2}\sum_{j=1}^{v}\binom{b_j}{2} \Big/ \binom{m}{2}\right]}{\frac{1}{2}\left[\sum_{i=1}^{u}\binom{a_i}{2} + \sum_{j=1}^{v}\binom{b_j}{2}\right] - \left[\sum_{i=1}^{u}\binom{a_i}{2}\sum_{j=1}^{v}\binom{b_j}{2} \Big/ \binom{m}{2}\right]},$$

where m denotes the number of samples of $\mathbf{X}$ as mentioned in Sect. 3.1. The ARI is bounded between the value of -1 and 1, with:

- The value of 1 indicates perfect matching between two clustering results.
- The value of 0 means agreement equivalent to random chance.
- Negative values correspond to worse than random agreement.

Based on [8], we define $\mathbf{L}_b^*$ is similar to $\mathbf{L}$ if $\mathrm{ARI}(\mathbf{L}, \mathbf{L}_b^*) \geq 0.5$. The overall clustering stability score S is computed as:

$$S = \frac{\#\left(\mathbf{L}_b^* | \mathrm{ARI}(\mathbf{L}, \mathbf{L}_b^*) \geq 0.5\right)}{B}.$$

While [6] originally named this stability score as a "p-value", we call it the S-score in this study to avoid confusion with hypothesis testing. An example of clustering stability evaluation algorithm is shown in Fig. 1. A higher S-score means that the original clustering result is more consistent under variations in the underlying population, indicating that the corresponding data structure is more suitable for clustering.

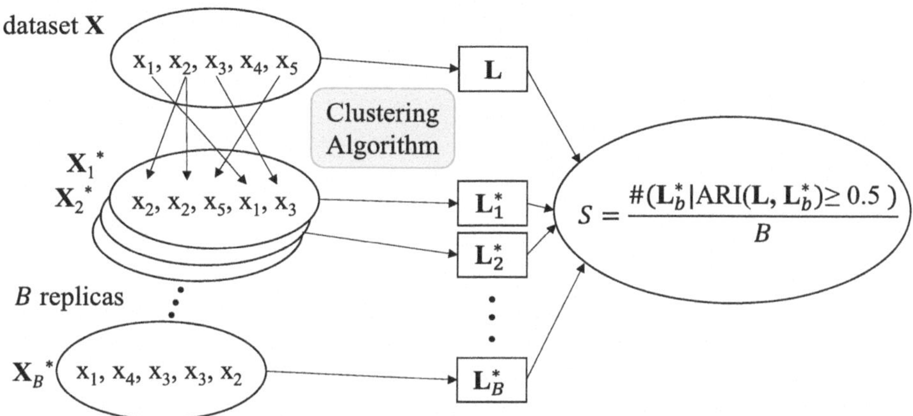

Fig. 1. Clustering stability evaluation when n=5

4 Experiments

4.1 Dataset

Based on [4,9], we use the publicly available **UNSW-NB15** dataset [10,11]. This dataset is generated in the Cyber Range Lab of the Australian Centre for Cyber Security (ACCS) by the IXIA PerfectStorm tool, which was employed to construct a hybrid of real modern normal activities and synthetic contemporary attack activities. The detailed information of the dataset used in our experiments is shown in Table 1.

4.2 Experimental Setup

We generate three types of datasets as described in Sect. 2.2 (see Fig. 2) and perform a grid search of clustering stability across multiple configurations, using a fixed random seed to ensure reproducibility:

Feature Extraction: Based on [9], we apply the pre-trained BIGBIRD Transformer [12] with batch size = 32 and max length = 1024 to extract payload features. The results have a fixed dimensionality of 768, determined by the model architecture.

Table 1. Feature composition of the experimental dataset

Type	Number of TCP stream	Ratio
Analysis	64	0.7
Backdoor	44	0.5
DoS	599	6.3
Exploits	4413	46.5
Fuzzers	2400	25.3
Generic	549	5.8
Shellcode	138	1.4
Reconnaissance	1254	13.2
Worms	27	0.3
Total	9488	100

Dimensionality Reduction: We apply UMAP to reduce the dimensionality of the extracted features, due to its capability in preserving data structure as mentioned in [13]. The number of output dimension is varied among $\{5, 15, 25, 35, 45\}$. The lower bound of 5 is selected as a balance to the header vector, which contains 5 components. Increasing the output dimension allows us to explore how richer representations affect clustering stability. The sequence $\{10x + 5\}$ is randomly selected to provide a balanced yet interpretable granularity of comparison.
Clustering Algorithm: Based on [4,9], we use HDBSCAN [14] for clustering, varying the `min_cluster_size` parameter among $\{5, 10, 15, 20\}$. The lower bound of 5 is inspired by [4], while the upper bound of 20 is set because the smallest attack category `Worm` contains only 27 streams (see Table 1).
Bootstrap Resampling: We apply column-wise bootstrap resampling with the number of bootstrap replicas B set to $\{100, 1000, 10000\}$, which follows common approaches for bootstrap-based inference.

These configurations allow us to analyze how each combination of parameters affected the clustering stability S-score. The average traffic size for each dataset and the original **UNSW-NB15** is shown in Fig. 2.

5 Analysis

To evaluate the suitability of clustering, we calculate the S-score of each dataset:

S_H: Clustering stability score of **HO**
S_F: Clustering stability score of **HFP**
S_A: Clustering stability score of **HAP**

Figures 3, 4, and 5 respectively show how the mean S-score of each dataset changes with increasing numbers of:

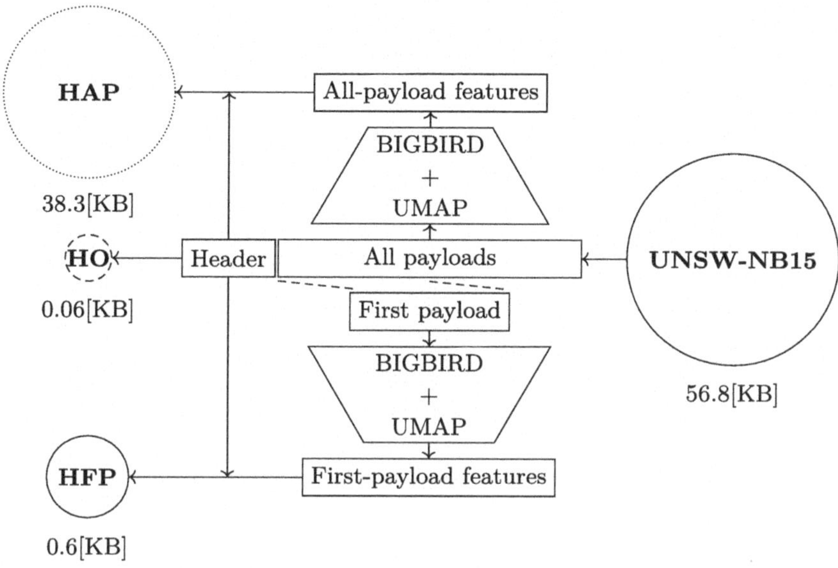

Fig. 2. Dataset construction ([KB] denotes the average traffic size)

1. Bootstrap replicas (B),
2. Dimension of UMAP projections (`dimension`) and
3. Minimum cluster size in HDBSCAN (`min_cluster_size`).

5.1 Comparative Clustering Stability Analysis

Across all experimental configurations, a consistent relationship of mean S-score is observed among the three datasets:

$$S_H < S_A < S_F$$

This order indicates that **HFP** derives the most stable clustering result. In contrast, **HO** shows relatively low stability, likely due to its limited representational capacity. Interestingly, **HAP** performs worse than **HFP** despite having more information. We predict that all-payload data contain a considerable proportion of excessive detail and noise, which may provide more biased or overly complex features when encoded by BIGBIRD. Consequently, the clustering result becomes less consistent when evaluated across different bootstrap samples, reflecting in a lower S-score.

5.2 Clustering Stability Under Varying Bootstrap Replicas

As shown in Fig. 3, increasing the number of bootstrap replicas from $B = 100$ to 1000 shows a remarkable improvement in clustering stability for all three datasets. This trend suggests that the underlying population of our experimental

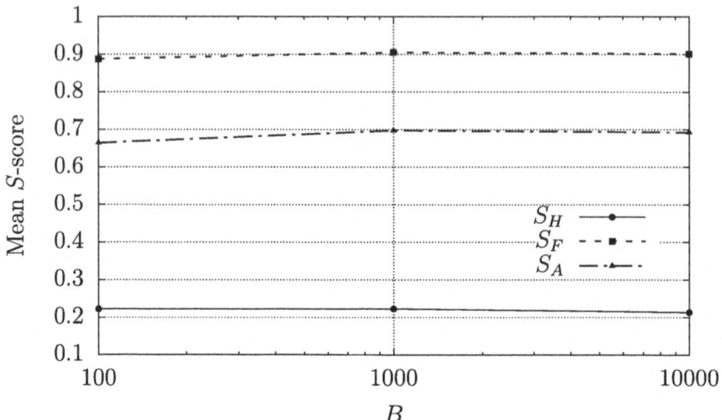

Fig. 3. Mean S-score with number of bootstrap replicas

data likely contains a substantial proportion of samples that derive clustering results similar to the one produced by our original dataset. Increasing the number of bootstrap replicas improves our ability to observe this stability.

Beyond $B = 1000$, the room for improvement decreases, with S_F—the highest S-score—converging to 0.9. This saturation point indicates that approximately 1000 bootstrap replicas are sufficient for our methodology, balancing both computational cost and statistical reliability.

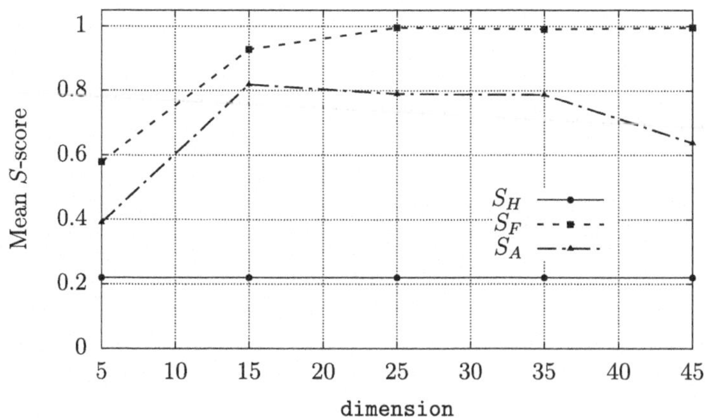

Fig. 4. Mean S-score with dimension of UMAP projections

5.3 Clustering Stability Under Varying UMAP Output Dimension

Since we apply UMAP technique only to payload-derived features, the stability score S_H remains invariant with increasing UMAP output dimension. Figure 4 focuses on the remaining two S-scores:

- S_F shows a consistent upward trend stabilizing near 1.0 when the UMAP output dimension reaches 25. This suggests that dimensions near 25 are optimal for representing first-payload features in our methodology.
- S_A improves initially but begins to decrease beyond `dimension`= 15. This drop likely reflects the adverse impact of overly complex features derived from all payloads.

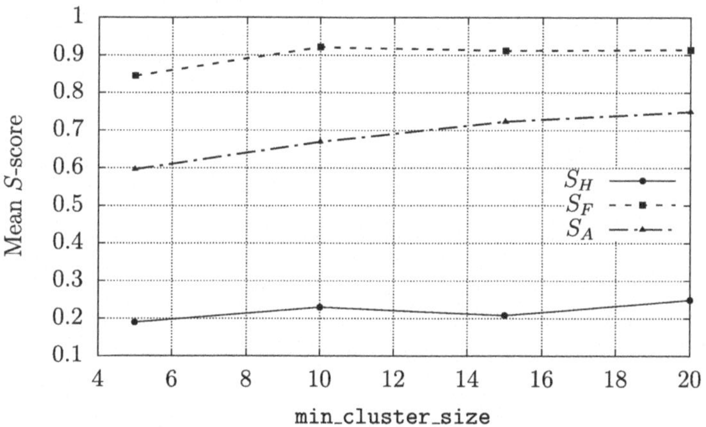

Fig. 5. Mean S-score with minimum cluster size

5.4 Clustering Stability Under Varying Minimum Cluster Size

As shown in Fig. 5, adjusting the `min_cluster_size` parameter results in different changes in clustering stability across our three datasets.

- S_H remains consistently low and does not benefit substantially from changes in this parameter, indicating a general weakness in supporting reliable clustering.
- S_F peaks around `min_cluster_size` = 10 and then declines slightly. This suggests that a minimum cluster size around 10 is optimal for our clustering pipeline.
- S_A increases steadily with larger `min_cluster_size`, possibly due to the filtering out of unstable micro-clusters. Notably, it may reach or bypass S_F under stricter clustering conditions, suggesting potential for further improvement in future research.

6 Discussion and Future Work

6.1 On the Use of Bootstrap Method

The bootstrap method has long been recognized as a powerful tool for estimating statistical parameters of the underlying population, especially in times when data volume is limited. In this study, we have shown its efficiency in evaluating the clustering stability of network traffic data in different structures. Even with only a single dataset per structural format, bootstrap resampling enables us to estimate the distribution of clustering results, offering a statistical basis for comparing clustering suitability among these datasets.

This approach is particularly relevant in many modern AI-based detection systems, where model performance evaluations are often doubted about reliability due to uncertainty about whether the test dataset adequately represents the underlying population. Bootstrap-based stability analysis offers a principled way to evaluate whether observed model behavior is stable, or it merely reflects overfitting or coincidental structure in a specific sample. We conclude that bootstrap method can play a critical role in advancing the evaluation of detection, classification, and clustering systems in cyber security.

6.2 Contribution: Insights Into Payload-Based Feature Design

A core discovery of this study is that the dataset created by combining header and first payload features achieves the highest clustering stability score across all experiment configurations. This result highlights how the first payload reflects the characteristics of a TCP stream, particularly where the sender has malicious intent. This insight has practical implications. Since working with the all-payload is resource-intensive, our result suggests that the first payload alone, combining with header information, provides a compact, yet expressive representation for downstream tasks. As shown in Fig. 2, our **HFP** dataset maintains an average traffic size of only 0.6 KB, which is approximately 1% of the original **UNSW-NB15** and just 1.6% of the **HAP** dataset, while outperforming **HAP** in clustering suitability. Furthermore, our estimation of optimal UMAP output dimensions and HDBSCAN parameters offers a potential foundation for future studies seeking optimal configurations for network traffic analysis.

6.3 Limitations

Use of a Single Dataset: The experiment is conducted using only one labeled dataset: A set of malicious TCP streams extracted from the **UNSW-NB15**. Although the dataset is widely used and well-structured, the generalizability of our findings to other traffic types, including benign or real-world operational traffic, remains to be validated.

Clustering-Centric Evaluation: We have been focusing on assessing which data structure is the most suitable for clustering, but we have not yet given any insights into how the resulting clusters can be used in practical tasks such as anomaly detection, protocol classification and so on. Future work should bridge this gap by connecting cluster quality to task-specific performance.

6.4 Future Work

Scaling to Real-World Traffic: To adapt our conclusions in more realistic environments, we plan to apply the proposed pipeline to the large-scale network traffic dataset collected from the darknet of a specific organization such as a government agency or university. Such a dataset includes both benign and malicious traffic, allowing a broader analysis of the representational capacity of the first payload across diverse traffic types.

Toward Intrusion Detection System: As shown in Fig. 2, we have constructed a proxy for network traffic that retains only 1% the original data volume. Based on the finding that this proxy supports stable clustering, we intend to design and evaluate an intrusion detection system (IDS). In addition, we aim to investigate whether this compact proxy is sufficient to support reliable detection performance, or if further optimization is required. The envisioned IDS would rely on early-packet features for fast and efficient traffic analysis, making it particularly suitable for deployment in edge or resource-constrained environments.

7 Conclusion

To address our research question, we developed a bootstrap-based framework to evaluate clustering stability of different feature configurations. This approach enabled us to quantitatively compare the three dataset: **HO**, **HFP**, and **HAP**.Our results clearly indicate that the dataset constructed from the first payload and packet header achieves the highest clustering stability across all experimental configurations. Thus, we conclude:

> **Answer for Research Question**
>
> The dataset created by combining first payload and packet header is the most suitable for clustering.

This finding supports our hypothesis and highlights the first payload as an effective proxy for client behavior. In contrast, all-payload data appears to be noisy and overly detailed, which degrades the reliability of the resulting clusters. Meanwhile, although the header-only configuration is lightweight and efficient, it may require a more specialized framework, such as those proposed in [1,2], to be able to fully play its role.

In addition, our analysis shows how clustering stability varies with model parameters, such as the number of bootstrap replicas, the dimensionality of UMAP projections, and the minimum cluster size in HDBSCAN. These observations can serve as preliminary data for future studies about optimization. Importantly, our study also emphasizes the value of bootstrap method in data analysis. Our use of bootstrap resampling is an example of statistical inference with limited data. As data scarcity remains a persistent problem, bootstrap method serves as an effective tool for improving downstream tasks and building more rigorous and reliable model evaluation.

In future work, our aim is to extend this framework to larger and more diverse network datasets as well as to explore downstream applications including intrusion detection systems.

References

1. Zhang, Y., Paxson, V.: Detecting stepping stones. In: USENIX Security Symposium, vol. 171, p. 184 (2000)
2. Goto, Y., Nakamura, Y.: A study of stepping stone detection using active scan an observation of darknet. In: Computer Security Symposium 2021 Proceedings. Information Processing Society of Japan, pp. 308–313 (2014)
3. Wang, K., Stolfo, S.J.: Anomalous payload-based network intrusion detection. In: International Workshop on Recent Advances in Intrusion Detection. Springer, pp. 203–222 (2004)
4. Ghiëtte, V., Doerr, C.: Clustering payloads: Grouping randomized scan probes into campaign templates. In: IFIP Networking Conference, IFIP Networking 2022, Catania, Italy, June 13–16, 2022. IEEE, pp. 1–9 (2022)
5. Efron, B., Tibshirani, R.J.: An introduction to the Bootstrap. Chapman and Hall/CRC (1994)
6. Shimodaira, H.: Approximately unbiased tests of regions using multistep-multiscale bootstrap resampling. Ann. Stat. **32**(6) (2004)
7. Hubert, L., Arabie, P.: Comparing partitions. J. Classif. **2**, 193–218 (1985)
8. Aaron, L., Davis, M., Keegan, K., et al.: Orchestrating single-cell analysis with bioconductor. https://bioconductor.org/books/3.12/OSCA/clustering.html#comparing-different-clusterings (2021), accessed: 2025-05-16
9. Pham, S., Nakamura, Y.: Efficient packet payload feature extraction using the bigbird model. Int. J. Comput. Theory Eng. **17**, 1–12 (01 2025)
10. Moustafa, N., Slay, J.: UNSW-NB15: a comprehensive data set for network intrusion detection systems (UNSW-NB15 network data set). In: 2015 Military Communications and Information Systems Conference (MilCIS). IEEE, pp. 1–6 (2015)
11. Moustafa, N., Slay, J.: The evaluation of network anomaly detection systems: statistical analysis of the UNSW-NB15 data set and the comparison with the kdd99 data set. Inf. Secur. J.: A Global Perspect. **25**(1–3), 18–31 (2016)
12. Zaheer, M., Guruganesh, G., Dubey, K.A., Ainslie, J., Alberti, C., Ontanon, S., Pham, P., Ravula, A., Wang, Q., Yang, L., et al.: Big bird: Transformers for longer sequences. Adv. Neural. Inf. Process. Syst. **33**, 17283–17297 (2020)
13. McInnes, L., Healy, J., Melville, J.: UMAP: Uniform manifold approximation and projection for dimension reduction (2018). arXiv:1802.03426
14. McInnes, L., Healy, J., Astels, S., et al.: HDBSCAN: Hierarchical density based clustering. J. Open Source Softw. **2**(11), 205 (2017)

Comparative Eval. of SSL Feature Extractors & Classifiers for DFAD

Seong-Bean Park and Hyun-Min Song(✉)

Dankook University, Yongin, South Korea
{seongbeanpark,hyunminsong}@dankook.ac.kr

Abstract. With recent advancements in artificial intelligence, generative AI technologies such as Text-to-Speech and Voice Conversion have become highly sophisticated, making it increasingly difficult to distinguish between deepfake audio and genuine human voices. As this technology becomes more accessible, its malicious use in crimes like social engineering is increasing, highlighting the urgent need for robust detection technologies. This study presents a comprehensive performance analysis of various deepfake audio detection models. We utilize large-scale Self-Supervised Learning models–specifically XLSR, HuBERT, and WavLM as feature extractors. These are paired with various classifier architectures, including AASIST, Conformer, and Transformer, which have demonstrated strong performance in audio-related tasks. Through experiments on the ASVspoof 2019 LA and ASVspoof 5 datasets, we demonstrate that SSL-based models significantly outperform traditional detection systems. On the ASVspoof 2019 dataset, the WavLM-Transformer combination achieved the best performance with an Equal Error Rate of 2.22%. For the more challenging ASVspoof 5 dataset, the XLSR-AASIST combination proved most robust, achieving an EER of 8.41%. Our experiments confirm that overall performance is not determined by the standalone superiority of a single component, but by the optimal pairing of an extractor and classifier, which varies depending on dataset characteristics. These findings provide a clear direction for developing more advanced and robust deepfake audio detection models.

Keywords: AI security · Deepfake audio detection · Self-supervised learning

1 Introduction

Advancements in artificial intelligence and deep learning have led to rapid progress in generative AI technologies such as Text-to-Speech (TTS) and Voice Conversion (VC). While deepfake audio created with previous technologies was largely distinguishable by humans, recent TTS and VC models can now generate deepfake audio that is virtually indistinguishable to the human ear. Furthermore, the growing accessibility of deepfake audio generation models has created

K.-W. Park and J. Park (Eds.): WISA 2025 2025, LNCS 16434, pp. 317–329, 2026.
https://doi.org/10.1007/978-981-95-6857-4_24

an environment where anyone can easily use this technology, and it is now possible to create deepfakes, including voice clones, with just a few seconds of audio. However, as the accessibility of generative AI models increases, cases of malicious use of deepfake creations are also on the rise. In fact, in 2020, a bank in the United Arab Emirates suffered a 35 million dollar loss due to deepfake audio that cloned the voice of a corporate director who was an existing client [1]. Although sophisticated deepfake audio generation technology can be utilized in positive domains such as entertainment and education, it can also be used for malicious purposes, including scams, the dissemination of misinformation, and privacy violations. Therefore, research into the development of deepfake audio detection technology is necessary not only to prevent the damage caused by such audio but also to ensure its safer use.

In this paper, we conduct experiments with large-scale self-supervised learning (SSL) speech representation models (XLS-R, HuBERT, and WavLM) and various detector architectures (AASIST, Conformer, and Transformer), which are commonly used in deepfake audio detection research. Through a comparative analysis of overall performance and performance by attack type, we aim to understand the interrelationship between the speech feature extraction models and the deepfake audio detectors, and to identify more robust extractor-detector combinations.

2 Related Work

Deepfake audio is speech data generated using artificial intelligence, a technology that creates new speech by imitating a specific individual's voice or manipulates the content of existing audio data. Early deepfake audio was relatively easy to detect due to artifacts such as unnatural intonation, mechanical sounds, and a lack of emotional expression. However, with recent advancements in generative AI, deepfake audio generation models can now produce far more natural and precise audio. In particular, the development of Audio Language Models (ALMs) has significantly lowered the barrier to entry for deepfake audio generation, enabling the creation of highly realistic and diverse deepfake audio [2].

Deepfake audio generation technology is broadly categorized into two main techniques: TTS and VC. TTS is a technology that converts text into a human voice; when text is input to a model, the corresponding speech is generated. VC is a technique that transforms the vocal characteristics of an utterance, such as tone and timbre, from a source speaker to those of a target speaker while preserving the linguistic content.

Previous research in deepfake audio detection has primarily used Mel Frequency Cepstral Coefficients (MFCC), Linear Frequency Cepstral Coefficients (LFCC), and Constant Q Cepstral Coefficients (CQCC) as methods for voice feature extraction [3]. MFCCs are the most representative speech feature, mimicking the human auditory system's perception of frequency (the Mel scale). They have long been used as effective features in various speech processing domains, such as speaker recognition and speech recognition. LFCCs are computed similarly to MFCCs but differ in their use of a filterbank on a linear scale instead of the Mel scale. LFCCs are known to exhibit superior performance to MFCCs, particularly in detecting spoofing attacks and certain types of synthetically generated audio. CQCCs are speech features based on the Constant Q Transform (CQT), which is characterized by higher temporal resolution at higher frequencies and lower frequency resolution at lower frequencies. This property enables a more effective analysis of dynamic changes in the high-frequency regions of a speech signal. These techniques, which are frequency analysis methods from signal processing used to extract meaningful information from signal data, have shown good performance in the field of deepfake audio detection [3].

Although traditional voice feature extraction techniques have shown considerable success in deepfake audio detection, they have limitations in effectively representing the features contained in the latest deepfake audio and lack generalization ability against unknown attack types [4]. In contrast, speech representation models based on SSL, pre-trained on large-scale datasets, are considered a powerful alternative. These models demonstrate strong generalization performance by extracting rich acoustic information that is difficult to capture with traditional methods [5].

3 Methodology

3.1 Self-supervised Learning Feature Extractor

The performance of a deepfake audio detection system is heavily dependent on the ability to extract meaningful features from audio data. In this paper, we utilized large-scale speech models based on SSL, a method primarily employed in modern speech processing, to extract features from audio data. Unlike traditional supervised learning models, SSL-based models are trained on large-scale unlabeled data, eliminating the need for labeled data, which enables them to create effective representations of input speech. As feature extractors for deepfake audio, we used three representative, large-scale, pre-trained SSL speech models from the speech processing domain: XLSR (300M), HuBERT Large, and WavLM Large.

XLS-R XLSR [6] is a multilingual speech representation model developed by Meta AI. Its architecture is based on Wav2Vec 2.0 [7] and comprises three main components: a Convolutional Neural Network (CNN) feature encoder, a transformer encoder, and a quantization module. The CNN feature encoder takes raw audio waveforms as input and converts them into latent speech representations. The transformer encoder then captures contextual information across the entire sequence of CNN-derived representations to produce richer embeddings. The quantization module discretizes the CNN outputs into finite units, which are used as targets during the self-supervised learning process.

HuBERT HuBERT [8] is a speech representation model based on self-supervised learning, developed by Meta AI. The architecture of HuBERT is based on BERT and consists of a CNN Feature Encoder that processes raw audio waveforms and a Transformer Encoder that learns contextual information. The CNN Feature Encoder converts the speech signal into latent representations, and the Transformer Encoder then masks portions of these representations, predicting the information in the masked sections by inferring from the context of the entire sequence. The core of this model is that it first converts speech frames into discrete hidden units using an offline clustering algorithm, such as k-means, and then utilizes these units as ground-truth labels for the model to predict during the self-supervised learning process.

WavLM WavLM [9], developed by Microsoft, is a general-purpose speech representation model designed for a wide range of downstream speech tasks, including not only speech recognition but also speaker identification and speech separation. The WavLM architecture is based on HuBERT and primarily consists of a CNN Feature Encoder and a Transformer Encoder. The CNN Feature Encoder is responsible for converting raw audio waveforms into latent representations of speech. The Transformer Encoder then captures the temporal and contextual relationships within the speech representations generated by the CNN to produce the final, richer representations. Instead of a separate Quantization Module, WavLM uses discrete pseudo-labels, generated via offline clustering, as the ground-truth targets during its self-supervised learning process. Notably, it enhances the model's robustness through a 'Masked Speech Denoising' approach, where the model learns to predict the original clean speech labels from noisy speech inputs.

3.2 Classifier

In this study, we selected the AASIST [10], Transformer [11], and Conformer [12] architectures as the classifiers to be used with the SSL-based feature extractors. AASIST is a graph network-based architecture widely utilized as a classifier in recent deepfake audio detection studies, demonstrating strong performance. Both the Transformer and Conformer architectures were selected as they have inherent strengths in processing time-series data, such as audio, and are primarily utilized in deepfake audio detection research. The Conformer architecture, which enhances the Transformer structure by adding a CNN Encoder, has also shown strong performance in deepfake audio detection [13]. Detailed information about the classifiers used in this study is presented in Tables 1 and 2.

3.3 Deepfake Audio Detector

Figure 1 illustrates the architecture of the Deepfake Audio Detection model proposed in this study. An input waveform is processed through an SSL-based feature extractor and converted into an audio embedding vector of shape (201, 1024), where 201 is the number of frames and 1024 is the dimension. The audio embedding vectors extracted from the training dataset are used to train the classifier. Subsequently, the audio features extracted from the evaluation dataset are fed as input to the trained classifier to be distinguished as either 'bona fide' or 'Spoof'.

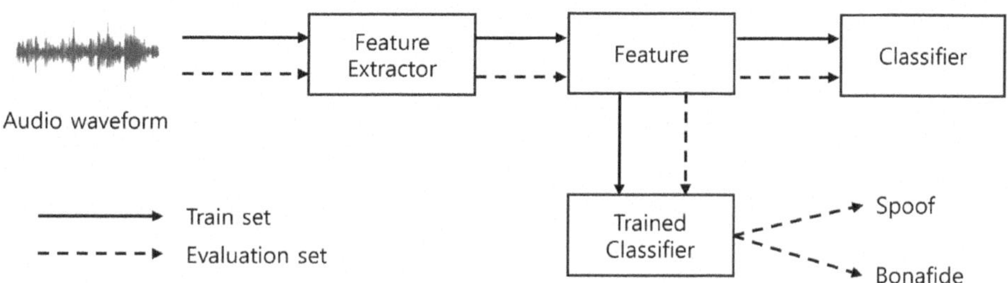

Fig. 1. A figure caption is a deepfake audio detection model structure proposed in the study.

Table 1. AASIST classifier architecture

Layer/module	Configuration/parameters
Input processing stage	
Input projection	Linear (feature_dim → 128)
Feature reshaping	BatchNorm2d, MaxPool2d(3,3), SELU
CNN encoder	
Residual blocks (x6)	Sequential filters: (1→32), (32→32), (32→64), (64→64) x3
Attention module	2x Conv2d to derive spectro-temporal weights
Initial graph module	
Graph attention (GAT)	2x GAT layers (S & T), out_dim: 64
Graph pooling	50% node reduction for both S & T graphs
Max graph operation block	
Structure	2 parallel branches, each with 2x (HtrgGAT + GraphPool)
HtrgGAT Layer	out_dim: 32
Graph Pooling (in MGO)	50% node reduction
Output stage (Readout)	
Aggregation	Max & Avg pooling on final graph nodes + master nodes
Output layer	Linear (32 × 5 → 2)

Table 2. Transformer and conformer classifier architectures

Layer/module	Transformer classifier	Conformer classifier
Input processing stage		
Input projection	Linear (1024 → 512)	
Class token	Learnable token (1, 1, 512)	
Positional encoding	Sine/Cosine based, Dropout = 0.1	
Encoder		
Encoder type	nn.TransformerEncoder	torchaudio.models.Conformer
Layers	6	2
Model/embedding dim	512	512
Attention heads	8	4
FFN dimension	2048	2048
Conv kernel size	–	31
Dropout	0.1	0.1
Classification head		
Normalization	LayerNorm (on CLS token)	–
Output layer	Linear (512 → 2)	

4 Experiment

4.1 Dataset

In this paper, we used the ASVspoof 2019 LA dataset and the ASVspoof 5 Track 1 dataset. Table 3 shows the number of bona fide audio samples, spoof audio samples, and the total number of samples for each dataset.

ASVspoof 2019 LA The ASVspoof 2019 LA dataset was created based on the Voice Cloning Toolkit (VCTK). The training dataset consists of 2,580 bona fide audio samples collected from 8 male and 12 female speakers, and 22,800 spoofed audio samples generated by deepfake audio. The evaluation dataset, used for model assessment, is composed of 7,355 bona fide audio samples from 21 male and 27 female speakers, and 63,882 spoofed audio samples. The deepfake audio samples were generated using two techniques: TTS and VC.

ASVspoof 5 Track1 The ASVspoof 5 dataset is generated based on the Multilingual Librispeech (MLS) dataset. MLS was collected from approximately 2,400 female and 2,300 male speakers and offers significantly greater acoustic diversity than the VCTK dataset, which was primarily used for previous ASVspoof datasets, as it was recorded across a wider variety of devices and environments. The ASVspoof 5 training dataset consists of 19,797 bona fide audio samples from 204 male and 196 female speakers, and 163,560 spoofed audio samples.

The evaluation dataset, used for model assessment, comprises 138,688 bona fide audio samples from 367 male and 370 female speakers, and 542,086 spoofed audio samples. The deepfake audio samples were created using nine types of TTS/VC attack techniques and seven types of adversarial attack techniques.

Table 3. Table shows the composition of the ASVspoof dataset used for the experiments.

Data set	Bona fide	Spoof	Total
Train (2019 LA)	2,580 (10.17%)	22,800 (89.83%)	25,380
Train (5 Track1)	19,797 (10.85%)	163,560 (96.64%)	182,357
Eval (2019 LA)	7,355 (10.33%)	63,882 (89.67%)	71,237
Eval (5 Track1)	138,688 (20.37%)	542,086 (79.63%)	680,774

5 Evaluation

5.1 Evaluation Matrix

A True Positive (TP) is a case where bona fide audio is correctly identified as bona fide. A True Negative (TN) is a case where spoof audio is correctly identified as a spoof. A False Positive (FP) is a case where spoof audio is incorrectly identified as bona fide. A False Negative (FN) is a case where bona fide audio is incorrectly identified as a spoof. The False Accept Rate (FAR) is the percentage of spoof audio samples that the deepfake audio detection system incorrectly classifies as bona fide, thereby granting access.

$$\mathrm{FAR} = \frac{\mathrm{FP}}{\mathrm{FP} + \mathrm{TN}} \times 100\% \tag{1}$$

The False Rejection Rate (FRR) is the percentage of bona fide audio samples that the deepfake audio detection system incorrectly classifies as spoof, thereby blocking access.

$$\mathrm{FRR} = \frac{\mathrm{FN}}{\mathrm{TP} + \mathrm{FN}} \times 100\% \tag{2}$$

The Equal Error Rate (EER) is the error rate at the point where the FAR and FRR are equal, which occurs by adjusting the system's decision threshold. This metric provides a comprehensive, single-value measure of the system's overall performance by considering the trade-off between FAR and FRR. In essence, it represents the most balanced performance point of the system. A lower EER value indicates that the system is better at distinguishing between bona fide and spoof audio.

$$\mathrm{EER} = \mathrm{FAR}(t_{\mathrm{EER}}) = \mathrm{FRR}(t_{\mathrm{EER}}) \tag{3}$$

Table 4. Table shows the experimental results for the ASVspoof 2019 LA dataset.

Dataset	Feature extractor	Classifier	EER (%)
ASVspoof 2019 LA Baseline system[14]	CQCC	GMM	9.57
	LFCC	GMM	8.09
ASVspoof 2019 LA	**XLSR**	**AASIST**	**2.22**
	XLSR	Conformer	5.83
	XLSR	Transformer	5.35
	HuBERT	AASIST	2.99
	HuBERT	Conformer	2.26
	HuBERT	Transformer	2.38
	WavLM	AASIST	2.68
	WavLM	Conformer	2.28
	WavLM	**Transformer**	**2.22**

5.2 Evaluation Result

We conducted an overall and attack-specific performance evaluation for combinations of SSL-based feature extractors and classifiers.

Table 4 presents the overall performance evaluation metrics for each model on the ASVspoof 2019 LA Evaluation dataset, which was trained on the ASVspoof 2019 LA Train dataset. The two baseline models from the ASVspoof 2019 LA Challenge, CQCC+GMM and LFCC+GMM, recorded EERs of 9.57% and 8.09%, respectively. In our experiments using SSL-based speech representation models as feature extractors, the EERs ranged from a minimum of 2.22% to a maximum of 5.83%, demonstrating vastly superior performance compared to deepfake audio detection systems based on traditional extraction techniques.

Analyzing each feature extractor, the XLSR model achieved the best performance among the models when paired with the AASIST-based classifier. However, when combined with the Conformer and Transformer classifiers, it showed EERs of 5.83% and 5.35%, respectively, marking the poorest performance among the different models. This indicates that the combination of the XLSR model and Transformer-based classifiers is relatively weak for the ASVspoof 2019 dataset. For the HuBERT and WavLM models, the Transformer-based classifier combinations showed relatively better performance than the AASIST architecture. In particular, the combination of WavLM and Transformer achieved an EER of 2.22%, which, along with the XLSR and AASIST combination, was the best performance.

Tables 5 and 6 show the evaluation metrics per attack type for the ASVspoof 2019 LA dataset. For most attack types, the WavLM and HuBERT models demonstrate superior performance and show significant potential compared to the XLSR model. However, experiments using the XLSR model reveal poor performance on specific attack types, indicating that its robustness is lower than that of the other models. Furthermore, all models exhibit a relatively high EER for the A19 attack type, suggesting that not only the XLSR model but also WavLM and HuBERT require improvements in robustness.

Table 5. Evaluation results for attack types A07-A13 on the ASVspoof 2019 evaluation dataset.

System	A07	A08	A09	A10	A11	A12	A13
XLSR + AASIST	0.91	1.87	0.69	5.10	3.52	1.49	0.57
XLSR + Conformer	1.44	1.57	0.77	29.49	10.01	4.96	0.72
XLSR + Transformer	1.04	4.91	0.84	1.47	1.30	1.30	0.72
HuBERT + AASIST	0.53	1.89	0.20	3.15	1.04	0.19	0.04
HuBERT + Conformer	1.39	4.01	1.44	3.42	1.47	1.43	1.49
HuBERT + Transformer	0.65	3.81	0.16	3.60	0.88	0.22	0.04
WavLM + AASIST	1.16	1.67	0.16	5.52	1.61	0.49	0.16
WavLM + Conformer	0.80	1.20	0.04	5.11	0.91	0.14	0.02
WavLM + Transformer	0.41	1.24	0.04	1.24	0.65	0.16	0.04

Table 6. Evaluation results for attack types A14-A19 on the ASVspoof 2019 evaluation dataset.

System	A14	A15	A16	A17	A18	A19
XLSR + AASIST	0.86	1.77	1.04	1.30	1.66	2.44
XLSR + Conformer	0.95	1.65	1.73	1.79	5.52	18.72
XLSR + Transformer	0.81	1.04	1.47	8.43	6.69	15.55
HuBERT + AASIST	0.91	0.71	0.72	2.79	6.43	8.99
HuBERT + Conformer	1.44	1.45	1.52	1.65	3.44	5.98
HuBERT + Transformer	0.71	0.71	0.91	0.53	2.54	6.81
WavLM + AASIST	0.90	1.30	0.79	2.03	2.40	7.64
WavLM + Conformer	0.26	0.88	0.69	1.55	1.58	6.98
WavLM + Transformer	0.04	0.57	0.61	1.48	2.00	7.85

The overall performance of each model on the ASVspoof 5 Track 1 Evaluation dataset is detailed in Table 7. All models were trained on the corresponding ASVspoof 5 Track 1 Train dataset. The official baselines for the challenge, AASIST and RawNet2, achieved EERs of 29.12% and 36.04%, respectively. Our experiments, which utilized SSL-based speech representation models as feature extractors, yielded EERs ranging from 8.41 to 30.2%. All tested combinations, barring the XLSR+Transformer model, vastly outperformed the baseline systems.

A closer look at each feature extractor reveals that for the XLSR model, combinations with the AASIST yielded respectable performance. This suggests that its approach of leveraging features from both the time and frequency domains is more effective for deepfake audio detection than Transformer-based classifiers, which primarily rely on sequential characteristics. In contrast, the Transformer combination resulted in a very high EER. Given that the Transformer-based

Conformer performed well, this suggests that the CNN Encoder in the Conformer architecture had a meaningful influence on the features extracted by the XLSR model. For experiments with HuBERT and WavLM, the WavLM-based models generally outperformed the HuBERT-based models. Overall, it is evident that models leveraging SSL-based feature extractors achieve significantly better performance than the baselines that do not.

Table 7. Table shows the experimental results for the ASVspoof 5 Track1 dataset.

Dataset	Feature extractor	Classifier	EER (%)
ASVspoof 5 baseline system[15]	AASIST		29.12
	RawNet2		36.04
ASVspoof 5 track1	**XLSR**	**AASIST**	**8.41**
	XLSR	Conformer	9.16
	XLSR	Transformer	30.2
	HuBERT	AASIST	12.87
	HuBERT	Conformer	14.02
	HuBERT	Transformer	12.98
	WavLM	AASIST	11.14
	WavLM	Conformer	11.98
	WavLM	Transformer	10.10

Table 8. Evaluation results for attack types A17-A24 on the ASVspoof 5 evaluation dataset.

System	A17	A18	A19	A20	A21	A22	A23	A24
XLSR + AASIST	4.23	8.31	4.74	4.90	2.69	4.16	6.46	8.97
XLSR + Conformer	5.44	9.26	5.67	5.59	5.45	5.70	9.48	16.45
XLSR + Transformer	38.09	39.56	28.11	22.31	27.18	30.31	27.27	37.82
HuBERT + AASIST	5.25	4.67	3.17	4.89	12.29	13.73	7.84	26.32
HuBERT + Conformer	5.34	6.19	5.73	7.99	11.69	14.22	9.52	24.24
HuBERT + Transformer	4.74	4.71	2.95	5.03	10.17	12.42	7.46	23.23
WavLM + AASIST	4.41	5.60	4.04	5.76	8.41	9.57	11.02	21.76
WavLM + Conformer	5.79	5.65	1.76	2.47	9.21	15.64	8.83	34.62
WavLM + Transformer	4.99	4.32	2.30	3.14	8.87	10.09	8.65	30.16

Table 9. Evaluation results for attack types A25-A32 on the ASVspoof 5 evaluation dataset.

System	A25	A26	A27	A28	A29	A30	A31	A32
XLSR + AASIST	2.34	2.99	9.28	20.51	3.56	10.68	11.36	9.01
XLSR + Conformer	5.48	5.51	5.73	22.96	5.47	9.26	12.01	5.53
XLSR + Transformer	26.38	34.81	17.67	51.21	35.31	20.95	22.44	12.47
HuBERT + AASIST	6.19	4.86	9.81	29.33	5.37	11.18	12.70	21.90
HuBERT + Conformer	7.63	7.37	13.43	28.64	4.70	15.81	16.11	25.64
HuBERT + Transformer	5.29	5.69	11.05	28.34	4.31	14.71	13.74	29.20
WavLM + AASIST	5.13	3.76	9.35	25.36	4.39	9.70	13.59	14.40
WavLM + Conformer	5.31	5.22	4.72	33.11	6.89	7.57	15.82	6.30
WavLM + Transformer	4.49	4.37	4.79	32.88	6.00	5.92	10.35	6.22

Tables 8 and 9 show the evaluation metrics per attack type for the ASVspoof 5 Track 1 Evaluation dataset. Compared to the results from ASVspoof 2019, the EERs for all systems have increased significantly overall. In particular, the significant drop in performance across all models against attack types 24 and 28 reveals a high dependency on the specific attack type. Therefore, to reduce this dependency and improve model robustness, it is essential to diversify the training dataset.

6 Conclusion

This study conducted a comprehensive evaluation and analysis of deepfake audio detection performance by combining SSL-based speech representation models with various classifier architectures.

On the relatively clean ASVspoof 2019 dataset, models such as WavLM and HuBERT demonstrated superior performance when combined with a Transformer-based classifier. In contrast, on the ASVspoof 5 dataset, which includes crowdsourced data and adversarial attacks, the XLSR feature extractor, with its cross-lingual characteristics, showed the most robust performance when paired with the AASIST classifier, a model specialized in voice anti-spoofing. Therefore, it seems advisable to use the XLSR and AASIST combination, which showed the best performance on the more recent ASVspoof 5 dataset. However, since the optimal combination depends on the characteristics of the dataset (e.g., noise, diversity of attack types) rather than the standalone superiority of a particular feature extractor or classifier, it is most recommended to find a pairing that is suitable for the specific dataset in use. Furthermore, since models exhibited vulnerabilities to specific attack types in both datasets, it highlights the need to create robust models with generally competent performance, rather than models that are strong only against specific attacks.

In this study, data augmentation techniques were intentionally excluded to facilitate a pure performance comparison between model architectures. Consequently, this research was unable to conduct comparative experiments with models that approach state-of-the-art (SOTA) performance. Future research will extend this work by applying various data augmentation and domain adaptation techniques to improve the model's generalization and robustness against unseen attacks and various acoustic variables that may be encountered in real-world environments.

Acknowledgments. This work was supported by the Institute of Information & Communications Technology Planning & Evaluation (IITP) grant funded by the Korea government (MSIT) (No.RS-2025-02215590, Development of AI implementation obfuscation technology to prevent information leakage in On-Device AI.

References

1. uniteai.: Deepfaked Voice Enabled $35 Million Bank Heist in 2020 (2020). https://www.unite.ai/deepfaked-voice-enabled-35-million-bank-heist-in-2020/. Accessed 26 June 2025
2. Xie, Y., Xiong, C., Wang, X., Wang, Z., Lu, Y., Qi, X., et al.: Does current deepfake audio detection model effectively detect alm-based deepfake audio? In: Proceedings of the ISCSLP, pp. 481–485. IEEE (2024)
3. Patil, A.T., Acharya, R., Sai, P.K.A., Patil, H.A.: Energy separation-based instantaneous frequency estimation for cochlear cepstral feature for replay spoof detection. In: Proceedings of the Interspeech, pp. 2898–2902 (2019)
4. Zhang, B., Cui, H., Nguyen, V., Whitty, M.: Audio deepfake detection: what has been achieved and what lies ahead. Sensors **25**(7), 1989 (2025)
5. Guo, Y., Huang, H., Chen, X., Zhao, H., Wang, Y.: Audio deepfake detection with self-supervised wavlm and multi-fusion attentive classifier. In: Proceedings of the ICASSP, pp. 12702–12706. IEEE (2024)
6. Conneau, A., Baevski, A., Collobert, R., Mohamed, A., Auli, M.: Unsupervised cross-lingual representation learning for speech recognition (2020). arXiv:2006.13979
7. Baevski, A., Zhou, Y., Mohamed, A., Auli, M.: wav2vec 2.0: a framework for self-supervised learning of speech representations. In: Proceedings of the NeurIPS, vol. 33, pp. 12449–12460 (2020)
8. Hsu, W.-N., Bolte, B., Tsai, Y.-H.H., Lakhotia, K., Salakhutdinov, R., Mohamed, A.: HuBERT: self-supervised speech representation learning by masked prediction of hidden units. IEEE/ACM Trans. Audio Speech Lang. Process. **29**, 3451–3460 (2021)
9. Chen, S., Wang, C., Zhengyang Chen, Y.W., Liu, S., Chen, Z., Li, J., Kanda, N., Yoshioka, T., Xiao, X., Jian, W., Zhou, L., Yang, S., Wei, F., Huang, Y., Luan, J., Hui-ling, L.: WavLM: large-scale self-supervised pre-training for full stack speech processing. IEEE J. Sel. Top. Signal Process. **16**(6), 1505–1518 (2022)
10. Jung, J., Heo, H.-S., Tak, H., Shim, H., Chung, J.-S., Lee, B.-J., Yu, H.-J., Evans, N.: AASIST: audio anti-spoofing using integrated spectro-temporal graph attention networks. In: Proceedings of the ICASSP, pp. 6367–6371. IEEE (2022)

11. Vaswani, A., Shazeer, N., Parmar, N., Uszkoreit, J., Jones, L., Gomez, A.N., Kaiser, L., Polosukhin, I.: Attention is all you need. Proc. NeurIPS **30**, 5998–6008 (2017)
12. Gulati, A., Qin, J., Chiu, C.C., Parmar, N., Zhang, Y., Yu, J., Han, W., Wang, S., Zhang, Z., Wu, Y., Pang, R.: Conformer: convolution-augmented transformer for speech recognition (2020). arXiv:2005.08100
13. Rosello, E., Gomez-Alanis, A., Gomez, A.M., Peinado, A.: A conformer-based classifier for variable-length utterance processing in anti-spoofing. In: Proceedings of the Interspeech, pp. 5281–5285. ISCA (2023)
14. Wang, X., Yamagishi, J., Todisco, M., Delgado, H., Nautsch, A., Evans, N., Kinnunen, T., Vestman, V., Lee, K.A., Doss, M.M., Juvela, L., Alku, P., Ling, Z.-H.: ASVspoof,: a large-scale public database of synthesized, converted and replayed speech. Comput. Speech Lang. **64**(101114), 2020 (2019)
15. Wang, X., Delgado, H., Tak, H., Jung, J.W., Shim, H.J., Todisco, M., Kukanov, I., Liu, X., Sahidullah, M., Kinnunen, T., Evans, N., Juvela, L., Alku, P.: ASVspoof 5: design, collection and validation of resources for spoofing, deepfake, and adversarial attack detection using crowdsourced speech. In: Proceedings of the Odyssey, pp. 1–8. ISCA (2022)

Author Index

K.-W. Park and J. Park (Eds.): WISA 2025 2025, LNCS 16434, pp. 331–332, 2026.
https://doi.org/10.1007/978-981-95-6857-4

The manufacturer's authorised representative in the EU is Springer Nature Customer Service Centre GmbH, Europaplatz 3, 69115 Heidelberg, Germany. If you have any concerns regarding our products, please contact ProductSafety@springernature.com

Printed and bound by CPI Group (UK) Ltd, Croydon, CR0 4YY

07/07/2026

02160913-0009